TOWARDS CONTINENTAL ENVIRONMENTAL POLICY?

SUNY series in Environmental Governance: Local-Regional-Global Interactions

Peter Stoett and Owen Temby, editors

TOWARDS CONTINENTAL ENVIRONMENTAL POLICY?

North American Transnational Networks and Governance

EDITED BY

Owen Temby and Peter Stoett

Published by
State University of New York Press, Albany

Printed in the United States of America

For information, contact State University of New York Press, Albany, NY
www.sunypress.edu

Production by Westchester Publishing Services
Marketing by Fran Keneston

Library of Congress Cataloging-in-Publication Data:

Names: Temby, Owen, 1979– editor. | Stoett, Peter J. (Peter John), 1965– editor.
Title: Towards continental environmental policy? : North American transnational networks and governance / edited by Owen Temby and Peter Stoett.
Description: Albany : State University of New York Press, [2017] | Series: SUNY series in environmental governance : local-regional-global interactions | Includes bibliographical references and index.
Identifiers: LCCN 2016059170 (print) | LCCN 2017026300 (ebook) | ISBN 9781438467597 (e-book) | ISBN 9781438467573 (hardcover : alk. paper) | ISBN 9781438467580 (paperback : alk. paper)
Subjects: LCSH: Environmental policy—North America—International cooperation. | Environmental management—North America—International cooperation. | Environmental protection—North America—International cooperation.
Classification: LCC GE190.N7 (ebook) | LCC GE190.N7 T69 2017 (print) | DDC 333.7097—dc23
LC record available at https://lccn.loc.gov/2016059170

10 9 8 7 6 5 4 3 2 1

Contents

List of Illustrations

List of Tables

Foreword

IRASEMA CORONADO

Can North America move resolutely towards truly continental environmental policy making? That is the central question examined in this informative and intriguing collection of essays on the stewardship of the North American environment.

Owen Temby and Peter Stoett have collected and coordinated contributions by leading scholars on North American environmental policy. This impressive and highly readable compendium highlights the historical antecedents that have led to the development of cross-border initiatives and other forms of environmental cooperation between the three countries. It also cites examples of where the United States, Canada, and Mexico have cooperated bilaterally or trilaterally across a broad range of environmental issues—from water to endangered species, from transborder pollution to concerns about fossils fuels to hopes for a successful continental transition towards clean energy production. If we are to continue to protect our environment and natural resources across North America in a meaningful way, these foundational institutions, policy initiatives, and international agreements can serve as a basis for the vital work we need to do, and urgently.

Thanks to political and economic developments of the past two-and-a-half decades, the North American continent is of a particularly meaningful scale at which to conceive of environmental governance. The North American Free Trade Agreement (NAFTA), which came into effect in 1994, has increasingly integrated the economies of Canada, Mexico, and the United States. Broader trade flows, however, have resulted in greater impacts on the North American environment.

Allow me to illustrate this with a personal anecdote. From 2012 to 2015, I had the privilege of serving as executive director of the

Commission for Environmental Cooperation. During my tenure, I lived and worked in Montreal. My transition from the U.S.-Mexican border city of El Paso to Canada's largest French-speaking city broadened my awareness of continental environmental issues. In Montreal, it was an eye-opening experience for me to go the local market and see watermelons imported from Mexico by marketers and shippers of fresh fruits and vegetables headquartered in my hometown of Nogales, Arizona. I understood that this high-quality, fresh produce was being transported from the Valle de Sinaloa, up Mexico's Federal Highway 15, to Nogales, Sonora, where, after waiting for hours to cross the border into the United States, they were trucked northward more than 4,000 kilometers to reach the market in Montreal. While it was great to have access to fresh fruits and vegetables, especially in the depth of Montreal's impressive winter, the environmental impact of that type of journey alone is significant because it produces a substantial amount of greenhouse gas emissions. This kind of economic integration has encroached into other key North American supply chains, such as the one for automotive parts and vehicles, and this too has an impact on the environment.

Fortunately, there is much to learn from the accomplishments of binational and trinational cooperation. For example, the International Boundary and Water Commission and its Mexican counterpart, the Comision Internacional de Limites y Aguas, on the U.S.-Mexican border, and the International Joint Commission, which helps Canada and the United States prevent disputes over their transboundary waters, are institutions that have helped us address issues related to the allocation of water across borders. Yet they still do not fully address environmental issues related to groundwater. Several other transboundary environmental issues similarly receive insufficient attention from international institutions on a binational or trinational scale.

Ideally, the North American Climate, Clean Energy, and Environment Partnership, announced by Canadian prime minister Justin Trudeau, U.S. president Barack Obama, and Mexican president Enrique Peña Nieto at the North American Leaders' summit in Ottawa on June 29, 2016, will pave the way for deepening and enhancing environment protection in North America. As this volume notes, given the broad international dimensions of environmental crises, the fact that the three countries are parties to the United Nations Framework Convention on Climate Change (and the Paris Agreement) further supports the North American trios' efforts to achieve each leader's respective domestic goals while meeting their international commitments on the environment. (At of the time of this writing, in December 2016, all three countries have ratified the Paris Agreement.)

One of the major contributions of this book is its historical perspective and chronicling of the domestic antecedents to environmental cooperation or conflict exhibited by the three countries. The contributors discuss how various interest groups and institutions have helped advance or stymied the environmental protection agenda. Consider the disdain of much of the U.S. Congress for environmental stewardship and regulation, or the substantial power of the fossil fuel energy lobby, or Mexico's recent energy sector reform, and the Province of Alberta's progressive energy policy changes since the election of Premier Rachel Notley of the leftist New Democratic Party. The challenge ahead is to ensure continuity in the conservation, protection, and enhancement of the North American environment despite changes in government leadership.

This volume also provides a broad review of examples of successful environmental cooperation at the local, state, provincial, and national levels, including cross-border cooperation. The authors elucidate issues such as fossil fuel extraction and the movement of oil between countries, the hope for renewable power, and the importance of respecting the social and cultural heritages of peoples that transcend our border regions. Success stories include the Mexico-Reducing Emissions from Deforestation and Forest Degradation Programme, the innovative subnational cap-and-trade system agreement between the province of Quebec and the state of California, and the successful electricity exchanges between Canada and the United States that have been in place for more than a century. Other subnational entities can replicate these models of environmental cooperation.

Despite this proliferation of national and subnational environmental agreements on the North American borderlands, there are fewer agreements at the continental level. This book raises several germane questions about ways in which we can transform bilateral cooperation on the environment into closer North American integration of policies, initiatives, and agreements. If the editors can bring together like-minded scholars on these issues, perhaps those of us in the growing community of people concerned about the continental environment can help policy makers do the same.

At the time of the writing of this foreword, the United States had just elected a president whose declared policy intentions represent a political sea change that is bound to have a huge impact on environmental stewardship in the United States, and perhaps even across North America. His campaign pronouncements, often made through social media channels, included assertions that climate change is a hoax, that NAFTA should be annulled or renegotiated, that the Environmental Protection Agency should be reined in or eliminated, and that a new wall should be built across the entire span of the U.S.-Mexican border. This new tack on environmental and trade policy is likely to pose new challenges for the environmental well-being of North America and its inhabitants.

This volume provides a historical context that frames the continents' common environmental concerns and reminds us of the value of seeing what can be possible in environmental policy making. From imagining a Colorado River that flows fully once again through the great delta at its mouth in the Gulf of California, to defining a truly clean energy future for North America, capitalizing on past successes can be the model for a hopeful future.

Acknowledgments

The empirical and conceptual focus of this volume is a corollary of our recent efforts to amass excellent research on the governance of transboundary environmental issues in North America. In the process, we organized panels at the 2014 conventions of the International Studies Association in Toronto and the International Political Science Association in Montreal, from which several of the chapters herein are taken. We thank Raul Pacheco-Vega and Stephen Bird for serving as discussants for each of these two panels. In late 2014 we worked with Concordia University's Loyola College for Diversity and Sustainability and the Loyola Sustainability Research Centre, and the Commission for Environmental Cooperation, to organize the Symposium on North American Environmental Governance, held in February 2015. The event's participants inspired some of the ideas represented in Chapters 1 and 16.

We also edited a special issue of the journal *Review of Policy Research* on natural resource and biodiversity governance in North America, published in January 2015. Many of the concepts underpinning this book, and some of the content in Chapter 1, are from the special issue's introductory article, and also from a review essay published in *Global Environmental Politics*:

Stoett, P., & Temby, O. (2015). Bilateral and trilateral natural resource and biodiversity governance in North America: Organizations, networks, and inclusion. *Review of Policy Research*, *32*(1), 1–18.

Temby, O. (2015). Limits of transnational environmental network governance in North America. *Global Environmental Politics*, *15*(3), 176–183.

In addition, revised and updated versions of three articles from the *Review of Policy Research* special issue have been included as chapters. An earlier version of Chapter 2 was published as:

Jinnah, S., & Lindsay, A. (2015). Secretariat influence on overlap management politics in North America: NAFTA and the Commission for Environmental Cooperation. *Review of Policy Research*, *32*(1), 124–145.

An earlier version of Chapter 5 was published as:

Mumme, S. P. (2015). The evolution of natural resource conservation capacity on the US–Mexico border: Bilateral and trilateral environmental agreements since La Paz. *Review of Policy Research*, *32*(1), 19–39.

An earlier version of Chapter 9 was published as:

Gerlak, A. K. (2015). Resistance and reform: Transboundary water governance in the Colorado River Delta. *Review of Policy Research*, *32*(1), 100–123.

We gratefully acknowledge the special issue's reviewers for helpful comments on these contributions.

And finally, we thank our colleagues at the Loyola Sustainability Research Centre at Concordia University, in particular its former coordinator, Adan Suazo; and our families for their endless support as we brought this project to fruition.

ONE

Research on Transboundary Environmental Governance in North America

New Approaches to Existing and Emerging Challenges

PETER STOETT AND OWEN TEMBY

INTRODUCTION[1]

North America territorially encompasses a diverse mosaic of interrelated ecosystems forming a larger and interdependent whole.[2] The Commission for Environmental Cooperation (CEC) counts 15 unique terrestrial ecoregions and 19 marine ecoregions, many of which cross national boundaries (CEC, 1997; Wilkinson et al., 2009). These ecosystems provide services vital to individual and community health, including an impressive array of fluvial systems, mineral and forest resources, and biodiversity. However, their management is complicated by the reality of multilayered territorial fragmentation, historical patterns of heavy industrialization, and oscillating levels of economic integration. The 1994 North American Free Trade Agreement (NAFTA) codified integrative processes that were already underway and have since intensified, and which have considerable implications for the living standards experienced by the inhabitants of the three nation-states. More than US$2.5 billion in merchandise crosses between Canada, the United States, and Mexico every day, and hundreds of billions of dollars of foreign direct investment have flowed into each country from the NAFTA trading partners since the treaty went into effect (NAFTANOW.org, 2013). This integration has evolved with limited explicit regard for the known ecoregions, yet it has substantial ecological implications. For example, electricity is often generated from natural resources in one country and consumed in another, the extraction and processing of petroleum for sale on the global market is continentally integrated, and toxic materials are regularly transported across the two borders.

While Canada, the United States, and Mexico have complex regulatory regimes for managing a wide range of environmental challenges, there is limited policy congruence and, of course, territorially demarcated policy realms limit administrative and regulatory reach. To address problems related to managing transboundary environmental issues in North America, governments have ratified agreements and created bilateral and trilateral organizations to ostensibly facilitate collaboration and policy coordination among stakeholders. Similarly, many transnational policy networks have evolved in the nonstate sectors as well. Yet the function of these organizations and networks in the broader policy process, and their geographic reach, is not always entirely clear. This volume sheds light on these evolving networks with academic rigor and empirical scope.

Specifically, this book examines the binational and trinational governance of transboundary environmental issues in North America. Given the proliferation of the international organizations and transnational networks with ostensive potential to facilitate continentally integrated policy making, we ask whether a transition is occurring "towards continental environmental policy." Do we see what Stephen Mumme and Pamela Duncan (1997) call "fragmented bilateralism" (p. 43) or is there increasing evidence of the "sub-state actor hypothesis," which is especially popular among North American climate change policy studies and posits that subnational actors (states and provinces, cities and towns) have become, by default, the key actors in transborder environmental governance today (Betsill & Bulkeley, 2004; Boychuck & VanNijnatten, 2004; Fry, 2004; Rabe, 2008; Selin & VanDeveer, 2009)? Similarly, has the "downscaling" observed by scholars of transboundary water governance, and the concomitant expansion of nongovernmental actor participation, occurred equally across binational relationships and in other environmental policy issue areas (Norman, 2015; Norman, Cohen, & Bakker, 2013)?[3] While seeking to answer these broad questions, the contributions provide tentative answers to the following questions:

- What transnational networks and international organizations are significant in the governance of transboundary environmental issues in North America?
- Has the proliferation of these networks and intergovernmental organizations facilitated a transition of North American environmental governance towards integrated continental environmental policy? And,

- To the extent this has happened, what is its scope in terms of stakeholder inclusion, organizational and network activities and functions, and issue comprehensiveness?
- To the extent this has *not* happened, what alternatives have proliferated, and which policy directions can take us closer to realizing coherent, sustainable arrangements?

Scholars studying North American environmental policy have asked these questions—increasingly—in recent years, and have begun to provide tentative answers for this evolving policy domain. This research has reflected a healthy coalescence in approaches to a perennial set of environmental problems (Temby, 2015). Drawing on literatures developing concurrently in both international relations (IR) and public administration on collaborative networks and governmental organizations as interactive bureaucracies (Agranoff & McGuire, 2001; Barnett & Finnemore, 2004; Biermann & Siebenhüner, 2009; Heckscher, 1994), recent studies underscore the role network participants perform in sharing knowledge and developing, coordinating, and implementing policy, and focus on the network and organizational properties likely to bring about successful outcomes (McLaughlin & Krantzberg, 2012; Pacheco-Vega, 2015; Temby, Rastogi, Sandall, Cooksey, & Hickey, 2015). They identify a place for subnational and federal government agencies, binational and trinational organizations, scientists, and economic stakeholders in governance arrangements facilitating mutual learning and adjustment so that complex environmental problems can be managed in an integrative, inclusive, and sustainable fashion (Craik, Studer, & VanNijnatten, 2013; Healy, VanNijnatten, & Lopez-Vallejo, 2014; Norman, Cohen, & Bakker, 2013).

In this book, we seek to advance this discourse by presenting current research on binational and trinational environmental policy in North America on a wide range of topics. These include the "commons" issues of transboundary biodiversity and natural resource governance on which so much recent research has focused, and also the related issues of transboundary energy policy and climate change mitigation. The latter retain special contemporary salience given the expansion (and, more recently, the productivity contraction) of the Canadian tar sands and the stated commitment of the United States, Canada, and Mexico to address planet warming greenhouse gas emissions (GHGs). Yet energy and climate change adaptation appear to be unique policy areas in relation to the others, with their own peculiar constellations of actors and governing arrangements at differing levels of development; accordingly, there is a clear need for variance in the analytical frameworks that can help us understand how they operate on a continental scale (Studer, 2013; Temby, 2015). We return to this issue later in this chapter and in these authors' respective chapters, as they seek to spell out the roles for the diversity of implicated actors in specific policy areas.

We introduce this edited collection by providing an overview of some of the recent conceptual innovation relevant to the study of North American environmental politics, including research represented by chapters in this volume. These are the "new approaches" referred to in the title. First, however, we briefly discuss some of the salient environmental issues for which continental governance is actively practiced and that are driving experimental governance arrangements. As the title of this chapter suggests, overlaying and interacting with the longstanding environmental issues are "emerging challenges" calling for institutional innovation in addressing them and developments in the scholarly understanding of how these institutions operate.

EXISTING AND EMERGING CHALLENGES: THE NORTH AMERICAN ECOPOLITICAL CONTEXT

The environmental challenges with continental and transboundary implications are numerous and relevant at different scales, from the management of transboundary ecoregions to "glocal" issues in which global economic processes entailing cross-border transactions degrade local environmental conditions. In North America there are several categories of natural resources and wildlife that cross political borders and for which management is a challenge of bilateral and potentially trilateral collaboration. Many of these are related to cross-border resources, and migratory species such as the gray whale and the monarch butterfly, and the intentional and incidental introduction of invasive alien species (IAS). Shared water resources are a primary example, and climate change further challenges the fragile governance structures that have been erected in this area during the past century. Problems include increases and decreases of water supplies, including new drought and flood patterns (Kling et al., 2006); the demand for more diversion projects with transborder consequences; increased ranges of IAS; shifts in fish habitat; and other threats to future water resources, riparian peoples, and relations between Canada, the United States, and Mexico.[4]

At the same time, perhaps more than any other area, binational institutionalism has been fairly strong in water relations, most notably in the Great Lakes region: the International Joint Commission (IJC) retains its reputation as a model of shared resource management (though see

Parrish, 2006), and the partial success of the Great Lakes Water Quality Agreement is encouraging. However, there are simmering and newly emerging transborder water disputes from the Pacific to the Atlantic (Bankes & Bourget, 2013; Brandson & Hearne, 2013; Locke & McKinney, 2013) as well as along the U.S.-Mexican border (Gerlak, Zamora-Arroyo, & Kahler, 2013; Mumme, 2003), and climate change promises to pose especially acute challenges in this issue area. Subnational units are certainly playing an important role in developing water management (Brown, 2015; Hall, 2006; Norman, 2015) and adaptation policy, but water is such a high priority for all three national governments we may see their influence diminished as adaptation needs are recognized.

In one of the nastier positive feedback loops that we face today, climate change poses a fundamental threat to biodiversity (Smith et al., 2012), the further loss of which drives continued climate change. We need to assess continent-wide policy responses, including cross-border habitat protection and peace parks, migratory wildlife conservation, border control for unwanted pests and other efforts to curtail the spread of IAS, such as Asian carp, purple loosestrife, pine beetles, zebra mussels, and others (Sanders & Stoett, 2006). Such policies will need to be particularly sensitive to the Canadian-U.S.-Mexican relationship and to communities dependent on wildlife and other forms of biodiversity in natural settings. We can expect to see the emergence of subnational units playing key roles here across the border regions, including scientists, farmers' associations, First Nations and American Indian communities, and voluntary recreational groups.

Beyond water and wildlife, other cross-border issues will continue to influence network development and political activity, including forestry, land degradation and desertification, mountain range conservation, and others. In the U.S.-Canadian case, uniquely, the question of Arctic resources is gaining prominence. More than just another shared border between the two countries, the Arctic bioregions represent one of the greatest challenges related to climate change and the pursuit of environmental justice, since the inhabitants of the Arctic have contributed so little to the risks they now face as ice sheets melt, sea levels rise, tundra softens, keystone species are displaced, and persistent organic pollutants continue their northward journeys (see Koivurova, Keskitalo, & Banks, 2009). The Arctic has also been a source of both prolonged territorial conflict and sustained cooperation between Canada, the United States, and other circumpolar states (Huebert, 2006). One would not anticipate subnational units having a great deal of influence in the development of bilateral Arctic relations, since they are relatively powerless communities; however, land claims processes have given First Nations new weight in negotiations, and

Alaska remains a decidedly powerful state within the American federation, due primarily to its oil wealth.

On the U.S.-Mexican border, the industrialization accompanying economic integration during the past 30 years has brought about substantial water and soil pollution and natural habitat loss. Making matters worse, the economic marginalization of the borderland inhabitants suffering this environmental degradation presents a challenge to the binational and trinational environmental organizations purportedly designed to integrate them into formal decision-making processes (Simon, 2014). The reluctance of the three governments to facilitate more inclusive environmental governance, coupled with the borderland region's pressing challenges, has called into question the legitimacy of the relevant regional binational and trinational institutions. This has improved only slightly in recent years with the increased transparency of the famously insular binational water management organization, the International Boundary and Water Commission (IBWC), to the involvement of nongovernmental stakeholders. Yet the extent of the unresolved challenges to habitat and public health that this organization must address (e.g., water allocation and quality) promises to keep it under increased scrutiny.

Finally, there are the considerable challenges associated with the regional (transboundary and continental) distribution of energy production and consumption. Outside of regional markets for electricity sales and distribution (e.g., Quebec and the northeast United States), little binational or trinational regulation of energy takes place. Yet the transmission of oil, coal, uranium, liquefied natural gas, and other energy resources is a constant issue and will remain so as long as, for example, Mexico's oil supplies deplete, Canada's become more available, substantial refining capacity remains in the United States, and all three countries participate in the extraction of natural gas from shale formations. The BP oil spill of 2011 provided ample evidence of the continued threat to biosafety presented by deepwater oil drilling platforms, and pipeline leaks and tragic train derailments further amplify legitimate concerns about the sustainability of energy resource transport systems (see Merry, 2014). Integrated efforts to move towards renewable energy resources, are occurring, however, and provide evidence of shared concerns and goal setting (Etcheverry, 2013; Rabe, 2013).

Understanding how Canada, the United States, and Mexico have responded to these complex sets of issues, what actors are important in the process, and where the deficiencies and opportunities for improvement exist requires enhanced analytical tools. We turn to the most significant recent conceptual developments by scholars working on these new approaches in the next section of this chapter.

NEW APPROACHES: CONCEPTUAL DEVELOPMENTS IN NORTH AMERICAN ENVIRONMENTAL GOVERNANCE

This book's subtitle, *North American Transnational Networks and Governance*, reflects significant conceptual developments in the study of North American politics and, more specifically, environmental governance. Largely extraneous to national regulatory processes, alternative "governance" arrangements are in play in binational, trinational, and international efforts to coordinate programs and share knowledge. They typically take the form of "networks" of actors, whose members are often state, provincial, or federal government agencies, municipal governments, scientists, economic stakeholders and, at times, multinational corporations. Given the arguable democratic deficit in the process, a more appropriate characterization is perhaps "(semi-) inclusive technocracy." Furthermore, often such networks feature the participation of one of the many North American international environmental organizations created and funded by two or three of the continent's nations.

In a recent volume marking the 20th anniversary of NAFTA, titled *Regional Governance in a Post-NAFTA North America*, Brian Bow and Greg Anderson (2015) observe that much of the early scholarly literature aimed at understanding the development of this trinational institution was "looking in the wrong places and expecting the wrong things" (p. 1). Their point is that research using the lens of international negotiation and formal policy infrastructure development failed to capture the wealth of changes in North American governance occurring during the past 20 years. However, more recent conceptual developments, occurring largely outside the study of North American politics, have revealed that actually quite a bit happened. Bow and Anderson specifically highlight the research commonly categorized under the label "multilevel governance" as important for locating governance and accounting for change.

Multilevel governance (MLG) was popularized by Liesbet Hooghe and Gary Marks (2003), who used the term to organize different approaches to research on governance "dispersed among multiple centers of authority" (p. 233). They classified contemporaneous literature depicting a disaggregated state and responses to the resulting coordination challenges into two categories, unimaginatively titled "Type I" and "Type II." Type I governance represents federally structured systems that include general-purpose jurisdictions (in particular, local jurisdictions), jurisdictionally defined (nonintersecting) organizational membership for policy actors, a limited number of jurisdictions, and a durable architecture that persists beyond the circumstances justifying its establishment (Hooghe & Marks, 2003). Type II governance represents shorter-term and more flexible arrangements. Here, governance operates on more scales, networks are formed around specific problems and may cease to exist when the problems are sufficiently addressed, they have overlapping members, and relationships are more informal. In Type II governance, working groups of bureaucrats from different organizations are one form of an evolving, depoliticized underbelly of governance.

These are, of course, ideal types, as Bow and Anderson point out. In the North American context, transnational networks address transnational issues, but it happens within the constraints of international treaties and with the participation of international organizations and federally arranged national and subnational agencies. And, as the contributions of this volume on environmental governance show, sometimes adaptive networks can reshape the durable bi- or trinational architecture. Given this dialectical relationship underpinning the "new mode of regional governance in North America," Bow and Anderson (2015, p. 3) observe that the extent to which binational relationships exhibit Type I or Type II arrangements should be a priority for empirical investigation.

Fortunately, recent research in the field of IR, augmented by studies of public administration, has provided useful concepts for making sense of this complex political space.[5] While these multilevel governance approaches to policy making have been applied to many different issue areas, their application in the environmental governance issue area has been particularly fruitful, and provides a conceptual basis for this volume's analyses. In IR, constructivist theory has expanded the field's research program by examining questions about the role of government agencies, intergovernmental institutions, and global activists in diffusing norms and framing knowledge (Finnemore & Sikkink, 1998; Hoffmann, 2005; Litfin, 1994; Price, 1998; Wapner, 1995). A common concern for scholars adhering to this approach involves examining who establishes rules used for governance and who is viewed as having authority to do so. For example, Peter Haas (1990), in a well-known study of Mediterranean Sea environmental management, discusses the role of "epistemic communities" providing technical expertise and framing scientific knowledge. These experts in government agencies, universities, and activist organizations facilitate the management of shared natural resources by filling a technical gap and enhancing government capacity by disseminating a shared understanding of how to address specific environmental challenges. The epistemic community's authority is derived from its perceived expertise and knowledge of the issue area. The recent establishment of the UN-based Intergovernmental Science-Policy Platform on Biodiversity and Ecosystem Services (IPBES) is an example of an epistemic community asserting policy relevance.[6]

Of late, an important branch within IR constructivist scholarship has examined international organizations and their secretariats as *bureaucracies*, exploring the ways in which this understanding can contribute to a research program examining international organizational dynamics and influence (Barnett & Finnemore, 2004; Biermann & Siebenhuner, 2009; Jinnah, 2014). These scholars argue that international organizations, as bureaucracies, derive their authority from their capacity to expertly develop impartial and technocratic rules governing their own behavior and the behavior of relevant external actors. This rational-legal authority is supplemental to (and potentially interacts with) whatever delegated authority such organizations explicitly receive from the governments that created them. It has several implications for the behavior of international environmental organizations (including the transboundary environmental institutions in North America). It grants them a degree of autonomy in relation to the governments that created them. Obviously North American transborder environmental organizations have *some* measure of autonomy, as the statutes creating the organizations typically outline the specific tasks that have been delegated to them by member states. However, as Finnemore and Barnett explain, international organizations possess a degree of discretion in exercising their authority by virtue of the fact that understandings of the complex problems they are expected to govern are often underdeveloped; and they tend to develop their own cultures and internal processes in carrying out their delegated tasks, which can lead them to pursue their own distinct interests (see also Jinnah, 2014). For example, as Stephen Mumme (1984) illustrates, the U.S. Section of the IBWC has exercised "substantial institutional autonomy" in mediating between the U.S. Department of State and the states along the U.S.-Mexican border in their relations with Mexico (p. 115). Despite being formally overseen by the U.S. Department of State, the IBWC's influence is a result of its clientele relations with the states and specialized expertise. Rational-legal authority also grants transboundary environmental organizations types of power that understandings based on regulatory capacity or the mere provision of information do not capture. International organizations can "use their authority to orient action and create social reality" by classifying information, defining concepts, constructing problems, and identifying actors (sometimes themselves) as qualified to address the problem (Barnett & Finnemore, 2004, p. 6).

This IR constructivist understanding of organizational influence permits consideration of the possibility that organizations' actions can contribute to policy innovation through interaction with other implicated public agencies and a contribution to learning through collaboration.

Indeed, the "new public management" scholarship has explicated a "post-bureaucratic" way for government organizations to function (Aucoin, 1995; Hecksher, 1994; Kernaghan, 2000). According to this view, postbureaucratic organizations operate on the basis of consensus rather than hierarchy, are concerned with relationships rather than specific tasks, and seek to innovate rather than maintain the status quo. Subsequently, a robust literature on policy networks developed into a mainstay of the public administration field, with scholars observing that environmental policy (among other complex issue areas) is increasingly formulated by diverse actors operating within such networks (see Isett, Mergel, LeRoux, Mischen, & Rethemeyer, 2011, for the state of the art).

Networks arguably fitting the postbureaucratic mold tend to be issue specific and include both public and private sector participants (such as public agencies from multiple levels of government) as well as arms-length nonprofits (Agranoff & McGuire, 2003; Edelenbos, van Buuren, & van Schie, 2011; Giebels, van Buuren, & Edelenbos, 2015; Imperial, 2005). They are utilized by governments to respond to complex and cross-cutting environmental issues in which the knowledge needed to inform decision making is highly specialized yet fragmented across bureaucratic agencies, and when regulatory jurisdiction is shared both horizontally (i.e., across governments and agencies within governments) and vertically across levels of government (Agranoff, 2007; Berardo, Heikkila, & Gerlak, 2014; Imperial, 2005). These networks enable agencies to share and integrate specialized knowledge and develop institutional capacity to address what Rittel and Webber (1973) refer to as "wicked" problems of modern governance. Their membership tends to be overlapping among issue areas, with public agencies typically participating in networks on a wide range of topics. For example, as Christopher Brown (2015) has shown, a network of more than 20 federal and state or provincial agencies and local governments formulate policy for the management of the transboundary Abbotsford-Sumas aquifer in the Salish Sea region on the U.S.-Canadian border. These environment, health, and agriculture departments operate at two levels of government and also with indigenous tribal governments. Moreover, not all of those involved are even formal governmental agencies; also participating are staff from Washington State University, nonprofit organizations, and industry groups with a stake in decision making on aquifer use.

The emergence of environmental management through issue-specific collaborative networks, and the ability of transboundary North American organizations to participate in them, suggests that bilateral and trilateral environmental governance may be a multiagency and multistakeholder affair. Rather than evaluating individual organizations or regimes for their effectiveness in compelling states to behave differently (i.e., as independent variables), we should consider the possibility that they operate within and thereby contribute to the construction of these networks: defining problems, framing knowledge, categorizing information, dedicating specialized personnel, and playing an intrinsic, if not a defining, role in the development of policy. Regulatory authority often rests with domestic agencies, but even then it is a decentralized array of agencies at several levels of government that (ideally) seek to coordinate policy making in addressing highly complex problems. In these situations, good information is in demand and in perpetually insufficient supply, and intergovernmental organizations and activists with technical expertise potentially play an important part.[7]

While this volume contains several examples of scholarship within this theoretical orientation, some recent attempts to specify loose conceptual frameworks are worth highlighting because they evidence the recent coalescence in approaches to North American environmental policy. First, in a recent special issue of the journal *Review of Policy Research* on North American natural resource and biodiversity governance, we proposed using two dimensions to distinguish between and categorize international environmental organizations: the extent to which they behave postbureaucratically, and whether their dominant function is regulatory or aimed at building capacity by channeling funds or information (Stoett & Temby, 2015). Following Charles Hecksher (1994), we called the bureaucratic/postbureaucratic dimension "interactiveness" (Table 1.1), and assessed in which of the four categories the binational and trinational North American environmental organizations examined in the special issue belong. We found organizations fitting into each of the four of the quadrants, albeit with a trend towards more postbureaucratic behavior.

Second, in their recent work, *Environmental Policy in North America: Approaches, Capacity, and the Management of Transboundary Issues*, Robert Healey, Debora VanNijnatten, and Marcela Lopez-Vallejo (2014)

Table 1.1
A Typology of International Environmental Organizations

	"Interactiveness"	
Dominant Function	**Bureaucratic**	**Post-Bureaucratic**
Regulatory	Siloed Regulator	Participatory Regulator
Capacity Building	Resource Depot	Collaborative Facilitator

Source: Stoett and Temby (2015).

engage in the ambitious project of circumscribing and defining North American environmental governance, and exploring the relevant domestic, bilateral, and trilateral institutions already in place. They argue that despite different legal frameworks and political cultures among Canada, the United States, and Mexico, their approach to addressing the diversity of environmental issues is not so pronounced that it presents a substantial hindrance for trilateral cooperation. Rather, the problem is one of environmental governance *capacity*, defined as "the ability to propose, plan, choose a course of action, implement, and evaluate an effective policy" (p. 6).[8] To enhance capacity and, to the extent necessary, bridge national policy differences, the authors propose three "critical functions for transboundary governance mechanisms" (i.e., organizations), namely, (1) creating comprehensive and stable transboundary networks, (2) enabling mutual learning and information exchange, and (3) facilitating the provision of resources (p. 7). The authors then proceed to assess the extent to which this has happened in four topical environmental issue areas: biodiversity, smog, greenhouse gas reduction, and genetically modified organisms (GMOs).

Third, Debora VanNijnatten and Neil Craik (2015) have recently shown that North American transgovernmental networks are often "bundled" by domestic leaders or international organizations seeking to harness this form of governance. Network bundling, they observe, "mobilizes bureaucratic resources toward network activities," and offers "considerable potential in terms of enabling higher levels of environmental policy coordination" (pp. 42–43). VanNijnatten and Craik give examples of formal plans or forums, presently underway, that bundle working groups under a moniker, specifically the 2009 U.S.-Canada Clean Energy Dialogue, Border 2020 (the U.S.-Mexican environmental plan), and working groups organized by the CEC.

These recent examples are indicative of the coalescence in approaches to the study of North American environmental policy (represented well by several contributions to this volume), especially with their focus on learning and capacity building through policy networks. However, evidence suggests that, despite its utility, this approach also has notable limitations in locating governance where it occurs. In a provocative study of indigenous communities and U.S.-Canadian water governance, Emma S. Norman (2015) underscored the deep normative and epistemological divides between these communities and policy makers. Norman's analysis takes the unraveling state and downscaling of governance as a given and explores the efforts of binational international institutions to adapt to these changes. But her main concern is to examine the activities of indigenous communities living in the borderland areas as they seek to reclaim and govern their traditional water resources while concurrently strengthening community bonds. Her expressed hope is that the ongoing transition in water governance, coupled with indigenous communities' empowerment, will contribute to the decolonialization of the boundary region—in particular, the dissolution of unjust scalar constructions such as national borders cutting across tribal land. However, insofar as this is happening and will happen, it does so outside the normal technocratic networks that govern these resources. Tellingly, Norman locates indigenous water governance through accounts of community gatherings and acts of defiance to scientists and government officials. Insofar as the influence of these important sovereign political actors is channeled through the networks governing transboundary aquatic ecosystems (and it is not entirely clear that it is), conceptual approaches illustrating how this occurs need to be developed.

Moreover, the cases of successful governance through networks and international organizations in North America that have been described are mostly in the areas of biodiversity and natural resource management (such as water and fisheries). Healey et al. (2014) found that biodiversity governance in particular exhibits well-developed networks facilitating the exchange of information and provision of resources. Their existence and effectiveness in the areas of smog and GHG abatement are more mixed; and in the area of GMO governance they are almost nonexistent. This is partially reflective of regulatory reluctance or gaps, but also suggests that some transboundary environmental issues are more apt to be examined with the "networks" lens than others (at least, networks consisting of government agencies and international organizations). Similarly, in a recent assessment of the extent to which such networks have worked to develop a continental climate change regime, Isabelle Studer (2013) observed:

> In the absence of both supply and demand for a climate change regime, bottom-up, transgovernmental collaborative networks are not strong enough to push for the emergence of such a regime, even if there were high levels of energy interdependence and strong linkages between energy security and vulnerabilities to climate change. (p. 58)

Analyzing these institutions to understand North American environmental policy appears to work well when policy coordination necessitates that transboundary interagency networks integrate scientific knowledge across organizational boundaries to manage a definable commons (land use policy, for example), and less well when the important actors operate outside of these networks and sidestep the relevant binational/trinational organizations (as in the case of greenhouse gas mitigation and energy policy). The contributions in this volume enable a further clarification of the utility of these organizations and networks, and of analytical frameworks that can enhance our understanding of their function, scope, and potential.

ORGANIZATION OF THE BOOK

The volume is divided into three parts, each briefly described below.

Part I: Bilateral and Trilateral Institutional Effectiveness

The first part of the book assesses the effectiveness of existing institutions and the political and organizational challenges they must overcome to bring about coordinated and inclusive international governance. Chapters 2 and 3 both focus on institutions created through the NAFTA environmental side accords, in particular the CEC, the continent's prime example of a trilateral environmental organization. Chapter 2 employs a similar approach to the one used in Sikina Jinnah's (2014) notable recent book on international organization influence and biodiversity governance, *Post-Treaty Politics*, but here it is applied to a North American institution addressing a broader suite of issues. Jinnah and Lindsay examine how the CEC's secretariat exercises influence through the production and dissemination of independent reports. Exploring this mechanism of technocratic governance illustrates the importance of North American international organizations in sharing information and building capacity within policy networks, despite an absence of regulatory authority, as in the case of the CEC.

In Chapter 3, Simon offers a striking alternative account of the CEC, as well as two other institutions established under the auspices of NAFTA: the North American Development Bank (NADB) and the Border Environmental Cooperation Commission (BECC). She highlights the side accords' objectives of more participatory environmental governance on the North American borderlands and the practical challenges the organizations have faced in integrating grassroots activists into the policy process. Using a case study of a failed attempt to involve a citizens' group in a grant proposal to the BECC and NADB, Simon highlights the barriers (in particular, the "digital divide") that hinders public participation in the organizations and networks at issue in this volume. It is a sobering account of some of the most important limitations of policy networks in North American environmental governance.

Chapter 4 highlights another shortcoming, namely the lack of transboundary environmental impact assessment processes and the problems caused by this lacuna. Collins and Kennedy explore Canada's and the United States' domestic policy regimes, highlight past binational disputes that could have been better addressed with more developed institutions, and argue for the desirability and feasibility of a bilateral transboundary environmental impact assessment agreement. They contend that North America should look to an existing international agreement, the Espoo Convention on transboundary environmental impact assessment (to which Canada is a party), for an example of how a successful systematic binational framework could operate, and suggest that projects along the U.S.-Mexican border would similarly benefit from such a framework. The end goal is not to curb development, but to enhance its legitimacy through public accountability and discourse.

Part II: Biodiversity and Natural Resource Governance

The second part contains contributions focused specifically on the governance of living natural resources and ecosystems. In Chapter 5, Mumme offers a "big picture" view of the bilateral and trilateral agreements facilitating the development of natural resource conservation capacity on the U.S.-Mexican border since the mid-1980s. These include not only executive agreements, such as the 1983 La Paz Agreement and the NAFTA environmental side accords, but also the binational and trinational organizations that have evolved through them. Focusing on capacity gains facilitated by these organizations, Mumme assesses them on multiple dimensions relevant to the study of transboundary environmental networks, including public participation inclusiveness, intersectoral integration, information sharing, and the provision of financial resources. He contends that while recent capacity gains have improved the management of transboundary natural resources, security measures taken post–9/11 have redirected funding away from conservation measures and led to activities that threaten transboundary wildlife (an issue to which he and Brown return in Chapter 10).

Olive delves into a more specific issue area in Chapter 6: the conservation of endangered species in Canada and the United States. Despite historical similarities and federal governments, two distinct regulatory regimes have evolved over the last five decades, and Olive's work, much of it based on numerous interviews with landholders in both countries, suggests that human–land relationships and culture play a pivotal role in the implementation and success of conservation programs. She emphasizes differences in approach to listing species as endangered as an obstacle to effective bilateral policy development. She identifies one issue, however, that is very congruent: the steady decrease in resources devoted to endangered species protection. While some readers may disagree with her characterization of the inherent differences between Canada and the United States, few would argue that there is both an urgent need for increased, as opposed to decreased, attention to the wildlife protection issue area. The need for more collaboration between Canada and the United States—and for this to extend to Mexico, which has a strong record of at least rhetorical prioritization of biodiversity protection—has never been stronger in light of the additional strain presented by climate change, continued land use intensification, and urbanization experienced across the continent.

Chapter 7 provides an overview of binational institutions participating in U.S.-Canadian transboundary fisheries governance. (Mexico and the United States, while claiming waters shared by various fish stocks, lack such institutions.) As Song, Temby, Krantzberg, and Hickey show, fisheries governance is unique as a wildlife stewardship challenge because fish stocks are managed differently depending on whether they are inland or in the marine environment, and also because of their commercial value (extending beyond the harvest value of the fish to that of the tourism industries supported by recreational fishing). In their contribution, the authors examine the networks and organizations managing the Pacific salmon fisheries, the Great Lakes fisheries, and the ground fisheries of the Atlantic northeast. They show that the informal character of relationships among civil servants and other stakeholders represents a critical dimension to how these networks and organizations function, pointing to the need for further research on this topic.

In Chapter 8, VanNijnatten and Stoett examine the policy networks that have developed during the last century in the fight against invasive alien species (IAS) across the continent. IAS are a pernicious threat to biodiversity, human health, the economy, and community identity. As major trading states, all three North American countries are highly vulnerable to their introduction in waterways and along other transportation corridors. Improper disposal of exotic pets and plants are further challenges. VanNijnatten and Stoett focus primarily on aquatic invasive species, and also delve into the more coherent network on plants. They find that extensive networks for collaboration exist, along with some formal and globally linked institutions such as the North American Plant Protection Organization. While Canada and the United States have made significant progress in moving towards the common goals of invasive species management, there is a great deal to be done as climate change and other emerging complications present new challenges, and some of the more fragile and isolated ecologies (such as the Arctic and the island state of Hawaii) face special threats to biosafety. Mexico has an enviable devotion to biodiversity in global terms, but can only advance its own counter-bioinvasion strategies with closer integration with its NAFTA partners' policies (and, of course, Mexico must look southward in a preventive fashion as well). A promised North American IAS strategy is in the works. The authors conclude that the interactions between networks and institutions in the prevention and early detection architecture for invasive species might be characterized as recursive and iterative in nature, a common pattern identified in other chapters as well.

The next two chapters offer case studies of recent political events affecting ecosystems on or near the U.S.-Mexican border. In Chapter 9, Gerlak examines the successful efforts of a transboundary network, the Delta Restoration Network, in addressing water governance issues in the binational Colorado River. Because the water in the river has been mostly diverted to cities and for agriculture, it no longer reaches the ocean. The area where it had connected with the ocean in the past, the Colorado River delta, nevertheless remains a wetlands ecosystem rich in biodiversity, serving as a habitat for numerous species of plants and birds. A substantial challenge for the network, as Gerlak explains, is that the binational organization governing U.S.-Mexican transboundary water utilization, the IBWC, is insular and bureaucratic. In this contribution, Gerlak traces the development of the network, including its changes in membership, and provides an account of how it was able to influence the IBWC and other policy makers to develop an international agreement to restore water to the delta.

In Chapter 10, Mumme and Brown present a less rosy view of binational environmental cooperation (or lack thereof) between Mexico and the United States. Their contribution covers the politics of the security fence on the U.S.-Mexican border. As they explain, this environmentally destructive project was not a result of bilateral policy coordination or cooperation, nor was it resisted or even problematized by environmental interests when it was under consideration. The authorization and regulatory path for this physically and symbolically imposing barrier occurred in an ironically stealthy way, with protests occurring only afterwards. This case study serves as an important reminder that, at times, security and immigration policy trump sound wildlife policy, and that the policy process can take place outside the reach of the environmentally concerned networks that have a stake in it.

Part III: Energy and Climate Change Mitigation

The third and final part of this volume contains contributions on energy governance, including the presently salient issues of sustainable energy and greenhouse gas mitigation. Chapter 11 describes a different role for government and the types of networks discussed elsewhere in this book. Gonzalez argues that the Canadian oil sands have been integrated into the American energy system through the efforts of elite policy-planning networks seeking to maintain low liquid fuel prices in the United States. He outlines these networks' operations at two different scales. First, during the early and middle years of the 20th century, a network consisting of the Alberta government and elites within the province developed the oil sands as a source of energy. Second, following World War II, as American oil demand increased—and especially following the 1973 oil shock—elite policy networks identified Alberta oil as a solution to supply shortages. As Gonzalez contends, this is important for the American understanding of its global hegemonic role. These networks sought to secure Alberta's unconventional oil as a way of fueling U.S. urban sprawl and consumption, a substantial source of U.S. global clout. This chapter suggests that some environmental issues (such as unconventional energy), while potentially employing the language of networks, beg for a political economy approach to understanding their political dynamics.

In Chapter 12, López-Vallejo examines the U.S.-Mexican energy relationship, in particular the extent to which programs in place for sustainable energy development are robust or instead relegated to the transnational production and distribution processes for fossil fuels. The chapter's central argument is that the relationship consists of two different "types, intensities, and rhythms," for fossil fuels and sustainable energy. In both cases a disparity in available technological capacity sets the tone, but is manifest in different ways. In the former, Mexico exports (like Canada) a substantial amount of its crude oil to the United States for refining, and then imports refined petroleum for consumption. Here the energy relationship develops as the industry adjusts to the evolving global demand and technological context for their product, which includes bilateral trade when expedient (as in case of different technologies and natural resources on either side of the border). In the latter, the two governments have created bilateral agreements ostensibly to facilitate the development of sustainable energy in Mexico, in part so that American states can purchase this electricity and satisfy their renewable energy quotas. As López-Vallejo shows, the technological capacity gap has manifested itself as Mexico has fallen behind in the development of these technologies—despite the organizational infrastructure appearing to be in place. The binational integration of sustainable energy development between Mexico and the United States has failed to materialize as promised, with clean energy addressed only tangentially in existing programs. López-Vallejo and Gonzalez paint a bleak picture of the prospect for environmentally concerned energy relations in North America.

The next two chapters return the focus to the U.S.-Canadian energy relationship but, rather than focusing on fossil fuels specifically, discuss electricity relations on the border. In Chapter 13, Macfarlane examines hydroelectric developments and the role of the IJC in approving them and mediating conflicts between the two countries. This is achieved through a historical overview of four regional groupings of border hydrostations, namely Great Lakes–St. Lawrence, Pacific Northwest, Maine–New Brunswick, and Rainy River/Lake of the Woods. As Macfarlane shows, the hydroelectric developments and the binational organization they necessitated have had substantial influence on U.S.-Canadian environmental and energy policy, particularly on the role of subnational governments. Furthermore, while bilateral relations have been "fluid," consisting of both conflict and cooperation, Canada's confrontational "hydro nationalism" has been a persistent trait with contemporary relevance.

Chapter 14 focuses on contemporary electricity relations in the Manitoba/Midwest and Québec/New York–New England regions. This is important because electricity generation is the United States' largest source of greenhouse gases, and thus opportunities for more efficient distribution systems (including efficiencies from buying and selling from cross-border neighbors) should be seized upon. In this chapter, Rowlands offers a review of the actors involved in the process of transboundary electricity trade and transmission, their interests, and the means through which they communicate. Similar to Song et al. in Chapter 7, Rowlands explores the extent to which stakeholders communicate through informal and formal means, and the conditions that lead to cooperation and conflict. This is of particular significance given that, as Rowlands notes, conflict is more common than cooperation, even though there are potential joint gains that could benefit both sides. He concludes with suggestions for managing these conflicts and improving the potential for the utilization of transboundary electricity transmission.

In Chapter 15, Huff offers a "case for continental" climate change policy integration. As noted elsewhere (see Studer, 2013; VanNijnatten & Craik, 2013), the case is not obvious or necessarily intuitive. After all, fossil fuel markets are *globally* integrated and electricity markets are mainly subnational. Huff acknowledges these and other drawbacks, yet contends that there is both a rationale and potential for an integrated North American climate regime. In making the case, he reviews existing domestic programs, regional initiatives, and multilateral institutions that might be implicated in the process, and constructs an account of a halting, piecemeal, yet potentially emergent and integrated system that might lower mitigation costs, facilitate the development of policy capacity, and improve the three countries' negotiating position in global abatement talks. Recent trilateral commitments are an exciting development, though seasoned observers will advise caution lest we become overly optimistic, especially after the election of Donald J. Trump to the presidency of the United States in 2016.

Finally, in Chapter 16, we conclude by reviewing our guiding questions and assessing the lessons learned from the contributions herein. We also point the way to potentially fruitful directions for future research on North American environmental transnational environmental governance.

CONCLUSION

If there is a "North American idea" premised on a continental future (Clarkson, 2008; Pastor, 2011), then the ecologically sustainable governance of the continent's ecosystems and energy systems is not optional. They are central to the project, and play a fundamental role in defining the thousands of communities that are found on the continent, including those located in the cross-border regions. While it is premature to speak of an integrated North America as one might refer to the European Union, economic and demographic trends indicate that, despite relatively rigid borders after September 11, 2001 (and ongoing border-related controversies on all three borders, including the Alaska-Canadian borderline), the continent can be viewed as integration in progress (on 9/11, see Farson, 2006; Konrad & Nicol, 2008). Mexico is culturally tied to its southern neighbors, Canada is similarly entwined with its European cousins, and the United States faces unique challenges as the most powerful state in the international system (and its power is partially a reflection of its northern and southern neighbors; see Clarkson & Mildenberger, 2011). Indeed there are vast cultural differences between citizens of these countries and, of course, equally pronounced differences within them (Adams, 2003). Yet the natural ties that bind are undeniable, and the institutional architecture that the three governments, substate political units, and transnational experts form today will affect the collective fate of all North Americans tomorrow, despite the political turbulence experienced after the November 2016 election in the United States.

We hope the chapters of this book will shed some light on an understudied topic: how cross-border institution building is shaping the contours of environmental governance in North America. No doubt, each contribution will raise as many questions as it answers, paving the way for more research in this area. But as all three countries face the common threat of climate change, it is more important than ever that the vast expertise and collaborative potential that exists in the transnational sphere can find an equally influential voice in the formal intergovernmental context.

NOTES

1. A 2015 special issue of *Review of Policy Research*, edited by the present editors of this volume, made an earlier effort to integrate contemporary research on transnational environmental governance in North America; this original volume furthers this agenda, though some of the material found here was first introduced there.
2. Note that, in accordance with the North American Free Trade Agreement (NAFTA), we include Mexico in not only the geophysical continent of North America, but also consider it a North American country in the political and economic sense, despite its close physical and cultural connection to Latin America, and despite the United Nations' exclusion of Mexico from what it generally considers the region of North America.
3. Tun Myint (2012) and Susanne Schmeier (2013) make similar observations about multistakeholder participation transboundary water governance in other international contexts. Myint labels the observed phenomenon "policycentric" and develops a useful theoretical approach for examining it.
4. Invasive species will become a particularly troublesome border control problem as their population ranges shift, posing threats to local habitat and human health. See Ameden, Cash, Vickers, and Zilberman (2007), Mainka and Howard (2010), and Smith et al. (2012).
5. It is worth underscoring the significance of these recent conceptual developments in the history of IR theory. For an overview and critique of existing state-centric approaches relevant to this volume, see Stoett and Temby (2015). Other useful critiques offering similar alternative accounts of, and approaches to, transnational environmental policy

include Verweij's (2000) application of grid-group theory, Myint's (2012) "polycentric governance," and Kütting and Cerny's (2015) "transnational neopluralism."

6. On IPBES, see www.ipbes.net. For an informative study on the interface between science, policy, and biodiversity in the Canadian context see Bocking (2004).
7. This need not be interpreted as the democratization of policy making. Many of these organizations are fairly elitist in nature, reflecting the need for higher educational attainment and years of networking.
8. For another useful study of international environmental organizations and transnational capacity building, albeit outside the North American context, see Heikka, Gerlak, Bell, and Schmeier (2013).

REFERENCES

Adams, M. (2003). *Fire and ice: The United States, Canada, and the myth of converging values*. Toronto, ON: Penguin.

Agranoff, R. (2007). *Managing within networks: Adding value to public organizations*. Washington, DC: Georgetown University Press.

Agranoff, R., & McGuire, M. (2001). Big questions in public network management research. *Journal of Public Administration Research and Theory*, *11*(3), 295–326.

Agranoff, R. & McGuire, M. (2003). *Collaborative public management: New strategies for local governments*. Washington, DC: Georgetown University Press.

Ameden, H., Cash, S., Vickers, D. A., & Zilberman, D. (2007). *Economics, policy, and border enforcement of invasive species*. Edmonton, AB: Alberta Institute for American Studies.

Aucoin, P. (1995). *The new public management: Canada in comparative perspective*. Montreal, QC: Institute for Research on Public Policy.

Bankes, N., & Bourget, E. (2013). Apportionment of the St. Mary and Milk Rivers. In E. S. Norman, A. Cohen, & K. Bakker (Eds.), *Water without borders? Canada, the United States, and shared waters* (pp. 159–178). Toronto, ON: University of Toronto Press.

Barnett, M., & Finnemore, M. (2004). *Rules for the world: International organizations in global politics*. Ithaca, NY: Cornell University Press.

Berardo, R., Heikkila, T., & Gerlak, A. K. (2014). Interorganizational engagement in collaborative environmental management: Evidence from the South Florida Ecosystem Restoration Task Force. *Journal of Public Administration Research and Theory*, *24*(3), 697–719.

Betsill, M., & Bulkeley, H. (2004). Transnational networks and global environmental governance: The cities for climate protection program. *International Studies Quarterly*, *48*(2), 471–493.

Biermann, F., & Siebenhuner, B. (Eds.). (2009). *Managers of global change: The influence of international environmental bureaucracies*. Cambridge, MA: MIT Press.

Bocking, S. (2004). *Nature's experts: Science, politics, and the environment*. New Brunswick, NJ: Rutgers University Press.

Bow, B., & Anderson, G. (2015). Building without architecture: Regional governance in post-NAFTA North America. In B. Bow & G. Anderson (Eds.), *Regional governance in post-NAFTA North America: Building without architecture* (pp. 1–30). New York, NY: Routledge.

Boychuck, G., & VanNijnatten, D. (2004). Economic integration and cross-border policy convergence: Social and environmental policy in Canadian provinces and American states. *Horizons*, *7*(1), 55–60.

Brandson, N., & Hearne, R. (2013). Devils Lake and Red River Basin. In E. S. Norman, A. Cohen, & K. Bakker (Eds.), *Water without borders? Canada, the United States, and shared waters* (pp. 179–192). Toronto, ON: University of Toronto Press.

Brown, C. (2015). Scale and subnational resource management: Transnational initiatives in the Salish Sea region. *Review of Policy Research*, *32*(1), 60–78.

Clarkson, S. (2008). *Does North American exist? Governing the continent after NAFTA and 9/11*. Toronto, ON and Washington, DC: University of Toronto and Woodrow Wilson Center Press.

Clarkson, S., & Mildenberger, M. (2011). *Dependent America? Now Canada and Mexico construct U.S. power*. Toronto, ON and Washington, DC: University of Toronto Press and Woodrow Wilson Center Press.

Commission for Environmental Cooperation. (1997). *Ecological regions of North America: Toward a common perspective*. Montreal, QC: CEC Secretariat.

Craik, N., Studer, I., & VanNijnatten, D. (Eds.). (2013). *Climate change policy in North America: Designing integration in a regional system*. Toronto, ON: University of Toronto Press.

Edelenbos, J., van Buuren, A., & van Schie, N. (2011). Co-producing knowledge: Joint knowledge production between experts, bureaucrats and stakeholders in Dutch water management projects. *Environmental Science & Policy*, *14*(6), 675–684.

Etcheverry, J. (2013). New approaches to climate mitigation: Collaborative strategies for developing renewable energy in North America. In

N. Craik, I. Studer, & D. VanNijnatten (Eds.), *Climate change policy in North America: Designing integration in a regional system* (pp. 157–181). Toronto, ON: University of Toronto Press.

Farson, S. (2006). Rethinking the North American frontier after 9/11. *Journal of Borderlands Studies*, *21*(1), 23–45.

Finnemore, M., & Sikkink, K. (1998). International norm dynamics and political change. *International Organization*, *52*(4), 887–917.

Fry, E. (2004). The role of subnational governments in North American integration. In T. J. Courchene, D. J. Savoie, & D. Schwanen (Eds.), *The art of the state II: Thinking North America*, no. 3 (pp. 3–31). Montreal, QC: Institute for Research on Public Policy.

Gerlak, A. K., Zamora-Arroyo, F., & Kahler, H. P. (2013). A delta in repair: Restoration, binational cooperation, and the future of the Colorado River Delta. *Environment: Science and Policy for Sustainable Development*, *55*(3), 29–40.

Giebels, D., van Buuren, A., & Edelenbos, J. (2015). Using knowledge in a complex decision-making process—Evidence and principles from the Danish Houting project's ecosystem-based management approach. *Environmental Science & Policy*, *47*, 53–67.

Haas, P. M. (1990). *Saving the Mediterranean: The politics of international environmental cooperation*. New York, NY: Columbia University Press.

Hall, N. (2006). Toward a new horizontal federalism: Interstate water management in the Great Lakes region. *University of Colorado Law Review*, *77*, 405–456.

Healy, R. G., VanNijnatten, D. L., & Lopez-Vallejo, M. (2014). *Environmental policy in North America: Approaches, capacity, and the management of transboundary issues*. Toronto, ON: University of Toronto Press.

Heckscher, C. (1994). Defining the post-bureaucratic type. In C. Heckscher & A. Donnellon (Eds.), *The post-bureaucratic organization: New perspectives on organizational change* (pp. 14–62). Thousand Oaks, CA: Sage.

Heikkila, T., Gerlak, A. K., Bell, A. R., & Schmeier, S. (2013). Adaptation in a transboundary river basin: Linking stressors and adaptive capacity within the Mekong River Commission. *Environmental Science & Policy*, *25*(1), 73–82.

Hoffmann, M. J. (2005). *Ozone depletion and climate change: Constructing a global response*. Albany, NY: State University of New York Press.

Hooghe, L., & Marks, G. (2003). Unraveling the central state, but how? Types of multi-level governance. *American Political Science Review*, *97*(2), 233–243.

Huebert, R. (2006). Canada-U.S. environmental Arctic policies: Sharing a northern continent. In P. LePrestre & P. Stoett (Eds.), *Bilateral ecopolitics: Continuity and change in Canadian-American environmental relations* (pp. 115–132). London, UK: Ashgate.

Imperial, M. T. (2005). Using collaboration as a governance strategy lessons from six watershed management programs. *Administration & Society*, *37*(3), 281–320.

Isett, K. R., Mergel, I. A., LeRoux, K., Mischen, P. A., & Rethemeyer, R. K. (2011). Networks in public administration scholarship: Understanding where we are and where we need to go [Supplement 1]. *Journal of Public Administration Research and Theory*, *21*, i157–i173.

Jinnah, S. (2014). *Post-Treaty politics: Secretariat influence in global environmental governance.* Cambridge, MA: MIT Press.

Kernaghan, K. (2000). The post-bureaucratic organization and public service values. *International Review of Administrative Sciences*, *66*(1), 91–104.

Kling, G., Hayhoe, K., Johnson, L. B., Magnuson, J. J., Polasky, S., Robinson, S. K., Zak, D. R. (2006). *Confronting climate change in the Great Lakes region: Impacts on our communities and ecosystems.* New York, NY: Union for Concerned Scientists and Ecological Society of America. Original report 2003, updated Executive Summary 2006.

Koivurova, T., Keskitalo, C., & Banks, N. (Eds.). (2009). *Climate governance in the Arctic.* New York, NY: Springer.

Konrad, V., & Nicol, H. (2008). *Beyond walls: Reinventing the Canada-United States borderlands.* Aldershot, UK: Ashgate.

Kütting, G., & Cerny, P. G. (2015). Rethinking global environmental policy: From global governance to transnational neopluralism. *Public Administration*, *93*(4), 907–921.

Litfin, K. T. (1994). *Ozone discourses.* New York, NY: Columbia University Press.

Locke, H., & McKinney, M. (2013). The Flathead River Basin. In E. S. Norman, A. Cohen, & K. Bakker (Eds.), *Water without borders? Canada, the United States, and shared waters* (pp. 193–220). Toronto, ON: University of Toronto Press.

Mainka, S., & Howard, G. (2010). Climate change and invasive species: Double jeopardy. *Integrative Zoology*, *5*(2), 102–111.

McLaughlin, C., & Krantzberg, G. (2012). An appraisal of management pathologies in the Great Lakes. *Science of the Total Environment*, *416*, 40–47.

Merry, M. K. (2014). *Framing environmental disaster: Environmental advocacy and the Deepwater Horizon oil spill.* New York, NY: Routledge.

Mumme, S. P. (1984). Regional power in national diplomacy: The case of the U.S. Section of the International Boundary and Water Commission. *Publius*, *14*(4), 115–135.

Mumme, S. P. (2003). Revising the 1944 water treaty: Reflections on the Rio Grande drought crises and other matters. *Journal of the Southwest*, *45*(4), 649–670.

Mumme, S. P., & Duncan, P. (1997). The Commission for Environmental Cooperation and environmental management in the Americas. *Journal of Interamerican Studies and World Affairs*, *39*(4), 41–62.

Myint, T. (2012). *Governing international rivers: Polycentric politics in the Mekong and the Rhine*. Northampton, UK: Edward Elgar.

NAFTANOW.org. (2013). Results: North Americans are better off after 15 years of NAFTA. Retrieved from http://www.naftanow.org/results/default_en.asp

Norman, E. S. (2015). *Governing transboundary waters: Canada, the United States, and indigenous communities*. New York, NY: Routledge.

Norman, E. S., Cohen, A., & Bakker, K. (Eds.). (2013). *Water without borders? Canada, the United States, and shared waters*. Toronto, ON: University of Toronto Press.

Pacheco-Vega, R. (2015). Transnational environmental activism in North America: Wielding soft power through knowledge sharing? *Review of Policy Research*, *32*(1), 146–162.

Parrish, A. (2006). Mixed blessings: The Great Lakes Compact and Agreement, the IJC, and international dispute resolution. *Michigan State Law Review*, *2006*(5), 1299–1321.

Pastor, R. (2011). *The North American idea: A view of a continental future*. Oxford, UK: Oxford University Press.

Price, R. (1998). Reversing the gun sights: Transnational civil society targets land mines. *International Organization*, *52*(3), 613–644.

Rabe, B. (2008). States on steroids: The intergovernmental odyssey of American climate policy. *Review of Policy Research*, *25*(2), 105–128.

Rabe, B. (2013). Building on sub-federal climate strategies: The challenges of regionalism. In N. Craik, I. Studer, & D. VanNijnatten (Eds.), *Climate change policy in North America: Designing integration in a regional system* (pp. 71–107). Toronto, ON: University of Toronto Press.

Rittel, H. W., & Webber, M. M. (1973). Dilemmas in a general theory of planning. *Policy Sciences*, *4*(2), 155–169.

Sanders, J., & Stoett, P. (2006). Fighting extinction and invasion: Transborder conservation efforts. In P. LePrestre & P. Stoett (Eds.), *Bilateral ecopolitics: Continuity and change in Canadian-American environmental relations* (pp. 157–178). London, UK: Ashgate.

Schmeier, S. (2013). *Governing international watercourses: River basin organizations and the sustainable governance of internationally shared rivers and lakes*. London, UK: Earthscan.

Selin, H., & VanDeveer, S. (Eds.). (2009). *Changing climates in North American politics: Institutions, policymaking, and multilevel governance*. Cambridge, MA: MIT Press.

Simon, S. (2014). *Sustaining the borderlands in the age of NAFTA: Development, politics, and participation on the US-Mexico border*. Nashville, TN: Vanderbilt University Press.

Smith, A., Hewitt, N., Klenk, N., Bazely, D. R., Yan, N., Wood, S., . . . Lipsig-Mumme, C. (2012). Effects of climate change on the distribution of invasive alien species in Canada: A knowledge synthesis of range change projections in a warming world. *Environmental Reviews*, *20*(1), 1–16.

Stoett, P., & Temby, O. (2015). Bilateral and trilateral natural resource and biodiversity governance in North America: Organizations, networks, and inclusion. *Review of Policy Research*, *32*(1), 1–18.

Studer, I. (2013). Supply and demand for a North American climate change regime. In N. Craik, I. Studer, & D. VanNijnatten (Eds.), *Climate change policy in North America: Designing integration in a regional system* (pp. 35–67). Toronto, ON: University of Toronto Press.

Temby, O. (2015). Limits of transnational environmental network governance in North America. *Global Environmental Politics*, *15*(3), 176–183.

Temby, O., Rastogi, A., Sandall, J., Cooksey, R., & Hickey, G. M. (2015). Interagency trust and communication in the transboundary governance of Pacific salmon fisheries. *Review of Policy Research*, *32*(1), 79–99.

VanNijnatten, D., & Craik, N. (2013). Designing integration: The system of climate change governance in North America. In N. Craik, I. Studer, & D. VanNijnatten (Eds.), *Climate change policy in North America: Designing integration in a regional system* (pp. 5–34). Toronto, ON: University of Toronto Press.

VanNijnatten, D., & Craik, N. (2015). "Bundled transgovernmentalism" and environmental governance in North America. In B. Bow & G. Anderson (Eds.), *Regional governance in post-NAFTA North America: Building without architecture* (pp. 31–48). New York, NY: Routledge.

Verweij, M. (2000). *Transboundary environmental problems and cultural theory: The protection of the Rhine and the Great Lakes*. New York, NY: Palgrave.

Wapner, P. (1995). Politics beyond the state: Environmental activism and world civic politics. *World Politics*, *47*(3), 311–340.

Wilkinson, T., Wilken, E., Bezaury-Creel, J., Hourigan, T., Agardy, T., Hermann, H., . . . Padilla, M. (2009). *Marine ecoregions of North America*. Montreal, QC: Commission for Environmental Cooperation.

PART I

BILATERAL AND TRILATERAL INSTITUTIONAL EFFECTIVENESS

TWO

Navigating Overlap Management under NAFTA

The Role of the CEC Secretariat

SIKINA JINNAH AND ABBY LINDSAY

INTRODUCTION

Although initially siloed into separate international regimes, trade and environmental issues have grown increasingly intertwined over the past few decades. Environmental treaties commonly use trade measures to secure environmental objectives and trade agreements increasingly incorporate environmental provisions, such as requirements to enforce domestic environmental laws (Jinnah & Lindsay, 2016). The increased interaction between trade and environmental issues is reflective of a broader trend in international politics wherein overlap between international regimes is increasingly common. Such overlap has prompted a growing body of literature on what overlap is (Gehring & Oberthür, 2006) and how it should be managed (Oberthür & Stokke, 2011). "Overlap management," as it has come to be called, has focused most recently on the role of nonstate actors, such as international bureaucracies (i.e., secretariats; see Jinnah, 2010; Selin, 2010). Recent literature has shown, for example, how secretariats can influence overlap management by creating new institutions or shaping the way states understand and respond to certain issues (Jinnah, 2014).

This chapter examines how overlap between trade and environmental issues is managed under the North American Free Trade Agreement (NAFTA), and specifically the role of the secretariat in this process. NAFTA (1993) itself does not have a secretariat. However, alongside NAFTA, Canada, Mexico, and the United States negotiated the North American

Agreement on Environmental Cooperation (NAAEC)[1] and set up its managing body, the Commission for Environmental Cooperation (CEC). The CEC does have a secretariat,[2] which is tasked with, inter alia, providing technical, administrative, and operational support on issues related to trade–environment overlap.

Much of the international relations literature ignores secretariats, assuming they are merely functionaries of member states (Abbott & Snidal, 1998). This study follows more recent scholarship, which highlights the potentially important roles that secretariats can play in international affairs (Barnett & Finnemore, 2004; Biermann & Siebenhuner, 2009; Jinnah, 2014) and the influence secretariats can have on overlap management. We argue that the CEC secretariat has influenced overlap management in ways that reflect "post-bureaucratic" behavior (Stoett & Temby, 2015), primarily through brokering knowledge, in ways that build state capacity to collaborate across borders on trade–environment issues. Specifically, we demonstrate how the secretariat has influenced decisions related to budget allocations, cooperative activities between member states, the creation of new institutions, and evaluating allegations of parties' failures to enforce environmental laws. Moreover, we argue that this case raises important questions about the appropriate role of secretariats in trade–environment politics (and beyond), and has important policy implications with several new secretariats currently being set up under the burgeoning number of regional trade agreements under negotiation by the United States and many others.

NAFTA'S ENVIRONMENTAL PROVISIONS

The focus of our analysis is on the environmental provisions contained in the NAAEC. Article 3 of this agreement guarantees the sovereignty of each country to develop its own domestic environmental laws and levels of environmental protection, commits parties to "high levels of environmental protection," and articulates that they "shall strive to continue to improve those laws and regulations" (NAAEC, 1993). Article 5 further commits each party to "effectively enforce its environmental laws and regulations through appropriate governmental action" and lists 12 specific actions governments can take to accomplish this.

The NAAEC also includes several provisions related to increasing public participation, resolving environmental conflicts, and promoting environmental cooperation. Alongside public participation in procedural matters (Article 7), the NAAEC includes a public "submissions on enforcement matters" (SEM) mechanism (Article 14). Through this mechanism, any nongovernmental organization or person[3] can submit documentation asserting that a country is failing to effectively enforce its environmental laws. If the submission warrants further investigation, there are procedures for developing a factual record (Article 15). For conflicts that arise between the parties on environmental matters, the NAAEC also provides an opportunity for state-to-state consultations and dispute resolution (Articles 22–36). Finally, to help implement these environmental provisions and improve environmental quality more broadly, the NAAEC provides a platform for cooperation and information sharing on environmental matters (Article 20).

Of central relevance to this study, the parties also established the CEC under the NAAEC. The CEC is an international organization for the three NAFTA countries, established to address North American environmental concerns, help prevent conflicts between trade and environmental issues, and strengthen effective enforcement of environmental laws (CEC, 1997b). It is one of three ministerial commissions in a complex web of trilateral intergovernmental institutions that also includes over 50 committees, subcommittees, and working groups (CEC, 1997b).[4] Specifically, the CEC cooperates with the NAFTA Free Trade Commission to implement NAFTA's environmental goals and assess the impacts of the trade agreement on the environment. It does this by acting as the contact point for environment-related inquiries, "contributing to the prevention or resolution of environment-related trade disputes," and engaging in other such activities (NAAEC, 1993, Article 10).

The CEC consists of three main bodies: the council, the joint public advisory committee (JPAC), and the secretariat.[5] The council is the CEC's governing body, composed of environment ministers from each country. These ministers are responsible for overseeing implementation of the NAAEC and meet at least annually to discuss North American environmental issues. The JPAC is a committee of 15 citizens, five from each country, which advise the council on any matter within scope of the NAAEC. They meet at least annually and often hold public meetings in the spirit of promoting public participation.

Finally, the parties established the secretariat to provide technical, administrative, and operational support for the CEC. The secretariat is governed by the council and is headquartered in Montreal with a liaison office in Mexico City. It is supported, along with other CEC activities, by the annual budget of the commission, which has been around US$9 million per year since 1996. Each party contributes an equal share of the annual budget, and the secretariat assists with planning for and managing those funds. The council is responsible for selecting the secretariat's executive director, who serves for a three-year term before it rotates to a national of another party (NAAEC, 1993, Article 11). The executive director appoints and supervises the rest of the staff of the secretariat, which consists of approximately 45 people who work on a variety of functions, including cooperation projects, communication, and administration and finances (CEC, 2017). In terms of its mandate relevant to managing trade–environment overlap, the CEC secretariat performs four key functions: writing independent reports, managing public submissions, producing factual records required under the NAEEC's SEM mechanism, and drafting annual programs and budgets.

The remainder of this chapter evaluates if and how the CEC secretariat influences trade–environment politics under the NAAEC and NAFTA, focusing on in its work producing independent reports.

METHODS AND ANALYTICAL APPROACH

Following Jinnah's (2014) previous work on this topic, our analysis of secretariat influence unfolds in three steps (Figure 2.1). Step 1 examines how the CEC secretariat *participates* in environmental governance, and if such participation reflects any mechanisms of secretariat influence. Subsequently, we analyze if the secretariat's mechanisms of influence can be traced to changes in political outcomes and thus actually reflect secretariat *influence* on trade–environment politics (step 2). If secretariat influence is identified, we conduct a counterfactual analysis to rule out alternative explanations for any such changes (step 3).

First, we examine how the CEC secretariat participates in environmental governance across its four central mandated functions. This analysis allows us to assess the secretariat's *potential* for influence. We do this by examining the secretariat's formal mandate and any other instructions from the CEC that outline additional responsibilities related to environmental governance. Additional instructions from the CEC include council decisions, instructions at council meetings, and council revisions of the annual work program and budget. Additionally, council members and their staff may give informal instructions to the secretariat intersessionally; however, these instructions are largely undocumented so they are not considered here. In other words, we use the secretariat's various mandates for action and any relevant documents produced in response to such mandates to ascertain what exactly the secretariat does to manage trade–environment overlap.

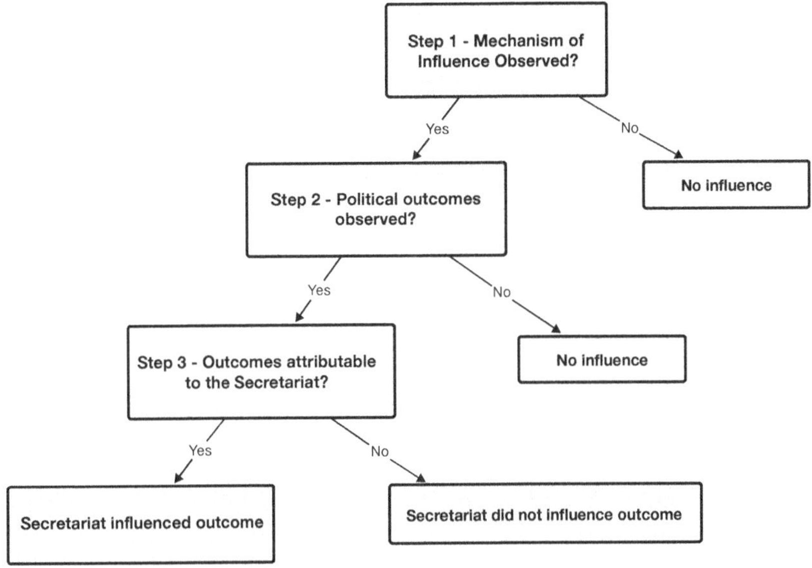

FIGURE 2.1 Secretariat Influence (Adapted from Jinnah, 2014).

The second step in this analysis involves determining if any mechanisms of influence identified in the first step resulted in any changes to political outcomes. Although tracing mechanisms of influence for all four secretariat functions would be ideal, such a detailed analysis is outside the scope of this chapter. Our analysis, therefore, is limited to one of the secretariat's four key functions: producing independent reports. We chose to focus on the production of independent reports because the data for tracing mechanisms of influence to changes in political outcomes is readily available in the time and budget allotted for this project and this mandated function is most unusual for secretariats. We are unaware of any other studies that evaluate the potential for influence of secretariat-produced independent reports, whereas the other three mandated functions, or closely related ones, are evaluated elsewhere. Therefore, the need for evaluation of this function is more immediate than for the other three functions at this time.

Finally, if the results from step 2 show that the secretariat did impact CEC activities, we proceed to the third step—a counterfactual analysis—to rule out alternative explanations for the observed changes in CEC activities.[6]

Secretariat Participation as a Mechanism of Influence (Analysis—Step 1)

The secretariat exercises various mechanisms of influence as it carries out each of its four main functions.[7] These mechanisms include capacity building, negotiation facilitation, litigation facilitation, knowledge brokering, and marketing. This section details the secretariat's work in producing independent reports. Again, mechanisms of influence only indicate a *potential* for influence.

In producing independent reports, the CEC secretariat's activities reflect potential influence via knowledge brokering. Under Article 13 of the NAAEC, the secretariat may prepare a report for the council on any topic within the scope of the annual work program without prior approval. It may also prepare reports on cooperative matters outside the scope of the annual work program but within the scope of the NAAEC, as long as it gives the council 30 days within which to object. To develop the reports, the secretariat may hire experts to assist and can draw on a wide range of sources, including any information that is publicly available, submitted by interested organizations, persons, or parties, or gathered through public consultations. The reports are then made public, or not, through a vote of the council. To date, the secretariat has prepared eight such reports, including one on long-range transport of air pollution, migratory bird habitat, and energy and the environment.

Knowledge brokering, which entails providing information and expertise, is the main mechanism of influence reflected through the secretariat's participation in this process. It is important to note that the secretariat has the autonomy to identify an environmental issue as significant, research and draft a report on the topic, and recommend actions to the council to address the issue. As with its work in other areas, such as on submissions, the secretariat may hire environmental experts to assist, gather, and synthesize information for the report (Jinnah & Lindsay, 2015). It can also hold public consultations, such as conferences, seminars, or symposia (NAAEC, 1993, Article 13.2(d)) to involve a range of viewpoints. Despite this wide-ranging effort to collect viewpoints and information, it is ultimately the secretariat's decision to determine how to present the information gathered in the final report. Thus, through its activities collecting information on important environmental issues, synthesizing data, and drafting reports for the council, we see that the secretariat engages in knowledge brokering.

Secretariat Influence (Analysis—Step 2)

This section analyzes whether the CEC secretariat's activities related to the production of independent reports under Article 13 have impacted CEC outcomes. If the knowledge-brokering mechanism of influence identified in the previous section can indeed be traced to changes in outcomes, then we can confirm that the secretariat influenced trade–environment politics.

We have analyzed seven of the eight independent reports the secretariat has produced to date. We have not included the eighth report because insufficient time has passed since its release to effectively evaluate any impacts resulting from it (Table 2.1).

The CEC secretariat's first independent report on the death of migratory birds at the Silva Reservoir was published in 1995 (CEC, 1995). The secretariat agreed to research and produce this report in response to a request from local community members concerned with bird die-off around the reservoir. Specifically, the report concluded that the mortality of 20,000 to 30,000 migratory waterbirds during the winter of 1994–1995 in the area was due to botulism. The secretariat made recommendations

Table 2.1
Commission for Environmental Cooperation Independent Reports

	Title	Date
1	CEC Secretariat Report on the Death of Migratory Birds at the Silva Reservoir	1995
2	Continental Pollutant Pathways	1997
3	Ribbon of Life: An Agenda for Preserving Transboundary Migratory Bird Habitat on the Upper San Pedro River	1999
4	Environmental Challenges and Opportunities of the Evolving North American Electricity Market	2002
5	Maize and Biodiversity: The Effects of Transgenetic Maize in Mexico	2004
6	Green Building in North America	2008
7	Designing Sustainability: Reducing Greenhouse Gas Emissions from Freight Transportation in North America	2011
8	Hazardous Trade? An Examination of US-Generated Spent Lead-Acid Battery Exports and Secondary Lead Recycling in Canada, Mexico, and the United States	2013

to the council to address the issue, such as altering the topography to be less conducive to botulism outbreaks, and pertaining more broadly to continental waterbird management, such as establishing a trilateral task force to monitor and respond to migratory bird disease outbreaks.

The *Annual report 1996* credits the Silva Reservoir report with a series of environmental management capacity-building activities for the Mexican state of Guanajuanto. These included developing the state's first environmental council (CEC, 1996). While not a direct recommendation of the secretariat's report, the *Annual report 1996* credits the secretariat's report with catalyzing these activities in Guanajuanto. Furthermore, the council adopted several broad initiatives that reflected some of the more specific recommendations from the secretariat's report shortly after it was published. For example, the council approved funding for the Cooperation on Migratory Birds project to identify important areas for migratory birds (CEC, 1995). In the following year, it also approved the North American Biodiversity Information Network and passed Council Resolution 96-02, which established a working group to develop a strategy and action plan for the conservation of North American birds (CEC, 1996; CEC Council, 1996). These CEC activities were new and followed the release of the secretariat's report, which suggests secretariat influence.

The secretariat's second independent report, released in 1997 (*Continental pollutant pathways*), addressed long-range transport of air pollution throughout North America, including acid deposition, mercury, ozone, particulate matter, and persistent organic pollutants (CEC, 1997a). The secretariat's core recommendation in the report was that although existing collaborative efforts to address air pollutants were only bilateral among the NAFTA countries at the time, these issues should be addressed on a continental scale. The secretariat argued that this was the most effective way to address the problem because Mexico, Canada, and the United States share affected terrestrial and aquatic ecosystems, weather patterns link the three countries, and they are affected by many of the same sources of air pollutants. The report also included nine specific recommendations to the council, such as collaborating in existing multilateral forums on air pollution issues and increasing funding to address continental air pollution.

Again, the council appeared to change the way it addressed these issues following the production of the report. In fact, prior to the secretariat's report, collaboration on air pollution issues between the NAFTA parties only occurred bilaterally and did not feature in CEC activities at all. For example, in 1998, the council revised its cooperation activities midyear to include cooperation on North American air quality, and in 1999 the council approved two additional air quality cooperation projects, one of which was specifically aimed at trilateral coordination (CEC, 1998). Similar air pollution cooperative efforts have continued to be a regular part of the CEC's activities since the secretariat's report was released, including in the most recent Operational Plan (CEC, 2013). This report appears to have influenced CEC activities.

The secretariat's third independent report (*Ribbon of life*) focused on areas of riparian habitat across the U.S.-Mexican border that were designated "globally important bird areas" under one of the cooperative migratory bird projects that was initiated following the secretariat's Silva Reservoir report. The report included five specific recommendations for the council, as well as additional recommendations provided by the advisory board of independent experts that the secretariat had created to assist with the report (CEC, 1999b). For example, the secretariat recommended that the council develop an interagency working group and organize a workshop on transboundary water management.

In this case, secretariat influence is quite clear. The *Annual report 1999* noted that many of the secretariat's recommendations were taken up directly by the council and were in the process of being implemented to protect specific habitats. These efforts included public–private initiatives, efforts to bring part of Mexico's riparian habitat under protected areas management, and a trust fund for future conservation efforts (CEC, 1999a). Additionally, on the basis of the secretariat's report, the CEC provided a grant to the Nature Conservatory to provide technical assistance to Mexico to assist with its efforts in the basin (CEC, 2014).

The secretariat's fourth report (*Environmental challenges and opportunities of the evolving North American electricity market*) had a broad issue-based focus on electricity and the environment (i.e., it was not geographically focused like the previous three reports). The report was released in 2002, at a time when the three North American countries were discussing electricity integration. It covered issues from cross-border impacts of electricity generation to standards and regulations, and identified opportunities for renewable energy and innovative economic instruments, among other recommendations (CEC, 2002b). In its response to the report, Canada noted that the countries had already started implementing steps similar to some of those suggested in the report. Mexico, on the other hand, noted the recommendations were very different from what its government was considering (CEC, 2002b).

Nevertheless, the report may have prompted additional council activities on this issue. One of the five broad recommendations in the report was to collaborate on increasing energy efficiency and renewable energy. Further, contemporaneously with the drafting of the report, the council approved a new cooperation project on carbon sequestration, energy efficiency, and renewable energy. Likewise, in the 2002 Annual Report, the council noted that it "agreed to a series of actions to promote health and environmental objectives within the context of expanding the generation and distribution of energy in North America and the trade of energy between [the] three countries" (CEC, 2002a). Finally, in 2005 energy and environmental officials from each country, along with a few other experts, met for the first of many times as the Renewable Energy Expert Committee (CEC, 2005). This suggests a possible causal relationship between secretariat recommendations and CEC activities, but we cannot confirm this causal link due to the ongoing surrounding political discussions on the topic and the multitude of actors involved in domestic policy making on this issue.

In contrast to the first four reports wherein the council approved new cooperation activities during or immediately following their release, there were no such activities following the fifth report (CEC, 2004) on the effects of transgenetic maize on biodiversity in Mexico. The report verified there was transgenetic corn in Oaxaca and Puebla despite the Mexican ban on it, and the report's extensive recommendations were not well received by the parties: all three council members were "concerned" that the recommendations were not supported by the scientific evidence in the report (CEC, 2004). Furthermore, the U.S. letter also stated it was ready "to improve procedures for implementing Article 13, as well as the content and quality of any future Article 13 reports" (CEC, 2004). Thus, the secretariat did not influence CEC activities through this report at all, with all three states explicitly rejecting the secretariat's recommendations.[8]

The sixth and seventh reports were both focused on opportunities to improve the environment, rather than remedy existing problems. The secretariat completed the reports *Green building in North America* and *Designing sustainability: Reducing greenhouse gas emissions from freight transportation in North America* in 2008 and 2011, respectively (CEC, 2008, 2011). Secretariat recommendations stemming from these reports included such things as developing a common vision for green building in North America and adopting incentives to support deployment of advanced fuel-saving technologies and freight transportation that will reduce carbon dioxide emissions as transportation of goods increases between the three countries.

Immediately after the green building report's release, the council approved cooperation projects on green buildings for the very first time. For example, the council followed the secretariat's recommendation to promote private sector financing for green buildings. The council even explicitly recognized that these activities were "kicked off" by the secretariat's report, suggesting strong secretariat influence stemming from it

(CEC, 2014). In contrast, the secretariat's report on greenhouse gas emissions from freight transport does not appear to have catalyzed any further actions by the council, suggesting limited, if any, secretariat influence.

In summary, the CEC secretariat's influence through independent reports varies. Many of the reports—on migratory birds, continental air pollutant pathways, riparian habitat, electricity and the environment, and green building—precipitated clear changes to CEC activities, with the council establishing projects based on secretariat recommendations. However, other reports—on greenhouse gas emissions from freight transport and maize and biodiversity in Mexico—appear to have had little to no impact on CEC activities, with states explicitly rejecting secretariat recommendations in some cases.

These results raise two important questions: Are there alternative explanations for the changes we observed in CEC activities following the secretariat reports? And if not, under what conditions are secretariats able to influence politics?

Alternative Explanations? (Counterfactual Analysis—Step 3)

As detailed in the previous section, council activities shifted following the release of five of the seven secretariat reports analyzed here—migratory birds, continental air pollutant pathways, riparian habitat, electricity and the environment, and green building. Immediately following the release of these reports the council approved and funded new cooperative activities reflecting the secretariat's recommendations in those reports, including a recommendation to set up a trust fund to support future efforts on these issues. This suggests that the secretariat's reports influenced CEC politics in these instances. However, it is of course possible that the council decided to make these changes for other reasons. Alternative explanations for these changes must therefore be considered and excluded in order to assert that the secretariat did in fact influence politics in this case.

Secretariat influence is most clear in the green building, migratory birds, and riparian habitat reports. On green building there is little, if any, doubt that the secretariat influenced the council's activities. As explained earlier, the council explicitly acknowledged the influence of the secretariat's report on its activities on this issue (CEC, 2014). In the latter two, the council adopted recommendations reflecting the secretariat's recommendations, such as bringing part of Mexico's riparian habitat under protected areas management, which was taken up directly by the council through a grant to the Nature Conservatory (CEC, 2014). Although it is certainly possible that other factors also influenced the council's decisions in these

Table 2.2
Summary of Results: Secretariat Influence (step 2)

Report Number	Title	Impact of Secretariat Knowledge Brokering on Outcome	Influence
1	Silva Reservoir Migratory Birds	Several new projects initiated afterwards, including Cooperation on Migratory Birds, North American Biodiversity Information Network, and environmental management capacity-building activities for Guanajuanto	Yes
2	Continental Air Pollutant Pathways	Council approved first trilateral air quality cooperation project Air quality projects became regular activities	Inconclusive
3	San Pedro River Riparian Habitat	Many secretariat recommendations for activities to protect specific important habitats were implemented following report	Yes
4	Electricity and the Environment	Council approved a new cooperation project on carbon sequestration, energy efficiency, and renewable energy	Inconclusive
5	Maize and Biodiversity	NA	No
6	Green Building	Report kicked off new cooperative projects on green buildings	Yes
7	Freight Transportation	NA	No

cases, the dearth of political activity surrounding these issues prior to the secretariat's reports suggest that the reports were at a minimum a contributing influence in both instances.

In contrast, the secretariat's influence is least clear in the report on electricity and the environment, wherein the issue was a topic of intense debate and discussion among the parties prior to the report being produced. In this instance additional data, perhaps through interviews with key informants, is needed to affirmatively claim secretariat influence.

Secretariat influence resulting from the report on air pollutant pathways is difficult to evaluate with the available data. Although the council appears to have followed the secretariat's recommendation that a continental approach was needed, it is certainly possible that the council was receiving similar recommendations from other sources. For example, the JPAC gives recommendations to the council solicited through public input and European countries were negotiating the continental-scale Convention on Long Range Transboundary Air Pollution (LTRAP) in parallel to the secretariat's work on this issue. Both of these sources could have influenced the council's actions following the secretariat's report. In this instance, therefore, secretariat influence is likely, but additional information is needed to make a more definitive determination (Table 2.2).

WHEN IS SECRETARIAT INFLUENCE LIKELY?

This variation in the CEC secretariat's influence across reports raises questions about the conditions under which secretariats are likely to influence politics. Jinnah (2014) has argued elsewhere that secretariats are likely to influence politics when the secretariat has little competition from other actors to carry out its activities and when state preferences are weak or underdeveloped. On competition, the CEC secretariat faced little competition from other actors to carry out its knowledge-brokering activities across at least three of the four core areas of its work—public submissions, drafting budgets and work programs, and facilitating environmental cooperation. No other organization has the mandate or level of access that the CEC secretariat does for these functions. The secretariat alone receives submissions and processes them. While other organizations have the skills to draft budgets and work programs or facilitate environmental cooperation, the council gives these responsibilities only to the secretariat.

Its fourth function—drafting independent reports—is a bit different. While the NAAEC mandates the secretariat to carry out this function, other nongovernmental organizations or academic institutions could generate such reports and send them to the council. In some cases, such as sustainable freight, there were a wide variety of other actors involved. Further, the JPAC can always develop or bring such reports to the council's attention and influence council priorities, thus resulting in competition for the secretariat. Although we did not carry out an analysis of the JPAC here, the timing and content of several JPAC events suggest that the JPAC and secretariat work closely together, not in competition. Competition is relatively high, therefore, with regard to the secretariat's work in producing independent reports, in comparison to the competition it faces in carrying out its other core functions. This suggests that secretariat influence is even more likely in the other core areas of its work and additional research on such activities is needed.

On state preferences, we might expect some variation across the secretariat's core functions in terms of the strength of state preferences and thus the secretariat's ability to influence outcomes. For example, we might expect states to have very strong preferences, and thus weak secretariat influence, on issues that are politically sensitive domestically or where the domestic decision making is complex, as is the case with greenhouse gas emissions from transportation and genetically modified crops, such as maize. Similarly, on budgetary decisions states may be resistant to secretariat input on how limited CEC finances should be spent, with an average of US$9 million allocated to the CEC each year.

In contrast, secretariat suggestions for environmental cooperation projects might be better received, especially in situations where secretariat expertise and capacity to analyze cooperation needs outstrips that of states. As a core focus of the CEC secretariat's work and merely one of many issues on responsible state agencies' docket, cooperation is an area where we might expect to see this dynamic at play. Thus secretariat influence in this area is likely. Similarly, it is not surprising that the secretariat was able to influence political outcomes through independent reports. The report on bird habitat in the San Pedro River Basin provides evidence of this. The secretariat used its capacity and experience with multistakeholder dialogues and public participation to convene local stakeholders on both sides of the U.S.-Mexican border—a process that involved more than 650 people from both countries (CEC, 1999b). Then, as a result of the report, the council approved financing technical assistance to Mexico to establish and implement a protected area along the San Pedro River. This case, therefore, comports with existing analyses of when secretariats are likely to influence political decision making and when such influence is less likely.

CONCLUSION

The CEC case supports recent findings that international secretariats are more than mere functionaries of state actors as international relations theory often assumes. Rather, they participate in political decision making in ways that are central to global governance processes. In this case, the CEC secretariat participates in environmental governance primarily by brokering knowledge that helps guide the council in making decisions on several important governance issues under the NAAEC. This includes decisions related to budget allocations, cooperative activities between member states, and allegations of parties' failures to enforce environmental laws (Jinnah & Lindsay, 2015).

Knowledge-brokering activities have been observed prolifically among other secretariats in recent studies. However, those undertaken by the CEC secretariat appear to reach a bit further in terms of their potential to impact institutions and core decisions made by the council. Although a full evaluation of the impact of the secretariat's knowledge-brokering activities on public submissions, budget drafting, and cooperation is outside the scope of this chapter, there are several ways in which we might expect these activities to influence CEC politics.

For example, as we have argued elsewhere, the secretariat's knowledge brokering shapes cooperative activities and provides capacity building through technical assistance to governments on domestic laws and regulations, some of which works across countries to address transboundary environmental issues or harmonize standards. Such activities can influence CEC politics when they impact governance structures and institutions through, for example, the trilateral task force to monitor and respond to migratory bird disease outbreaks. Furthermore, because capacity-building programs shape the way states understand environmental governance issues, these workshops can also influence CEC politics when they affect how states distribute resources. The secretariat's work in drafting the CEC annual report and budget is also a potential source of influence. Done hand-in-hand with the development of cooperation activities, the CEC annual report and budget has the ability to shape CEC politics by shaping the council's governance plans and priorities for the upcoming year. Finally, SEMs and factual records can also influence governance decisions and allocation of resources when they expose lack of environmental law enforcement (Jinnah & Lindsay, 2015).

The focus of our analysis here, however, is the CEC secretariat's role in producing independent reports. As with the other core secretariat functions in this case, knowledge brokering is central. In identifying important topics to research and report on, the secretariat plays a critical role in shaping the council's agenda. For example, in response to the secretariat's reports on the bird die-off in the Silva Reservoir and migratory bird habitat in the San Pedro River Basin, the council pursued actions to implement the secretariat's recommendations. Likewise, after the report on green building the council approved new cooperation activities on this issue and credited the secretariat's report directly with "kick starting" this work (CEC, 2014). New cooperative activities arose after five of seven independent reports examined here, with secretariat influence on council activities likely in three of them—that is, the green building, migratory birds, and riparian habitat reports.

Specifically, these activities suggest that the secretariat influenced political outcomes by providing the council with recommendations for cooperative activities to address migratory bird conservation and green building initiatives. In response to these secretariat recommendations the CEC allotted new resources to projects on these issues and developed rules and institutions, such as working groups or committees, to guide future work in these areas. There were also of course areas in which the secretariat clearly did *not* influence CEC politics. Notably there were no changes in CEC activities following the *Maize and biodiversity* report nor the *Sustainable freight* report, with parties rejecting the secretariat's recommendations in the former entirely.

There are several policy implications that arise out of this analysis, both for the CEC and for broader trade–environment policy. The amount of control governments can exert over secretariats, and correspondingly the amount of secretariat autonomy, are based in part on the secretariat's mandate and in part on how that mandate is operationalized over time. For example, the CEC secretariat's mandate for independent reports was drafted such that the secretariat has the autonomy to select the topic of the reports within the scope of the annual work program. Although this mandate is broad, it is also carefully limited by including topics the council has already approved through the annual work program. Nevertheless, as we saw in the *Maize and biodiversity* report, this mandate leaves a substantial amount of room for the secretariat to maneuver. In that case, the secretariat chose a topic that was included in the work program (i.e., biodiversity) likely as a means to draw attention to an issue that was politically controversial and not included (i.e., genetically modified crops). Although the council ultimately rejected the secretariat's recommendations in that report, these activities suggest that if states are concerned about increasing secretariat autonomy, more careful consideration to secretariat mandates is needed in establishing new agreements and organizations.

Thus, our analysis illustrates how a secretariat can use its mandate to create room to maneuver and often can even design its own mandate by catalyzing new cooperation activities. Through independent reports, the CEC secretariat brought new topics to the attention of the council, and the secretariat paired those with simultaneously proposing parallel cooperation projects in the annual work program and budget. This also raises the question of where secretariat preferences originate. Are they derived from mandate? Are they an attempt to make trade and environmental protection more compatible? Or do the council, states, JPAC, or other actors influence the secretariat's preferences? The answer is likely a combination of all of these rationales and would be an interesting focus for future research.

This study sheds light on the role of secretariats in environmental governance, the importance of design in secretariat mandates and, more broadly, secretariat–state relationships. These questions are particularly timely now that the United States is in the process of operationalizing broad provisions in free trade agreements with Peru, Panama, and Colombia that call for secretariats to be created for functions such as processing submissions and developing factual records. This study provides an in-depth example of one potential mechanism of influence secretariats can exert and how they potentially shape environmental governance decisions of relevance to these agreements. Following the international relations literature on secretariats, many previous agreements have largely followed broad cookie-cutter language regarding secretariat mandates. However, as our empirical and theoretical understanding of how secretariats actually do participate in global governance grows, these new trade negotiations still have the ability to redefine the appropriate role for secretariats. On the one hand, as state governments are squeezed for funding and are stretched to cover a wide variety of international agreements, secretariats can use their expertise and networks to improve regime implementation and manage overlap with other regimes. On the other hand, providing autonomy to largely unaccountable international bureaucrats raises some important questions about the legitimacy of environmental governance decisions, and as has been demonstrated elsewhere in the literature, can result in unintended consequences related to equity and distribution of power (Jinnah, 2014).

NOTES

1. Often referred to as NAFTA's environmental "side agreement." Although legally two separate agreements, the NAAEC was negotiated alongside NAFTA in response to concerns about NAFTA's environmental impact, so we often refer to NAFTA for both.
2. In this chapter, the CEC secretariat refers to the environmental secretariat established under the NAAEC. This is to distinguish it from secretariats established under other parts of NAFTA.
3. Per NAAEC (1993) Article 14.1(f), the submission must be "filed by a person or organization residing or established in the territory of a Party."
4. This provides a stark contrast to the relationships between the three countries prior to NAFTA, which were primarily bilateral and done

through informal or diplomatic channels rather than institutionalized processes and bodies. For more information see CEC, 1997b.

5. During the NAFTA negotiations two additional environmental institutions were created, the North American Development Bank and the Border Environment Cooperation Commission, both of which were established to address environmental issues along the U.S.-Mexican border. Given their bilateral nature, they are not included in this study, but are important interlocutors for the CEC on those specific issues.
6. A more detailed explanation of our methodological approach can be found in Jinnah and Lindsay (2015).
7. For more details on the mechanisms of influence, see Jinnah, 2014.
8. States' dissatisfaction with the secretariat's report was perhaps also reflected in their rejection of the secretariat's proposal the following year to draft an independent report on Transboundary Environmental Impact Assessments (TEIAs; CEC Council, 2005), despite the JPAC's support for it (Gardner, 2005).

REFERENCES

Abbott, K. W., & Snidal, D. (1998). Why states act through formal international organizations. *Journal of Conflict Resolution*, *42*(1), 3–32.

Barnett, M., & Finnemore, M. (2004). *Rules for the world: International organizations in global politics*. Ithaca, NY: Cornell University Press.

Biermann, F., & Siebenhüner, B. (Eds.). (2009). *Managers of global change: The influence of international environmental bureaucracies*. Cambridge, MA: MIT Press.

Commission for Environmental Cooperation. (1995). *CEC secretariat report on the death of migratory bird mortality at the Silva Reservoir*. Montreal, QC: CEC Secretariat.

Commission for Environmental Cooperation. (1996). *Annual report 1996*. Montreal, QC: CEC Secretariat.

Commission for Environmental Cooperation. (1997a). *Continental pollutant pathways*. Montreal, QC: CEC Secretariat.

Commission for Environmental Cooperation. (1997b). *NAFTA's institutions: The environmental potential and performance of the NAFTA Free Trade Commission and related bodies*. Montreal, QC: CEC Secretariat.

Commission for Environmental Cooperation. (1998). *Annual report 1998*. Montreal, QC: CEC Secretariat.

Commission for Environmental Cooperation. (1999a). *Annual report 1999*. Montreal, QC: CEC Secretariat.

Commission for Environmental Cooperation. (1999b). *Ribbon of life: An agenda for preserving transboundary migratory bird habitat on the Upper San Pedro River*. Montreal, QC: CEC Secretariat.

Commission for Environmental Cooperation. (2002a). *Annual report 2002*. Montreal, QC: CEC Secretariat.

Commission for Environmental Cooperation. (2002b). *Environmental challenges and opportunities of the evolving North American electricity market*. Montreal, QC: CEC Secretariat.

Commission for Environmental Cooperation. (2004). *Maize and biodiversity: The effects of transgenetic maize in Mexico*. Montreal, QC: CEC Secretariat.

Commission for Environmental Cooperation. (2005). *Annual report 2005*. Montreal, QC: CEC Secretariat.

Commission for Environmental Cooperation. (2008). *Green building in North America*. Montreal, Canada: QC Secretariat.

Commission for Environmental Cooperation. (2011). *Designing sustainability: Reducing greenhouse gas emissions from freight transportation in North America*. Montreal, QC: CEC Secretariat.

Commission for Environmental Cooperation. (2013). *Operational plan of the Commission for Environmental Cooperation: 2013–2014*. Montreal, QC: CEC Secretariat.

Commission for Environmental Cooperation. (2017). Secretariat. Retrieved from http://www.cec.org/about-us/secretariat/staff-directory

Commission for Environmental Cooperation Council. (1996). *Cooperation for the conservation of the birds of North America* (Council Resolution 96-02). Montreal, QC: CEC Secretariat.

Commission for Environmental Cooperation Council. (2005). *Decision regarding the proposal by the secretariat of the Commission for Environmental Cooperation (CEC) to prepare an Article 13 report on case studies on transboundary environmental impact assessment* (Council Resolution 05-07). Montreal, QC: CEC Secretariat.

Gardner, J. (2005). Letter to Council Members. August 22. Retrieved from http://www.cec.org/sites/default/files/documents/jpac_advice_council/1645_JPAC-letter-Article-13-TEIA_en.pdf

Gehring, T., & Oberthür, S. (Eds.). (2006). *Institutional interaction in global environmental governance: Synergy and conflict among international and EU policies*. Cambridge, MA: MIT Press.

Jinnah, S. (2010). Overlap management in the World Trade Organization: Secretariat influence on trade-environment politics. *Global Environmental Politics*, *10*(2): 64–79.

Jinnah, S. (2014). *Post-treaty politics: Secretariat influence in global environmental governance*. Cambridge, MA: MIT Press.

Jinnah, S., & Lindsay, A. (2015). Secretariat influence on overlap management politics in North America: NAFTA and the Commission for Environmental Cooperation. *Review of Policy Research*, *32*(1): 124–145.

Jinnah, S., & Lindsay, A. (2016). Diffusion through issue linkage: Environmental norms in US trade agreements. *Global Environmental Politics*, *16*(3), 41–61.

North American Free Trade Agreement, 32 I.L.M. 289, 605. (1993). Retrieved from https://www.nafta-sec-alena.org/Home/Legal-Texts/North-American-Free-Trade-Agreement

North American Agreement on Environmental Cooperation, 32 I.L.M. 1482. (1993). Retrieved from http://www.cec.org/sites/default/files/naaec.pdf

Oberthür, S., & Stokke, O. S. (Eds.). (2011). *Managing institutional complexity: Regime interplay and global environmental change*. Cambridge, MA: MIT Press.

Selin, H. (2010). *Global governance of hazardous chemicals: Challenges of multilevel governance*. Cambridge, MA: MIT Press.

Stoett, P., & Temby, O. (2015). Bilateral and trilateral natural resource and biodiversity governance in North America: Organizations, networks, and inclusion. *Review of Policy Research*, *32*(1): 1–18.

THREE

The CEC, Digital Divides, and Participatory Challenges in the U.S.-Mexican Borderlands

SUZANNE SIMON

INTRODUCTION

The North American Free Trade Agreement (NAFTA) was an innovative trade treaty because it included two side agreements, the Environmental Side Agreement (ESA) and Labor Side Agreement (LSA), as supplemental accords to the trade treaty itself. Both accords emerged in response to widespread popular opposition to NAFTA, which questioned the degree to which the environmental, labor, and human costs of free trade were outweighed by its purported benefits. While the labor accord was intended to ensure that NAFTA would neither extend existing violations of Mexican workers' rights, nor create a labor race to the bottom, the environmental agreement was created to encourage trilateral environmental cooperation throughout North America. The creation of environmentally cooperative opportunities was especially important for the historically fractious U.S.-Mexican border region where, in the famous words of Gloria Anzaldua, the "Third World grates up against the first and bleeds" (1987, p. 3). Environmental cooperation in this region has been hindered by its extraordinary social, cultural, political, and economic divisions.

The ESA's relative accomplishments continue to be weighed and debated. NAFTA was hailed by some in the 1990s as the "greenest trade treaty in history" (Thomas & Weber, 1999, p. 134) and a harbinger of a new era in which environmental concerns would increasingly be written into international trade treaties (Deere & Esty, 2002; Esty, 2001, 2004).

While early observers may have overestimated NAFTA's possibilities for hemispheric or global harmonization of trade and environmental interests, there can be little doubt that the ESA was a policy and institutional level improvement on previously existing mechanisms. Unlike the LSA, which has fallen into disuse because of its lack of effectiveness, the organizations, citizens, nongovernmental organizations (NGOs) or environmental NGOs (ENGOs), networks, and academic and government bodies that cluster around the ESA have grown more robust and vibrant over time. These robust, bi- and trilateral conversations may help to forge greater cooperative possibilities in the future, and perhaps even serve as building blocks or a roadmap for environmental diplomacy in the climate change era.

NAFTA's ESA was created to encourage cross-border cooperation and environmental dispute resolution equally for Canada, the United States, and Mexico. However, the majority of the opposition that eventuated in both accords focused on existing and potential conflicts between the United States and Mexico and, in particular, on the environmental and labor degradation that two decades' worth of offshore manufacturing had already brought to the border region. The status of the United States (and Canada) as "first world" nations, and Mexico as "third world" figured highly in the rationale for the accords, which, due to their participatory structure and ideals, were believed by proponents to encourage Mexican democratization (Simon, 2007, 2014). Therefore, while the environmental side and its companion institutions have become integral and productive components of the North American environmental policy-making landscape, it is important to remember that they emerged from a specific historical moment and problematization of Mexico as a uniquely corrupt, "third world," and transitional nation.

The purpose of this chapter is to introduce the reader to a small slice of the complex political, cultural, and border-specific context anterior to the creation of the ESA. I will demonstrate the ways in which fundamental inequalities that existed from NAFTA's inception continue to percolate throughout the practice of the side accord in the border region. Rather than a sea that lifts all boats, free-market capitalism in Mexico has been experienced by many as a tsunami of increasing impoverishment and marginalization. When poverty means digital and social isolation, it prevents people from participating in otherwise democratic processes. Therefore, this chapter provides an ethnographic example of a Mexican environmental organization that was incapable of participating with side accord–created institutions because of its members' digital and social isolation.

This chapter is divided into five sections. Since environmental regimes take root in social, cultural, and political landscapes, the first section provides a cursory review of the history and making of the U.S.-Mexican borderlands. The region's post-1970 history is particularly important because globalization brought clusters of offshore assembly plants (*maquilas*, in Spanish) to several Mexican border cities. This extraordinary concentration of multinationally owned factories ultimately produced the pervasive environmental contamination that NAFTA opponents would subsequently point to as evidence for their arguments. The second section discusses the unique historical conjuncture that allowed trilateral environmental cooperation to be debated as part and parcel of a strategy for mapping Mexico's political trajectory. Neither Canada nor the United States received this special treatment. The primary reason for singling out Mexico comes directly from development ideology that holds that some nations in the world are developed while others are undeveloped, and it is the duty and burden of developed nations to help undeveloped nations develop. The third section briefly describes the structure and function of the ESA and its companion institutions. This is followed by ethnographic data I collected while conducting fieldwork in the border city of Matamoros, Tamaulipas, for a period of 16 months from November 2001 until March 2003. During this period, I conducted participant-observation fieldwork with a Matamoros-based grassroots environmental justice organization, which I call "Las Caracaras." I describe the opportunities and challenges that the organization encountered when the city's water and sanitation department engaged in public outreach as part of its plans for a North American Development Bank (NADBank) loan which, in turn, would allow for the rehabilitation of the city's antiquated water and sanitation system. Using Las Caracaras's experiences as an example, the final section discusses the ways in which digital, economic, and social status fault lines can radically curtail opportunities for the vast majority of Mexican border populations to participate in ESA processes, thus undercutting the side agreement's mission of encouraging democratic participation and cross-border cooperation. Neither the labor nor the environmental side accords' crafters accounted for these fault lines when the accords were written because the ideological assumption was that free trade would suture these chasms. Twenty years after the fact, the basic issue of digital (dis)connectedness and literacy must be addressed if policy makers are interested in the possibility of the environmental side accord fulfilling its original mandate.

THE *MAQUILA* INDUSTRY AND THE MAKING OF THE CONTEMPORARY BORDERLANDS

The early 20th-century historian Herbert Bolton first used the term "borderlands" to describe the shifting frontiers between French, English, and Spanish settler populations in North America (he ignored the indigenous populations) (Truett, 1997). The U.S.-Mexican borderlands have historically functioned as a cultural contact zone (Alvarez, 1995), a "diffuse zone of acculturation" and a "complex zone of cultural, social, economic, genetic, military, political, religious and linguistic interaction between many different groups of people" (Stern, 1998, p. 157). Partly because of the status of the border as a frontier, its peoples have often been considered marginal to their respective countries (Worcester, 1998, p. 7). Those at the center are considered more "pure" and possessed of nationally desired characteristics, while those at the margins are frequently viewed as less pure or culturally anemic (Das & Poole, 2004).

Within the border regions's tumultuous history, it is impossible to overstate the eventual importance of the actual *border*, once defined by the 1846 Treaty of Guadalupe Hidalgo, to the production and reproduction of the *borderlands* as a culturally, economically, and environmentally marginal region within North America. Borders are territorial markers designating sovereign limits; the U.S.-Mexican border region is unique for the degree to which nonlocal forces have historically produced the locale of border life, and continue to do so (as immigration debates, post–9/11 security measures, and the cartel wars make evident; Brady, 2002; Buchanan, 2001; Ortiz, 1999). The significance of nonlocal forces to border life and culture is perhaps most evident in the massive developmental upheavals that took root on the Mexican side of the border in the mid-1960s, and have continued to shape virtually all aspects of the border's natural, cultural, and political landscapes since then. Noted border scholar and native, Ramon Eduardo Ruiz (2000), succinctly conveys this epochal shift:

> Today, life on the Mexican side of the borderlands only rarely conjures up that of the 1920s. For those of us who knew the old, the dissimilarity is striking. Since the 1960s, the arrival of assembly plants, an adjunct of the global economy, has radically altered the contours of Mexican border society. (p. 61)

Two events came together to ineradicably alter the border region in this period. The first was the creation of the joint U.S.-Mexican Border Industrialization Program (BIP; cf. Baerresen, 1971) of 1965. The BIP was intended to provide employment to former Mexican guest workers who, at the end of the Bracero program in 1964, found themselves and their families clustered on the Mexican side of the border without work. It was supposed to provide factory employment, thus discouraging immigration and creating an "economic fence" (Rivera-Batiz, 1986, p. 263).

The second force that emerged in the early 1970s was the restructuring of the global economy as the U.S. and other core economies shifted to flexible production (cf. Harvey, 1989, pp. 121–197) and offshore manufacture. Briefly, a fundamental aspect of our contemporary global economy is the global commodity production chains that were forged during this period, and which continue to proliferate and entangle different regions of the globe in novel ways. The U.S.-Mexican border region was dramatically transformed by this reorganization of commodity production processes. Multinational corporations' two principal motivations for relocating manufacturing processes from the "first world" to the "third world" are the cheaper labor costs and, typically, more lenient environmental protections. Assembly plants began migrating to the Mexican frontier during this period because Mexico offered all this and more. In particular, its proximity ensured that even transportation costs were minimal, and factory managers could easily live in the United States while commuting to work across the border. Since the early 1970s, the northern Mexico *maquila* sector has grown into an enclave economy with few productive backward or forward linkages with the Mexican economy (Cooney, 2001, pp. 75–76; Delgado Wise & Cypher, 2007, p. 126; Hart-Landsberg, 2002, p. 21).

These twin, intertwined forces came together to produce many of the pollution problems that plague the U.S.-Mexican border region to this day. The *maquilization* of the frontier produced such rapid urbanization and migration to the borderlands that the building and maintenance of basic urban infrastructure could not keep pace. The border has provided a virtual, if unfortunate, living laboratory for the study of the effects of any number of organic and inorganic air, water, and soil pollutants on human health. One example of organic pollution is *aguas negras*, or sewage. As Mexicans migrate to border cities, they typically settle into squatter camps that become incorporated into cities as *colonias*. Until these cities are incorporated, the glacially slow process of establishing basic services leaves people to dig canals or ditches that serve a single household or a settlement. These ditches can be dug anywhere, and often link up with city canals and frequently drain into larger waterways such as the Rio Grande.

Inorganic pollution is pervasive because of the *maquila* industry. Hundreds of toxins and chemicals are used in border factories. High levels of xylene, toluene, benzene, mercury, lead, arsenic and DDT are common in the air, waters, and soils. Border literary theorist, Jose David Saldivar

(1997), provides a wrenching account of the *maquilas*' impacts on the border environment:

> In my childhood in Cameron County in South Texas, I saw the Texas-Mexico borderlands turn into an ecological wasteland, with more than ninety-three *maquiladoras* pouring out toxic waste and endangering life chances and life experiences on both sides of the border. (1997, p. 19)

These environmental health problems were well documented by the time of the NAFTA debates and strategically used by NAFTA opponents (see e.g., Barry, 1994; Brenner, Ross, Simmons, & Zaidi, 2000; Ellis, 1996; Moure-Eraso, et al., 1994; Simon, 1997; Stebbins, 1992).[1]

Transboundary environmental cooperation is difficult at policy and local levels under any circumstances. However, the U.S.-Mexican border presents unique challenges precisely because the border itself has been such a constitutive factor in producing the environmental threats and pollution that pervade the region. Offshore assembly plants move to the Mexican side of the border precisely because of the border. Economic development and environmental protections are rarely seen at such stark cross-purposes. The border is materially and symbolically productive because it produces a "third world" that can be ritually contrasted with a "first," and an automatic power imbalance that was amply present in the NAFTA debates and side accord negotiations.

MEXICO'S DUAL TRANSITION AND THE NAFTA DEBATES

By the time of the NAFTA deliberations in the early 1990s, Mexico had been undergoing a sustained process of dual economic and political transition for at least two decades. The NAFTA debates discursively alloyed this dual transition to the trade treaty and its side accords; the first would guarantee the complete liberalization of Mexico's economy, while the second would encourage the country's ongoing democratization (Simon, 2007, 2014).

Due to the influence of the *maquila* sector, Mexico's economy had been in the process of economic liberalization since the early 1970s. Until then, the economy was governed by the same principles of protectionism and Keynesian economic development practices that guided many developing countries' economies following the Great Depression (Escobar, 1995; Harvey, 1989). The Mexican economy was also isolated from foreign investment or influence because of the ideology of the Institutional Revolutionary Party (*Partido Revolucionario Institucional*, or PRI), which took power in the aftermath of the Mexican Revolution of 1910–1920. Based on populist, socialist, and corporatist principles, the party was staunchly opposed to foreign investment until the inner architecture of Mexico's economy and political system began to crumble in the late 1960s and early 1970s.

Mexico was also in a period of political transition at the time of the NAFTA debates. From the late 1960s onward, there had been growing popular discontent, which the PRI, the world's "perfect authoritarian regime," sought to squash. Certain critical events—the 1968 Tlaltelolco massacre, the crushing of independent labor unions, and the 1985 Mexico City earthquake in which the government left tens of thousands in the rubble—had made both the gross negligence and repressive potential of the PRI apparent (Fox & Hernandez, 1992; La Botz, 1995; Lawson, 2000; Lorena Cook, 1995; Teichman, 1997). In 2000, the National Action Party's candidate, Vincente Fox, won the presidency in the first ostensibly free election in seven decades. The relative levels of fraudulence or fairness of national elections has remained a subject of national debate in the two elections since (2006 and 2012), and the PRI is currently back in charge as Mexico's ruling party. The democratization processes that were occurring within Mexico for decades prior to the NAFTA debates remained largely invisible to American and Canadian public eyes, thus indirectly supporting the morality play narrative that America, in particular, had a responsibility to introduce democracy to its southern neighbor.

Mexico's democratization processes supported the creation of the environmental and labor side accords in at least two ways. First, their internally generated democratic opening allowed expression of Mexican dissent to NAFTA, which joined with and supported opposition in Canada and the United States. Second, the accords were anchored in a discourse that claimed that the side agreements, with their provisions for dispute resolution, accountability, and public participation, would aid Mexico's political transition to democracy, accountability, and modernity (Simon, 2007).

While negotiations had been in the works for years between President H. W. Bush and Mexican president Carlos Salinas de Gortari, these talks did not crash the American public scene until the U.S. election campaigns pitting Bush, Perot, and Clinton against each other (MacArthur, 2000). The debates of the early 1990s were shaped by two competing stances. NAFTA opponents argued that the treaty would continue this degradation and extend southward to all of Mexico. Environmental groups specifically feared that NAFTA would legitimate existing "pollution haven" tactics (Leonard, 1988; Mayer, 2002, pp. 97–118). Mexican resistance was rooted in similar issues, while also nested within a larger agenda of strengthening civil society, protecting human rights, and opposing neoliberal free trade policies and globalization (Brooks & Fox, 2002; Graubart, 2005, pp. 109–110, Hoggenboom, 1996; Lorena Cook, 1997).

NAFTA proponents agreed that environmental abuse had been a standard operating procedure in the preceding years, but assiduously maintained that the wealth created by free trade would result in the more efficient running of Mexico's environmental regulatory institutions, thus prohibiting future environmental abuses. Supporters maintained that the agreement would promote democratization in Mexico (Chambers & Smith, 2002) by encouraging participation and transparency and flushing corruption from the political system (Garcia Urrutia, 2002, p. 80; MacArthur, 2000; Warnock, 1995, p. 155).

As the debates proceeded, it became clear that the problem was not that Mexico's laws were weak, but, rather, that they were unenforced. Accordingly, in 1992 presidential candidate Clinton announced his intention to negotiate supplemental agreements that would satisfy both free trade advocates and environmentalists. This push for ancillary accords was based on negative perceptions of Mexico, not the United States or Canada (Mayer, 2002, pp. 104, 108). Trade negotiators worked on the agreements throughout 1993, eventually mollifying U.S. environmental and labor groups, while frustrating Mexican policy makers who did not appreciate the eleventh -hour monkey wrench that was redolent of potential and insulting national sovereignty threats (Abbott, 2001; Araya, 2002). Of the two agreements, the environmental side was ultimately more critical than the labor agreement in guaranteeing U.S. congressional support, even as congressional approval sealed the fate of labor as well (Dreiling, 1998, p. 221).

In sum, the circumstances surrounding the creation of NAFTA's ESA did not radiate ideals of cooperation, trust, and mutual respect. Nested within Mexico's political transition, proponents of NAFTA and the side agreements argued that they would accelerate and entrench this transition. This transitional phase built on Mexico's status at the time as a "third world" nation, while simultaneously positioning the United States, in particular, as a democracy coach. Hatched in response to U.S. and Canadian opposition, the accord was redolent of northern environmental imperialism. Referred to by Araya as "Mexico's NAFTA Trauma" (2002), the eleventh-hour brokering of side agreements put Mexico in a one-down position vis-à-vis its northern neighbors.

THE NORTH AMERICAN AGREEMENT ON ENVIRONMENTAL COOPERATION

The environmental side accord functions in two principal ways. First, it provides an institutional framework for trinational, cross-border cooperation and for the resolution of environmental disputes arising from NAFTA-inspired economic integration. Second, it created border-specific development institutions to address the environmental issues raised in the NAFTA debates.

At the first level, the environmental side is intended to foster cooperation and assist in environmental dispute resolution. Since the debates had revealed lack of enforcement of Mexican laws as a problem, the petitioning mechanisms within the Commission for Environmental Cooperation (CEC) exist to ensure that each signatory nation enforces its own actually existing environmental laws. The CEC does not harmonize laws. Although Mexican environmental laws were once very weak, they have become much stronger since the early 1970s (Mumme, Bath, & Assetto, 1988; Vasquez, 1993, p. 363). The accord and the CEC rely on cooperation, accountability, and transparency and possess only weak or nonexistent enforcement tools. While the absence of enforcement mechanisms within the agreements drew the ire of NAFTA critics (Evans, 2000; MacArthur, 2000, pp. 184–185; Mayer, 2002; Pomeroy, 1996, pp. 791–792), the accord's "sunshine effect" was presumed to guarantee that the "agreement would achieve enforcement of domestic labor [and environmental] laws through exposure of problems and exchange of information" (Pomeroy, 1996, p. 789).

The ideals of transparency and the "sunshine effect" powerfully influenced the accord's emphasis on accountability, public participation, and sustainability. This is because the NAFTA debates took place at a time when "sustainability" was gaining deeper traction within the environmental and development communities (Dreiling, 1998, p. 231), and development was becoming more closely linked with democracy, relying "heavily on the rhetoric of participation, empowerment, human rights, and democracy as essential aspects of supposedly authentic 'development' " (Rajagopal, 2003, p. 146; cf. Cleaver, 2001, p. 36). However, the fact that the CEC, BECC, or other side accord–related institutions post all documents to their websites or distribute them via listservs (e.g., BECCnet) does not guarantee public participation or bottom-to-top accountability. Vast swaths of the Mexican population lack internet access and digital literacy. In the next section, I describe how one Mexican border environmental justice group became incapable of participating in an important side accord inspired institution—the municipal citizens' committee—because they lacked access to the digital world.

The trinational CEC, which is the environmental accord's primary governing body, is made up of a council, the Joint Public Advisory Committee (JPAC), and the Secretariat. The secretariat provides technical input for the JPAC, receives the submissions and petitions filed by individuals, citizens' groups, and nongovernmental organizations, and produces secretariat reports (see Chapter 2). Submitters must first exhaust all domestic environmental regulatory institutions and possibilities before appealing to the CEC. If an organization files a complaint with the secretariat of the CEC, stipulating precisely which environmental laws are being violated and by whom, the CEC is required to investigate the allegations, consult environmental ministries, mediate or resolve the dispute, and produce a factual record.

The accord is often lauded for containing "mechanisms for public participation and transparency that are unparalleled in any other international agreement or institution" (Ferreti, 2002, p. 85; cf. Goldschmidt, 2002). However, a brief perusal of the petitions makes evident that a vast amount of technical, legal, scientific, medical, and toxicological expertise is necessary simply to prepare a petition. On the one hand, this encourages citizens or lay organizations to rely on NGOs, ENGOs, or others with professional status and knowledge to facilitate their concerns. On the other hand, the vast majority of citizens are, by default, excluded, because they do not have the knowledge or expertise, nor do they have access to NGOs or ENGOs. If they do not have any of these, then it is highly likely that they are poor, uneducated, without social status or connections, and without access to the internet and the world of knowledge and information contained within it. In that case, the level of transparency practiced by the CEC and its institutions does not matter. Additional measures must be applied to ensure that those on the far side of the digital fault lines must be able to participate if the accord is to fulfill its mandate of encouraging cooperation and democratization.

The ESA also created two border institutions: the North American Development Bank (NADBank) and the Border Environment Cooperation Commission (BECC). The BECC reviews loan applications to ensure that projects meet the accord's sustainability and participatory requirements. Projects must comply with minimum standards in the areas of human health, environment, technical and financial feasibility, community participation, sustainable development, and "provision to the affected community [of] a comprehensive document explaining the proposal and project in addition to documentation of the applicant's fulfillment of participatory requirements" (McKinney, 2000, pp. 166–167). Once a project has been certified, loan funds are dispersed from the NADBank.

An important part of that certification involves demonstration of public participation. Section 4 of the joint BECC/NADBank, titled "Relationship with the Public," states that the "commission shall establish procedures" ensuring "public availability of documentary information on all projects for which a request for assistance or an application for certification is made," and opportunities for public comment and complaints (McKinney, 2000, p. 183). The community participation component requires that "the project applicant [must] submit a comprehensive community participation plan," establish a steering committee composed of community organizations, and meet with local affected organizations "to inform the public about the project and to develop support for it" (McKinney, 2000, p. 167). Any municipality requesting a loan must establish a so-called citizens' committee that ostensibly represents the interests of all sectors of the town or city. Leaders of the citizens' committees report to the JPAC. The citizens' committee is one of the most important conduits for NADBank applicants to ensure community participation. It is intended to function as an informational and educative node within the cross-cutting and complicated requirements of the BECC, and it is also the only requirement targeted specifically at community participation. In the next section, I describe one of Matamoros's environmental justice organization's experiences with the city's citizens' committee (*Comite Ciudadano*).

PARTICIPATORY POSSIBILITIES AND PRACTICAL CONSTRAINTS FOR A MATAMOROS ENVIRONMENTAL JUSTICE ORGANIZATION

Here I describe Las Caracaras's experience with a Matamoros development project that, by virtue of the BECC mandate for public participation, involved them initially and should have included their participation throughout. In early 2002, the city of Matamoros began public outreach for a project and loan application they were preparing for a project called PIAPS (*Plan Integral de Aguas Potables y Saneamiento*, or Integrated Plan for Potable Water and Sanitation). The project aimed to repair the city's many collapsed underground pipes, which allowed sewage to flow through the streets during the rainy season. It also sought the creation of an additional wastewater treatment plant, since at the time there was only one for a city of close to one million people. The project was housed within the Water and Sanitation Department, or JAD (*Junta de Aguas y Drenaje*). To receive a NADBank loan, the city of Matamoros and the JAD had to comply with the BECC and CEC requirements of public outreach, participation, and support.

It was this novel nexus of funding, participation, and environmental improvement that brought the JAD and Las Caracaras together. As part of their funding application process, the city and the JAD had to form a citizens' committee to hold public meetings, receive public comment, sustain dialogue, and otherwise maintain transparency. A JAD engineer also provided a presentation for Las Caracaras in the latter's office. People within Las Caracaras were on a first name basis with many within the JAD because they frequently traveled downtown to city hall to remind sanitation workers to remove the garbage from their neighborhoods. This engineer came at the request of one of the few middle-class members of the group who was also an aspiring politician who spent considerable time at city hall.

The engineer appeared at the appointed time on one steamy May evening. He was equipped with graphs, a projector, PowerPoint presentation, and slides. With a very professional presentation, he explained PIAPS to the group in the following way: The city was working on a 50-year plan to provide clean and potable water for all of its citizens, and the city was proposing this project to BECC and NADBank. The most important part of this plan involved repairing at least 30 *caidas* that plagued the city. *Caidas*, he explained, were broken and leaking wastewater pipes made of inferior quality (French) materials. They had constricted through time, leaving thin pipes running through larger caverns that collapsed under the weight of ever heavier traffic, a result of the city's population explosion. These are sewage pipes that contaminated all of the subsoils and groundwater. The city regularly flooded during the rainy season, leaving residents to literally canoe their way around or wade through sometimes waist-high water. Echoing the concerns of Las Caracaras about the malodorous canal polluting their neighborhoods, he noted that many drains originally constructed for flood prevention were now used for sewage, as well as "possible" clandestine dumping by *maquilas*. The plan would help resolve the public health problems caused by sewage draining indiscriminately because "an epidemic does not recognize a border," he declared. Finally, the engineer provided a flowchart of the BECC/NADBank loan application process, introducing and explaining acronyms and institutions that, until this meeting, most members of the organization had never encountered, including those of the ESA. He explained that one of the JAD's obligations was public outreach, and he was frank about his motivation for this presentation for Las Caracaras. He explained BECC requirements for a NADBank loan, including the constitution of a citizens' committee, and went so far as to say that a BECC committee might pose these questions to members of the citizens' committee: "Do you know what the problem is? Do you know what the solution should be?" If the JAD were to prove that it had fulfilled its requirements for participation in the BECC certification process, the proof would be in a fully informed citizenry. He hoped that Las Caracaras might be willing to participate in the committee and, if they did, that his presentation had prepared them to answer those questions.

During the question-and-answer session that followed, some in the audience could not resist making jokes about his and the JAD's sudden interest in these neighborhoods and in poor people like Caracaras members. They reminded the engineer of the irony of the situation; typically so ignored by city hall and the JAD that they had to visit their offices weekly to beg them to come and collect trash, the tables had suddenly turned and it was the JAD now being solicitous. As one forthright member put it, "It will be difficult to gain support since everyone in the city knows that the JAD has typically favored the needs of the wealthier communities. Why should we believe that things would be any different now? More importantly, why should we help to bring to fruition a project which would have no benefits for us, but only for the rich?"

The engineer rather sheepishly admitted that, yes, the city had traditionally favored wealthier neighborhoods, but "if the people would just give the city and the JAD a chance, we are ready to democratize, change our image and change our practices." Additionally, "the city government is trying to be less corrupt, more democratic, more transparent, but it needs the '*gente*' to give them a chance first."[2] He guaranteed that, in addition to transparent discussions prior to the signing of a NADBank loan, the citizens' committee, once formed, would also provide follow up ("*seguimiento*") on JAD activities to ensure that the JAD acted in accordance with its obligations to the city's citizens. He admitted that he had never visited this neighborhood before, which he had difficulty navigating because of the lack of street signs and perpetually winding streets. That comment, as well as the offhand one that he lived across the river in Brownsville, Texas (made without a hint or irony), failed to elicit laughter, however.

In early September 2002, the Matamoros citizens' committee was announced.[3] According to the two Caracaras members who attended the first meetings, the committee consisted largely of representatives of business, education, industry, and civic organizations, all of whom constituted the local social elite. They had felt out of place as likely afterthoughts: "Our names were definitely at the bottom of the list." It was never revealed how these "representatives" of a thin and notably elite slice of Matamoros's demographic profile were selected, but if the selection process was anything like that of the Matamoros Good Neighbor Environmental Board (GNEB) meeting that other Caracaras members and I had attended one month before, these "public" representatives were the recipients of private email invitations.

Las Caracaras's participation in the citizens' committee was short-lived, however, due to internal frictions that were also part of a pattern within the group. The one person who could guarantee continued access to the citizens' committee was accused of pilfering funds and other nefarious activities. When Las Caracaras parted ways with him, they also lost their committee connection. With few middle-class members, the opportunities that Las Caracaras gained to escape their information-voided world—lack of access to newspapers, the internet, political influence, and social connections—came from these individuals and this fieldworker.

Throughout the time that I observed and worked with Las Caracaras, it was clear that the overwhelmingly dislocating and deleterious effects of poverty, educational differences, class, and differential access to the digital universe proved to be the organization's Achilles' heel in a variety of contexts. These ranged from a local, cross-border, environmental coalition-building effort in which suspicions abounded as to why and how a particular cross-border activist was representing Las Caracaras to Brownsville's only environmental group, to Las Caracaras's sustained relationship with the Sierra Club over a period of years. In both cases, Las Caracaras's founding members—who were also the organization's poorest, least educated, and least digitally connected—thought that *their* participatory possibilities were compromised by their class, ethnicity, and gender, as well as their glaring lack of access to the digital world. The vast majority did not have telephones, never mind computers. When one has neither telephones nor computers, and lives in a poor *colonia* with unpaved roads and limited running water, it is unlikely that one has either the funds to visit a cyber-café or the requisite digital literacy to make that visit useful. The organization frequently imploded because of the class, ethnic, educational, gender, and digital tensions that continually strained it, and it seemed to disband temporarily or lose members completely whenever it was on the cusp of receiving some type of symbolic or material support. Within a political economy of scarce resources, the very possibility of resources and support—or even contact with others beyond the poverty-induced information void in which they lived—forced all subterranean divisions to the surface and, typically, ripped the group asunder.

PARTICIPATORY CHALLENGES AND THE DIGITAL DIVIDE

A kaleidoscope of issues served to exclude Las Caracaras from effective participation in the Matamoros citizens committee: class, race, migrant status, educational levels, location, and social status. These factors in turn determined the degree to which Las Caracaras members had digital access and literacy. Only a tiny fraction did, and they were all middle or lower middle class professionals of whom other Caracaras members were frequently suspect. Warf and others have observed that the structural inequalities of the nondigital world get reinscribed in the digital universe, effectively compounding existing social gaps: "All the existing social categories of wealth and power are replicated in cyberspace, at least in terms of access to the equipment and technical know-how necessary to gain entry" (Warf, 2001, pp. 16–17). Digital access might have greatly increased the odds of Las Caracaras's continued participation in the citizens' committee, as well as many other environmental endeavors from which they became effectively excluded because of digital disconnectedness and their own shame about their "ignorance."

Critics of participatory development frequently maintain that "participation" is executed in a top-down manner and largely just to fulfill funders' requirements, thus producing an illusion or "performance" of participation, rather than genuine engagement (see e.g., Cooke & Kothari, 2001; Peters, 2000). That would seem to be the logical conclusion to reach regarding the composition and practices of the Matamoros citizens' committee and JAD, as outlined in this chapter. However, the fact that participation is a requirement does not make it any less real. Similarly, it is not possible or reasonable to assume the intentions of those working in government or development institutions. Thus, while mandated participation can frequently produce the appearance of simply being an exercise in bureaucracy, to assume that those in charge of executing participatory practices (such as the JAD and City Hall) are uniformly uninterested in substantive participation from those most marginalized does a disservice to the diversity of agency present even in government and development institutions. Having observed mandated participation in a variety of settings, I have tentatively concluded that hasty assumptions of official disinterestedness are just that—hasty assumptions. Rather, there are a number of structural factors that encourage participation from certain sectors of the local population and discourage others.

NAFTA and the side agreements went into effect around the same time that the internet took root as an ineluctable aspect of modern life, including hopes for its "inherently democratic impacts, facilitating equal access to data and knowledge regardless of social standing or geographic location" (Warf, 2001, p. 4; cf. Norris, 2002). However, in all the primary side accord documents reviewed by this author, digital obstacles have never come up as a practical, participatory gap requiring redress. In the 16 months of fieldwork in Matamoros, purchasing the local daily newspaper virtually every day (*El Bravo*), not once was a public announcement for an upcoming citizens' committee, BECC, or GNEB meeting found. Instead, announcements of meetings and their accomplishments were made after the fact. Participatory opportunities were heavily circumscribed by class, status, and access to the digital world. The accords' crafters seemingly assumed that the "market alone [would] take care of any perceived" digital divide (Mariscal, 2005, p. 210) just as it would take care of all other social and economic problems. There is a dramatic and growing digital divide in Mexico. This disparity deleteriously affects participatory capacities. Most of the "public" dialogue carried out by the CEC, BECC, and other environmental accord takes place on the far side of a digital divide that communities most in need of help often cannot bridge.

CONCLUSION

NAFTA's ESA made bold headways in the area of bi- and trilateral environmental cooperation. At the same time, the side accord was discursively, temporally, and politically tied to Mexico's democratization and was brokered under less than ideal conditions. In spite of that, trilateral conversations and cooperation grounded in the environmental agreement seem to have grown more robust and sustainable with time. A persistent weakness in the effectiveness of the side accord remains the fact that it is unreachable for, and unknown to, the vast majority of the digitally disenfranchised Mexican population. Due to the poverty that continues to pervade the country, and the vast rural and urban lifestyle divides, the Mexican "public" that the environmental accord might reach is a very thin and select slice. If the accord is to become a democratic tool for cross-border environmental cooperation and decision making, some effort must be made to increase the transparency of the CEC and border development institutions, as well as to bridge the abyss that poverty, lack of education, and digital disconnectedness create to exclude most Mexican border populations from a conversation in which they should be principal participants.

NOTES

1. The toxicological, environmental, biological, and epidemiological border pollution literature is so vast that the interested reader is advised to consult the resources discussed in Brenner, Ross, Simmons, & Zaidi (2000).

2. Literally, "the people," but used as a reference to the *clase popular* (poor, working poor, lower middle and, less so, middle class peoples).
3. "The Creation of the Executive and Citizens' Committee for Matamoros' Plan Integral." *El Bravo*, September 5, 2002.

REFERENCES

Abbott, F. M. (2001). NAFTA and the legalization of world politics: A case study. In J. Goldstein, M. Kahler, R. O. Keohane, & A. M. Slaughter (Eds.), *Legalization and world politics* (pp. 135–164). Cambridge, MA: MIT Press.

Alvarez, R. (1995). The Mexican–U.S. border: The making of an anthropology of borderlands. *Annual Review of Anthropology*, *24*, 447–470.

Anzaldua, G. (1987). *Borderlands: The new mestiza = la frontera*. San Francisco, CA: Aunt Lute Books.

Araya, M. (2002). Mexico's NAFTA trauma: Myth and reality. In C. Deere and D. Esty (Eds.), *Greening the Americas: NAFTA's lessons for hemispheric trade* (pp. 61–78). Cambridge, MA: MIT Press.

Baerresen, D. W. (1971). *The border industrialization program of Mexico*. Lexington, MA: Heath Lexington Press.

Barry, T. (1994). *The challenge of cross-border environmentalism: The U.S.-Mexico case*. Albuquerque, NM: Resource Center Press.

Brady, M. P. (2002). *Extinct lands, temporal geographies: Chicana literature and the urgency of space*. Durham, NC: Duke University Press.

Brenner, J., Ross, J., Simmons, J., & Zaidi, S. (2000). Neoliberal trade and investment and the health of Maquiladora workers on the US-Mexico border. In J. Y. Kim, J. Millen, A. Irwin, & J. Gershman (Eds.), *Dying for growth: Global inequality and the health of the poor* (pp. 261–292). Monroe, ME: Common Courage Press.

Brooks, D., & Fox, J. (2002). Movements across the border: An overview. In D. Brooks & J. Fox (Eds.), *Cross-border dialogues: U.S.-Mexico social movement networking* (pp. 1–68). San Diego, CA: Center for US-Mexican Studies.

Buchanan, R. (2001). Border crossings: NAFTA, regulatory restructuring, and the politics of place. In N. Blomley, D. Delaney, and R. T. Ford (Eds.), *The legal geographies reader: Law, power, and space* (pp. 285–297). Malden, MA: Blackwell Publishers.

Chambers, E. J., & Smith, P. H. (2002). NAFTA in the new millennium: Questions and contexts. In E. Chambers & P. Smith (Eds.), *NAFTA in the new millenium* (pp. 1–27). La Jolla, CA: Center for U.S.-Mexican Studies.

Cleaver, F. (2001). Institutions, agency and the limitations of participatory approaches to development. In B. Cooke & U. Kothari (Eds.), *Participation: The new tyranny?* (pp. 36–55). London, UK: Zed Books.

Cooke, B., & Kothari, U. (Eds.). (2001). *Participation: The new tyranny?* London, UK: Zed Books.

Cooney, P. (2001). The Mexican crisis and the Maquiladora boom: A paradox of development or the logic of neoliberalism? *Latin American Perspectives*, *28*(3), 55–83.

Das, V., & Poole, D. (2004). State and its margins: Comparative ethnographies. In V. Das & D. Poole (Eds.), *Anthropology in the margins of the state* (pp. 3–33). Santa Fe, NM: School for American Research Press.

Deere, C., & Esty, D. C. (Eds.). (2002). *Greening the Americas: NAFTA's lessons for hemispheric trade.* Cambridge, MA: MIT Press.

Delgado Wise, R., & Cypher, J. M. (2007). The strategic role of Mexican labor under NAFTA: Critical perspectives on current economic integration. *Annals of the American Academy of Political and Social Science*, *610*(1), 119–142.

Dreiling, M. (1998). Remapping North American environmentalism: Contending visions and divergent practices in the fight over NAFTA. In D. Faber (Ed.), *The struggle for ecological democracy: Environmental justice movements in the United States* (pp. 218–247). New York, NY: Guilford Press.

Ellis, E. A. (1996). Bordering on disaster: A new attempt to control the transboundary effects of Maquiladora pollution. *Valparaiso Law Review*, *30*, 621.

Escobar, A. (1996). *Encountering development: The making and unmaking of the third world.* Princeton, NJ: Princeton University Press.

Etsy, D. C. (2001). Bridging the trade-environment divide. *Journal of Economic Perspectives*, *15*(3), 113–130.

Esty, D. C. (2004). The environmental dimension of economic integration: The FTAA and beyond. In A. Estevadeordal, D. Rodik, A. M. Taylor, & A. Velasco (Eds.), *Integrating the Americas: FTAA and beyond* (pp. 673–694). Cambridge, MA: Harvard University Press.

Evans, P. (2000). Fighting marginalization with transnational networks: Counter-hegemonic globalization. *Contemporary Sociology*, *29*(1), 230–241.

Ferretti, J. (2002). NAFTA and the environment: An update. *Canada-United States Law Journal*, *28*, 81–89.

Fox, J., & Hernandez, L. (1992). Mexico's difficult democracy: Grassroots movements, NGOs, and local government. *Alternatives*, *17*(2), 165–208.

Garcia Urrutia, M. (2002). The authentic labor front in the NAFTA-era regional integration process. In D. Brooks & J. Fox (Eds.), *Cross-border dialogues: U.S.-Mexico social movement networking* (pp. 77–86). San Diego, CA: Center for U.S.-Mexican Studies.

Goldschmidt, M. (2002). The role of transparency and public participation in international environmental agreements: The North American agreement on environmental cooperation. *Boston College Environmental Affairs Law Review*, *29*, 343.

Graubart, J. (2005). Politicizing a new breed of "legalized" transnational political opportunity structures: Labor activists' uses of NAFTA's citizen-petition mechanism. *Berkeley Journal of Employment and Labor Law*, *26*(1), 97–142.

Hart-Landsberg, M. (2002). Challenging neoliberal myths: A critical look at the Mexican experience. *Monthly Review*, *54*(7), 14–27.

Harvey, D. (1989). *The condition of postmodernity*. Cambridge, MA: Blackwell Press.

Hogenboom, B. (1996). Cooperation and polarisation beyond borders: The transnationalization of Mexican environmental issues during the NAFTA negotiations. *Third World Quarterly*, *17*(5), 989–1005.

La Botz, D. (1995). *Democracy in Mexico: Peasant rebellion and political reform*. Boston, MA: South End Press.

Lawson, C. (2000). Mexico's unfinished transition: Democratization and authoritarian enclaves in Mexico. *Mexican Studies/Estudios Mexicanos*, *16*(2), 267–287.

Leonard, H. J. (1988). *Pollution and the struggle for the world product: Multinational corporations, environment, and international comparative advantage*. Cambridge, MA: Cambridge University Press.

Lorena Cook, M. (1995). Mexican state-labor relations and the political implications of free trade. *Latin American Perspectives*, *22*(1), 77–94.

Lorena Cook, M. (1997). Regional integration and transnational politics: Popular sector strategies in the NAFTA era. In D. Chambers (Ed.), *The new politics of inequality in Latin America* (pp. 516–540). Oxford, UK: Oxford University Press.

MacArthur, J. (2000). *The selling of free trade: NAFTA, Washington, and the subversion of democracy*. Berkeley, CA: University of California Press.

Mariscal, J. (2005). Digital divide in a developing country. *Telecommunications Policy*, *29*(5), 409–428.

Mayer, F. W. (2002). Negotiating the NAFTA: Political lessons for the FTAA. In C. Deere & D. C. Esty (Eds.), *Greening the Americas: NAFTA's lessons for hemispheric trade* (pp. 97–118). Cambridge, MA: MIT Press.

McKinney, J. (2000). *Created from NAFTA: The structure, function, and significance of the treaty's related institutions.* Armonk, NY: M. E. Sharpe.

Moure-Eraso, R., Wilcox, M., Punnett, L., Copeland, L., & Levenstein, C. (1994). Back to the future: Sweatshop conditions on the Mexico-U.S. border. I. Community health impact of Maquiladora industrial activity. *American Journal of Industrial Medicine*, *25*(3), 311–324.

Mumme, S., Bath, R., & Assetto, V. J. (1988). Political development and environmental policy in Mexico. *Latin American Research Review*, *23*(1), 7–34.

Norris, P. (2002). *Digital divide: Civic engagement, information poverty, and the internet worldwide.* Cambridge, UK: Cambridge University Press.

Ortiz, V. (1999). Only time can tell if geography is still destiny: Time, space, and NAFTA in a U.S.-Mexican border city. *Human Organization*, *58*(2), 173–181.

Peters, P. E. (Ed.). (2000). *Development encounters: Sites of participation and knowledge.* Cambridge, MA: Harvard University Press.

Pomeroy, L. O. (1996). The labor side agreement under the NAFTA: Analysis of its failure to include strong enforcement provisions and recommendations for future labor agreements negotiated with developing countries. *George Washington Journal of International Law and Economics*, *29*, 769–801.

Rajagopal, B. (2003). *International law from below: Development, social movements and third world resistance.* Cambridge, MA: MIT Press.

Rivera-Battiz, F. (1986). Can border industries be a substitute for immigration? *The American Economic Review*, *76*(2), 263–268.

Ruiz, R. E. (2000). *On the rim of Mexico: Encounters of the rich and poor.* Boulder, CO: Westview Press.

Saldivar, J. D. (1997). *Border matters: Remapping American cultural studies.* Berkeley, CA: University of California Press.

Simon, J. (1997). *Endangered Mexico: An environment on the edge.* San Francisco, CA: Sierra Club Books.

Simon, S. (2007). Framing the nation: Law and the cultivation of national character stereotypes in the NAFTA debate and beyond. *Political and Legal Anthropology Review*, *30*(1), 22–45.

Simon, S. (2014). *Sustaining the borderlands in the age of NAFTA: Development, politics and participation on the U.S.-Mexico border.* Nashville, TN: Vanderbilt University Press.

Stebbins, K. R. (1992). Garbage imperialism: Health implications of dumping hazardous waste in third world countries. *Medical Anthropology*, *15*(1), 81–102.

Stern, P. (1998). Marginals and acculturation in frontier society. In R. Jackson (Ed.), *New views of borderlands history* (pp. 157–188). Albuquerque, NM: University of New Mexico Press.

Teichman, J. (1997). Neoliberalism and the transformation of Mexican authoritarianism. *Mexican Studies/Estudios Mexicanos, 13*(1), 121–147.

Thomas, C., & Weber, M. (1999). New values and international organizations: Balancing trade and environment in the North American Free Trade Agreement. In A. Taylor & C. Thomas (Eds.), *Global trade and global social issues* (pp. 134–150). New York, NY: Routledge Press.

Truett, S. (1997). Neighbors by nature: Rethinking region, nation, and environmental history in the U.S.–Mexico borderlands. *Environmental History*, *2*(2), 160–178.

Vasquez, X. C. (1993). The North American Free Trade Agreement and environmental racism. *Harvard International Law Journal*, *34*(2), 357–379.

Warf, B. (2001). Segues into cyberspace: Multiple geographies of the digital divide. *Environment and Planning B: Planning and Design*, *28*(1), 3–19.

Warnock, J. W. (1995). *The other Mexico: The North American triangle completed*. New York, NY: Black Rose Books.

Worcester, D. (1988). The significance of the Spanish borderlands to the United States. In D. Weber (Ed.), *New Spain's far northern frontier: Essays on Spain in the American West, 1540–1821* (2nd ed., pp. 1–16). Dallas, TX: First Southern Methodist University Press.

FOUR

The Absence of—and Need for—a Transboundary Environmental Impact Assessment Agreement between the United States and Canada

OLIVIA COLLINS AND WILLIAM V. KENNEDY

INTRODUCTION

Environmental impact assessment (EIA) is a key component to understanding the current underdevelopment of binational and trinational environmental governance in North America.[1] While many networks have been formed across issue areas, often related to resource management, there is no common approach—much less an institutionalized form of ongoing collaboration—on what many would consider the most fundamental role governments can play in assessing proposed projects that may have serious impacts on both ecology and society.

From the time of its origin in the U.S. National Environmental Policy Act (NEPA) of 1969, EIA has proliferated globally and is currently incorporated in the environmental and sustainable development policies of almost all countries. It is carried out on both public and private sector projects, plans, and programs at local, regional, and national levels of government and is increasingly used as a requirement for project funding by development and commercial banks. Both the United States and Canada have well-established EIA systems operating at both the national and state or provincial level; Mexico also has an EIA regime in place, which came into force much later. However, despite a long history of cooperation in addressing environmental issues and coordinated management of transboundary impacts and resources, the United States and Canada have no formal transboundary environmental impact assessment (TEIA) *agreement* to deal with project-specific transnational environmental issues.

Maintaining healthy border regions is crucial for both countries from an economic, social, and environmental point of view. Management of shared natural resources must therefore be carried out effectively to prevent further damage to already stressed ecosystems. For example, water use and water diversion have become increasingly important issues (Brown, 2015). Groundwater is a critical resource and the aquifers in North America are often polluted. In several regions, groundwater is being used faster than it can be regenerated (Kidd, 2002, p. 1). Air pollution also continues to be a problem despite existing legislation to reduce pollutants. Ozone and particulate matter (PM) are especially worrisome because of their potential effect on human health. Compounding these problems is climate change, the consequences of which are already being felt across the entire transboundary region. These are all issues that are typically addressed in an environmental impact assessment regardless of its scope—local, regional, national, or transboundary. Although a treaty dealing with TEIA would not solve the environmental conundrum, it could certainly draw much needed attention to problems directly related to projects with transboundary impacts, increasing awareness and providing critical information to those involved in the decision-making process. If large projects were subject to a joint assessment process, together with increased transparency and public involvement on both sides of the border, overall environmental quality would be improved.

The objective of this chapter is to demonstrate that there is not only a need for a TEIA agreement, but that the construction and implementation of such an agreement is also highly feasible within the political boundaries of Canada and the United States. We begin by looking briefly at North America, demonstrating that historically the three nations have favored a bilateral, rather than a trilateral approach to transboundary resource management. We then focus on the United States and Canada and explore their laws on EIA and the extent to which they address transboundary issues. This is followed by a section describing a few recent projects on the border with potentially significant impacts on both countries, but which failed to consider the transboundary effects. Finally, we provide a description of the Convention on Environmental Impact Assessment in a Transboundary Context (more commonly known as the Espoo Convention), which was adopted by the member states of the UN Economic Commission for Europe (UNECE) and could serve as a model for a transboundary EIA agreement between the United States and Canada.

ENVIRONMENTAL MANAGEMENT ACROSS NORTH AMERICA: A BRIEF SURVEY

All three North American countries are vast in size and share the common challenge of managing their resources adequately. Even though their respective environmental regimes were established at different times—Mexico nearly two decades after the United States and Canada—many similarities in environmental policy do exist between them. They all have national agencies that promote forest conservation and all of them created large national parks systems in the 19th century. In addition, they all have environmental pollution control regimes that regulate air, water, and soil. However, there are substantive differences as well.

A brief look at their respective legal systems illustrates these substantive differences well. In the United States, the courts "rule not only on the constitutionality of laws, but also on details of how administrative agencies interpret legislative directions" (Healy, VanNijnatten, & Lopez-Vallejo, 2014, p. 31). As a result, the court system in the United States is generally perceived as just another stage in the policy process, albeit one that can take years or even decades to surpass. In contrast to the United States, Canadian courts have been very reluctant to dispute political decisions, including those made at the bureaucratic level; and the restrictive rules of standing have severely limited the capacity of environmental interest groups to dispute government decisions. And in Mexico, there is a comprehensive set of civil laws and codes, leaving little room for interpretation by the courts. Environmental management is therefore addressed differently across the three countries, in addition to being shaped by the different degrees of financial resources available for this purpose (Mexico having considerably less to contribute than the other two).

Political, geographical, and economic differences aside, the three nations have cooperatively managed transboundary resources in the last century, adopting a bilateral rather than a trilateral approach. Between the United States and Canada, there exist more than 10 major agreements regulating a wide range of environmental issues beginning with the Boundary Waters Treaty (BWT) of 1909; between the United States and Mexico, there exist several agreements covering a comprehensive range of transboundary environmental problems, the first of which was signed as long ago as 1889. Trilateral environmental negotiations on the other hand have often met with opposition and have rarely been achieved. For example, an attempt to create a tripartite commission in 1895 to "adjudicate rights on streams of an international character" was vetoed by the U.S.

State Department (Healy et al., 2014, p. 47). Another attempt in 1909 by President Theodore Roosevelt to create a trilateral plan on natural resource management across North America was eventually dissolved by President Taft, who entered office only months after the proposed plan. More relevant to the discussion on TEIA is a recent attempt to create a trilateral TEIA agreement, proposed by the Commission on Environmental Cooperation (CEC) in the late 1990s, which also failed. Article 10(7) of the North American Agreement on Environmental Cooperation (NAAEC), which created the CEC, directs the three governments to develop an agreement on TEIA with respect to:

> (a) Assessing the environmental impact of proposed projects subject to decisions by a competent governmental authority and likely to cause significant adverse trans-boundary effects, including a full evaluation of comments provided by other Parties and persons of other Parties;
> (b) Notification, provision of relevant information and consultation between Parties with respect to such projects; and
> (c) Mitigation of the potential adverse effects of such projects. (CEC, 1997)

In the mid-1990s a trilateral expert group was established by the CEC to begin the negotiation process, and in 1997 a draft agreement was published. Although each of the three countries possessed federal systems of government with EIA legislation at both the national and state or provincial level, the draft agreement applied solely to national-level EIA requirements. Mexico was insistent on the inclusion of state and provincial actions while Canada and the United States were opposed; this difference led to a breakdown in negotiations. In 2005 the CEC Secretariat attempted to revive interest in an agreement with a proposal to its council to carry out a special report (under Article 13 of the NAAEC) which would cover six to eight case studies related to TEA; but the three governments voted against the proposal.

With the exception of the NAAEC, the environmental side agreement to NAFTA, the United States, Canada, and Mexico have undoubtedly had more success with bilateral environmental arrangements. Given that the United States and Canada have well-established EIA regimes and have signed many environmental agreements in the past, it is conceivable to imagine a bilateral TEIA agreement that would satisfy both parties.

DOMESTIC LEGISLATION, TRANSBOUNDARY LACUNA

Very few countries have EIA legislation that outlines procedures on how to proceed with transboundary assessments, and Canada and the United States are no exception. The U.S. NEPA and the Canadian Environmental Assessment Act (CEAA) fail to address TEIA adequately. Both omit detailed provisions on how to proceed with projects resulting in transboundary impacts (Garver & Podhora, 2008). On the international level, Canada has ratified the Espoo Convention on TEIA but the United States has not. In most transboundary pollution disputes, the United States and Canada have relied mostly on their bilateral agreements, their domestic EIA systems, and their respective legal systems to settle disputes.

The lack of provisions detailing TEIA in their EIA systems indicates that a TEIA agreement would contribute to improved environmental management, especially from a planning point of view. Research has shown that EIA, despite being a more informative than substantive process, could "contribute to greater consideration of environmental concerns in the future, both by proponents, whose plans may become more environmentally acceptable from the outset and by decision makers who may come to demand higher standards of environmental protection" (Sassman, 2012, n. 221). Moreover, given that the EIA process is "self regulatory and reflexive, requiring decision makers to account for and respond to the views of affected persons" (Craik, 2007, p. 383), a TEIA agreement could be used as a tool to improve accountability using cooperative management mechanisms such as inclusive public consultations and information-sharing sessions, further reducing the risk of conflict. Many experts consider stakeholder participation to be "a means to improve public acceptance and developmental decisions, particularly those involving complex technology, uncertain risks, and contending values" (Kasperson & Ram, 2013, p. 92). In cases that provoke opposition or resistance, this could be a valuable approach.

The U.S. National Environmental Policy Act of 1969

In the United States, domestic EIA is dictated by the NEPA of 1969, which is regarded as the first environmental impact assessment policy and has been used as a model for many other nations worldwide (Hall, 2007; Sassman, 2012; Tweedie, 2006). The Council on Environmental Quality (CEQ) was created alongside NEPA to ensure that the federal agencies conducting environmental impact statements (EIS) comply with NEPA procedures (Hall, 2007). The language of NEPA does not directly refer to transboundary assessments or detail specific obligations.[2] However, in 1997 the CEQ "issued a guidance on NEPA Analyses for Transboundary Impacts" (Hall, 2007, p. 701). This guidance effectively states that NEPA policy should include the assessment of transboundary impacts but includes no provisions on how to proceed with TEIA (Craik, 2008; Rosenberg, 2000).[3]

Even before the 1997 guidance was issued, "the application of NEPA to transboundary environmental impacts . . . generated a large body of case law" (Tweedie, 2006, p. 870). Scholars have noted over the years that the U.S. courts have not favored the extraterritorial application of U.S. domestic laws, including NEPA (Cassar & Bruch, 2004; Parrish, 2005; Popiel, 1995; Tweedie, 2006). In particular, even though lower-level courts have been more willing to apply NEPA extraterritorially, it is believed that "the narrow interpretation it has received in the US Supreme Court" specifically has limited its application to transboundary impacts (Tweedie, 2006, p. 875).[4] Subsequently, critics argue that the limited value given to TEIA under NEPA makes domestic EIA unsuited to serve as a model for a TEIA agreement (Knox, 2002; Tweedie, 2006).

The Canadian Environmental Assessment Act

In Canada, EIA policy is governed by the CEAA. According to the act, proponents must conduct an EIA for any designated projects that are found in the "Regulations Designating Physical Activities" list. Similar to NEPA, the CEAA makes only a vague reference to transboundary impact assessment in the presence or possibility of transboundary harm.[5] While the language prescribed by the CEAA does encourage the minister to enter into some sort of TEIA agreement with another nation if he or she deems it appropriate, no provisions are provided on how to proceed with TEIA. Even though the CEAA goes one step further than NEPA by including such a provision, "the significance of the CEAA's transboundary provisions remains uncertain" because of its limited practice (Tweedie, 2006, p. 885).

Despite the fact that both nations have strong EIA regulations in place, both fail to outline meaningful procedures for applying them in transboundary situations. This provides a strong argument to develop a mechanism that will help bridge that gap. Transboundary projects "necessarily implicate the environment on both sides of the border, without regard to political boundaries. Yet because boundaries exist, there is a danger that harms will be unduly overlooked or dismissed" (Fang, 2012, p. 297). And a failure to assess *all* the significant environmental impacts of a project can lead to unintended consequences for both nations, especially when the impacts are more global in nature, such as GHG emissions (Fang, 2012). It is therefore in the environmental, social, and economic interest of the United States and Canada to conduct TEIAs for large projects, to avoid the associated costs of unexpected environmental impacts. A TEIA agreement could also improve the planning side of resource management where other treaties dealing with transboundary pollution fall short, by providing a more transparent assessment process for projects with potentially harmful impacts. An agreement with clear, mutually developed guidelines would potentially improve interagency coordination and ensure that the TEIA was carried out more effectively, reducing obstacles or conflict that often arise from such large projects. The same logic would apply to projects along the U.S.-Mexican border, though EIA in Mexico is still in its infancy.[6]

ENVIRONMENTAL DISPUTES BETWEEN CANADA AND THE UNITED STATES

Numerous conflicts that have occurred throughout the decades between the United States and Canada when dealing with transboundary resource issues. Many of these disputes are project-specific and demonstrate that there is a need for further negotiations regarding TEIA. In many controversial transboundary cases, the parties have deferred to litigation to solve the disputes. While relying on the legal system has certain advantages, the process is usually lengthy and costly for both governments and can also cause internal discord between federal agencies. There is also an inherent risk that can manifest in a variety of ways: a successful outcome is very hard to predict; the environmental outcome may not be favorable even to the plaintiff; and once a final decision is made by the ruling body, there may not be any opportunity for further negotiations, should the ruling prove challenging to implement or incite a negative reaction from the public (Springer, 2007).

Avoiding litigation when possible and relying instead on well-designed TEIA process that encourages a deliberative approach will improve the climate for productive negotiations, promote an atmosphere of cooperation and potentially prevent disputes and any tainting of good relationships. The enormous and increasingly difficult task of managing transboundary resources requires that parties on both sides of the border continue to engage in a spirit of compromise regarding large projects with potentially significant environmental impacts. In addition, a TEIA agreement could help streamline the process and prevent the duplication of EIAs, which often results from subsequent transboundary disagreements. Furthermore, if the two EIAs conflict, this can raise questions about the legitimacy of a specific review and provoke further disagreement. The following section highlights four transboundary disputes between Canada and the United States. Each case is different, yet demonstrates that a TEIA agreement could fill a gap in resource management along the U.S.-Canadian border. A summary all of four examples can be found in Table 4.1.

Sumas Energy Dispute

A commonly discussed transboundary dispute is the Sumas Energy case that took place between the province of British Columbia (BC) and the State of Washington. In 1999, the Sumas Energy 2 electric company suggested the construction and operation of "a 660-megawatt combined-cycle combustion turbine facility (the Sumas Energy 2 Generation Facility) in the City of Sumas, Washington" (Buckley & Belec, 2011, p. 58; Washington State EFSEC, 2001, pp. 1–4). The project proposal included an electrical transmission line to be built across the border into BC. There was quite a bit of opposition to the project from both sides of the border, for fear that the facility would cause unwanted air pollution, even though the EIS produced by Washington State indicated that air emissions would fall within acceptable thresholds (Buckley & Belec, 2011). The government of BC and Environment Canada even appealed to the U.S. Environmental Protection Agency (EPA) appeals board to have the U.S. EIS denied (Buckley & Belec, 2011, p. 69). Notwithstanding the efforts of the Canadian governments and other stakeholders to convince Washington State to deny the permit for the facility, one was issued to build the facility (Kersten, 2009).

Despite this outcome, the electric transmission line included in the project triggered the need for a permit by the Canadian National Energy Board (NEB) (Kersten, 2009). As a result, the NEB had to conduct its own EIA for the transmission line. The province of BC appealed to the NEB and subsequently, the NEB decided to include not only the impacts of the transmission line in the EIA, but the entire generation facility that was to be built exclusively on the U.S. side of the border (Buckley & Belec, 2011). The choice to do so proved influential, as the NEB's 2004 final EIA determined "that the Sumas 2 plan was not environmentally acceptable" (Kersten, 2009, p. 189). Soon after, the electric company "appealed to Canadian Court of Appeals, challenging the NEB's decision to deny building a connection to the grid based on the pollution generated on the US side of the border" (Buckley & Belec, 2011, p. 69). The energy company

Table 4.1
Summary of Four Case Studies Describing Transboundary Disputes between Canada and the United States

Dispute	Summary	EIA	Outcome	Possible Benefit of a TEIA
Sumas 2 Energy Facility	**1999:** Construction of an energy facility and 8.5 km-long power line from the U.S.-Canadian border to a hydrosubstation in Abbotsford, BC	U.S.: EFSEC; Canada: NEB	**Resolved in favor of BC, 2004:** U.S. Supreme Court supported the NEB's decision to prevent the power line; Project abandoned by proponent	Improved public opinion; Improved relations between Sumas and Abbotsford
Devil's Lake Outlet	**1999:** Construction of an outlet to allow water from Devil's Lake to drain into the Sheyenne River, which flows into the Red River into the state of Minnesota and the province of Manitoba	No EIA conducted	**Temporarily resolved, 2005:** Agreement signed to allow emergency outlet; Two outlets constructed along with other flood relief structures; Canada continues to oppose the chosen outlet options	More appropriate alternatives; Improved public opinion; Improved relations; More transparency
Portland-Montreal Pipeline Reversal	**2014:** Reversal of the pipeline flow to transport Canadian tar sands oil east, through to Portland's port for international export	No EIA conducted	**Temporarily resolved, 2014:** Clear Skies Ordinance passed to prevent pipeline reversal; Final outcome pending resolution in court between pipeline company and City of Portland	Improved public opinion; Better understanding of environmental impacts; Proposed alternatives; More transparency
Keystone XL Pipeline	**2008:** Construction of a trans-boundary pipeline carrying tar sands crude from Alberta to Texas refineries	US: NEPA; Canada: NEB	**Unresolved, 2015:** Approved in Canada; U.S. Presidential Permit is denied; TransCanada Corp. sues United States under NAFTA	Improved public opinion; Better understanding of environmental impacts; More transparency

Abbreviations: BC, British Columbia; EFSEC, Washington State Energy Facility Site Evaluation Council; EIA, environmental impact assessment; NAFTA, North America Free Trade Agreement; NEB, Canadian National Energy Board; NEPA, U.S. National Environmental Policy Act; TEIA, transboundary environmental impact assessment.

argued that the NEB's ruling exceeded its jurisdiction, but the court sided with the NEB and the proposal was eventually withdrawn and the project abandoned (Buckley & Belec, 2011, p. 69; Kersten, 2009).[7] Beyond the courts, the dispute caused a "cooling of relations between the cities of Sumas and Abbotsford," both of which share the responsibility to effectively manage transboundary resources (Buckley & Belec, 2011, p. 69).

With a TEIA agreement in place, a joint assessment could have helped increase transparency by adopting an inclusive framework, reducing opposition to the project, and helping to foster an atmosphere of cooperation. For example, a single TEIA covering the entire transboundary project would have not only prevented the duplication of EIAs, reducing costs for both governments, but it would have also triggered public forums and discussions that included participants from both sides of the border. Using a more participatory approach, where information is shared in an open, nonconfrontational setting, may have benefited both cities given the strong opposition to the project. This is especially true for the city of Sumas, which was counting on this project to help revive its economy. Cross-boundary meetings may have even helped to dispel certain environmental fears related to the project and been used as an opportunity for the public and experts to propose and exchange interesting alternatives. Two-way information-sharing sessions could also have been perceived as an act of good will, easing some of the built-up tension. Without a collaborative strategy in place that encourages a transboundary, inclusive decision-making process, these disputes are likely to continue to generate divisive outcomes.

Although it is obvious that the economic impacts of this project would have disproportionately benefited the State of Washington (an element that played an important role in the NEB's final decision), a TEIA agreement could have paved the way for a compromise that would have reduced legal and administrative costs for both governments and helped preserve good political relations.

Devil's Lake Dispute

Another example of transboundary conflict is the Devil's Lake dispute. Not only is this a complicated case blending interstate and international transboundary issues, but the dispute is also closely linked to the Garrison Diversion project, a transboundary controversy in the region that took place in the early 1970s (Springer, 2007). To a certain degree, "the breadth and depth of the opposition to the Devil's Lake project is explained, in part, by its historic connection to the much larger Garrison Diversion" project (Springer, 2007, p. 87).[8] However the Devil's Lake matter was approached differently, since no joint reference to the International Joint Commission (IJC) was ever made to study the issue, suggesting that relying on a more cooperative mechanism, such as a TEIA agreement, could help settle a project-related disagreement and lead to better overall cross-border relations in a region with a contentious history.

Devil's Lake is located in North Dakota and is the largest freshwater lake in the state (Flanders, 2006). However, due to reduced natural drainage, the lake contains high levels of salinity and has risen nearly 24 feet in the last two decades. The rising waters have cost the U.S. government millions of dollars and the flooding has displaced hundreds of residents and forced businesses to close. In the late 1990s, the government of North Dakota proposed to build a water-diversion outlet "to relieve flooding pressure" on those living nearby. Controversy arose because the outlet would cause the lake's water to drain into the Sheyenne River, which flows into the Red River into the state of Minnesota and the province of Manitoba. The construction of the outlet raised major concerns from environmental groups and state and provincial governments regarding the environmental consequences of Devil's Lake waters seeping into these other water bodies. Many feared that the outlet would introduce "foreign biota and other environmentally harmful water . . . which will in turn infect the waters of Lake Winnipeg and the Nelson River system, both part of the Hudson Bay watershed leading to the Atlantic Ocean" (Flanders 2006, p. 1003). This would have economic as well as environmental consequences for regions that depend on commercial and sport fishery revenues from these water systems (Rosenberg, 2000).

North Dakota's stance was that the threat of water contamination and transfer of invasive species was inexistent, because it was based on "faulty science" (Brandson & Hearne, 2013). In addition, North Dakota refused to refer the case to the IJC (based on how long it took the commission to solve similar disputes in the past) and therefore did not consider the outlet to be a Boundary Waters Treaty matter. On the other hand, Manitoba felt that the possibility of contamination from dissolved solids and the introduction of foreign biota was a serious threat and that no outlet option would remedy the potential impacts. In the end, no joint reference to the IJC was ever carried out and efforts at mediation failed.[9]

What ensued was a very long and complex legal battle and eventually an initial outlet was built following an unbinding agreement reached between the United States, Canada, North Dakota, Minnesota, and Manitoba (Brandson & Hearne, 2013). However, shortly before it was completed in 2005, the Canadian government continued its efforts to delay the plan. As a compromise, North Dakota installed a special filter at the emergency outlet that would help decrease "the danger of biota transfer through the outlet, and the U.S. Government agreed to design and construct a more advanced water treatment system that would eventually replace the gravel filter" that is currently in place (Paris, 2008, p. 3). Even today, "discussions on the design and financing of the more advanced treatment system" have been left unresolved (Paris, 2008, p. 3). In this case, no official EIAs were ever conducted. Although the U.S. Army Corps of Engineers invited the government of Manitoba to participate in an environmental review of the outlet project, the provincial government refused, stating that any review would need to follow NEPA procedures and comply with the BWT (Paris, 2008). Because this was a state-funded project, it did not legally require the involvement of the federal government. Instead, a rapid bioassessment was conducted to determine the risk of water contamination downstream, which concluded that the outlet did not pose any immediate danger. Later, in 2011, North Dakota announced plans to build another outlet, this time with no mention of a filter to decrease the transfer of contaminants and foreign biota (Brandson & Hearne, 2013). The completion of the initial outlet in 2005 (which was expanded in 2010) was followed by a second outlet in 2012, along with other flood relief structures aimed at draining water from Devil's Lake (North Dakota SWC, 2016). Canada continues to oppose the outlet projects (Brandson & Hearne, 2013).

This is a particularly complex case because it involves international transboundary matters in a region with a history of transboundary conflict. North Dakota and Manitoba continue to cooperate on other water management issues, but the Devil's Lake dispute tainted their political relations in a way similar to the Sumas Energy case between the cities of Sumas and Abbotsford. Subsequently, it is believed that North Dakota and Manitoba's "failure to allow for mediation has created a legacy of bitterness between the two neighbors, which will inevitably taint future water relations and provide an unfortunate precedent to other governments contemplating water projects that may pose a risk across the border" (Brandson & Hearne, 2013, p. 190). This example clearly demonstrates that a joint assessment, exploring well-researched and scientifically sound alternatives, could have helped the two countries reach a more timely and agreeable compromise on the project. A TEIA process with well-defined steps that requires equal participation and input from both parties would help improve the climate for future negotiations and the effective management of vital natural resources. Equally as important, producing a TEIA report with sound environmental alternatives that both parties contribute to and agree upon can also set a positive precedent in environmental management and lead to better environmental quality in the long run. If the

TEIA is more environmentally acceptable from the outset, it is likely to meet with less opposition and be carried out more efficiently.

Portland-Montreal Pipeline Reversal

Another example of a transboundary dispute, this one involving the controversial topic of energy pipelines, is the case of the Portland–Montreal pipeline reversal. The issue garnered attention in July 2014 when a vote by the city council in Portland, Maine, voted 6 to 1 in favor of the South Portland Clear Skies Ordinance,[10] which "prohibits the bulk loading of crude oil onto any marine tank vessel in the Shipyard Zoning District or Shoreland Overlay District" (City of South Portland, 2015). This ordinance effectively prevents ExxonMobil and other partners from transporting Canadian tar sands oil east through their pipelines to South Portland's waterfront (Drouin, 2014). The pipeline network, built in the 1940s, currently flows west and transports nearly 150,000 barrels a day of light crude oil from South Portland to Montreal (Bagley, 2014). The oil companies in question are trying to reverse the flow of the pipeline. Although the two Portland pipelines can together carry up to 600,000 barrels a day, business has slowed significantly in the last 30 years (Banerjee, 2014). In fact, according to state data, the flow of oil through the Montreal-Portland pipeline had dropped to zero in January 2016 (Bell, 2016). A flow reversal would allow Exxon and its partners to benefit from the Alberta oil boom and generate more income (Banerjee, 2014). The U.S. State Department approved the reversal of the Portland-Montreal section in 2008, without issuing a permit or conducting an environmental impact review. However, the project was put on hold because of the economic downturn (Murphy & Brown, 2015).

In Canada, the NEB authorized the reversal of Line 9 in 2014, the section of pipeline that connects to the Portland-Montreal pipeline, linking Alberta's tar sands oil to Montreal. Initially, the city of Montreal objected to the approval, holding Enbridge accountable and pointing out that it had not met all the conditions of approval. Enbridge reviewed the NEB's conditions and began operating the Line 9 pipeline in December 2015 (Nelson, 2015). However, the Chippewas of the Thames First Nation appealed the NEB's decision and the Supreme Court of Canada heard the appeal in late 2016 (National Energy Board, 2016; the case is ongoing at press). It remains to be seen what the NEB's role will be in regard to the reversal of the Portland-Montreal pipeline to allow the tar sands crude to flow past Montreal and reach Portland. What is clear is that opposition to the proposed reversal has been strong on both sides of the border, with citizens, local governments, and environmental groups expressing profound concerns over a project whose potentially significant impacts have not been adequately evaluated through an EIA.

The top concerns revolve around the risks involved with transporting the heavier tar sands oil in the aging pipeline (which has exceeded its estimated 60-year life span) that runs through sensitive ecosystems and watersheds. For example, the Portland-Montreal pipeline crosses a watershed for a major tributary into Sebago Lake, the main source of drinking water for the greater Portland Area. There is also apprehension regarding the environmental impacts related to the release of toxic fumes caused by the off-loading of tar sands oil at port, a process that releases toxins into the air such as benzene, a known human carcinogen; close to the export hub in South Portland are an elementary school, a park, and residential neighborhoods (Bagley, 2014).

It stands to reason that the city of South Portland continued to contest the reversal and eventually passed the Clear Skies Ordinance. While this is a big victory for the residents and city council members, it also signals the beginning of a drawn out, costly legal battle. In February 2015, the Portland Pipe Line Corporation, a subsidiary of ExxonMobil, and the American Waterways Operators filed a lawsuit against the City of Portland in an effort to overturn the ordinance (City of South Portland, 2015). The City of Portland's motion to dismiss the lawsuit on technical grounds was denied and the lawsuit was allowed to go forward (Bouchard, 2016). In addition to this lawsuit, others speculate that the Canadian government will challenge the decision as the Canadian industry expects to increase its tar sands production and will need pipelines to transport the bitumen to ports in order to effectively get its product to the international market (Drouin, 2014). Until the lawsuit is settled, it is unlikely that much oil will flow through the Portland-Montreal pipeline (Bell, 2016).

Although this is just one example and part of the larger context of the ongoing dispute about pipelines and the transport of Canadian tar sands oil, a detailed TEIA would outline several important aspects about the project and trigger some public discussions on the matter. Without an EIA on either side of border, the proponents, the governments, and the public were deprived of the opportunity to understand the potential environmental impacts related to the flow reversal; the construction of the related infrastructure needed to process the oil sands crude at port; and the transport of tar sands oil instead of conventional oil. In addition, a properly managed TEIA process would include the submission of comprehensive and environmentally sound alternatives, allowing parties to weigh their options within the sociopolitical, environmental, and economic context. A TEIA would also include in-depth, cross-border public consultation sessions that would address the communities' concerns and provide a platform for open and fair exchange. Trust in corporations is at an all-time low, especially for those in the oil and gas industries (Kasperson & Ram, 2013). It would therefore be in the best interest of all parties to adopt a precautionary and deliberative strategy, putting a special emphasis on stakeholder involvement. Overall, a TEIA may have allowed a participatory, inclusive, and informed approach that would influence public perception of the project and the outcome of the Clear Skies Ordinance.

The Keystone XL Pipeline

Perhaps the most well-known and controversial development project affecting the U.S.-Canadian border in recent years is the Keystone XL oil pipeline. This project, proposed in 2008, has garnered a great deal of media attention because of its size, its transboundary nature, and the pivotal role is has played on the political stage. This case may have evolved beyond the scope of a TEIA, but it still highlights the gap in bilateral management between the United States and Canada and where transboundary project-related issues are dealt with in an ad hoc way, costing parties time, money, and in some instances harming good relations.

The proposed American portion of the pipeline would stretch 875 miles running from Morgan, Montana, to Steele City, Nebraska, with a maximum capacity of 830,000 barrels per day and with a cost of US$3.3 billion to be paid for by Keystone, a subsidiary of TransCanada Pipeline, Ltd. The project would also include ancillary infrastructure related to the construction, repair, and operation of the pipeline including pump stations, new roads, and transmission lines. The project would also include a section to be constructed in Canada, which would cross the Alberta-Saskatchewan border near McNeill, Alberta, with about 267 kilometers of pipeline in Alberta and 259 in Saskatchewan, estimated to cost US$7 billion. Although the physical characteristics of the pipeline and its related structures (as well as the types of environmental impacts associated with its construction) would be similar in both counties, two different EIAs were prepared in compliance with the two federal environmental assessment acts, neither of which assessed the impacts on the neighboring country.

The full U.S. EIA triggered by NEPA is made up of 11 volumes that far exceed 1,000 pages each, with comprehensive additional studies and data. Those interested in reading the full EIS can find it published in its entirety on the U.S. State Department website for the Keystone XL Project.[11] The Canadian portion of the project was approved in February 2009 and construction is pending the decision on the American portion. A two-page summary is provided on the Canadian Environmental Assessment Agency's website.

The Canadian NEB's 168-page "Reasons for Decision" document summarizes their assessment (National Energy Board, 2010). The project did not qualify for a full EIA under the CEAA. However, an Environmental Screening Report was required and submitted to the NEB by the applicant and other interested parties including Environment Alberta and Environment Saskatchewan. The NEB also carried out public hearings that did not include extensive dialogue with First Nations communities. The NEB's public consultation process has come under fire as a result of the 2012 changes to their review policy, which limits public participation to those who are "directly affected" by the project or who possess "relevant information or expertise" (Leahy, 2015). The definition of these terms is highly contested and not clearly defined. Participants must apply to participate and the NEB has the final say on whether or not to allow them an opportunity to partake in the process. This has caused conflict in recent cases related to pipelines and challenged the process by which the public has a right to be involved in important assessments.

There are many factors that influenced the direction this project has taken. Oil pipeline projects all over North America face resistance, and the tar sands in Canada are no exception. Another issue is that TransCanada "has a history of spills associated with its other pipelines," creating a legacy of distrust and an increased risk for environmental disasters in ecologically sensitive areas (Parker, 2013, p. 236). In addition, "TransCanada used eminent domain to route the pipeline through private land in some instances in Texas" creating further conflict and opposition to the pipeline (Henry, 2014).

In the United States, the final EIS provided a comprehensive overview of the critical environmental and socioeconomic considerations, including an extensive assessment of climate change impacts. The State Department received more than 1.5 million letters on the draft EIS released in 2012. Most were concerned that the department did not adequately address the greenhouse gas and climate change effects of the project. It is estimated that "the process of extracting, refining and shipping tar sands oil results in about 17 percent more greenhouse gas emissions than regular oil" (Henry, 2014). However, because a section of the Keystone pipeline crosses the U.S.-Canadian border, it requires a presidential permit before it can be constructed (Parfomak, Pirog, Luther, & Van, 2013). President Obama, however, did not believe that the project was in the best economic interest of the United States and that its economic benefits had been exaggerated (Daly, 2013). In February 2015 he vetoed legislation passed by the U.S. Congress that approved the pipeline and in November of that same year he denied the required presidential permit. TransCanada is fighting back. In January 2016, the company announced its plans to sue the United States under the North American Free Trade Agreement (NAFTA) and "also initiated Constitutional litigation against the U.S. Administration" (TransCanada Corporation, 2016). One year later, in January 2017, newly elected President Trump revived the pipeline by signing an executive memorandum inviting TransCanada to resubmit its application, indicating that a presidential permit would be granted (Baker & Davenport, 2017).

Given the sheer size of the pipeline and the numerous concerns expressed by communities and stakeholders on both sides of the border, it is possible that a more open conversation focused on the environmental impacts, alternatives, and solutions would have reduced opposition. A joint assessment would have streamlined the process by preventing duplication of assessments and avoided producing two diverging EIAs, which is also cause for confusion. The joint approach would have forced both governments to work together, gaining a more comprehensive understanding of the project itself, as well as the broader implications and environmental issues related to pipelines. Sharing expertise and experiences can lead to productive political and environmental outcomes and set a positive precedent in political negotiations. Combining this with thorough public participation would have increased transparency throughout the process and possibly contributed to a more favorable outcome overall.

Pipelines are controversial and their impacts on the environment have already been felt across the continent. Even in the best of circumstances, this project would have elicited opposition, if only because of TransCanada's poor environmental record and the resistance to the production and transport of tar sands oil. However, the environmental assessment of the Keystone XL pipeline has been carried out in an isolated and disjointed manner that, while being in compliance with domestic legislation in Canada and the United States (with the Canadian side being significantly less rigorous than the American), has led to a political controversy that a more cooperative transboundary approach might have ameliorated.

THE ESPOO CONVENTION: A SUCCESSFUL TEIA MODEL

The lack of domestic attention to TEIA and the fact that Canada and the United States have historically dealt with transboundary disputes in an unsystematic way points to the need for a formalized approach to address transboundary environmental impacts, with an emphasis on planning. A good example of TEIA can be found in the Espoo Convention. This agreement could serve as a model as it contains some key elements that could help form an effective TEIA agreement between Canada and the United States. In addition, the Espoo Convention incorporates essential provisions that increase transparency, encourage political accountability and promote more meaningful exchange between the stakeholders, all of which could promote better relations and dispel disputes. These elements would specifically address the failure of their domestic EIA regimes to adequately address TEIA and fill the gaps where their bilateral environmental protection treaties fall short. Although it was drawn up in a European context, the Espoo Convention could be a suitable model for North America because it deals with TEIA agreements between sovereign nations and it has been successfully implemented.[12]

Some of the key elements in the Espoo Convention include requirements for public participation and dispute resolution mechanisms to help coordinate the process. Fortunately, several of these elements are already present in Canadian and U.S. EIA policies, making the possibility of a TEIA agreement more likely.

Public Participation Provisions

Public participation is a key component to any EIA regime, especially in transboundary situations that require more diplomacy. As highlighted throughout this chapter, involving the public in a meaningful way can be beneficial. Broad stakeholder participation can be used as a tool to increase "public acceptance, leading to ongoing decisions that are better informed . . . and that assure greater implementation of needed projects and development" (Kasperson & Ram, 2013, p. 92). Including provisions for public participation and information sharing are therefore paramount, especially in an international context where interests may conflict. Some of the Espoo Convention's strongest elements can be found in Article 3, *notification*, and Article 5, *consultation*.

In an international context, notification would require information sharing between governments as well as with the public. As the initial step, its importance should not be underestimated. Article 3 in the Espoo Convention describes the process of notification, and requires the party of origin to "notify any Party which it considers may be an affected Party as early as possible and no later than when informing its own public about that proposed activity" (UNECE, 1991). In addition, Article 3(8) also states that "the concerned Parties shall ensure that the public of the affected Party . . . be provided with possibilities for making comments or objections on, the proposed activity, and for the transmittal of these comments or objections to the competent authority of the Party of origin" (UNECE, 1991).

Including a provision for notification is especially important because, although it is not common to all TEIA regimes, it has proven to be an essential element in the process (Ebbesson, 1999). Although the Espoo Convention does not set a timeframe in which this is to be accomplished, it does indicate that it should be done according to the country of origin's own EIA system. An added benefit to this clause is that early notification, especially in a case of transboundary harm, can also be seen as an act of good will on the part of the country of origin. Doing so creates an atmosphere of cooperation and promotes a more transparent approach that may ease any existing tensions and prevent confrontation or disagreement that would otherwise occur later in the process.

Both the Canadian and U.S. EIA regimes outline notification procedures that involve public input at this stage of the process. Under NEPA, the Notice of Intent (NOI) triggers the opportunity for public comment before the draft EIS is prepared (McCuin, Schultz, & Orr, 2009); similarly, in Canada, the act allows for a 20-day public comment period on a project description (CEAA, 2013). Therefore, both nations already have a comparable requirement in place, and including such a provision in a bilateral agreement would not likely meet with any opposition.

Consultation is the heart of public participation and the outcome of consultations can easily sway public opinion on projects. If consultation is carried out effectively, it can prevent unnecessary conflict. Article 5 of the Espoo Convention states that the "Party of origin shall . . . without undue delay enter into consultations with the affected Party concerning, inter alia, the potential transboundary impact of the proposed activity and measures to reduce or eliminate its impact" (UNECE, 1991, Article 5). This requirement is further strengthened by Article 2(6) of the convention, which clarifies that "the Party of origin . . . shall ensure that the opportunity provided to the public of the affected Party is equivalent to that provided to the public of the Party of origin" (UNECE, 1991). This clause stresses the principle of nondiscrimination,[13] an important component to a TEIA agreement to guarantee a fair process (Cassar & Bruch, 2004; Knox, 2002).

Not only does the Espoo Convention encourage and require notification and consultation, it also mentions that the final decision regarding the project must consider the comments that were received during the notification and consultation processes (UNECE, 1991, Article 6(1)). There is no way to guarantee that the affected party's opinion will be adopted in the final decision, but such a provision at least provides for a fair exchange and further supports the principle of nondiscrimination.

Both NEPA and the CEAA provide for public participation throughout their respective domestic EIA processes. Under the newest amendments to the CEAA, public participation is required on four different occasions. The public has its first opportunity during the notification process as mentioned earlier, and is given 20 days to comment on the project description. Afterward, the public is allowed to comment on both the draft and the final version of the EIS guidelines and, finally, there is a period open for comment on the draft of the environmental assessment (CEAA, 2013). Under NEPA, there are three opportunities: during the scoping process or on the NOI, on the draft of the assessment, and on the final EIS (Environmental Protection Agency, 2012). Given that both domestic regimes provide for public participation, this provision would only require a joint body to facilitate the coordination of the process on either side.

Settlement of Disputes

One important element of a successful TEIA process is the inclusion of a dispute resolution mechanism or grievance mechanism so that governments and the public have recourse to challenge the decision of a TEIA. This is essential for a functional EIA process to maintain political accountability and to provide an alternative to litigation. There are a variety of ways to approach this issue in TEIA. The Espoo Convention suggests the creation of an arbitration committee to help resolve conflicts.

The Espoo Convention addresses dispute resolution in Article 15 and Appendix VII, suggesting the creation of an arbitration committee. The stipulations are designed for an international context, offering the possibility of bringing a dispute to the International Court of Justice, but it suggests bringing the problem to an arbitration committee beforehand (UNECE, 1991). This type of mechanism could easily be tailored to the needs of Canada and the United States. For example, the convention suggests creating an arbitration committee of three representatives selected through a mutually agreed mechanism.

Members of an arbitration committee could be chosen from the Canadian Environmental Assessment Agency, in the case of Canada; and for the United States, members could be elected from the Council on Environmental Quality or the EPA. As an alternative to the Canadian Environmental Assessment Agency, the EPA, and the CEQ, commissioners from the IJC could be also elected to form an arbitration committee, given that the framework is already in place and that the IJC has decades of experience dealing with bilateral environmental disputes. This "tribunal" would act as a quasi-judicial body to help resolve disputes before they reached the courts. The quasi-judicial nature of the tribunal would not impede on the autonomy of either nation, helping to prevent issues of sovereignty from obstructing the process; and it would reduce the need for litigation, therefore reducing administrative and legal costs for both governments. These agencies are suited to fulfill this role and could be called upon to serve in TEIA disputes.

CONCLUSION

Managing resources and environmental impacts across the U.S.-Canadian border regions is a mammoth task. The border regions across North America face serious environmental challenges that need to be carefully managed. Historically, the three nations have favored a bilateral approach to environmental management over a trilateral approach. Canada and the United States have often cooperated, signing more than 10 environmental agreements in the last century, demonstrating that the nations are capable of compromise and opening the door to the possibility of a treaty for transboundary project assessment. A TEIA agreement is not only feasible given their political history—there is also a need. Their domestic EIA systems do not adequately address the assessment of transboundary harm, creating a large gap in environmental management for project-related impacts. In the United States, NEPA makes no mention of TEIA and U.S. courts have been reluctant to apply the act's provisions extraterritorially. In Canada, the CEAA briefly refers to TEIA, but includes no clear provisions on how to carry out the process. In addition, many transboundary resource conflicts have erupted in the last several years, leading to long, drawn-out legal battles and in some instances harming good relations. If the two countries want to preserve their resources and improve their management approach, they will need to implement tools, such as a TEIA process, that foster information sharing and open participation.

Fortunately, an existing TEIA regime, such as the Espoo Convention, can serve as a positive example for Canada and the United States. This agreement has not only been successful in practice, but it also contains other key elements, such as requirements for notification and public consultation, dispute resolution mechanisms, and more. Conveniently, many of these provisions are already in place in Canadian and U.S. EIA legislation, making the transition into a TEIA agreement not only possible but also conceivable. Obviously, concerns about sovereignty would need to be addressed.

Additionally, a TEIA agreement would have far-reaching benefits for both nations. It would strengthen and improve the management of the shared resources, all of which face serious risk from human pressures and climate change. For example, a TEIA agreement would increase TEIA practice, allowing experience to improve the process, which could increase overall environmental quality. Signing a TEIA agreement would also increase transparency in U.S.-Canadian relations and help reduce costly and lengthy conflicts. With more information shared in an open process, increased public awareness and participation would lead to improved political accountability and therefore result in more transparent planning outcomes.

NOTES

1. There is no single, universally accepted definition of "environmental impact assessment" and the term is often interchangeably used with "environmental assessment." The International Association for Impact Assessment (IAIA), the leading global authority on the use and best practice of impact assessment, defines EIA as "the process of identifying, predicting, evaluating and mitigating the biophysical, social and other relevant effects of development proposals prior to major decisions being taken and commitments made" (IAIA, 1999).
2. In section 102 [42 USC § 4332] of NEPA, the act states that

   > all agencies of the Federal Government shall . . . recognize the worldwide and long-range character of environmental problems and, where consistent with the foreign policy of the United States, lend appropriate support to initiatives, resolutions, and programs designed to maximize international cooperation in anticipating and preventing a decline in the quality of mankind's world environment.
3. According to the 1997 guidance document,

   > The entire body of NEPA law directs federal agencies to analyze the effects of proposed actions to the extent they are reasonably foreseeable consequences of the proposed action, regardless of where those impacts might occur. . . . Case law interpreting NEPA has reinforced the need to analyze impacts regardless of geographic boundaries within the United States, and has also assumed that NEPA requires analysis of major federal actions that take place entirely outside of the United States but could have environmental effects within the United States. (Council on Environmental Quality, 1997)

4. In addition, the CEQ's guidance document did not "receive concurrence of the State and Defense Departments" which calls into question the guidance's legal effect, because neither department recognizes that the "CEQ has unilateral authority to decide whether NEPA applies extraterritorially" (Knox, 2002, p. 299).
5. In subsection 68(a) of CEAA 2012, the act stipulates, "a federal authority must not carry out a project outside Canada . . . unless the federal authority determines that the carrying out of the project is not likely to cause significant adverse environmental effects" (Government of Canada, 2012). Further on in subsection 73, the act continues and suggests that if the minister deems it appropriate to "conduct a study of the effects of existing or future physical activities carried out in a region that is entirely outside federal lands," that the "Minister may enter into an agreement or arrangement with any jurisdiction" (Government of Canada, 2012). Under Section 2(1) of the Canadian Environmental Assessment Act, the term "jurisdiction" is defined as "a government of a foreign state or of a subdivision of a foreign state, or any institution of such a government; and an international organization of states or any institution of such an organization" (Government of Canada, 2012).
6. EIA was adopted in Mexico following international agreements such as the 1992 Rio Summit on sustainable development and the signing of NAFTA (Perevochtchikova & André, 2013). At the federal level, EIA is dictated by the General Law of Ecological Equilibrium and Environmental Protection (LGEEPA) and "EIA Regulation" (Craik, 2008). The Mexican Environment Ministry oversees the EIA process (Perevochtchikova & André, 2013). EIA is triggered not only by the federal government's involvement in projects, but also by the 23 sectors outlined by LGEEPA that require an EIA. Mexican states therefore only have jurisdiction over the projects that lie outside of what is established by LGEEPA. Among the noted weaknesses in Mexican EIA policy is that no specific environmental indicators are outlined to guide the scientific analysis. Instead, the EIA legislation lays out only four general groups of criteria such as air, water, soil, and vegetation. Furthermore, although public participation and post-project evaluation provisions are included in the legislation, they are both lacking in practice. Similar to Canada and the United States, Mexican EIA policy recognizes the importance of transboundary impacts, yet provides no guidelines on how to adequately address them.
7. It should be noted however that this is a special case as most countries are rarely able to veto a project and often "must endure whatever consequences the originating nation deems acceptable" (Kersten, 2009,

p. 190). But because a portion of the project was to be built on Canadian soil, Canada's influence on the final decision was substantially larger.

8. The Garrison Division was a major engineering proposal with far-reaching implications.

   The Garrison Diversion would have used waters stored in the large reservoir behind the massive Garrison Dam, completed in 1955 along the Missouri River, to irrigate farms in eastern North Dakota. Water from the Missouri was to be channeled into Devil's Lake, creating an inlet that could be use to stabilize lake levels in times of drought. With an outlet on the other side of the lake, the project would have connected the Missouri River and all its tributaries, with the entire Hudson Bay watershed, effectively linking two major water systems otherwise separated by the continental divide. (Springer, 2007, p. 87)

9. Issues jointly referred to the IJC usually result in reports and studies, similar to EIA, upon which the commission makes a recommendation to both nations regarding their dispute. Although the commission has been criticized because of the limited powers it has been granted, it has, to some degree, set the stage for TEIA. The IJC has dealt successfully with many disputes resembling EIA over the years. For example, in the early 1970s, the commission was assigned to evaluate the environmental consequences of raising a dam in the Washington State, which would result in flooding in BC. Canadians were unhappy with the proposed compensation plan from Washington. Both governments submitted a request to the IJC to conduct an assessment. Based on the assessment, the IJC eventually demanded that the City of Seattle postpone raising the dam for one year. Later on in the 1980s, BC and the Washington State finally came to an agreement regarding the dispute, which led to the High Ross Dam treaty (Cassar & Bruch, 2004).

10. In the draft ordinance committee's recommendations, this new zoning amendment is

    consistent with the City's traditional land use authority, to protect the health and welfare of its residents and visitors and to promote future development consistent with the City's Comprehensive Plan by prohibiting within the City *the bulk loading of crude oil onto marine tank vessels*, and also by prohibiting construction or installation of related facilities, structures, or equipment that would create significant new sources of air pollution, adversely impact or obstruct ocean views and scenic viewsheds, and impede or adversely impact the City's land use and planning goals. (City of South Portland, 2014, p. 11)

11. U.S. Department of State. Keystone XL Pipeline Project Final Environmental Impact Statement is available at http://keystonepipeline-xl.state.gov/archive/dos_docs/feis/.
12. For more details on the documented challenges related to the implementation of the Espoo Convention, refer to the "Review of Implementation of the Convention on Environmental Impact Assessment in a Transboundary Context (2010–2012)," available at http://www.unece.org/env/eia/implementation/review_implementation.html.
13. The principle of nondiscrimination essentially states that "countries should apply the same environmental protection to potential harm in other countries that they apply to such harm in their own" (Knox, 2002, p. 292).

REFERENCES

Bagley, K. (2014, July 28). Maine Port votes to block tar sands exports. But will it matter? *Inside Climate News*. Retrieved from http://insideclimatenews.org/news/20140728/maine-port-votes-block-tar-sands-exports-will-it-matter

Baker, P., & Davenport, C. (2017, January 25). Trump revives Keystone pipeline rejected by Obama. *New York Times*. Retrieved from https://www.nytimes.com/2017/01/24/us/politics/keystone-dakota-pipeline-trump.html

Banerjee, N. (2014, July 21). Maine town fights plan to use pipeline to export oil sands crude. *Los Angeles Times*. Retrieved from http://www.latimes.com/nation/la-na-portland-pipeline-20140721-story.html#page=1

Bell, T. (2016, March 9). South Portland-to-Montreal crude oil pipeline shut down. *Portland Press Herald*. Retrieved from http://www.pressherald.com/2016/03/08/portland-to-montreal-crude-oil-pipeline-shut-down/

Bouchard, K. (2016, March 29). South Portland prepares for potentially costly legal fights over pipeline, LPG depot. *Portland Press Herald*. Retrieved from http://www.pressherald.com/2016/03/28/south-portland-braces-for-increased-legal-fees/

Brandson, N., & Hearne, R. (2013). Devils Lake and Red River Basin. In E. S. Norman, A. Cohen, & K. Bakker (Eds.), *Water without borders?*

Canada, the United States, and shared waters (pp. 179–192). Toronto, ON: University of Toronto Press.

Brown, C. (2015). Scale and subnational resource management: Transnational initiatives in the Salish Sea region. *Review of Policy Research, 32*(1), 60–78.

Buckley, P., & Belec, J. (2011). Cascadia reconsidered: Questioning micro-scale cross-border integration in the Fraser Lowland. *University of the Fraser Valley Research Review, 3*(3), 57–80. Retrieved from http://journals.ucfv.ca/rr/RR33/article-PDFs/4-buckley.pdf

Canadian Environmental Assessment Agency. (2013). Process diagram: Environmental assessments process managed by the agency. Retrieved from http://www.ceaa-acee.gc.ca/Content/1/6/2/16254939-1C3C-48A4-B99D-77E34A5DF1EE/EA_processes-Processus.pdf

Cassar, A. Z., & Bruch, C. (2004). Transboundary environmental impact assessment in international watercourse management. *NYU Environmental Law Journal, 12*, 170–244. Retrieved from http://heinonline.org/HOL/LandingPage?handle=hein.journals/nyuev12&div=13&id=&page=

City of South Portland. (2014). *Draft ordinance committee recommendations: Part 1. Recommended ordinance changes* (Ordinance #1-14/15). Retrieved from http://www.southportland.org/files/8114/0580/7459/08_-_ORDINANCE__1-14-15.pdf

City of South Portland. (2015). *Clear skies legal fund*. Retrieved from http://www.southportland.org/departments/city-clerk/draft_ordinance_committee/clear-skies-legal-fund/

Commission for Environmental Cooperation. (1997). *Draft North American agreement on transboundary environmental impact assessment*. Retrieved from http://www.cec.org/Page.asp?PageID=122&ContentID=1906&SiteNodeID=366

Council on Environmental Quality. (1997). *Guidance on NEPA analysis for transboundary impacts*. Washington, DC. Retrieved from http://www.gc.noaa.gov/documents/transguide.pdf

Craik, N. (2007). Deliberation and legitimacy in transnational governance: The case of environmental impact assessments. *Victoria University of Wellington Law Review, 38*(2), 381–402. Retrieved from http://www.victoria.ac.nz/law/research/publications/vuwlr/prev-issues/pdf/vol-38-2007/issue-2/deliberation-craik.pdf

Craik, N. (2008). Transboundary environmental assessment in North America: Obstacles and opportunities. In K. Bastmeijer & T. Koivurova (Eds.), *Theory and practice of transboundary environmental impact assessment*. Retrieved from SSRN: http://ssrn.com/abstract=1285509

Daly, M. (2013, March 14). Obama says Keystone XL pipeline not major jobs creator. *Associated Press*. Retrieved from http://www.ctvnews.ca/obama-sayskeystone-xl-pipeline-not-major-jobs-creator-1.1195042

Drouin, R. (2014, July 23). How a town in Maine is blocking an Exxon tar-sands pipeline. *Grist*. Retrieved from http://grist.org/climate-energy/how-a-town-in-maine-is-blocking-an-exxon-tar-sands-pipeline/

Ebbesson, J. (1999). Innovative elements and expected effectiveness of the 1991 EIA convention. *Environmental Impact Assessment Review*, *19*(1), 47–55. Retrieved from http://0-www.sciencedirect.com.mercury.concordia.ca/science/article/pii/S0195925598000286

Environmental Protection Agency. (2012). *NEPA: Basic information*. Retrieved from http://www.epa.gov/compliance/basics/nepa.html#publicrole

Fang, L. (2012). Environmental review problems of cross-boundary projects under NEPA: Lessons from the tar sands pipelines. *Stanford Environmental Law Journal*, *31*, 285–313.

Flanders, J. M. (2006). Transboundary water disputes on an international and state platform: A controversial resolution to North Dakota's Devil's Lake dilemma. *North Dakota Law Review*, *82*(3), 101–136. Retrieved from http://papers.ssrn.com/sol3/papers.cfm?abstract_id=902467

Garver, G., & Podhora, A. (2008). Transboundary environmental impact assessment as part of the North American agreement on environmental cooperation. *Impact Assessment and Project Appraisal*, *26*(4), 253–263. Retrieved from http://www.tandfonline.com/doi/abs/10.3152/146155108X366013#.Uscwr2RDthw

Government of Canada Justice Laws. (2012). Canadian Environmental Assessment Act, 2012, S.C. 2012, c. 19, s. 52. Retrieved from http://laws-lois.justice.gc.ca/eng/acts/C-15.21/page-1.html

Hall, N. D. (2007). Transboundary pollution: Harmonizing international and domestic law. *University of Michigan Journal of Law Reform*, *40*(4), 680–746.

Healy, R. G., VanNijnatten, D. L., & Lopez-Vallejo, M. (2014). *Environmental policy in North America: Approaches, capacity, and the management of transboundary issues*. Toronto, ON: University of Toronto Press.

Henry, T. (2014, January 14). Keystone XL will impact climate, but isn't make or break, state dept. says. *State Impact, NPR*. Retrieved from http://stateimpact.npr.org/texas/2014/01/31/keystone-xl-will-impact-climate-but-isnt-make-or-break-state-dept-says/

International Association for Impact Assessment. (1999). *Principles of environmental impact assessment best practices*. Retrieved from https://www.iaia.org/publicdocuments/special-publications/Principles%20of%20IA_web.pdf?AspxAutoDetectCookieSupport=1

Kasperson, R. E., & Ram, B. J. (2013). The public acceptance of new energy technologies. *Daedalus, the Journal of the American Academy of Arts & Sciences*, *142*(1), 90–96.

Kersten, C. M. (2009). Rethinking transboundary environmental impact assessment. *Yale Journal of International Law*, *34*, 173–206. Retrieved from http://heinonline.org/HOL/LandingPage?handle=hein.journals/yjil34&div=7&id=&page

Kidd, J. (2002). Groundwater: A North American resource [online]. Expert workshop on freshwater in North America, Program on Water Issues, University of Toronto. Retrieved from http://www. powi.ca/pdfs/groundwater/water_disucssion-e1.pdf

Knox, J. H. (2002). The myth and reality of transboundary environmental impact assessment. *American Journal of International Law*, *96*(2), 291–319. Retrieved from http://www.jstor.org/discover/10.2307/2693925?uid=3739464&uid=2&uid=3737720&uid=4&sid=21103291887613

Leahy, Derek. (2015, February 10). Canada's pipeline review process broken but still important, critics say. *DesmogCanada*. Retrieved from http://www.desmog.ca/2015/02/10/canadas-pipeline-review-process-broken-still-important-critics-say

McCuin, G., Schultz, B., & Orr, R. (2009). *Know NEPA: Important points for public participation* (Special Publication 09-14). University of Nevada Cooperative Extension. Retrieved from http://www.unce.unr.edu/publications/files/nr/2009/sp0914.pdf

Murphy, J., & Brown, S. (2015). Tar sands at our doorstep: The threat to the Lake Champlain region's waters, wildlife and climate. Merrifield, VA: National Wildlife Federation. Retrieved from http://www.nwf.org/News-and-Magazines/Media-Center/Reports/Archive/2015/05-28-2015-Tar-Sands-at-our-doorstep.aspx

National Energy Board. (2016). *Court challenges to National Energy Board or governor in council decisions: Recent court challenges*. Calgary, Alberta: NEB. Retrieved from http://www.neb-one.gc.ca/pplctnflng/crt/index-eng.html

Nelson, J. (2015, December 18). Reversing Enbridge and Big Oil's pipeline plans. *Counter Punch*. Retrieved from http://www.counterpunch.org/2015/12/18/reversing-enbridge-big-oils-pipeline-plans/

North Dakota State Water Commission. (2016). *Devil's Lake fact sheet*. Retrieved from http://www.swc.nd.gov/pdfs/dl_fact_sheet.pdf

Parfomak, P. W., Pirog, R., Luther, L., & Van, A. (2013). *Keystone XL pipeline project: Key issues* [Congressional research service report]. Retrieved from https://fas.org/sgp/crs/misc/R41668.pdf

Paris, R. (2008). The Devils Lake dispute between Canada and the United States: Lessons for Canadian government officials [Center for International Policy Studies working paper]. Retrieved from http://aix1.uottawa.ca/~rparis/CIPS_Devils_Lake_Feb2008.pdf

Parker, K. (2013). Keystone XL: Reviewability of transboundary permits in the United States. *Colorado Journal of International Law and Policy*, *14*(1), 231–260.

Parrish, A. L. (2005). Trail smelter déjà vu: Extraterritoriality, international environmental law, and the search for solutions to Canadian-U.S. transboundary water pollution disputes. *Boston University Law Review*, *85*(355), 363–428. Retrieved from http://heinonline.org/HOL/Print?collection=journals&handle=hein.journals/bulr85&id=377

Perevochtchikiva, M., & André, P. (2013). Environmental impact assessment in Mexico and Canada: Comparative analysis at national and regional levels of federal district and Quebec. *International Journal of Environmental Protection*, *3*(8), 1–12. Retrieved from http://www.colmex.mx/academicos/cedua/mariap/pdfs/Articulos/2013-Environmental%20Impact%20Assessment%20in%20Mexico%20and%20Canada%20Comparative%20Analysis%20at%20National%20and%20Regional%20Levels%20of%20Federal%20District%20and%20Quebec.pdf

Popiel, B. R. (1995). From customary law to environmental impact assessment: A new approach to avoiding transboundary environmental damage between Canada and the United States. *B.C. Environmental Affairs Law Review*, *22*(2), 447–478. Retrieved from http://lawdigitalcommons.bc.edu/ealr/vol22/iss2/8

Rosenberg, S. A. (2000). A Canadian perspective on the Devils Lake outlet: Towards an environmental assessment model for the management of transboundary disputes. *North Dakota Law Review*, *76*, 817–859.

Sassman, W. (2012). The grass is always greener: Keystone XL, transboundary harms, and guidelines for cooperative environmental-impact assessment. *Vanderbilt Journal of Transnational Law*, *45*, 1489–1528. Retrieved from https://litigation-essentials.lexisnexis.com/webcd/app?action=DocumentDisplay&crawlid=1&doctype=cite&docid=45+Vand.+J.+Transnat'l+L.+1489&srctype=smi&srcid=3B15&key=9de6e5ece763c1ff624d25dc3aa8aea1

Springer, A. L. (2007). From trail smelter to Devils Lake: The need for effective federal involvement in Canadian-American environmental disputes. *American Review of Canadian Studies*, *37*(1), 77–102.

TransCanada Corporation. (2016). Keystone XL: Timeline. Retrieved from http://www.keystone-xl.com/timeline/

Tweedie, J. (2006). Transboundary environmental impact assessment under the North American Free Trade Agreement. *Washington & Lee Law*

Review, *63*, 849–910. Retrieved from http://heinonline.org/HOL/LandingPage?handle=hein.journals/waslee63&div=25&id=&page=

UN Economic Commission for Europe. (2014). Espoo convention 1991, 1989 U.N.T.S. 309. Retrieved from http://www.unece.org/index.php?id=38339

Washington State Energy Facility Site Evaluation Council. (2001). Sumas Energy 2 Generation facility—EFSEC application No. 99-01: Final environmental impact statement. Retrieved from http://www.efsec.wa.gov/Sumas2/eis/feisvol1.shtml

PART II

BIODIVERSITY AND NATURAL RESOURCE GOVERNANCE

FIVE

The Evolution of Natural Resource Conservation Capacity on the U.S.-Mexican Border

Bilateral and Trilateral Environmental Agreements since La Paz

STEPHEN P. MUMME

INTRODUCTION

The development of natural resources conservation along the U.S.-Mexican border closely corresponds to the emergence of the environmental era. The signature resource in this complex policy domain is water, and the emergence of environmental concern along the U.S.-Mexican border tracks directly to a Colorado River water agreement in 1973, signed just one year after the United Nation's Stockholm meeting that placed "The Environment" on the world's agenda. This agreement, the International Boundary and Water Commission's (IBWC's) Minute 242, settled a protracted binational dispute over salinity (IBWC, 1973). It is also the first U.S.-Mexican agreement on record to be reached in the context of a cross-border controversy over what would come to be understood as "ecological sustainability" (Ward, 2003). A decade later the United States and Mexico would sign a landmark pact, the 1983 La Paz Agreement, which committed both nations to sustained diplomatic engagement on matters of environmental concern (Agreement, 1983). The La Paz Agreement and the free trade negotiations that followed were the catalyst for more intensive bilateral cooperation on natural resources management in the border region.

This chapter examines the accrual of binational conservation governance capacity along the border after the La Paz Agreement. Following the lead of noted environmental governance scholar Martin Janicke (2002, pp. 4–7), conservation governance capacity is defined structurally and contextually. Janicke defines the structural/contextual dimension of environmental governance in terms of institutional context, informational context, and economic context. While Janicke's framework focuses on domestic environmental governance, it is quite adaptable for tracking the progress of binational initiatives. It invites the analyst to track the governance impact of binational and multilateral agreements on border regional natural resources management in terms of the institutional effect of specific agreements, the availability and access to information bearing on natural resources management, and the participating governments' investment in the implementation of these agreements.

BINATIONAL CAPACITY FOR NATURAL RESOURCES MANAGEMENT ON THE BORDER

Binational cooperation on natural resources is often held up as one of the most amicable elements of the U.S.-Mexican relationship. That view tracks to developments in the first half of the 20th century, landmark agreements on water in 1906 and 1944 and wildlife conservation in 1936 and 1941. While this sanguine assessment glosses over many specific points of contention, it is fair to say that during this period the United States and Mexico were able to achieve important commitments on international rivers and migratory wildlife that would strengthen their relationship and contribute to the development of the border region. For most of the 20th century, however, binational cooperation related to natural resources remained closely centered on the acquisition and control of these resources and not their sustainable management.

Beginning with the salinity crisis, however, the two countries forged a series of international agreements that gradually intruded on the developmentalist approach to managing the border's resources. These agreements, reviewed in this chapter, have strengthened binational natural resources governance. Since 1983 a succession of international agreements and binational programs have been layered onto older agreements and institutions, producing a multigovernmental mix of mandates and practices that amplify the scope of bilateral cooperation on natural resources management along the border.

These trends notwithstanding, the development of binational capacity for natural resources governance at the U.S.-Mexican border has received scant scholarly attention. A number of scholars have focused on the institutional development of binational water management (Brown, 2002; Ingram, Laney, & Gillilan, 1995; Mumme & Aguilar, 2003) and binational environmental cooperation (Liverman, Varady, Chavez, &

Sanchez, 1999; Mumme, 2003; Sanchez-Rodriguez & Mumme, 2013; Van Schoik, Lelea, & Cunningham, 2006). A few others, (Chester & McGovern, 2009; Salazar & Spalding, 2006; Sammet & Quinn, n.d.; Valdez, Guzman-Aranda, Abarca, Tarango-Arambula, & Sanchez, 2006) examine institutional progress in binational conservation of migratory birds and wildlife. A few of these studies approached the subject from an applied theoretical perspective, drawing on policy theory to explore and explain institutional development, but none have taken a systematic look at the development of institutional capacity in this binational issue area.

To better understand the evolution and accrual of enhanced governance capacity in this issue area it is necessary to consider the binational institutions in place at the time the La Paz Agreement was adopted and then examine successive agreements for how they add to or modify the management regime. Following Janicke's definition of structural/contextual capacity, this chapter is particularly attentive to changes in institutional context (defined here as programs, agencies, intersectoral cooperation, and public participation), informational context (assessment, data sharing, transparency), and economic context (government commitment of financial resources to the implementation of binational agreements).

THE LA PAZ FRAMEWORK FOR ENVIRONMENTAL COOPERATION: A BASELINE FOR ASSESSING BINATIONAL CAPACITY FOR NATURAL RESOURCES GOVERNANCE

Viewed from a structural capacity perspective, natural resources governance along the U.S.-Mexican border tends to be uneven when water management and conservation management are compared. Water, vital for border development, has absorbed the lion's share of the governments' attention and conservation has lagged behind. This is reflected in binational institutions. The 1944 Water Treaty, for example, established an influential binational agency, the International Boundary and Water Commission (IBWC), with a mandate for treaty interpretation and dispute resolution. Functions of the IBWC include protecting water quality in international rivers and streams, preventing pollution, and conserving international water resources for wildlife. By contrast, the 1936 U.S.-Mexican Convention for the Protection of Migratory Birds and Game Animals, by which the two countries pledged to set aside and protect wildlife refuges, came with no institutional architecture to speak of. In this institutional context, the intersectoral policy link between water management and wildlife conservation remained quite weak until modern environmentalism began to impact the management of natural resources. Both the Colorado

River Salinity Crisis, resolved in 1973 (IBWC, 1973), and industrial pollution of transboundary streams like the San Pedro River on the Arizona-Sonora border (Jamail & Ullery, 1979) highlighted the critical link between biodiversity and water resources. In 1975, the governments concluded the Agreement for Cooperation in the Conservation of Wildlife, establishing a U.S.-Mexican Joint Committee on Wildlife Conservation and Plant Conservation to better coordinate conservation efforts across and along the international boundary (Chester & McGovern, 2009) and in 1979 the IBWC was authorized to address transboundary pollution problems (IBWC, 1979). The La Paz Agreement springs from these issues, among others.

The La Paz Agreement sets a useful baseline for assessing the accrual of natural resources governance capacity along the border because it was configured as a framework for binational environmental cooperation. It aimed at establishing a diplomatic process for identifying and resolving environmental problems in the border region. It is an unusual type of executive agreement, occupying the highest rung on the ladder of executive agreements: one signed by the presidents themselves and not their subalterns. It is also functionally comprehensive, contributing to its potential scope and importance. Its language is broad enough to encompass all conceivable environmental problems and quite arguably, by referencing "conservation" as a goal, extends to the protection of the border's ecology and the natural environment in the border area. Its text enjoins the parties to address problems that may affect their neighbor's border zone. Administratively, the agreement's importance is enhanced by defining the border as extending 100 kilometers north and south of the boundary, the first official definition and one that would be adopted by other government agencies (Hajost, 1984, p. 9).

In its particulars, the La Paz Agreement frames its commitments in the UN's Stockholm Declaration and previous agreements. It requires monitoring pollution that may potentially impact the other country with an obligation to share the data with its neighbor state. The La Paz Agreement was the first U.S.-Mexican agreement to require that the national governments consult with their subsidiary governments on cooperative actions and it provides for the participation of states, local governments, and citizen-based organizations in its annual meetings and their inclusion in other government initiatives. The governments' national environmental agencies are designated as national coordinators for the agreement and are required to meet at least annually in public forums. Finally, the agreement provides for the conclusion of more specific implementing agreements as "annexes" to the main agreement.

The La Paz Agreement marks a significant departure from previous practice and introduces a new set of obligations and modes of problem solving in an issue domain.

As it affects natural resources management, the agreement applies primarily to water quality and contamination, to include the waters of transboundary rivers and streams, international sanitation, and water contamination problems located in the border region that are not fluvially international but have international implications for environmental health and the protection of biodiversity. The agreement acknowledges the IBWC's leading role in water management, reflecting an awareness of the ecological importance of water and the agreement's extension to this aspect of the natural environment. With respect to fauna and flora, however, the agreement's application is less evident. During the negotiations, it is known that Mexico, jealous of its international sovereignty, objected to including natural resources administration, though U.S. negotiators hoped to do so (Hajost, 1984). The resulting language can be read as a compromise, leaving a door open to addressing biodiversity.

Viewed diplomatically, the La Paz Agreement ushers in the modern era of environmental cooperation along the border (Varady & Ward, 2009, p. 18). It is the starting point for thinking about accrual of governance capacity for natural resources conservation along the border. More recent environmental and conservation agreements can be described, in part, as responses to La Paz and its implementation after 1983.

BINATIONAL AND TRINATIONAL AGREEMENTS IN THE 1990S

As a framework agreement, the La Paz Agreement had the immediate effect of legitimizing environmental concern along the U.S.-Mexican border. It also stimulated bilateral cooperation on conservation. As Salazar and Spalding observe, "most attempts to coordinate natural protected areas along the border before 1983 were unsuccessful" (2006, p. 81). In 1984, the two countries revised their 1975 agreement on wildlife with a further executive protocol to coordinate their transboundary wildlife conservation efforts and coordinate with the La Paz process (EPA, 1992, p. III-34). In 1988, Mexico's environmental ministry signed another Memorandum of Understanding (MOU) with the U.S. National Park Service, an agreement on Cooperation in Management and Protection of National Parks and Other Protected Areas and Cultural Sites (EPA, 1992, p. III-35), creating another coordinating mechanism, the Joint Committee for Management and Protection of National Parks and Other Protected Natural and Cultural Sites. Mexico's Directorate General for the Conservation of Natural Resources (DGCERN) and the U.S. Fish and Wildlife Service (FWS) were designated coordinators for both executive agreements. A related protocol on wetlands conservation was also signed in 1988 between DGCERN, FWS, and the Canadian Wildlife Service (CWS) (EPA, 1992, p. III-35). These conservation agreements established joint management mechanisms for co-adjacent protected areas and migratory wildlife, strengthened information sharing, and directed modest funds towards supporting these initiatives.

But the La Paz process was criticized by environmentalists. It was faulted for not addressing many environmental issues on the border agenda, failing to prioritize solutions, and failing to invest in environmental protection and remediation (Mumme, 1992). The North American Free Trade Agreement (NAFTA) negotiations drew attention to these shortcomings and afforded an opportunity to strengthen the La Paz process and broaden its application. By 1996, two new bilateral agreements, two trilateral agreements, and other initiatives combined to significantly strengthen binational conservation capacity along the border.

Bilateral Agreements

At the bilateral level two important agreements issued from the NAFTA debate that strengthened natural resources governance. The first of these agreements, in 1991, was the Integrated Border Environmental Plan (IBEP), 1992–1994 (EPA, 1992). An outcome of a 1990 presidential summit in Monterrey, IBEP was largely a compendium of existing bilateral environmental activities and a commitment to strengthen the La Paz process. No reference to sustainable development or conservation is found in the initial draft of the agreement, but the final draft, reflecting the input of border environmentalists, contains both. Noting that Mexico's environmental ministry was endowed with more direct responsibility for conservation than its U.S. counterpart, the document describes "a long history of cooperating on wildlife protection and the conservation of natural resources in the Border Area" and effectively framed these initiatives as falling within the scope of the La Paz Agreement (EPA, 1992, p. III-33). It also emphasized water quality protection.

Reinforcing IBEP's commitments, its successor, the Border XXI Program, placed natural resources on its list of borderwide issues and objectives in 1996. Border XXI set out an ambitious five-year agenda for strengthening biodiversity and protected areas, forest and soil conservation, and protecting marine and aquatic resources. It established "Natural Resources" as one of nine bilateral working groups under the La Paz protocol. The range of issues assigned the Water Working Group—a La Paz process working group since 1983—was extended to address ecosystem issues with the following statement:

> The development of a comprehensive understanding of the quantity and quality of water resources that are present in the region is critical to the selection of conservation and management alternatives. Any future water supply studies should include multipurpose use including fish and wildlife needs. (EPA, 1996, p. III-15)

Border XXI ambitiously sought to strengthen binational and intersectoral agency cooperation building on the post-NAFTA momentum of greater bilateral attention to the La Paz Agreement. Under this umbrella, the two countries signed a landmark Letter of Intent to Cooperate on Border Region Protected Areas in 1997 that assigned the Border XXI Natural Resources Working Group the responsibility for monitoring these activities (Salazar & Spalding, 2006, p. 82).

The second bilateral agreement, the 1993 Agreement to Establish a Border Environment Cooperation Commission (BECC) and a North American Development Bank (NADB), established two new linked agencies for the purpose of developing and financing needed environmental infrastructure projects in the border zone (BECC/NADB Charter, 1993). In this division of labor BECC was to provide technical support and receive and certify viable proposals for financing employing sustainable development criteria. NADB was to play a key role in financing certified projects. Under the agreement the range of eligible environmental infrastructure projects was potentially broad but initially the governments limited proposals to water supply and wastewater treatment. Conservation projects were not included. Some of the wastewater projects, however, such as those involving constructed wetlands, had conservation benefits. BECC's potential for funding water-related conservation projects was clearly identified in the Border XXI Framework Document (EPA, 1996). In 2002, BECC and NADB's mandate was extended, enabling these binational agencies to consider financing ecosystem/biodiversity projects (BECC/NADB Charter, 2002).

Trilateral Agreements

In addition to these binational initiatives, the NAFTA debate also generated two trilateral agreements between Canada, the United States, and Mexico that strengthened structural capacity for natural resources governance in the border area. One established a new regulatory institution focused broadly on North American environmental cooperation, the other, building on past binational arrangements, created a new trinational interagency committee aimed more narrowly on conservation of the region's fauna and flora.

The first of these agreements, the North American Agreement on Environmental Cooperation (NAAEC), signed in 1993, commits the three parties to a comprehensive agenda of environmental cooperation for the sustainable development of the region and provides a mechanism for citizen participation in the enforcement of national environmental laws—defined to include applicable natural resources and conservation legislation (NAAEC, 1993). The agreement also establishes a permanent secretariat, the Commission for Environmental Cooperation (CEC), based in Montreal, Canada, to oversee its implementation.

The CEC's formal policy mandate is vast but in practice its functions are restricted by the governments. From its inception, however, with limited financial support from the governments, the CEC has carved a niche for itself by examining environmental issues at the scale of the region's eco-zones, which are commonly international in scope. It has played a useful role in organizing stakeholders to address these international issues and has successfully drawn attention to shared environmental problems through its citizen- and secretariat-initiated investigations, spotlighting problems of common North American concern. Budget limitations have fixed the CEC's work program on a few problems selected for their North American relevance and scope and synergies with the work of other environmental and conservation agencies in the region. Within these constraints, conservation has consistently been a CEC policy priority.

The second agreement, an MOU to establish a Canada-Mexico-United States Trilateral Committee for Wildlife and Ecosystem Conservation and Management (1996), was to a significant extent motivated by the NAAEC. It may also reflect the interest of national wildlife agencies in asserting their jurisdiction in relation to the national environmental agencies and the new NAAEC and the CEC. Officially, it replaced the two international agreements previously guiding international interagency cooperation among the parties, the 1975 Mexico-U.S. Joint Committee on Wildlife and Plant Conservation and the Tripartite Committee for the Conservation of Migratory Birds and their Habitat, which were both established in 1988.

Comprised of the lead wildlife agencies of each government—the Canadian Wildlife Service, the International Affairs division of Mexico's Secretariat of Environment and Natural Resources (SEMARNAT), and the FWS—the Trilateral Committee (TC) was to meet annually to implement the MOU, develop and implement specific cooperative conservation projects, integrate these into national conservation policies, and address any other issues the parties should agree upon. The MOU was to remain in effect for five years and be automatically renewed for another five-year term unless one or more parties determined to withdraw. It has been renewed without controversy since 1996.

Much like the La Paz Agreement the TC MOU is designed more in the mode of a framework agreement. Its preamble locates the committee's authority in various international agreements on wildlife and biodiversity including the 1936 U.S.-Mexico Migratory Bird Convention, the 1940 Western Hemisphere Treaty, the international conventions on endangered species and biodiversity, and the NAAEC. It establishes a diplomatic procedure for the design and adoption of specific conservation projects and practices requiring international cooperation among the parties without otherwise committing to specific projects or funding mechanisms. The TC's former Wildlife without Borders-Mexico Program (U.S. Fish and Wildlife Service, 2013), its functions now merged into other TC working tables, is evidence that a number of the more visible North American cooperative programs for wildlife conservation are located in U.S.-Mexican border region (Trilateral Committee, 2016). From a diplomatic perspective the agreement is an advance over the more balkanized arrangements for trinational conservation cooperation that preceded it. But it did not fully incorporate all wildlife cooperative functions—for example, the brief does not include wetlands management or maritime issues associated with North America's semi-enclosed seas. The agreement was not meant to fully synergize or extend the authority of the CEC. Designed as a partnership between the domestic agencies of each country, the TC was clearly meant to be the more powerful and operational partner to the NAAEC and the CEC where trinational conservation cooperation was concerned.

Impact on the IBWC

The preceding agreements strengthened structural capacity at other agencies, most notably the IBWC. The IBWC continued to be incorporated into the La Paz Process through the Water Working Group. It was also drawn directly into BECC decision making as an ex-officio member of its governing board, participating in project certification decisions. In the 1990s this led to greater intersectoral cooperation between the IBWC's U.S. Section and the EPA, with interagency memoranda reached on financing international sanitation projects and greater attention paid by IBWC to the importance of public participation in validating and supporting IBWC initiatives. At the U.S. Section, IBWC Commissioner John Bernal took the unprecedented step of developing a formal strategic plan that situated the section's work in the language of sustainable development (IBWC, U.S. Section, 2000). In 1999, the U.S. Section also created new citizen advisory forums for the border's major international watersheds. At the Mexican Section (CILA), Commissioner Arturo Herrera steered the agency to embrace sustainability, while taking care to avoid bilateral confrontation over technical interpretation of the water treaties. It is fair to say that the 1990s saw advances in intersectoral cooperation and the incorporation of environmental concern in IBWC operations, though these reforms were modest from the perspective of some environmental advocacy organizations for whom IBWC was more an obstacle to conservation than its steward.

Capacity Gains in the 1990s

The number of agreements related to border region conservation and natural resources adopted in the 1990s was unprecedented in U.S.-Mexican relations. When these various initiatives are bundled, it is evident that the border region saw major gains in natural resources conservation capacity in this period. Some were border specific and situated in the orbit of the lead environmental agencies of the two governments. Some were a function of the new and strengthened multilateralism and trinational partnerships that impacted the border region. Some derived from corresponding changes at the IBWC. What emerged in the 1990s was an unprecedented matrix of cooperative initiatives related to binational cooperation in managing natural resources along the border.

Table 5.1 presents a simple typology based on Janicke's capacity-based analytical framework for environmental policy assessment (2002, p. 4). Three broad structural elements of environmental capacity can be used to take a snapshot of these gains. With just a few exceptions, capacity gains are found almost across the board in the three areas of structural capacity that affect natural resources management at the border: institutional context, informational context, and economic context.

With respect to the institutional context we see an array of new programs and projects created at each of the six listed institutions, four of which (BECC, NADB, CEC, and the TC) were established in this period. These agencies came with new or enhanced jurisdictions and mandates

Table 5.1
Capacity Gains in Natural Resources Management in the 1990s

Capacity Type	La Paz Program	BECC	NADB	IBWC	CEC	TC
Institutional Context						
New programs or projects	Yes	Yes	Yes	Yes	Yes	Yes
New agencies/mandates		Yes	Yes		Yes	Yes
Intersectoral integration	Promotes integration	With EPA and IBWC	With EPA and IBWC	With EPA and BECC	Promotes integration	
Public participation	Enhanced	New opportunity		New opportunity	New opportunity	
Informational Context						
Monitoring, assessment, and data gathering	New programs such as Border Environmental Indicators Project	Project-based data gathering			Citizen-initiated investigations and secretariat-initiated investigations; Work program assessments	New cooperative programs
Data sharing/info access	Increased	New commitments			New commitments/ facilities	
Transparency	Increased	New commitments			New commitments/ committees	
Economic Context						
Financial resources	BEIF funds and other investments	New project investments	New project investments	Increased investment partnering with EPA/SEMARNAT		

Abbreviations: BECC, Border Environment Cooperation Commission; CEC, Commission for Environmental Cooperation; EPA, U.S. Environmental Protection Agency; IBWC, International Boundary and Water Commission; NADB, North American Development Bank; SEMARNAT, Mexican Secretariat of Environment and Natural Resources; TC, Trilateral Committee.

that extended the scope of natural resources governance along the border. Even the USIBWC added a new environmental assessment unit and its Mexican counterpart, CILA, augmented coordination with SEMARNAT. These institutions embraced intersectoral integration in principle and to some extent in practice. Public participation in natural resources management also received a boost.

The 1990s also saw major gains in the informational context affecting natural resource management on the border. The La Paz programs, beginning with the Border XXI Program, placed new emphasis on monitoring environmental conditions along the border, including a new binational border environmental indicators project, new environmental information centers accessible to the public, and new commitments by working groups to aggregate and share information in their program areas. Its Natural Resources Working Group drew attention to border area conservation issues. It prodded U.S. and Mexican conservation units to devote additional resources to scientific assessment and wildlife management training programs and to strengthen cooperative enforcement of conservation regulations (EPA, 2000, pp. 102–103; Van Schoik et al., 2006, p. 46). New initiatives were mounted to generate binational geographic information systems (GIS) mapping of border ecosystems, map vegetation in the Colorado River Delta, characterize the flow of the Rio Grande, and conduct a borderwide assessment of conservation information gaps.

These efforts both supported and benefited from initiatives at the CEC and the Trilateral Committee. This is evident in the 1998 initiative to study and strengthen riparian habit along the San Pedro River on the Arizona-Sonora border. The EPA published annual reports on the environmental status of the border environment. At BECC, project certification was based on detailed and publicly accessible information on projects, to include their environmental sustainability and financing. The CEC's citizen- and secretariat-initiated investigations produced detailed studies of environmental problems. Its work programs on air quality, toxics, and biodiversity, ecosystems, environmental enforcement, and environmental law made data and information available that had previously been privileged or hard to access. The TC's five topical working tables (Species of Common Concern, Migratory Birds, Ecosystem Conservation, Law Enforcement, and CITES) provided a platform supporting new binational and trinational cooperative studies of transboundary wildlife (Trilateral Committee, 2011). Both the La Paz programs, BECC, and CEC also advanced a new ethic of institutional transparency and public accountability that enriched the informational mix.

A significant boost to financial capacity also accompanied these reforms although gains were greatest for institutions dealing with urban water resources and sanitation. Through BECC and NADB with EPA La Paz program support and additional funds from the IBWC, more than US$660 million was invested in sanitation and potable water projects by 2004, some of which favorably impacted border region conservation capacity (BECC/NADB, 2004, p. 2). The new infusion of public funds helped leverage private sector resources, strengthening the resource base for environmental infrastructure in the border zone. Sanitation projects at San Diego, San Luis Rio Colorado, Nogales, Cd. Juarez, and Nuevo Laredo improved water quality in border rivers protecting human health and riparian ecosystems. Other areas of natural resources management also saw additional investment if growth in border-focused conservation programs can be taken as a proxy of additional spending. The governments' limited operational support for the CEC, to the extent that CEC investigations and programs affected the border, should be factored in as a net gain benefiting conservation in the border region.

NATURAL RESOURCES MANAGEMENT CAPACITY TRENDS ALONG THE BORDER SINCE 2000

The natural resources capacity gains realized in the 1990s are substantial and represent long-term improvement in conservation management for the border region. Developments since 2001, however, have chipped away at binational capacity in this issue area. While the institutions that were created or strengthened in the 1990s have endured, the contraction or elimination of certain programs, fiscal shrinkage, and border security interventions have eroded some of the gains. These trends (see Table 5.2) are seen in the downsizing of the La Paz programs, cutbacks in funds available to BECC and NADB water projects along the border, fund stasis at CEC, some shrinkage in the venues for public participation in the relatively new border environmental institutions, and the imposition of national security measures on border conservation practices. Partially offsetting these trends are a few gains, mainly related to the management of water resources on the Rio Grande and the Colorado River, new commitments to protected areas, and a binational peace park at Big Bend.

Several factors are associated with the retreat from post-NAFTA La Paz commitments after 2000, including the election of conservative governments in Mexico and the United States, a post-9/11 shift in border priorities, economic contraction after 2007, and in the United States a notable decline in national interest in border environmental issues and their subordination to national security concerns. An early indicator of this

Table 5.2
Capacity Trends in Natural Resources Management in the 2000s

Capacity Type	La Paz Program	BECC	NADB	IBWC	CEC	Trilateral Commission
Institutional Context						
New programs or projects	Yes	Yes	Yes	Yes	Yes	Yes
New agencies/ mandates	New Border 2012 decentralized approach based on policy forums, working groups, and local area task forces	BECC/NADB board merger	BECC/NADB board merger	IBWC Minutes 308 and 317–319 authority for new advisory bodies for Rio Grande and Colorado Rivers	Narrowed work program	New sister-protected areas framework agreement
Intersectoral integration	Natural resources dropped from Border 2012 portfolio; Shrinking federal involvement	Sustained with EPA; IBWC dropped from new board	Sustained with EPA; IBWC dropped from new board	Sustained with EPA and strengthened with BECC	Sustained efforts to promote greater conservation policy integration	No change
Public participation	Decentralization; Tribal government inclusion; Less federal support to task forces; Complications due to U.S. border security measures	Sustained support at project certification level; NGOs lose board representative with board merger	No gains	U.S. section adds new citizen advisory boards	Sustained commitment tempered by loss of grant funds for NGOs	No change

Informational Context						
Monitoring, assessment, and data gathering	Sustained; no new advances; no new annexes	Sustained project-based data gathering		Minutes 308 and 317–319 on Rio Grande and Colorado Rivers	Sustained investigations but TEIA initiative abandoned	New cooperative programs
Data sharing/ Info access	Sustained; No new advances	Sustained	Arguably even less open to public scrutiny	Strengthened data sharing on Rio Grande and Colorado Rivers	Pollution data improvements; Grasslands initiative	Support for international conservation networks
Transparency	No new advances	No new commitments	Less transparency	No change	No change	No change
Economic Context						
Financial resources	Fund shrinkage at BEIF, elsewhere	Static operating budget; Shrinking BEIF; New CAP program	Shrinking BEIF funds; New WCIF; New CAP	Further partnering EPA/SEMARNAT; BECC/NADB	Fixed budget shrinking due to inflation	No fixed commitment of funds from the governments

Abbreviations: BECC, Border Environment Cooperation Commission; BEIF, BECC/NADB Border Environment Infrastructure Fund; CAP, NADB Community Assistance [grant] Program; CEC, Commission for Environmental Cooperation; EPA, U.S. Environmental Protection Agency; IBWC, International Boundary and Water Commission; NADB, North American Development Bank; NGO, non-governmental organization; SEMARNAT, Mexican Secretariat of Environment and Natural Resources; TEIA, transboundary environmental impact assessment; WCIF, Water Conservation Investment Fund.

retreat is seen in the restructuring of the cooperative border environmental programs in 2002 with the rollout of the new 10-year Border 2012 Program (EPA, 2012a). Border 2012 significantly reduced binational commitments, abandoning the nine working group model in favor of a new set of air, water, and toxics border-level policy forums and functional working groups, four regional working groups, and a number of local issue-based task forces, all strategically centered on five goals. These goals—controlling water pollution, controlling air pollution, preventing soil contamination, ensuring chemical safety, and reducing pesticide exposure—did not include conservation of natural resources. Though tribal and state governments were better incorporated in Border 2012 as stakeholders and participants, the direct collaboration of the U.S. Department of the Interior (DOI) and the EPA was suspended in favor of a more ad hoc and independent articulation of activities in the context of the DOI's new internal interagency mechanism, the DOI U.S.-Mexico Border Field Coordinating Committee. Thus, despite GNEB's observation that cross-sectoral cooperation was particularly vital for the conservation of renewable natural resources (Good Neighbor Environmental Board [GNEB], 2003, p. 32), Border 2012 represents a setback in intersectoral policy collaboration in regard to border environment and conservation. This trend is sustained in the latest La Paz program, Border 2020 (EPA, 2012b), which was unveiled in August 2012. Support for Border 2012 Task Forces also declined sharply after 2004 (GNEB, 2008, p. 55).

More evidence of policy retreat is seen in reduced binational subsidies to environmental infrastructure projects developed through the BECC and NADB. The EPA's core subsidies to the NADB's Border Environmental Infrastructure Fund declined steadily after peaking in 1997, falling 90% by 2008 (GNEB, 2008, p. 51). The curtailment of funds was partly offset by the creation of several new funds, most notably an US$80 million Water Conservation Investment Fund (WCIF) developed to help resolve a prolonged dispute over Mexico's treaty water obligations on the Rio Grande (BECC/NABD, 2004), and a small Community Assistance [grant] Program (CAP) at NADB. Even so, the fund reduction weighs most heavily on border region water infrastructure development, forcing the BECC and NADB to limit project support. Ironically, the funding contraction adversely affects these agencies' operational capacity to support conservation at the very time their authority in this area has amplified.

The CEC's scope of work continues to emphasize conservation programs, collaborating with the Trilateral Committee's efforts in this regard. Yet its capacity to do so is ever more restricted by the governments' failure to augment its budget, frozen at US$9 million since it opened its doors in 1994. In spite of these limits the CEC has done extraordinary work in supporting and publicizing trinational and binational wildlife conservation activities on a continental basis, but its ability to undertake special investigations, including those that respond to citizen-initiated complaints, is circumscribed. Funds matter. The CEC's diplomatic potential has also been frustrated, revealing its structural dependency on the decentralized policy making that dominates much binational and trinational water and conservation governance along the borders. This is perhaps best seen in its abandonment of an initiative to craft a new transboundary environmental impact assessment agreement for the North American region (Craik, 2007, p. 23).

In addition to these developments, some venues for public participation have closed or contracted along the border, victims of policy adjustments and funding cuts (Mumme, 2009). The most high-profile change came in 2002 with a merger of the BECC and NADB Boards which became effective in January 2006 (Ganster, 2006). The merger eliminated an important platform for the articulation of environmental concerns by culling out direct NGO representation on the board. It also diminished intersectoral coordination by eliminating the IBWC's ex-officio membership. These trends are reinforced by the governments' 2015 decision to fully merge the two institutions (BECC/NADB, 2014; Mosbrucker, 2015). The reduction in funds for border programs was also felt at the level of Border 2012 Task Forces, which was reflected in reduced support for binational travel and engagement. Heightened security measures along the border have also thwarted binational collaboration and public participation in joint activities.

The ramping up of U.S. national security concerns at the border, particularly the passage of the Real ID and Secure Fence acts in 2005 and 2006 respectively, may well pose the most serious threat to border wildlife conservation since the heyday of the reclamation era. The Real ID Act endowed the U.S. Department of Homeland Security with sweeping authority to override any domestic law that might in its determination obstruct the expeditious construction of tactical security infrastructure (TSI) along U.S. boundaries (de la Parra & Cordova, 2007, pp. 175–181; Mumme & Ibanez, 2009). The Secure Fence Act authorized construction of up to 700 miles of hard fencing along the boundary with Mexico. Condemned by environmentalists and conservation advocacy groups, criticized by Mexican public officials, and resisted by U.S. conservation agencies (Segee & Cordova, 2009, pp. 241–244), the unilateral construction of TSI along the border has gone forward largely unchecked, destroying and fragmenting habitats, disrupting migration corridors, and threatening or complicating important wildlife protection measures borderwide. In 2008, the DHS Bureau of Customs and Border Protection (CBP) attempted to deflect environmental criticism from its border fence by rolling out a series of Environmental Stewardship Plans to signify its determination to mitigate environmental effects. These were widely criticized as little more than compilations of existing biodiversity knowledge for different sections of the border, wanting in commitment to altering planned construction, partnering with conservation agencies, and funding long-term studies of the fence's impact on species along the international boundary. Instead of directing additional funds to U.S. conservation agencies to deal with adverse TSI impacts, the U.S. Congress appropriated US$50 million in 2010 for CBP to invest in conservation (Vitiello, 2011), intentionally subordinating federal and state conservation agencies to DHS oversight in prioritizing mitigation activities along the border. Security hawks in the U.S. Congress continue to seek even more authority to override conservation concerns in border-protected areas, including the potential wall the Trump administration has vowed repeatedly to construct.

While binational management of natural resources has suffered from the aforementioned trends, it is important to note that many of the institutional capacity gains that came with the burst of binational cooperative developments in the 1990s remain. Unilateral security measures, destructive as they are, have not undone the earlier binational commitments, though they have hindered implementation. In a few areas, border natural resources management has seen real progress, mostly related to water resources management but also touching on protected areas.

Gains in the area of water resources management are seen in several agreements roughly a decade apart, the first in the IBWC's Minute 308 resolving a water supply dispute on the Rio Grande in 2002 and the second in a series of agreements beginning in 2000 and culminating in 2010 and 2012 related to water conservation on the Colorado River. In brief, the Rio Grande water delivery agreement established the aforementioned WCIF at NADB for the development of several water conservation projects on Mexico's Rio Conchos (IBWC, 2002; BECC/NADB, 2004). It also committed to an as yet unfulfilled objective of establishing a basin-wide international water advisory body to the IBWC to ensure the sustainable management of the river's water resources and cooperative responses to drought. On the Colorado River, beginning with an agreement in 2000 authorizing a study of the Colorado River Delta's ecological water needs (IBWC, 2000), the two governments, partnering with NGOs and established stakeholders on the river, strengthened their advisory process for riparian conservation on the lower Colorado. The opportunity to capitalize on this effort came in April 2010 when a damaging earthquake destroyed water conveyance infrastructure in the Mexicali Valley, causing Mexico to approach the United States for additional water storage in upstream dams. That, in turn, produced an unprecedented series of agreements that, for the first time, recognized a treaty-based ecological responsibility for the river. These agreements, Minute 317, 318, and 319 also create a permanent advisory group to the IBWC and provide a temporary formula for drought sharing on the Colorado River and needed water supply for riparian vegetation south of the international boundary (IBWC, 2010a, 2010b, 2012). Minute 319 sunsets in 2017 but authorizes the governments to seek a lasting solution.

Another favorable development in binational water resources management is seen in U.S. domestic legislation. In 2006, passage of the Transboundary Groundwater Assessment Act authorized a limited study of transboundary groundwater basins along the New Mexico-Arizona border, with provision for consulting Mexican officials and water experts in developing basin assessments and authorizing US$10 million for the effort (United States-Mexico Transboundary Aquifer Assessment Act, 2006).

Binational cooperation on protected areas has also been furthered by a 2009 agreement strengthening cooperation across coadjacent protected areas and a U.S.-Mexican MOU, signed in May 2010, that pledged to move forward with long proposed plans to develop the adjacent Santa Elena Canyon and Big Bend protected areas as "a natural area of binational interest" (White House, 2010). This is a critical step towards having these remarkable natural areas designated as an international peace park. The MOU is one of the few bilateral agreements in natural resources management since 2000 beyond water resources protocols.

CONCLUSION

This review of post-La Paz natural resources conservation capacity development (institutional, informational, and economic) along the U.S.-Mexican border describes significant gains since 1983, particularly the extraordinary burst of diplomatic activity in the 1990s. These gains are evident in new institutions and programs, new commitments from established institutions, informational gains in the form of new monitoring, reporting, data sharing, and transparency arrangements, and direct and indirect gains in financial support for programs affecting conservation, particularly in water management.

It is fair to say that many of these gains have been consolidated and sustained over the past decade, setting a new floor for thinking about natural resources management governance along the border. Yet, as seen in this chapter, the post-2001 period has not been particularly kind to natural resources management along the border. Diminished funding through the agencies and programs created in the 1990s has affected the management of natural resources. The sharp decrease in EPA support for border water infrastructure, if partly offset by initiatives like the WCIF and fewer restrictions on NADB's lending, still constrain BECC and NADB capacity to support conservation functions in the border region. CEC's financial paralysis has meant steady erosion in its overall capabilities, including conservation. Diminished support for La Paz program participation now limits the governments' ability to create and convene environmental task forces along the border. The unilateral prioritization of border security has seen billions of dollars flow into TSI as opposed to other border functions, and funds aimed at mitigating conservation damage are held at the DHS rather than the FWS or other U.S. domestic conservation agencies. Unilateral action on security has unquestionably complicated the implementation of bilateral agreements aimed at protecting border wildlife even if these formal structures for binational and trinational cooperation remain in place.

A notable setback was seen in the withdrawal of U.S. natural resources agencies from the La Paz programs, diminishing much-needed policy integration related to conservation management on the border. While some intersectoral gains remain, the closer cooperation between national environmental agencies and the IBWC, for example, the BECC and NADB's ability to certify and fund conservation-related infrastructure needs, and the effort to harmonize the bilateral activities of the various U.S. Interior Department natural resources agencies through its U.S.-Mexico Border Field Coordinating Committee, the conservation sectors' status as a highly balkanized policy arena remains.

This intersectoral integration problem points to one of the enduring challenges in natural resources conservation along the border. As border environmental analyst Mark Spalding (2006), there is as yet no strategic plan or vision for the binational management of this policy sector. The new post–La Paz tapestry of border-focused institutions and programs has generated more tools and opportunities for binational cooperation but falls well short of any comprehensive vision and strategic commitment to sustaining water resources and wildlife along the border. Instead, natural resources management along the border remains an assemblage of trinational, binational, national, and state and local agencies and programs with related and partially overlapping mandates. Managing binational water resources is the greatest priority in this policy mix but its importance for fauna and flora remains secondary to human purposes.

In sum, the La Paz process and NAFTA-related innovations have strengthened binational cooperation and governance capacity for biodiversity protection but their application still falls well short of a systematic plan or strategy for natural resources conservation along the border. For all the progress realized to date, events in the past decade highlight the vulnerability of natural resources management to the intrusion of other compelling policy priorities and the structural asymmetries of natural resources administration and economic development along the border. The enduring challenge for the United States and Mexico is to develop a more integrated approach to managing natural resources at the border in the context of a strategic commitment to the border's sustainable development.

REFERENCES

Agreement between the United States of America and the United Mexican States on cooperation for the protection and improvement of the environment in the border area. (1983). T.I.A.S. No. 10827. Retrieved from https://www.epa.gov/sites/production/files/2015-09/documents/lapazagreement.pdf

Border Environment Cooperation Commission and North American Development Bank. (2004). *BECC/NADB 2004 Joint Status Report.* Ciudad Juarez, Chihuahua, Mexico: Author.

Border Environment Cooperation Commission and North American Development Bank. (2014). *Discussion paper: Institutional integration of the Border Environment Cooperation Commission and the North American Development Bank.* Retrieved from http://www.nadb.org/pdfs/FreqUpdates/DRAFT%20BECC-NADB%20Reform%20Proposal.pdf

Border Environment Cooperation Commission and North American Development Bank Charter. (1993). Agreement concerning the establishment of a Border Environment Cooperation Commission and a North American Development Bank. *International Legal Materials, 32*, 1545.

Border Environment Cooperation Commission and North American Development Bank Charter (2002). Protocol of amendment to the agreement between the United States of America and the United Mexican States concerning the establishment of a Border Environment Cooperation Commission and a North American Development Bank. Retrieved from http://www.cocef.org/uploads/content/images/convenio%20SPAN.pdf

Brown, C. (2002). New directions in binational water resource management in the U.S.-Mexico borderlands. *Natural Resources Journal, 32*(3), 555–572.

Chester, C. C., & McGovern, E. D. (2009). Open skies over a closing border: U.S.-Mexico efforts to protect migratory birds. In L. Lopez-Hoffman, E. D. McGovern, R. G. Varady, & K. W. Flessa (Eds.), *Conservation of shared environments: Learning from the United States and Mexico* (pp. 100–114). Tucson, AZ: University of Arizona Press.

Craik, N. (2007). Transboundary environmental assessment in North America: Obstacles and opportunities. In K. Bastmeijer & T. Koivu rova (Eds.), *Theory and practice of transboundary environmental assessment*. Amsterdam, the Netherlands: Martinus Nijhoff.

de la Parra, C. A., & Cordova, A. (2007). The border fence and the assault on principles. In A. Cordova & C. A. de la Parra (Eds.), *A barrier to our shared environment: The border fence between the United States and Mexico* (pp. 175–181). Mexico City, DF: Secretariat of Environment and Natural Resources.

Environmental Protection Agency. (1992). *Integrated environmental plan for the Mexican-U.S. border area, 1992–1994*. Washington, DC: Author.

Environmental Protection Agency. (1996). *U.S.-Mexico Border XXI program framework document*. Washington, DC: Author.

Environmental Protection Agency. (2000). *U.S.-Mexican Border XXI program: Progress report, 1996–2000*. Washington, DC: Author. Retrieved from www.epa.gov

Environmental Protection Agency. (2012a). *Border 2012: Accomplishment report (2010–2012)*. Washington, DC: Author. Retrieved from http://www.epa.gov/2012

Environmental Protection Agency. (2012b). *Border 2020: U.S.-Mexico environmental program*. Washington, DC: Author. Retrieved from http://www.epa.gov/region9/border/pdf/border2020summary.pdf

Ganster, P. (2006, April 14). Good Neighbor Environmental Board letter to the president of the United States. Retrieved from https://www.epa.gov/faca/good-neighbor-environmental-board-comment-letter-2006

Good Neighbor Environmental Board. (2003). *U.S.-Mexico border environment 2002. Sixth report of the Good Neighbor Environmental Board to the president and congress of the United States* (EPA 130-R-03-001). Washington, DC: U.S. Environmental Protection Agency.

Good Neighbor Environmental Board. (2008). *Natural disasters and the environment along the U.S.-Mexico border* (EPA 130-R-08-001). Washington, DC: U.S. Environmental Protection Agency.

Hajost, S. A. (1984). U.S.-Mexico environmental cooperation: Agreement between the United States of America and the United Mexican States on cooperation for the protection and improvement of the border area. *Environmental Law*, *1984*(Spring), 1–3.

Ingram, H., Laney, N. K., & Gillilan, D. (1995). *Divided waters*. Tucson, AZ: University of Arizona Press.

International Boundary and Water Commission. (1973, August 30). Minute 242. Permanent and definitive solution to the international problem of the salinity of the Colorado River. Mexico, DF: Author. Retrieved from https://www.ibwc.gov/Files/Minutes/Min242.pdf

International Boundary and Water Commission. (1979, September 24). Minute 261. Recommendations for the solution to the border sanitation problems. El Paso, TX: Author. Retrieved from https://www.ibwc.gov/Files/Minutes/Min261.pdf

International Boundary and Water Commission. (2000, December 12). Minute 306. Conceptual framework for United States-Mexico studies for future recommendations concerning riparian and estuarine ecology of the limitrophe section of the Colorado River and its associated delta. El Paso, TX: Author. Retrieved from https://www.ibwc.gov/Files/Minutes/Min306.pdf

International Boundary and Water Commission. (2002, June 28). Minute 308. United States allocation of Rio Grande waters during the last year of the current cycle. Ciudad Juarez, Mexico: Author. Retrieved from https://www.ibwc.gov/Files/Minutes/Minute308.pdf

International Boundary and Water Commission. (2010a, June 17). Minute 317. Conceptual framework for U.S.-Mexico discussions on Colorado River cooperative actions. Ciudad Juarez, Mexico: Author. Retrieved from https://www.ibwc.gov/Files/Minutes/Minute_317.pdf

International Boundary and Water Commission. (2010b, December 17). Minute 318. Adjustment of delivery schedules for water allocation to Mexico for the years 2010 through 2013 as a result of infrastructure damage in Irrigation District 014, Rio Colorado, caused by the April 2010 earthquake in the Mexicali Valley, Baja California. El Paso, TX: Author. Retrieved from https://www.ibwc.gov/Files/Minutes/Min_318.pdf

International Boundary and Water Commission. (2012, November 20). Minute 319. Interim international cooperative measures in the Colorado River Basin through 2017 and extension of Minute 318, Cooperative measures to address the continued effects of the April 2010 earthquake in the Mexicali Valley, Baja California. Coronado, CA: Author. Retrieved from https://www.ibwc.gov/Files/Minutes/Minute_319.pdf

International Boundary and Water Commission, United States Section. (2000). *Strategic plan* [Author's copy]. El Paso, TX: Author.

Jamail, M., & Ullery, S. J. (1979). *International water use relations along the Sonoran Desert borderlands.* Arid Lands Resource Information (Paper No. 14). Tucson, AZ: University of Arizona Office of Arid Land Studies.

Janicke, M. (2002). The political system's capacity for environmental policy: The framework for comparison. In M. Janicke and H. Weidner (Eds.), *Capacity building in national environmental policy* (pp. 1–18). Berlin, Germany: Springer.

Liverman, D. M., Varady, R. G., Chavez, O., & Sanchez, R. (1999). Environmental issues along the United States border: Drivers of change and responses of citizens and institutions. *Annual Review of Energy and Environment*, *24*, 607–643.

Mosbrucker, K. (2015, December 17). North American Development Bank to merge with bi-national counterpart, rake in $900M investments. *San Antonio Business Journal.* Retrieved from http://www.bizjournals.com/sanantonio/news/2015/12/03/north-american-development-bank-to-merge-with.html?s=print

Mumme, S. P. (1992). New directions in transboundary environmental management: A critique of current proposals. *Natural Resources Journal*, *32*(3), 539–562.

Mumme, S. P. (2003). Environmental politics and policy on the U.S.-Mexican border studies: Developments, achievements, and trends. *Social Science Journal*, *40*(4), 593–606.

Mumme, S. P. (2009). Reflections on public participation in environmental protection policy on the U.S.-Mexico border. In Departamento de Estudios Urbanos y Medio Ambiente (Eds.), *Retos ambientales y desarrollo urbano en la frontera Mexico-Estados Unidos* (pp. 227–252). Tijuana, Mexico: Colegio de la Frontera Norte.

Mumme, S. P., & Aguilar, I. (2003). Managing border water to the year 2020: The challenge of sustainable development. In S. Michel (Ed.), *Binational Water Management Planning* (pp. 51–94). San Diego, CA: San Diego State University Southwest Center for Environmental Research and Policy.

Mumme, S. P., & Ibanez, O. (2009). U.S.-Mexico environmental treaty impediments to tactical security infrastructure along the international boundary. *Natural Resources Journal*, *49*(3–4), 801–824.

North American Agreement for Environmental Cooperation, 32 I.L.M. 1482. (1993). Retrieved from http://www.cec.org/sites/default/files/naaec.pdf

Salazar, J., & Spalding, M. (2006). Adjacent U.S.-Mexican border natural protected areas: Protection, management, and cooperation. In K. Hoffman (Ed.), *The U.S.-Mexican border environment: Transbound-*

ary ecosystem management (pp. 69–108). San Diego, CA: San Diego State University Press.

Sammet, A. M., & Quinn, M. S. (n.d.). *The influence of multi-level governance on national and regional conservation policy: Mexico and Canada*. Calgary, AB: University of Calgary.

Sánchez-Rodríguez, R., & Mumme, S. P. (2013). Environmental protection and natural resources. In P. Smith & A. Seeley (Eds.), *Mexico and the United States: The politics of partnership* (pp. 202–231). Boulder, CO: Lynne-Rienner Press.

Segee, B., & Cordova, A. (2009). A fence runs through it. In L. Lopez-Hoffman, E. McGovern, R. Varady, & K. Flessa (Eds.), *Conservation of shared environments: Learning from the United States and Mexico* (pp. 241–255). Tucson, AZ: University of Arizona Press

Trilateral Committee for Wildlife and Ecosystem Conservation and Management. (1996). Memorandum of Understanding establishing the Canada/Mexico/United States Trilateral Committee for Wildlife and Ecosystem Conservation and Management. Retrieved from http://www.trilat.org/index.php?view=download&alias=70-trilateral-mou&category_slug=about-the-trilateral&option=com_docman&Itemid=254

Trilateral Committee for Wildlife and Ecosystem Conservation and Management. (2011). *Association of Fish and Wildlife Agencies and State Agencies report to the executive table*. XVI meeting of the Canada/Mexico/U.S. Trilateral Committee for Wildlife and Ecosystem Conservation and Management, Oaxaca, Mexico.

Trilateral Committee for Wildlife and Ecosystem Conservation and Management. (2016). *Working Tables*. Retrieved from http://www.trilat.org/index.php?option=com_content&view=article&id=42&Itemid=117

United States-Mexico Transboundary Aquifer Assessment Act, PL 109-448. (2006). Retrieved from https://www.congress.gov/109/plaws/publ448/PLAW-109publ448.pdf

U.S. Fish and Wildlife Service. (2013). *Mexico*. Retrieved from https://www.fws.gov/international/pdf/factsheet-mexico.pdf

Valdez, R. J., Guzman-Aranda, C., Abarca, F. J., Tarango-Arambula, L. A., & Sanchez, F. C. (2006). Wildlife conservation and management in Mexico. *Wildlife Society Bulletin*, *34*(2), 270–282.

Van Schoik, D. R., Lelea, E., & Cunningham, J. (2006). Sovereignty, borders, and transboundary biodiversity: Turning a potential tragedy into true partnership. An introduction to the theory and practice of conservation biology in the security bisected U.S.-Mexican border region. In K. Hoffman (Ed.), *The U.S.-Mexican border environment: Transboundary ecosystem management* (pp. 1–68). San Diego, CA: San Diego State University Press.

Varady, R., & Ward, E. (2009). Transboundary conservation in the borderlands: What drives environmental change. In L. Lopez-Hoffman, E. D. McGovern, R. G. Varady, & K. W. Flessa (Eds.), *Conservation of shared environments: Learning from the United States and Mexico* (pp. 9–22). Tucson, AZ: University of Arizona Press.

Vitiello, R. (2011, April 14). Border: Are environmental laws and regulations impeding security and harming the environment? [Testimony of Deputy Chief Ronald Vitiello, U.S. Customs and Border Protection, before the U.S. Subcommittee on Natural Resources, Forests, and Public Lands, and the U.S. House Committee on Oversight and Government Reform, Subcommittee on National Security, Homeland Defense, and Foreign Operations]. Washington, DC: U.S. Congress. Retrieved from https://www.dhs.gov/news/2011/04/14/testimony-deputy-chief-ronald-vitiello-us-customs-and-border-protection-us-house

Ward, E. (2003). *Desert oasis*. Tucson, AZ: University of Arizona Press.

White House. (2010, May 19). Joint statement from President Barack Obama and President Felipe Calderon. Washington, DC: White House, Office of the Press Secretary. Retrieved from http://www.whitehouse.gov/the-press-office/joint-statement-president-barack-obama-and-president-felipe-calder-n

SIX

Biodiversity without Borders?

Acknowledging and Overcoming Obstacles in the Transboundary Governance of Endangered Species

ANDREA OLIVE

INTRODUCTION

The North American continent contains a vast array of biodiversity and its potential loss "is simultaneously a national problem, a transboundary issue, and a continental dilemma" (Healy, VanNijnatten, & Lopez-Vallejo, 2014, p. 100). To protect this natural resource, Canada, the United States, and Mexico have worked bilaterally and trilaterally to protect native flora and fauna. Despite these efforts, saving endangered species is an increasing challenge on the continent. The response in each country has been predominately at the domestic level, although all three are signatories to the Convention on the International Trade of Endangered Species (CITES) and together they maintain the Trilateral Committee for Wildlife and Ecosystem Conservation and Management (TCWECM). Canada and Mexico are also signatories to the United Nations Convention on Biological Diversity (UNCBD).

Out of the 15 distinct ecoregions that exist in North America, only one is shared trilaterally: the Great Plains (Commission for Environmental Cooperation [CEC], 2012). The United States and Canada share eight ecoregions[1] and both countries have well-established national legislation in place to protect and recover species at risk. In the United States the relevant legislation is the Endangered Species Act of 1973 (ESA), and in Canada it is the 2002 Species at Risk Act (SARA). Mexico regulates endangered species protection through its more general Ecology Law, which applies to all flora and fauna in Mexico.[2]

As former British colonies, Canada and the United States developed a similar liberal democratic system of governance. They are the world's largest trading partners, and share the world's longest border as well as the Great Lakes and three oceans (Bow, 2010). Given the institutional and economic similarities (see Clarkson & Mildenberger, 2011; Morales & Medina, 2011) and their longer histories with endangered species protection, this chapter focuses primarily on these two countries and seeks to offer an explanation as to why (more) cooperation on this issue is a challenge. As someone who has lived on both sides of the border in various locations, I possess a deep appreciation for the variation in geography, property norms, stewardship ethos, ideology, and economic realities. Since 2007 I have conducted more than 100 landowner interviews as well as a dozen interviews with field officers in various parts of the United States. In Canada I have conducted 50 landowner interviews, mail-surveyed 5,000 Canadian residents, and interviewed 19 wildlife and government agents as well as 15 individuals working with nongovernment interest groups aimed at the protection of species at risk. Building on this research, this chapter pulls together a synopsis of the major challenges facing bilateral collaboration.

While many of the components necessary for cooperation are present, and there are examples of success, cooperation can also be rare, inconsistent, and undervalued. This is similar to other bilateral natural resource management efforts in Canada and the United States. In the case of water, for example, there are jurisdictional and political barriers that hinder cooperation in governance (Norman, Cohen, & Bakker, 2013). As a result, in both countries management has "undergone a twofold rescaling: 'down' from national governments to local decision makers and 'out' from government-led decision-making structures to nongovernment actors" (Norman & Bakker, 2013, p. 47). This chapter examines trends in endangered species protection governance, where "governance" is taken to be a "continuous evolving decision-making process, including meetings, reports, data collection, public feedback, decisions, elections" (Norman et al., 2013, p. 12). Governance challenges for species at risk are thematically grouped into institutional, interest based, and ideational challenges in this chapter. For many of the same reasons that "water without borders" (Norman et al., 2013) is complicated, the idea of "biodiversity without borders" is equally challenged by problems of governance. Ultimately, it is argued that federalism on both sides of the border must find new ways to bend and stretch so that cross-border networks can form, new actors can enter the policy arena, information can flow, and resources can be leveraged and shared.

BIODIVERSITY AND BILATERAL RELATIONS

The turn of the 20th century is known as the "dawn of conservation diplomacy" in North America (Dorsey, 1998) because Canada and the United States worked together to create national parks and forests. It also marked the beginning of a shared history of long-standing cooperation in the area of biodiversity (see Healy et al., 2014, Chapter 3). Britain (on Canada's behalf) and the United States signed the North Pacific Fur Seal Convention in 1911 and the Migratory Bird Treaty in 1916. Two world wars paused further progress on conservation, but following World War II a second wave of environmentalism swept across the United States and Canada, and numerous domestic and bilateral agreements were created with many aimed at the protection of species under threat of extinction on the continent. See Table 6.1 for a list of existing policies for wildlife in Canada and the United States, which also includes overlap into some trilateral agreements with Mexico as well as international agreements.

The United States passed the 1966 Endangered Species Preservation Act, the 1969 Endangered Species Conservation Act, and the 1973 Endangered Species Act. The United States also led the international effort to establish CITES, to which 180 countries are signatories in 2015, including Canada. The North American Waterfowl Agreement was signed in 1986, followed in 1987 by an Agreement on the Conservation of the Porcupine Caribou Head; and in 1999 the two countries renewed the U.S.-Canadian Pacific Salmon Treaty. After Ottawa ratified the UNCBD in 1993, it signed the 1996 Accord for the Protection of the Species at Risk with nine provinces (Quebec did not sign) and two territories (Nunavut did not exist). In 2002 Canada passed SARA. Taken all together these treaties and laws compromise the two countries' primary efforts to protect and restore flora and fauna.

This track record of cooperation and collaboration for biodiversity and endangered species speaks not just to the close relationship between Canada and the United States, but also to a shared problem. There are 513 listed endangered or threatened species in Canada and 1,380 endangered or threatened species in the United States (Olive, 2014a). There is also consensus in the scientific community that grasslands, wetlands, and old-growth forests are under threat in North America (Brandt, 2009; Government of Canada, 2010). The primary reasons for biodiversity loss in both countries are habitat fragmentation, invasive species, agricultural practices (land use and pesticide use), and pollution (Czech & Krausman, 2001; Vaughn, 2011; Venter et al., 2006). Both countries are facing biodiversity

Table 6.1
Summary of Existing National Wildlife Legislation and Policy in Canada and the United States by Year and Type

Legislation/Policy	United States	Canadian	Bilateral	Trilateral	International
1911 Pacific Fur Seal Convention	Yes	Yes	Yes		
1916 Migratory Bird Treaty	Yes	Yes	Yes		
1954 Convention on Great Lakes Fisheries	Yes	Yes	Yes		
1966 Endangered Species Preservation Act	Yes				
1969 Endangered Species Conservation Act	Yes				
1973 Endangered Species Act	Yes				
1973 Convention on the International Trade in Endangered Species	Yes	Yes			Yes
1976 Magnuson-Stevens Fisheries Conservation and Management Act	Yes				
1986 North American Waterfowl Agreement	Yes	Yes		Yes	
1987 Agreement on the Conservation of the Porcupine Caribou Herd	Yes	Yes	Yes		
1992 UN Convention on Biological Diversity	Signed, not ratified	Yes			Yes
1994 Commission for Environmental Cooperation	Yes	Yes		Yes	
1996 MOU (Trilateral Committee for Wildlife and Ecosystem Conservation and Management)	Yes	Yes		Yes	
2002 Species at Risk Act		Yes			
2007 International Recovery Plan for the Whooping Crane	Yes	Yes	Yes		
2008 North American Monarch Conservation Plan	Yes	Yes		Yes	

Categories: United States only, Canada only, Bilateral Canada-United States, Trilateral Canada-United States-Mexico, International.

loss at a rapid and increasing rate. This is part of what Leaky and Lewin (1996) call the sixth extinction, whereby human beings are putting immense pressure on earth ecosystems and contributing to a mass extinction of other species.

Canadians and Americans are concerned about the extinction of other species for various reasons. Some individuals value the intrinsic worth of other living things while others value other species for medicinal applications, recreational uses, aesthetic value, or spiritual value (Beazley, 2001). From a pragmatic political level, and beyond reasons of vote capturing or public salience, the leaders of Canada and the United States must concern themselves with biodiversity loss for reasons of ecosystem services, ecotourism, pharmaceutical potential, and other anthropocentric uses. The American ESA uses the language of "aesthetic, ecological, educational, historical, recreational, and scientific value," while the Canadian SARA indicates that wildlife has "value in itself and is valued by Canadians for aesthetic, cultural, spiritual, recreational, education, historical, medical, ecological and scientific reasons." There is clear overlap and agreement that Canada and the United States should protect biodiversity, or at least endangered species, for both anthropocentric and ecocentric reasons. Unfortunately, specific institution, interest-based, and ideational obstacles challenge cooperation and prevent the establishment of cross-border networks for the purposes of conservation. These challenges are summarized in Table 6.2 and discussed in greater detail in the following sections.

Table 6.2
Summary of Institutional, Interest-based, and Ideational Factors Impacting Cooperation between Canada and the United States

	Institutional	**Interest-based**	**Ideational**
Key difference(s)	Federalism	Ownership of genetic resources; Inclusion of aboriginals/natives	Precautionary principle; Private property norms
Obstacles	Different listing/recovery process; Incongruent bilateral relationships	Sharing data; Type of knowledge used to make decisions; Set of actors included in governance	Different listing/recovering standards; Regulation of land as habitat

Institutional Challenges

Canada and the United States are both administered as federations but their respective constitutions organize power very differently between levels of government. In the United States, the federal government has immense power over wildlife and conservation. The second clause of Article 6 of the U.S. Constitution, known as the Supremacy Clause, indicates that federal law is the supreme law of the land and that it binds all judges in every state. However, the supremacy of the federal government over state law only applies in the context of the constitutionally authorized and divided power. In the case of endangered species, the federal government has authorized power to regulate land and wildlife, thus making the federal Endangered Species Act the law of the land in all states and across all land parcels (see Easley, Holtman, Scancarelli, & Schmidt, 2001).[3]

The Canadian Constitution grants jurisdiction over natural resources, private lands, and provincial crown land to the provinces. This gives provinces the balance of power when it comes to biodiversity and endangered species conservation. The federal government, through Section 92 of the constitution, has jurisdiction over federal crown lands (about 5% of the country outside the Northern Territories) and aquatic species. Through its exclusive treaty-making power the federal government also has jurisdiction over migratory birds and responsibility for aboriginal relations across the country. This essentially means that power over wildlife is divided and shared between the provinces and the federal government. Since there is no equivalent to the U.S. Supremacy Clause in Canada, the federal law for endangered species does not take precedent over provincial law. The result is a federal law (SARA), six provincial endangered species laws, and one territorial law. Four provinces (British Columbia, Alberta, Saskatchewan, and Prince Edward Island) and two territories (Yukon and Nunavut) have no stand-alone legislation for endangered species at all (Olive, 2014b). While the United States has one law for endangered species, Canada has a patchwork of regulations that vary across the country.

These constitutional differences have significant impact on endangered species protection and the implications for bilateral cooperation are plentiful. First, the different levels of authority at the federal level have led to different laws with significant variation in how species are listed and how species are protected and recovered in each country (Mooers, et al. 2010; Olive, 2014a). In the United States, the process is fairly straightforward. While any individual in the United States can petition to have a species listed on the ESA, more often than not it is the U.S. Fish and Wildlife Service (USFWS) or the National Oceanic and Atmospheric Administration

(NOAA) that initiates a listing since they are the lead federal agencies. In both cases a 12-month process using only "the best scientific and commercial data available" is completed to determine if a listing is warranted (Endangered Species Act of 1973, 2012, section 4). If a species is listed, a core area of habitat necessary to prevent extinction is automatically protected and anything beyond that depends on a cost-benefit analysis conducted by the agency. Importantly, a species' critical habitat is protected no matter where it is found—federal land, state land, or private land.

Once listed, the lead agency must oversee the creation and subsequent implementation of a recovery plan. The plan is considered a guiding document that describes the species and explains its reasons for endangerment. There is no set timeline for creating or implementing the recovery plan and often species wait years and years for such a plan. For example, the blue whale (*Balaenoptera musclulus*) and the wood bison (*Bison bison athabascae*) were both listed in 1970; the giant whale received a recovery plan in 1998 while the bison is still waiting. Nevertheless, even in this state of limbo the bison is protected along with the core habitat determined at the time of listing. The federal government can enforce ESA prohibitions for the bison indefinitely regardless of private or state landowner property rights.

In Canada, the listing process and recovery strategy process is comparatively more complicated. An independent scientific body created in 1977 called the Committee on the Status of Endangered Wildlife in Canada (COSEWIC) assesses flora and fauna in Canada. COSEWIC will make a recommendation to the Minister of Environment about the status of a species and the minister has nine months to accept or decline the recommendation (see Mooers et al., 2010). If the time elapses without a decision, the species is automatically listed on SARA with the status granted to it by COSEWIC. When a species is listed it is granted protection against harm and its residence is protected on federal lands (but critical habitat is not identified or protected at this stage).

Once listed on SARA the species is supposed to be given a recovery strategy and an action plan. In the strategy, the species is described, reasons for endangerment are provided, and a description of what exactly needs to be done to reverse the decline of the species is given. Only scientific information, including local knowledge and aboriginal traditional knowledge, can be used when writing a recovery strategy. During the next stage—the action plan stage—detailed planning is completed whereby economic and political factors are used to determine the best course of action to protect and recover the species (see Moores et al., 2010). Since more often than not the habitat identified for recovery is not federal land the completion of an action plan requires cooperation from provinces, private landowners, industry stakeholders, and aboriginal bands. This is a problem of domestic collaboration for endangered species. To date, only 13 species have an action plan in place (see Species at Risk Public Registry, 2015).

The difference in listing and recovery processes is of consequence for bilateral cooperation because transboundary species have inconsistent recovery processes. There are 30 species listed in both Canada and the United States as domestically endangered or threatened but that have range in the other country (Olive, 2014a). There are likely many more shared species, but different listing processes have different species in various stages of the listing process, with different status or in complete listing limbo. For example, the wolverine (*Gulo gulo*) is a species native to North America whose population is declining in its natural range. COSEWIC designated the wolverine as endangered in 2003 and it was listed as such under SARA. In 2014 Environment Canada proposed a recovery plan for the species. In the United States, conservation agencies petitioned the USFWS to list the species in 1995 but it was not until 2010 that the species was even considered as a candidate for listing. Thus, between 2003 and 2010 the species was caught in the institutional complexities of the two countries' conservation laws and held the status of endangered in Canada but no status in the United States. Ultimately, the USFWS withdrew its intent to list but is presently being sued by the Western Environmental Law Center on behalf of a handful of conservation agencies (Western Environmental Law Center [WELC], 2014).

Another implication of the different laws, stemming from distinctive constitutional powers, is that the two federal governments face challenges in working together collaboratively because of the differing scales of government. In the United States, the federal government is the key actor, but in Canada the sub-state actor hypothesis is validated because it is the provinces that have most of the power and responsibility for wildlife (Boychuck & VanNijnatten, 2004). This is a problem for creating networks of actors. In the case of the aquatic species, collaboration is more straightforward because NOAA can reach across the border and work with the Canadian Department of Fisheries and Oceans. For terrestrial wildlife, the USFWS must work with the Canadian Wildlife Service (CWS), which is responsible for SARA. However, if the transboundary species in question is on provincial or privately held lands, then the USFWS must work with a provincial wildlife or natural resource agency. And this only works in the six provinces that have stand-alone legislation for species at risk. For example, in the case of Peary caribou, the USFWS in Alaska should work with a wildlife agency in the Yukon, but since the Yukon lacks comparable legislation this makes collaboration quite difficult.

Moreover, even if the province has legislation, the different scales of government pose a challenge for creating and sustaining networks. Two examples are helpful. The Lake Erie water snake is a recently delisted endangered species in Ohio but a presently listed threatened species in the province of Ontario under its Endangered Species Act (2007) as well as nationally in Canada under SARA. The jurisdiction in Ohio falls predominately to the USFWS. In Ontario, jurisdiction is divided between the CWS and the Ontario Ministry of Natural Resources and Forestry (OMNRF). Thus, Ontario has jurisdiction on private lands and provincial crown lands, but on federal lands the federal government has jurisdiction. The responsibility is truly shared.

The consequence is that the USFWS may reach out to its sister organization, CWS, to cooperate in the case of the snake. In fact, it did so in 1997 after Canada and the United States signed a "Framework for Cooperation between the U.S. Department of the Interior and Environment Canada for the Protection and Recovery of Wild Species at Risk." The water snake was one of the 10 species included in the framework (Minister of Public Works, 1997). But cooperation was never realized. The longtime lead biologist for the water snake in the United States said her agency met only once with the Canadian team, but no relationship was ever forged (personal communication, August 2007). This is largely because the USFWS instead needed to forge a relationship with OMNRF since it is really the lead agency for the project. Aside from one attempt at federal cooperation, there was no effort to work bilaterally. Interviews with field officers in Ontario suggest they had no information about the Ohio snake population and no awareness of the recovery plan in the United States. Where the two countries could easily have shared a plan and worked together, cooperation never happened. The Lake Erie water snake remains a listed species in Canada.

Another example is the Roseate tern (*Sterna dougallii*), a migratory seabird that is endangered in both Canada and the United States. The USFWS wrote a recovery plan in 1993 and updated the plan in 1998. The CWS wrote a recovery strategy in 2010 with cooperation from relevant provinces, aboriginal groups, environmental groups, industry stakeholders, and private landowners. The Canadian plan specifically mentions the U.S. plan and a desire to "complement the recently updated United States Recovery Plan" (Environment Canada, 2010, p. iv) in terms of consistent scientific evidence and habitat information. Both the U.S. plan and the Canadian strategy focus exclusively on domestic populations. Neither document mentions team members nor colleagues across the border and neither document discusses any need nor desire for a joint recovery team nor even cooperation across the border. A CWS agent explained that

Canada's recovery team and the U.S. recovery team "have tried to have joint meetings every two years but logistics (timing, travel approvals, funding) have been an issue and so have some changes to the leadership of the U.S. team" (personal communication, August 2007). This was a common refrain among wildlife agents. Even when the countries have the same listed species and have both written recovery plans, cooperation is still difficult because of limited resources.

Interest-based Challenges

Canadian and U.S. interests have diverged internationally on conservation matters and this does have implications for collaboration in North America. In 1992 Canada signed and ratified the UN Convention on Biological Diversity (UNCBD), which is an international agreement predicated on three goals: conserve biological diversity across the globe, promote sustainable use and development, and share the benefits derived from the use of biological diversity and genetic resources—namely medical, agricultural and technological benefits (UNCBD, 2014). Making a commitment under this agreement entails monitoring and reporting of ecosystem health and national biological diversity. It also commits signatories to attending Conventions of the Parties to discuss progress on conservation issues.

The United States, under President George H. W. Bush, refrained from signing the treaty as a result of "pressures from the pharmaceutical industries concerned with intellectual property rights" and a related unwillingness to "enter into any open and automatic financial arrangement around the sharing of benefits" from genetic diversity and resources (Le Prestre & Stoett, 2001, p. 209). In 2000 the United States signed the Convention under President Bill Clinton, but the U.S. Senate has yet to ratify the treaty for likely the same reasons. These concerns did not prevent Canada from becoming the first industrialized country to ratify the UNCBD. The extent to which Canada is concerned about the pharmaceutical implications is less clear and it is likely the United States and Canada do not share this interest, or at least not to the same extent.

The United States is unwilling to share information about genetic resources as well as share the actual physical resources. Based on interviews with federal employees from the Department of Agriculture working in Saskatchewan and provincial employees of the Saskatchewan Ministry of Agriculture, it is clear that the United States has national security interests that prevent the sharing of scientific information across the border (personal communication, April 15, 2012). There are dedicated federal labs in the prairie regions working on a variety of projects around climate change adaptation. Government scientists in Canada indicated that the United States has a strict policy against sending seeds or other genetic material across the border. There is also a problem of sharing data or emailing computer files. Canadian scientists suggested that the best way to get information and learn from U.S. scientists is through attending scientific conferences and reading scientific journals (personal communication, April 15, 2012). Conservation is hindered by this design as the reality of the border makes communication and knowledge sharing difficult.

The second interest-based difference for Canada and United States conservation is also related to Canada's signature to the UNCBD as well as domestic developments in aboriginal law. Article 8j of the UNCBD commits signatories to the meaningful inclusion of indigenous peoples and their knowledge in conservation policy. What this means in practice is that COSEWIC must use traditional knowledge in the assessment of wildlife and that a SARA-listed species on or near aboriginal lands must have traditional knowledge as part of the recovery strategy and action plan (see Olive, 2012). Since all aboriginal land is federal land in Canada, SARA directly applies to reserve land. In 2000 the government created a stewardship fund specifically earmarked for projects on aboriginal lands and projects that involve the collection of traditional knowledge.

This is a huge responsibility and speaks to a major difference between federal responsibility and interest in Canada and the United States. While it is true that Canada struggles to include aboriginals and their knowledge in conservation policy (Olive, 2014a), the United States is making much less of an effort to include Native Americans. The ESA does provide some possible exemptions for Alaska Natives to subsistence hunt and fish. And in 1997, the U.S. federal government implemented an order, entitled Working with Tribes, to set the legal parameters of federal-tribal relationships in the context of the ESA. Nevertheless, the U.S. effort pales in comparison to Canada's effort (and other UNCBD signatories).

This can make cross-border collaboration difficult. It is not just that Canadian listing decisions will take longer (because aboriginal consultation takes time) and recovery plans will include and value different forms of knowledge, but that governance of endangered species includes different sets of potential actors across the border. This can contribute to the problem of incongruent relationships and also to the closing off of potentially valuable knowledge and ways of protecting endangered species. For example, in the case of water management there has been an "increasing prominence of Aboriginal actors as sovereign" (Cohen, Norman, & Bakker, 2013, p. 248) on both sides of the border. And this has in part lead to "new management paradigms that incorporate ecosystem management" (Cohen et al., 2013, p. 248). SARA and the ESA tend to take a species-specific approach, while aboriginal knowledge works to inform a more holistic ecosystem approach to the recovery and protection of endangered species (Olive, 2012). By opening governance opportunities to Native Americans and aboriginal Canadians, the two countries could establish new networks and gather new knowledge about ecosystems.

Ideational Challenges

In general, Canada and the United States share a similar culture predicated upon the same capitalist liberal democratic tradition. However, in the realm of conservation there are notable norm-based differences that permeate their approaches to species at risk. Most notably, Canada has opted for a precautionary approach to conservation and opted to avoid the regulation of private property for the sake of conservation. When not mutually shared, these principles impede cross-border governance.

Canada's SARA adopts the language of the precautionary principle; the preamble explicitly states that "if there are threats of serious or irreversible damage to a wildlife species, cost-effective measures to prevent the reduction or loss of the species should not be postponed for a lack of full scientific certainty." Moreover, Section 38 of SARA makes clear that protection, and the costs associated with it, should not be postponed because of a lack of science. This is a much different starting place than the American ESA, which historically has demanded listing and habitat decisions on the basis of "best scientific information available" with an option of "warranted but precluded" status that allows for another year of scientific evaluation (Easley et al., 2001). If the USFWS is not certain about a species' status they err on the side of gathering more science. If COSEWIC is not sure, the government is supposed to error on the side of protection. Since Canada ratified the 1992 Earth Summit Agenda 21 as well as the UNCBD, it is formally committed to applying the precautionary approach to issues of sustainable development. To that end, the language of precaution is found in numerous federal laws, such as the Oceans Act and the Environmental Protection Act. The United States has no federal environmental law that includes the language of the precautionary principle.

However, the degree to which Canada lives up to the precautionary principle in conservation efforts is questionable. Wojciechowski, McKee, Brassard, Findlay and Elgie (2011) argue that species are not being protected even though "the threshold of plausibility required to trigger a precautionary obligation has been exceeded" (p. 219). Instead, it has been left to the courts to force the government to apply a precautionary approach to listing and habitat decisions. Two examples, as examined by the University of Victoria Environmental Law Centre, include: *Alberta Wilderness Assn. v. Canada (Minister of Environment)*, which is known as the *Sage Grouse* case and *Environmental Defence Canada v. Canada (Minister of Fisheries & Oceans)*, which is known as the *Nooksack Dace* case. In *Sage Grouse* the court determined that the Minister of the Environment cannot postpone a recovery strategy simply because critical habitat cannot be conclusively or clearly identified. The Court used a prior ruling as justification. *Canada Ltée (Spray-Tech, Société d'arrosage) v. Hudson (Ville)* determined that the precautionary principle must be used to prevent environmental degradation in Canada vis-á -vis its commitments through international treaties. In *Nook Dace*, the court again decided that a recovery strategy is necessary even in the face of some scientific uncertainty. Here the court invoked SARA's preamble and also pointed out that as a signatory to the UNCBD, Canada is bound to the precautionary principle in domestic legislation (see Environmental Law Centre, 2010). Using the courts to enforce the precautionary principle does not necessarily mean that Canada uses a precautionary approach to conservation. However, the threat of court-mandated listings on the basis of the principle does set Canada down a different path than the United States.

Does this make U.S.-Canadian cooperation more difficult? Similar to differences in the listing and recovery process mentioned earlier, the Canadian use of the precautionary principle means there are inconsistent methods of listing and protecting habitat. It should technically be easier for a species and its habitat to qualify as listed in Canada if the precautionary principle is the guiding decision tool. Thus, Canada will find itself protecting species in North America that the United States does not because science is sometimes uncertain. If both countries used the same procedures and approaches to listing and habitat identification then there could at least be bilateral agreement on which species are endangered, threatened, and special concern. Such agreement would make streamlining recovery plans much easier and more efficient.

There are also differences in the country's approach to private property. While traditionally considered an institution and a main economic interest, private property can also act as an idea. Ever since its passage in 1973 the ESA has been contentious because it arguably violates the American norm of control over private property (Olive, 2014b; Raymond & Olive, 2008). The institution of private property has similar origins in Canada and the United States as John Locke's and Adam Smith's ideas took root in both countries. As is well known, Locke argued that individuals have a natural right to appropriation and ownership of nature, such as land. Building upon this, Smith, in *Wealth of Nations*, argued that the economy and the efficient allocation of resources necessitates property rights. Locke justified ownership and Smith justified a system of property rights. The U.S. Declaration of Independence is in part predicated on these ideas of individual right to "life, liberty, and the pursuit of happiness," where the latter is intended to mean "private property." Today both the United States and Canada have a system of private property rights that defines and protects an individual right to own and use property within the bounds of national law.

The institution is similar in both countries, but in the United States the idea of private property is part of the fabric of society. The right to own land is an essential component of identity and nationalism. In fact, it has been said that "to be an American is to own and control private property" (Jacobs, 1998, p. 36). Countless landowners in the United States used a similar refrain when discussing the ESA and stewardship during personal interviews. For example, a landowner in Ohio said, "I truly believe that in all circumstances, the bond between man and land is supreme" (personal communication, August 2007). Time and again, American landowners drew a connection between private property and democracy, identity, and freedom (see Olive, 2014b). Land is not just a part of an institution of property rights, it is part of the American story and what separates American culture from other cultures.

Illicial and Harrison (2007) argue that Canada avoided the issues of private property in SARA intentionally—through learning negative lessons from the U.S. experience of the ESA. This is to say, the Canadian federal government avoided regulating private property not because of constitutional limitations, but because it drew lessons from the U.S. government's 30 years of struggle to regulate private land for the sake of conservation. However, there is evidence to suggest that Canadians do not share American attitudes towards private property. In interviews with landowners, more Americans than Canadians claimed that private property is an absolute inalienable right (Olive, 2014b). This is likely because outright ownership of land is rare in Canada. As one Ontario land manager said "you don't buy land in Canada—you just lease it from the government" (personal communication, May 2009). This is largely true. Almost 90% of land in Canada is owned by the federal or provincial governments and leased to private individuals or firms for a period of up to 99 years. On the whole, this means that Canadians are less likely to reject conservation policy on the grounds of private property norms.

Different conceptions of private property in the two countries means that policy approaches to conservation will be different in each. If and when the USFWS decides to work with provincial wildlife agencies on joint recovery plans, the agencies will need to take different approaches to achieving cooperation and compliance from private landowners. For example, Furbish's lousewort (*Pedicularis fubishlaie*) is an endangered plant in New Brunswick and Maine. Although the plant obviously does not move back and forth across the border, it is the same species of plant in the same ecoregion of North America—it just happens to be in two different countries. The USFWS can protect the plant anywhere it is found whereas the CWS can only protect it on federal lands. The province of New Brunswick has an Endangered Species Act and the plant was listed in 1982 making it illegal to harm the plant and its critical habitat. The New Brunswick Department of Natural Resources wrote a recovery plan in 2006 (without input from the USFWS). Of the five known plant sites, three are found on private land. The province can legally regulate private land, but instead the recovery plan speaks only to the need to educate landowners and seek their voluntary stewardship. The U.S. Recovery Plan, written in 1991, seeks to oversee the permanent protection of 50% of the plant's habitat through land acquisition—either by the government or by environmental groups like the Nature Conservancy, which has purchased eight square miles of plant habitat (McCollough, 2007). The difference in approach is notable. The USFWS assumes that landowners will not voluntarily steward the species so land must be purchased. New Brunswick assumes that landowners will voluntarily steward the species so education and outreach must be conducted. The difference in approaches is a result of the differing ideas about property on the two sides of the border.

NAVIGATING COOPERATION

The whooping crane (*Grus Americana*) is a critically endangered bird in North America. In 1941 there were only 16 wild cranes remaining. By cooperatively writing and implementing a recovery strategy for the bird, a joint U.S.-Canadian recovery team has overseen a rise in population to an estimated 600 birds in the wild and 165 in captivity (International Crane Foundation, 2011). The CWS and the USFWS signed a 1990 memorandum of understanding entitled "Conservation of the Whooping Crane Related to Coordinated Management Activities." And in 2007 they created an International Recovery Plan. The success to date of this joint effort is emblematic of the potential of cross-border collaboration premised on governance. The joint plan relies not just on government sister-institutions (CWS and USFWS) but an astounding number of environmental organizations and indigenous groups (see CWS & USFWS, 2007, viii–ix). If a joint U.S.-Canadian recovery team can recover the cranes, why not the Roseate stern? Why not any species in North America?

There are significant challenges, as outlined earlier, that preclude collaborative transboundary governance of endangered species. These challenges are not insurmountable but they are real. Healy et al. (2014) argue that effective transboundary environmental governance entails creating stable binational networks, sharing a knowledge and information base, and addressing the problem of resources (p. 101). This is a good framework for discussing how and where we might look for ways around existing obstacles. First, the creation of binational networks in Canada and the United States is challenged by inconsistent procedures, a lack of resources, and by the inclusion of different actors in conservation politics. In the United States, private property owners are often front and center in ESA efforts alongside industry stakeholders and the federal government. In Canada, the circle of actors is much larger and emphasizes different participants. The federal government is often not important whereas provincial actors and aboriginal groups are key players. This prevents the formation of networks with similar conservation interests in the two countries. Moreover, the Canadian provinces that lack legislation will need to create policy and designate channels of authority such that cooperation with sister agencies can form. It is difficult for the USFWS to work with Alberta and Saskatchewan to conserve a species like the black-footed ferret when there is no formal process in those provinces to write and implement recovery plans.

So how can government agencies begin to cooperate and open up space to include more actors in conservation governance? Collaboration in the area of climate change might help build new networks. In the past few years the government in Canada, under the leadership of Stephen Harper and the Conservative Party, has committed to streamlining Canada's climate-related environmental policy to U.S. policy. More recently, Prime Minister Justin Trudeau and President Barack Obama released a U.S.-Canadian Joint Statement on Climate, Energy, and Arctic Leadership (Government of Canada, 2016). This might help create and sustain relationships between environmental groups and governments on both sides of the border. More promising, however, might be the creation of state-to-province relationships through climate partnerships and the already up-and-running cap-and-trade program between California, Quebec, and Ontario. Relationships between environmental agencies in states and provinces or federal-to-federal agencies can only help biodiversity. And since climate change is deeply connected to biodiversity as reason for possible endangerment of many species, agency and nongovernment organization relationships will be necessary for consistent attention and policy.

Beyond spillover cooperation from climate change, cooperation would be lubricated by the United States ratifying the UNCBD. This is because such a commitment would set in motion the UNCBD's requirements to share scientific information, include indigenous North Americans in conservation, and use a precautionary approach to the listing and protection of at-risk species. Mexico and Canada have already ratified the UNCBD, and if the United States did so trilateral governance could improve under the agreement. U.S. ratification would mean consistent monitoring and reporting on ecosystem status and trends. These documents could create benchmarks and be developed trilaterally to begin the process of addressing shared ecosystems in decline. Essentially, information could more easily flow across the three borders (even in cases where physical genetic resources are not shared). Moreover, U.S. ratification of UNCBD would entail including Native Americans in conservation and adopting a precautionary approach to listing, which would help streamline the recovery process bilaterally (and trilaterally).

However, even without UNCBD ratification from the United States, bi- and trilateral governance can be emboldened through two other biodiversity-centric agreements: the Canada-Mexico-U.S. Trilateral Committee for Wildlife and Ecosystem Conservation and Management (TCWECM) and the Commission for Environmental Cooperation (CEC). As noted in Table 6.1, the TCWECM was created in 1996 through a memorandum of understanding among wildlife agencies in the three countries (see Healy et al., 2014). The mission of the TCWECM is to "enhance cooperation and coordination . . . in projects and programs for the conservation and management of wildlife, plants, biological diversity, and ecosystems of mutual interest" (Trilateral Committee [TCWECM], 2012a). Since this is an agency-to-agency committee, asymmetrical institutions among the three countries hamper its scope and success. Environment Canada and the Canadian Wildlife Service has very little jurisdiction over wildlife, as mentioned earlier. To have a large impact on biodiversity in Canada the TCWECM would need partnerships with the 10 provincial and three territorial wildlife agencies (or aboriginal wildlife management boards). Nevertheless, the TCWECM has been able to focus on migratory birds (which are in the jurisdictional purview of all three federal wildlife agencies), some shared species of common concern (see TCWECM, 2012b), and activities related to CITES.

Running parallel to the North American Free Trade Agreement, the 1994 North American Agreement on Environmental Cooperation created the CEC. The mission of the organization is to facilitate "collaboration and public participation to foster conservation . . . in the context of increasing economic, trade, and social links" among the three countries

(CEC, 2014). To date, the CEC's work has been focused on ecosystem health, migratory birds, and marine protected areas. By and large the CEC helps to address knowledge sharing and capacity building. And while it may not directly address endangered species in United States and Canada, it does help sustain bilateral networks and communication channels between governments. However, as Healy, VanNijnatten, and Lopez-Vallejo (2014) point out, the "lack of resources (and political support) is a continuing problem, which limits the extent to which the CEC can realize its objectives" (p. 60) (see also Mumme, Chapter 5 in this volume). This would also extend to the TCWECM since wildlife agencies depend upon federal funding for support of species-at-risk programs and related activities.

Indeed, the problem of resources will be a significant challenge in both Canada and the United States (and Mexico). The USFWS reports annually on total federal and state funding on endangered species. The 2012 spending indicates a return to 2007 (pre-recession) spending levels. In the 2012 fiscal year federal agencies spent US$1.6 billion on endangered species programs, up from US$1.5 billion in 2011 and US$1.4 billion in 2010.[4] However, even in good economic conditions the funding of endangered species programs is limited. The ESA expired in 1993 and it is reliant on continual funding by Congress on an annual basis to remain legally enforceable. Every year the law is funded; but without a commitment to long-term funding it is difficult for the USFWS to make a commitment to staff and programs. Lack of funding was the primary complaint among wildlife field officers interviewed and was identified numerous times as the primary reason that cooperation with Canadian recovery teams was not possible or sustainable (Olive, 2014a).

On the Canadian side the funding situation is not significantly better. Nationally, the federal government funds SARA and in the 2012 budget $50 million (CAD) was allotted over a two-year period for species-at-risk programs (Environment Canada, 2012). While this is significantly less than the ESA, the jurisdiction of SARA is significantly smaller. It is provincial funding for endangered species that is most important as provinces mainly manage habitat. Unfortunately, no comparable data is available. Provincial governments do not report on species-at-risk funding each year. That said, Ontario is Canada's largest province (13.1 million people, roughly 40% of the total population) and its Ministry of Natural Resources and Forestry had an operating budget of $713 million (CAD) in 2012 (Ontario Ministry of Finance, 2013). That is all the money the province spent on activities and programs related to natural resources and endangered species conservation, which is half of what the United States spent on endangered species programs alone in 2012. So, comparatively, Canada is spending far less on species at risk. However, the larger problem in Canada is the overall lack of policy and the lack of habitat protection from coast to coast. There needs to be more dedicated funding for research and habitat protection. Both countries need resources, people, and finances in order to commit to cross-border cooperation.

CONCLUSION

Norman, Cohen, and Bakker (2013) emphasize the need for a new conception of transboundary water governance in Canada and the United States that requires policy makers to reframe this natural resource as "water without borders." This common understanding of a shared resource would allow policy actors to better integrate and coordinate their actions. In many ways, biodiversity is a similar resource, as it too moves across the continent without respect to political boundaries. A "biodiversity without borders" approach premised on the same notions of governance posed by Norman, Cohen, and Bakker (2013) and outlined here would be a novel way for Canada, the United States, and Mexico to address conservation.

That said, there are numerous obstacles to transboundary governance and cross-border institution building in Canada and the United States. The countries have established domestic programs for endangered species and have made some international, trilateral, and bilateral efforts to recover at risk species. But the differences between their institutions, interests, and ideas make further cooperation difficult. Transboundary endangered species governance cannot flourish when different actors hold different interests and values across the border. Canadian provinces need to create and implement consistent policies from coast to coast. Once clear lines of authority and rules have been established networks can be created and sustained—both among provinces and across the border. The United States needs to ratify the UNCBD, include Native Americans in the process of conservation, and adopt a precautionary approach to listing species and their habitat. Moreover, the two countries need to make serious ongoing financial commitments to endangered species programs, including scientific research.

There also needs to be greater attention paid to private property and conceptions of land in North America. In both Canada and the United States, the vast majority of endangered species rely on private lands for survival (Olive, 2014b). More research needs to be devoted to landowners' willingness to conserve biodiversity, especially in light of limited government resources. "Biodiversity without borders" imagines a continent where government agencies, scientific communities, and citizen groups can work together with fewer bureaucratic barriers, but it does not imagine a continent without private property rights. Significant mapping of property norms is required so that agencies (private or public) can better fit policy tools to conservation programs. Sometimes it might be necessary for the USFWS and the CWS to initiate land acquisition for habitat protection, but in other contexts voluntary commitment by private landowners could be a viable strategy. At present, questions of landowner motivation, especially nonagricultural landowners, remain underspecified and in need of more empirical case-study research.

The whooping crane case suggests that networks can be created and sustained and that resources, when provided, can be pooled and effectively used to protect a transboundary species.

However, the health and vitality of North American ecosystems is in the interest of more than two countries. Mexico contains the most biodiversity on the continent (Healy et al., 2014). Canada and the United States need to apply lessons of bilateral governance to a trilateral framework. The North American Monarch Conservation Plan for the monarch butterfly (*Danaus plexippus*) is exemplary of the potential of trilateral species conservation. The butterfly is not just found in each country, but migrates throughout all three countries each year. Mexico provides winter habitat while Canada and the United States provide summer habitat. There is a wide array of cooperation among "government agencies, nongovernmental organizations, the public, and the scientific community" (CEC, 2008, p. 6). In 2008 the CEC published the joint plan, which outlines the trilateral commitment to decrease deforestation and other types of habitat loss or fragmentation, as well as create new protected areas and monitoring of the monarch population across its entire range. By working together and building on existing networks, both at the government and nongovernment organizations level, the three countries will not only increase knowledge of the species, but protect this shared resource. North America needs more conservation initiatives like this, despite the existing obstacles.

NOTES

1. The eight ecoregions are: Arctic tundra, Taiga, Northern (boreal) forest, Northwest Forested Mountains, Eastern Temperate Forests, Great Plains, North American deserts, and Maine West Coast Forest ecosystem (CEC, 2012).
2. The Ecology Law was formally The General Law of Ecological Balance and Environmental Protection (Ley General del Equilibirio Ecologico y Proteccion al Ambiente).

3. However, this is not to say that states play no role in the protection or recovery of at-risk species. In fact, states collectively have more resources, especially human capacity, for wildlife (Thompson, 2006). States spent $135 million in aggregate in 1998 compared to the USFWS budget of $29 million that year (Niles & Korth, 2005). Section 6 of the ESA instructs the Departments of the Interior and Commerce to cooperate with states to the maximum extent possible for endangered species. Thus, the ESA is the supreme law of the land, but the states have an important, if not critical, role to play in the overall success of the act.
4. See expenditure reports at http://www.fws.gov/endangered/esa-library/index.html.

REFERENCES

Beazley, K. (2001). Why should we protect endangered species? Philosophical and ecological rationale. In K. Beazley & R. Boardman (Eds.), *Politics of the wild: Canada and endangered species* (pp. 9–25). Oxford, UK: Oxford University Press.

Bow, B. (2010). *The politics of linkage: Power, interdependence, and ideas in Canada-US relations*. Vancouver, BC: UBC Press.

Boychuck, G., & VanNijnatten, D. (2004). Economic integration and cross-border policy convergence: Social and environmental policy in Canadian provinces and American states. *Horizons*, 7(1), 55–60.

Brandt, J. P. (2009). The extent of the North American boreal zone. *Environmental Reviews*, *17*, 101–161.

Canadian Wildlife Service & U.S. Fish and Wildlife Service. (2007). International recovery plan for the whooping crane. Ottawa, ON: Recovery of Nationally Endangered Wildlife (RENEW) and Albuquerque, NM: U.S. Fish and Wildlife Service.

Clarkson, S., & Mildenberger, M. (2011). *Dependent America? How Canada and Mexico construct US power*. Toronto, ON: University of Toronto Press.

Cohen, A., Norman, E. S., & Bakker, K. (2013). Conclusion. In E. S. Norman, A. Cohen, & K. Bakker (Eds.), *Water without borders: Canada, the United States, and shared waters* (pp. 247–258). Toronto, ON: University of Toronto Press.

Commission for Environmental Cooperation. (2008). North American monarch conservation plan. Retrieved from http://www.mlmp.org/Resources/pdf/5431_Monarch_en.pdf

Commission for Environmental Cooperation. (2012). North American environmental atlas. Montreal, QC: CEC Secretariat. Retrieved from http://www.cec.org/Page.asp?PageID=924&SiteNodeID=495&AA_SiteLanguageID=1

Commission for Environmental Cooperation. (2014). About the CEC: Commission for environmental cooperation. Retrieved from http://www.cec.org/Page.asp?PageID=1226&SiteNodeID=310&BL_ExpandID=878

Czech, B., & Krausmen, P. (2001). *The endangered species act: History, conservation biology, and public policy*. Baltimore, MD: Johns Hopkins University Press.

Dorsey, K. (1998). *The dawn of conservation diplomacy: US-Canadian wildlife protection treaties in the progressive era*. Seattle, WA: University of Washington Press.

Easley, S., Holtman, J. P., Scancarelli, J., & Schmidt, B. A. (Eds). (2001). *The endangered species act: A Stanford environmental law society handbook*. Stanford, CA: Stanford University Press.

Endangered Species Act of 1973, 16 U.S.C. § 1531 et seq. (2012). Retrieved from https://www.fws.gov/endangered/laws-policies/esa.html

Environment Canada. (2010). *Amended recovery strategy for the roseate tern (Sterna dougallii) in Canada. Species at Risk Act recovery strategy series*. Ottawa, ON: Author.

Environment Canada. (2012). *Evaluation of programs and activities in support of the Species at Risk Act*. Ottawa, ON: Author. Retrieved from https://www.ec.gc.ca/ae-ve/6AE7146E-0991-4C2F-BE2F-E89DF4F8ED1E/13-018_EC_ID_1568_PDF_accessible_ANG.pdf

Environment Canada. (2014). *Recovery strategy for the wolverine (Gulo gulo), eastern population, in Canada [Proposed]. Species at Risk Act recovery strategy series*. Ottawa, ON: Author.

Environmental Law Centre. (2010). The precautionary principle. Victoria, BC: University of Victoria. Retrieved from http://www.elc.uvic.ca/associates/documents/Jun14.10-Precautionary-Principle-Backgrounder.pdf

Government of Canada. (2010). *Canadian biodiversity: Ecosystem status and trends 2010*. Ottawa, ON: Canadian Council of Resource Ministers.

Government of Canada. (2016). *US-Canada joint statement on climate, energy, and artic leadership*. Retrieved from http://pm.gc.ca/eng/news/2016/03/10/us-canada-joint-statement-climate-energy-and-arctic-leadership

Healy, R. G., VanNignatten, D. L., & Lopez-Vallejo, M. (2014). *Environmental policy in North America: Approaches, capacity and the management of transboundary issues*. Toronto, ON: University of Toronto Press.

Illical, M., & Harrison, K. (2007). Protecting endangered species in the US and Canada: The role of negative lesson drawing. *Canadian Journal of Political Science*, *40*(2), 367–394.

International Crane Foundation. (2011). *Whooping crane*. Bariboo, WI: Author. Retrieved from https://www.savingcranes.org/whooping-crane.html

Jacobs, H. M. (1998). The wisdom, but uncertain future, of the wise-use movement. In H. M. Jacobs (Ed.), *Who owns America? Social conflict over property rights* (pp. 29–44). Madison, WI: University of Wisconsin Press.

Le Prestre, P., & Stoett, P. J. (2001). International initiatives, commitments, and disappointments: Canada, CITES, and the CBD. In K. Beazley & R. Boardman (Eds.), *Politics of the wildlife: Canada and endangered species* (pp.190–216). Oxford, UK: Oxford University Press.

Leaky, R. E., & Lewin, R. (1996). *The sixth extinction: Patterns of life and the future of humankind*. New York, NY: Anchor.

McCollough, M. (2007). Furbish's Lousewort, five-year review: Summary and evaluation. Old Town, ME: U.S. Fish and Wildlife Service. Retrieved from http://www.fws.gov/northeast/endangered/PDF/Final%20Lousewort%205_yr%20Review.pdf

Minister of Public Works and Government Services Canada in cooperation with the U.S. Fish and Wildlife Service. (2001). Conserving borderline species: A partnership between Canada and the United States. Retrieved from http://publications.gc.ca/site/eng/415280/publication.html

Mooers, A. O., Doak, D. F., Findlay, C. S., Green, D. M., Grouios, C., Manne, L. L., . . . Whitton, J. (2010). Science, policy, and species at risk in Canada. *BioScience*, *60*(11), 843–849.

Morales, D. S., & Medina, L. A. (2011). *U.S. economic and trade relations with Canada and Mexico*. Hauppauge, NY: Nova Science Publishers.

Niles, L., & Korth, K. (2005). State wildlife diversity programs. In D. D. Goble, M. Scott, & F. W. Davis (Eds.), *The endangered species act at thirty: Lessons and prospects* (pp. 141–155). Washington, DC: Island Press.

Norman, E. S., & Bakker, K. (2013). Rise of the local? Delegation and devolution in transboundary water governance. In E. S. Norman, A. Cohen, & K. Bakker (Eds.), *Water without borders: Canada, the United States, and shared waters* (pp. 47–69). Toronto, ON: University of Toronto Press.

Norman, E. S., Cohen, A., & Bakker, K. (Eds.). (2013). *Water without borders: Canada, the United States, and shared waters.* Toronto, ON: University of Toronto Press.

Olive, A. (2012). Does Canada's species at risk act live up to Article 8? *Canadian Journal of Native Studies, 32*(1), 173–189.

Olive, A. (2014a). Comparing recovery in Canada and the US: The case of endangered species conservation. *Canadian Geographer, 58*(3), 263–275.

Olive, A. (2014b). *Land, stewardship & legitimacy: Endangered species policy in Canada and the United States.* Toronto, ON: University of Toronto Press.

Ontario Ministry of Finance. (2013). Ontario's outlooks and fiscal plan. In 2013 Ontario budget. Retrieved from http://www.fin.gov.on.ca/en/budget/ontariobudgets/2013/ch2g.html#ch2_t2-24

Raymond, L., & Olive, A. (2008). Landowner beliefs regarding biodiversity protection on private property: An Indiana case study. *Society and Natural Resources, 21*(6), 483–497.

Species at Risk Public Registry. (2015). Action plans. Retrieved from http://www.registrelep-sararegistry.gc.ca/sar/recovery/actionPlansTimelines_e.cfm

Thompson, B. H., Jr. (2006). Managing the working landscape. In D. D. Goble, M. J. Scott, & F. W. Davis (Eds.), *The endangered species act at thirty: Renewing the conservation promise* (pp. 103–126). Washington, DC: Island Press.

Trilateral Committee for Wildlife and Ecosystem Conservation and Management. (2012a). Background: About the trilateral committee. Retrieved from http://www.trilat.org/about-the-trilateral

Trilateral Committee for Wildlife and Ecosystem Conservation and Management. (2012b). Species of common concern working table. Retrieved from http://www.trilat.org/working-tables/shared-species-of-concern

UN Convention on Biological Diversity. (2010). Subnational and local implementation. Retrieved from http://www.cbd.int/en/ subnational/partners-and-initiatives/cbo/overview

Vaughn, J. (2011). *Environmental politics: Domestic and global dimensions.* Boston, MA: Wadsworth.

Venter, O., Brodeur, N. N., Nemiroff, L., Belland, B., Dolinsek, I. J., & Grant, J. W. A. (2006). Threats to endangered species in Canada. *BioScience, 56*(11), 903–910.

Western Environmental Law Center. (2014). Broad alliance of conservationists to sue feds over wolverine. Retrieved from http://www.westernlaw

.org/article/broad-alliance-conservationists-sue-feds-over-wolverine-press-release-81314

Wojciechowski, S., McKee, S., Brassard, C., Findlay S., & Elgie, S. (2011). SARA's safety net provisions and the effectiveness of species at risk protection on non-federal lands. *Journal of Environmental Law and Practice*, 22(3), 203–222.

SEVEN

Institutional Features of U.S.-Canadian Transboundary Fisheries Governance

Organizations and Networks, Formal and Informal

ANDREW M. SONG, OWEN TEMBY, GAIL KRANTZBERG, AND GORDON M. HICKEY

INTRODUCTION

Many of the fish harvested by commercial enterprises, recreationists, and indigenous groups in North America live and travel through shared or boundary waters. Prominent examples include Pacific salmon in the Pacific Northwest, cod and halibut in the Atlantic Northeast, and red snapper in the Gulf of Mexico. In addition to being an integral part of an aquatic ecosystem, transboundary fish are of tremendous economic value, representing billions of dollars for the regional economies they support through fishing and ancillary industries. Their interjurisdictional nature is clear: for example, the anadromous life cycle of the sockeye salmon (*Oncorhynchus nerka*) begins in freshwater streams and lakes from northern California, moves through British Columbia, Yukon, and into Alaska, then progresses to the Pacific Ocean, and then back to the original freshwater habitat.

Successfully governing sustainable fisheries is a challenging task even in the absence of binational complexities, which is well noted by many examples of inland and ocean fisheries (Allan et al., 2005; Cochrane, 2000; Myers & Worm, 2003; Pauly et al., 2002). Problems confounding the effective management of fisheries include the inadequate and unreliable assessment of stock and capture data, complex interactions with environmental changes (such as the effects of climate change), and perverse government and market incentives that lead to overcapacity and illegal fishing (Beddington, Agnew, & Clark, 2007; Ficke, Myrick, &

Hansen, 2007; Mora et al., 2009; Sumaila, Alder, & Keith, 2006; Watson & Pauly, 2001). While sound institutional mechanisms to maneuver these difficulties are of critical importance, grasping what institutions mean and how they perform has not been an easy task (Acheson, 2006; Chuenpagdee & Song, 2012; Jentoft, 2004; Walker et al., 2009). Increasingly, sustainable fisheries governance is recognized as a "wicked problem" with no clear and neat solutions to attended complex and adaptive challenges (Jentoft & Chuenpagdee, 2009). How to best design and support institutions for sustainable fisheries remains a contentious issue: should a single agency, such as the Canadian Department of Fisheries and Oceans, or multiple levels of organizations, such as the U.S. regional fishery management councils and federal agencies, the National Marine Fisheries Service, and the U.S. Fish and Wildlife Service, assume legitimate responsibility?

In the context of transboundary fisheries governance, an additional set of challenges related to international cooperation emerges. These challenges include problems of diffuse responsibilities, lack of clear accountability, tendency to free-ride, and overlapping sovereign claims. Not surprisingly, there have been widespread failures to conserve fish stocks in the high seas, with regional fisheries management organizations largely unable to obtain collective action among distant fishing nations (Cullis-Suzuki & Pauly, 2010; Meltzer, 1994). Likewise, in the binational North American context, there is a recognized need for institutional innovation to effectively bridge the potential political and management discrepancies and facilitate the implementation of sustainability measures (see Olive, Chapter 6; VanNijnatten & Stoett, Chapter 8).

As other chapters in this book highlight, transboundary environmental issues are indeed governable despite these complexities (see, especially, Jinnah & Lindsay, Chapter 2; Mumme, Chapter 5; Gerlak, Chapter 9; and Macfarlane, Chapter 13). While bi- and trinational environmental governance is substantially limited by territorial sovereignty and the related differences in domestic administrative approaches, it is not reducible to them. In a recent book on North American environmental policy, Healy, VanNijnatten, and Lopez-Vallejo (2014) show that transnational networks participate in the governance of a wide range of environmental issues, such as energy, air pollution, and, most successfully, natural resources and biodiversity, of which fisheries are an example (see also Temby, 2015). These networks are mostly interagency (what Isett et al. [2011] call "collaborative") bi- and trinational networks that facilitate mutual learning and adjustment among members and build capacity by facilitating informational transmission and, in some cases, distributing material resources (see also Agranoff & McGuire, 2001; Imperial, 2005). While they operate within the context of international treaties and other legal frameworks that define the roles and jurisdiction of implicated actors, their activities often exhibit an informal dimension (what Agranoff & McGuire [2001] call "groupware") that is also necessary for successful governance (Jinnah, 2014). For instance, in a recent study of these informal dimensions in the binational management of U.S.-Canadian Pacific salmon fisheries, Temby, Rastogi, Sandall, Cooksey, and Hickey (2015) show that civil servants from numerous agencies in several states and provinces from the two countries regularly communicate through both formal and informal channels on issues related to the shared management of these resources. Such micro-level interactions are understood as a key network element that influences institutional dynamics and efficacy (Owen-Smith & Powell, 2008).

This chapter builds on existing studies of North American environmental network governance by examining the institutional features of the collaborative networks managing transboundary U.S.-Canadian fisheries. As such, some important facets of fisheries governance, such as economic stakeholder demands and the ways in which they filter through the political system, are outside the scope of this chapter. Rather, the analysis herein seeks an understanding of the way transbounary networks of government agencies, binational organizations, and the professionals staffing them have contributed to facilitating binational cooperation. To do so, we focus on three shared fisheries between the United States and Canada: (1) the Pacific salmon fishery in the Pacific Northwest, (2) the Great Lakes fisheries, and (3) the ground fisheries in the Gulf of Maine in the Atlantic Northeast. While these cases are relatively well discussed in the literature—including their successes and challenges—less attention has been paid to the informal institutional dimension (i.e., untraced long-term working relationships, informal modes of interaction) that influence their ongoing development. Hence, we ask: What types of mechanisms (both formal and informal) have been relied upon in the governance of transboundary U.S.-Canadian fisheries in obtaining institutional outcomes in the years of their formation and operation?

Our review begins by defining transboundary fisheries in greater detail and outlines the extensiveness of this resource governance system internationally. Next, the three shared U.S.-Canadian fisheries are described in terms of their resource contexts, recent history, and the development of institutional arrangements they have exhibited, as well as some of the main achievements and challenges. Based on this account, we compare the three binational fishery networks in terms of several institutional features and discuss how a distinction based on the formality and informality of network dimensions can enhance scholarly understanding of how institutions manage transboundary natural resources such as fisheries. Our aim is to generate a more nuanced interpretation of the institutional arrangements that operate in North American transboundary fisheries.

TRANSBOUNDARY FISHERIES IN MARINE AND INLAND WATERS

Transboundary fisheries are dependent on fish stocks that occur within waters of two or more coastal states (e.g., the territorial waters, contiguous zone and, most typically, the exclusive economic zones [EEZs]). They can be broader in distribution to include "straddling stocks," if the same fish stocks also move between coastal states' EEZs and the high seas, as well as highly migratory species such as tuna. Other more specific circumstances concern anadromous species such as Pacific salmon and catadromous species like American eels, whose spawning and migration patterns may cross several internal waters, the EEZ, and the high sea boundaries (Meltzer, 1994; Russell & VanderZwaag, 2010). This migratory behavior of fish stocks, traversing both marine and inland settings, implicates different legal and political contexts.

In the marine setting, the 1982 UN Convention on the Law of the Sea (UNCLOS) provides coastal states an internationally recognized legal basis for claiming sovereign rights to natural resources found in the EEZ (see Article 56, 61, 66, and 67 of the UNCLOS). Under this legal regime, coastal states thus acquired the management and enforcement responsibilities in addition to the exclusive exploitation rights to fishing stocks found in the EEZ (Meltzer, 1994). This change has brought a massive amount (nearly 90%) of previously international or common marine resources into national jurisdiction (McConnell, 2010), reinforcing the role of coastal states, including Canada and the United States, as a major actor in the governance of the world's marine fisheries and raising an acute need for states to enter into cooperative frameworks in the conservation and management of transboundary fisheries.

Transboundary fisheries are also a significant topic in inland waters. Nearly 60% of the world's freshwater falls within a transboundary basin, in which at least one of the tributaries crosses a political boundary (Wolf, Natharius, Danielson, Ward, & Pender, 1999). The many shared lake and river systems, such as the Great Lakes, the Mekong River, and the Zambezi River are vital sources of freshwater, fish, and livelihoods for millions of people, in addition to myriad ecosystem services and benefits (Postel & Carpenter, 1997; Welcomme et al., 2010). Inland waters are classified as "internal waters," which means they are under the total sovereignty of the state as if they were an actual part of its land territory. Hence, it is the prerogative of the bordering countries to formulate a cooperative plan to manage the shared fish stocks. As a result, each locale has depended on place-specific institutional arrangements (or lack thereof) to oversee transboundary coordination, which has typically taken the shape of a joint management regime or interjurisdictional commissions, such as the Mekong River Commission (in Southeast Asia) and the Great Lakes Fishery Commission in North America. As such, they are designed to be the key enabling body of multilateral management actions based on mutual agreement and cooperation.

Domestically, both the United States and Canada have national policy regimes for the management of fisheries. The U.S. regime is bifurcated between marine waters and the Great Lakes. Marine fisheries policy is based on the 1976 Magnuson Fisheries Conservation and Management Act (Magnuson Act) and its 1996 and 2006 amendments. The act created eight regional fisheries management councils, composed of economic stakeholders and other interests and charged with developing fishery management plans (FMPs) for maximizing sustainable yield and restoring depleted fish stocks. These FMPs are evaluated and approved by NOAA Fisheries (commonly known by its formal name, the National Marine Fisheries Service [NMFS]), which serves as the overarching regulatory agency that ultimately determines how much of a fish species within the regional council's zone may be withdrawn (NMFS, n.d.). By contrast, in the Great Lakes fisheries are managed without a robust U.S. federal regulatory framework. State and tribal governments have the primary management authority for fish and wildlife resources within their boundaries. Wherein state jurisdiction ends three nautical miles from the shores in the marine realm, in the Great Lakes, state boundaries extend to the international border obviating the existence of U.S. federal waters (Gaden, Goddard, & Read, 2013). The federal mandate instead provides the authorization for the various federal agencies, such as the U.S. Fish and Wildlife Service and the U.S. Geological Survey, to conduct complementary, albeit critical, activities in a number of areas, including research, stock rehabilitation, and invasive species control, and to assist the work of the Great Lakes Fishery Commission and nonfederal governments (U.S. Fish and Wildlife Service, 2011).

In Canada, the management regime also differs between marine waters and the Great Lakes. Whereas the federal government, through the Department of Fisheries and Oceans (DFO), is the central authority in regulating marine fishery resources, the Great Lakes feature a more co-dependent arrangement between the federal and provincial (Ontario) government. The province, through the Ontario Ministry of Natural Resources and Forestry, generally takes a lead by drafting regulations as to who can fish and how the fish can be caught, as they assume the ownership of the fish in their waters. The federal government incorporates those regulations into the 1985 Fisheries Act (last amended in 2013) and implements them in a quasi-joint manner with provincial agencies (Gaden et al., 2013). Jurisdictional overlap therefore remains significant with responsibilities that are not always clear-cut (Fisheries and Oceans Canada, 2012, 2015). While these (U.S. and Canadian) policy frameworks are designed primarily as domestic policy, they comprise part of the institutional context in which binational networks and organizations must operate.

Given the wide-ranging geographic distribution and movement of fish stocks in both marine and inland waters, the essence of transboundary fisheries lies in dealing with the dynamic characteristics of the shared fish stocks whose natural migration patterns transcend political boundaries. Cooperation and reciprocity are required to negotiate this complex political-ecological challenge, fostered through effective institutional mechanisms. As the following three case studies of transboundary fishery governance show, the presence and the shape of such mechanisms can vary considerably.

PACIFIC SALMON IN THE NORTHWEST

The Pacific salmon is an anadromous species that migrates outwards and inwards along the coastal waters of the Pacific Northwest of North America. Consisting of seven species—chinook, sockeye, coho, pink, chum, steelhead, and cutthroat,[1] it mainly originates from the Columbia, the Fraser, and the Skeena river systems, in addition to three other rivers that flow from Canada to United States. Since the return migratory pattern is from north to south, and because salmon originating in the rivers of one country swim through and can be harvested in the coastal waters of the other (known as "interception"), the state of Alaska (United States) has the first opportunity to intercept salmon bound for Canadian rivers, followed by British Columbia (Canada), then the United States again in the states of Washington and Oregon (Munro, McDorman, & McKelvey, 1998). The interception of salmon has long caused friction between the multiple jurisdictions of the two countries. It therefore requires a carefully negotiated binational harvest allocation and conservation plan to account for the distinct biological characteristics of the Pacific salmon.

In an effort to expand the Fraser River Convention signed in 1930, which only covered salmon in the Fraser River and was limited to sockeye and pink salmon species, the two countries undertook a decades-long negotiation and finally reached an agreement in 1985 to create the Pacific Salmon Treaty. The elimination of high seas salmon fisheries in 1982 by the promulgation of the UNCLOS further supported the cause, making Pacific salmon a bilateral issue just between Canada and the United States (i.e., Article 66). The treaty is implemented by its regulatory body, the Pacific Salmon Commission (PSC), whose 16 commissioners meet three times a year (PSC, 2016a). Its operation also relies on the work of its committees, such as standing committees and technical committees as well as four geographical panels (Northern, Southern, Transboundary, and Fraser River panel).

Each year, the PSC receives stock and biological information from the two governments, which is analyzed by the technical committees and then sent to the panels. The panels provide fishery recommendations to the group of commissioners, which then reviews the recommendations and forwards the negotiated plans to the governments for final approval and regulatory implementation. The panels, composed of government fisheries managers, fisheries scientists, and representatives of fishing industry, are responsible for monitoring the state of the fishery and commenting on its management in their area of responsibility. The Fraser River Panel is an exception since it also engages in the in-season day-to-day management of the fishery including the decisions to open or close the fishery (PSC, 2016b).

Although the treaty proved effective in facilitating bilateral cooperation in the first several years, by the early 1990s the PSC became largely dysfunctional as the two countries were locked into a hard-nosed dispute over catch allocation principles underlying "interception." Uncompromising positions were maintained, which even led to retaliatory actions (Barkin, 2006; Munro et al., 1998). The trouble compounded as stock declines and collapses in the late 1990s forced a closure of the Canadian fishery. In 1999, a revision to the treaty (the "1999 Agreement") was signed, which renegotiated catch allocations in favor of conservation and rebuilding of the stock rather than the optimal level of capture (Barkin, 2006; McDorman, 2009). It is widely acknowledged that since the 1999 agreement the PSC has functioned relatively effectively (McRae, 2010). The most recent agreement in 2008, to be effective through the end of 2018, has reinforced this positive renewal effort by further committing to science-based conservation and harvest sharing plans. In addition, this new agreement is a reflection of the present stability and confidence that resides in the PSC as it was negotiated entirely within the commission process, unlike the 1999 agreement in which the two governments were forced to intervene to resolve the differences (PSC, 2008).

The success of the PSC in recent years is attributable to the formal integration of scientific assessment and evaluation with industry and government agencies, created through the framework of a bilateral treaty and a number of relevant committees and panels. Yet, aspects of informality have also formed a crucial element to its functioning. Substantial consultation and informal discussion is a long-standing feature representing a significant mode of interactions in the way PSC work is carried out (McRae, 2010; Temby et al., 2015). In addition, there appears to be a robust sense of willingness to cooperate among various binational stakeholders. For instance, the Restoration and Enhancement Funds established as part of the 1999 agreement to fund habitat and stock restoration research and training have been distributed roughly equally on both sides of the border, which has enhanced a sense of collective endeavor (McRae, 2010). Referring to a much greater sharing of information and openness than had existed in the past, one government representative commented about the way that fund committees operate, "you can't tell who is the Canadian member and who is the U.S. member" (quoted in McRae, 2010, p. 111). Such observations clearly emphasize the informal mechanisms that facilitate the nitty-gritty of PSC operation. Even the stalled negotiations in the 1990s are regarded as something of a friendly squabble with no malicious or distrustful intention to undercut the position of the other country, as illuminated by McRae's statement: "the government representatives on the Commission know each other well. The industry representatives in all of the sectors, commercial, recreational and aboriginal, see each other frequently and have had longstanding relationships. In this respect, the differences of the 1990s were somewhat in the nature of a family dispute!" (2010, p. 110).

GREAT LAKES FISHERIES

The Great Lakes fishery is one marked by drastic change. In the last 200 years, the structure of the fish community has been modified by extinction, depletion, and substitution of native species, and also has been heavily impacted by overfishing as well as the introduction of non-native species (Hudson & Ziegler, 2014; McCrimmon, 2002). In the region, the main target species included yellow perch, white perch, rainbow smelt, walleye, cisco, lake whitefish, lake trout, and chubs. Commercial fishing, which is currently dominated by yellow perch, has faced considerable reductions as a whole, while recreational fishing grew to be an economically significant industry beginning in the 1960s. For instance, in 2011, recreational fishing was worth over US$7 billion a year to the Great Lakes regional economy, while the commercial fishing industry contributed less than 1% of that amount (Hudson & Ziegler, 2014; Southwick Associates, 2013). Also since the 1960s, aboriginal fisheries were growing in stature as their fishing rights were reaffirmed through a series of landmark court decisions (Brenden, Brown, Ebener, Reid, & Newcomb, 2013). As a result, government management focus had been shifting to accommodate these changing balances in sector significance.

The international border bisects four of the five Great Lakes (Lakes Superior, Huron, Erie, and Ontario, with Lake Michigan entirely within the United States). The Great Lakes are a complex mosaic of more than 650 jurisdictional units including, most notably, two federal governments, eight U.S. states, the province of Ontario, two intertribal authorities, and several large metropolitan areas (McCrimmon, 2002). The state and provincial governments along with the intertribal agencies have the primary management authority, as they can establish and enforce harvest regulations, issue fishing licenses, stock fish, and carry out fish population assessment and habitat restoration plans (Gaden et al., 2013). Until the 1950s, the various agencies managed the Great Lakes fishery with little or no formal cooperation, which led to parochial and incoherent fishery practices (Gaden et al., 2013). Despite repeated attempts to coordinate a common guideline, which began as early as 1892, the self-desire to protect the jurisdictional independence of nonfederal authority, such as the U.S. states, prevented an establishment of a binational institution (Fetterolf, 1980). Two crises served as a catalyst to prompting collaboration in the mid-20th century—the severe impacts of the sea lamprey (*Petromyzon marinus*) invasion, which decimated the lake trout fishery by the late 1940s, and a perceived federal challenge to state-driven management authority within the United States (Gaden et al., 2013).

The Canadian and U.S. federal governments signed a treaty in 1954—the Convention on Great Lakes Fisheries—and created the Great Lakes Fishery Commission (GLFC). Further, a Joint Strategic Plan for Management of Great Lakes Fisheries was developed and signed by all major jurisdictions in 1981 (updated in 1997) to provide a strategic, though nonbinding, means with which to manage the Great Lakes fishery across political boundaries as an ecosystem. While these formal efforts reflect the acute need to cooperate to achieve shared goals, it nevertheless retained the existing structure of state, provincial, and federal authorities by giving the GLFC limited responsibilities that pertain to research duties and provision of management recommendations (Gaden et al., 2013). Supported by a technical committee, a lake committee exists for each of the Great Lakes to focus on the lake-specific management of fish communities. The lake committee representatives from all five lakes then form the Council of Lake Committees, representing a unifying body to address basin-wide issues such as sea lamprey control. Gaden, Krueger, Goddard, and Barnhart (2008) have stated that the Council of Lake Committees, the lake committees, and the technical committees are the key strength of the joint strategic plan, and "through these committees, agencies come together to share information, to strategize, and to commit to implementing their shared goals" (p. 58).

The GLFC's work on controlling sea lamprey population has been generally regarded as a success. A combination of three approaches—lampricides, stream barriers, and male-sterile-release, had shown to reduce its population by 90% by the late 1970s (Hudson & Ziegler, 2014; McCrimmon, 2002; VanNijnatten & Stoett, Chapter 8). Since then, the GLFC has expanded its activities to include the rehabilitation of affected species in collaboration with the various governments' efforts to stock and restore fish populations. While some consider that the GLFC has also proven to be a major force in the preservation of Great Lakes biodiversity (Ryder & Orendorff, 1999), cumulative effects of nonindigenous species and habitat/water quality degradation together with climate change-induced uncertainties pose a constant threat to the safeguarding of the many commercially important fish species. Although there have been some notable stock recoveries—for instance, lake whitefish in Lakes Michigan and Huron, and lake trout and cisco in Lake Superior—the question of whether these recoveries will endure remains an issue, given the ongoing and unpredictable changes occurring in the Great Lakes ecosystem (Brenden et al., 2013).

In a complex transboundary setting such as the Great Lakes, where multiple levels and types of governments have authority over their portions of the Great Lakes waters, and where the GLFC is largely set up as a research and recommendation-generating body, *voluntary* interjurisdictional cooperation becomes an essential requirement to achieving a politically coherent and ecologically sound management of the fishery. While the acute problem of the sea lamprey invasion had initially brought together the separate actors, it is also relevant to examine what keeps this cooperative structure on course. The case of the lake committee can be illuminating in this regard. Gaden et al. (2013) report that the meetings of the GLFC and the Lake Committee meetings have become a popular venue for various representatives since the 1960s. These committee meetings are conducive to fostering informal interactions, as they generally entail overnight stays and social events. The meetings of different lake committees are also scheduled sequentially in the same location to encourage participants to attend committee meetings other than their own and to learn about the activities of other jurisdictions and the research they are conducting (Leonard et al., 2011).

Although the GLFC was not established to harmonize regulations, it quickly became the focal point for information exchange and building rapport with one another. Gaden et al. (2013) succinctly explains:

> one of the main reasons cooperation among the jurisdictions continues to flourish today is because the fishery managers of the Great Lakes basin have this long history of working together. They expect to work together, they generally like and respect each other, and they operate as a professional "epistemic community," a community of professionals who "speak the same language." (p. 324)

Within the nonbinding framework of the joint strategic plan, well-integrated social ties have been noted that serve as a key to the effectiveness of this governance institution (Leonard et al., 2011). Hence, "a culture of cooperation" resides in the work of the lake committees, and informal approaches such as consensus building, openness, peer pressure, or other gentle ways of achieving accountability and sharing information have been fostered to help different agencies stay committed to the formal agreement of the GLFC (Gaden et al., 2008).

GROUNDFISHERIES IN THE GULF OF MAINE IN THE ATLANTIC NORTHEAST

The Gulf of Maine is a semi-enclosed sea bordered by two Canadian provinces (Nova Scotia and New Brunswick) and three U.S. states (Maine, New Hampshire, and Massachusetts), and supports a distinct and highly productive ecosystem with the presence of Georges Bank and Browns Bank. Fishing is an important commercial activity; about 505,000 metric tons of finfish and shellfish were harvested at a landed value of over US$1 billion in 2009 (Lapointe, 2013). Major fisheries target groundfish species such as cod and haddock, while other valuable species include scallops and lobster.

In 1977, with the introduction of the EEZ regime, the gulf became the exclusive domain of the Canadian and U.S. fisheries. Jurisdictional claims of the two countries, however, overlapped in an approximately 30,000 square kilometer area of key fishing ground, and the boundary dispute also involved unresolved ownership of Machias Seal Island (Cook, 2005). Following the ruling of the International Court of Justice in 1984 to delineate the international maritime boundary, Canadian and U.S. fishing activities were confined to their respective national EEZs with each country managing its fisheries resources separately. Yet, Georges Bank groundfish species are transboundary in nature. Not only do the stocks' distributions straddle the maritime boundary, individual fish also migrate substantially across the line (Pudden & VanderZwaag, 2010). Hence, many fishers (mostly U.S. fishing vessels in Canadian waters) were reported to commit boundary violations and subsequently engage in illegal fishing (Herbert, 1995). Especially, the high value of scallops provided a major incentive for U.S. scallop fishers to fish on the Canadian side, many of whom were dissatisfied with the location of the adjudicated boundary. Nevertheless, in 1990, unofficial cooperation and consultation on surveillance and enforcement of the boundary between Department of Fisheries and Oceans (Canada) and the U.S. Coast Guard eventually led to the signing of the U.S.-Canadian Fisheries Enforcement Agreement (Herbert, 1995).[2]

Despite achieving a high level of deterrence against boundary infractions, the narrow and largely protectionist and reactionary focus of the enforcement agreement had proved insufficient in conserving the commercial stocks, which had faced large-scale moratoria by the early 1990s. Herbert (1995) stated that the boundary dispute and the adjudication process had left a negative influence on U.S.-Canadian fisheries relations in the Gulf of Maine. The history of political wrangling, together with a disparate set of fisheries management philosophies and systems on either side of the border,[3] had precluded any formal agreement on the management and conservation of transboundary fisheries resources.

With the growing concerns of stock collapse, in which maintaining the status quo was not seen as a viable option, what emerged in 1994 was a series of informal discussions between Canadian and U.S. managers towards a joint commitment to reduce fishing levels and rebuild transboundary stocks in the vicinity of Georges Bank (Pudden & VanderZwaag, 2010). The U.S.-Canadian Transboundary Resources Steering Committee was created in 1995 and through its biannual meetings it began compiling joint stock assessments for cod, haddock, and yellowtail flounder in 1997. The success of this collaborative effort led to the formation of the Transboundary Resources Assessment Committee (TRAC) in 1998 and Transboundary Management Guidance Committee (TMGC) in 2000. The TRAC, co-chaired by respective federal agencies, NMFS (United States), and Department of Fisheries and Oceans (Canada), serves as the scientific arm of the TMGC, which, as a government-industry committee, then prepares guidance documents on resource sharing allocation and provides Canada and U.S. management authorities nonbinding, consensus-based advice on the management of the transboundary commercial species (Bedford Institute of Oceanography [BIO], 2015b).

The work of the TRAC and TMGC has proven successful in developing joint scientific stock assessments for a number of species and a sharing agreement for eastern Georges Bank groundfishes (Pudden & VanderZwaag, 2010). Affirming its influential role in 2003, Canadian and U.S. management authorities officially agreed to apply the TMGC's resource-sharing allocation formula for Georges Bank cod, haddock, and yellowtail flounder to their Gulf of Maine FMPs. The TRAC and TMGC processes have been sectorally oriented, however, relying on single stock assessments rather than approaching with an ecosystem-based perspective. In response to this growing recognition, the Steering Committee established an integration committee in 2005. Also, three working groups on species at risk, fish habitat, and oceans management have been formed to address collaborative opportunities beyond the focused realm of fisheries management (BIO, 2015a). Hence, this bilateral institutional arrangement currently operating in the Gulf of Maine is geared towards creating a more integrated management system.

Pudden and Vanderzwaag (2010) have described the development of the bilateral fisheries management institution in the Gulf of Maine as "'under the radar' navigations towards cooperative fisheries management with initiatives being largely of an informal nature" (p. 178). Due to the antagonistic history of the boundary dispute, which is in part still ongoing as it relates to the unresolved sovereignty claim of Machias Seal Island, and other political and technical differences in the way fisheries are managed on either side of the border, long-lasting and durable formal agreements have failed to take root. What filled the institutional void in light of the deepening concerns about stock collapses were informal discussions at the regional level between Canadian and U.S. scientists, resource managers, and fishing industry representatives. This effort brought increased communication and cooperation on fisheries management issues, which eventually led to the establishment of the U.S.-Canadian Transboundary Steering Committee acting as an informal advisory group (McDorman, 2009; Pudden & VanderZwaag, 2010). The work of the committee and its subcommittee has served to promote collaborative resource management in the area, and "scientific and bureaucratic cooperation has been achieved without high costs of administration and formalized structures" (Pudden & VanderZwaag, 2010, p. 197). With these informal arrangements based on "good neighborliness" persevering into the future, further opportunities for strengthening the bilateral relationship may develop, leading to more robust transboundary management mechanisms for key groundfish species as well as the marine ecosystem as an integrated whole. Such a vision appears to be a crucial one to pursue, given the continued difficulties in rebuilding the fish stocks in the region (see Ames, 2004; Layzer, 2011). The near collapse of the cod fishery in the Gulf of Maine and a subsequent fishing moratorium in 2014 have reiterated the dire status of this increasingly fragile resource (Abel, 2014; NMFS, 2014). An uncertain trajectory for future governance remains, which suggests a need to revisit the institutional arrangement that has set the process in motion.

DISCUSSION

Government organizations and collaborative networks are the central political and management mechanism with which to elicit bilateral cooperation; that is, countries must rely on them to manage shared resources. Hence, an enhanced understanding of their characteristics that can inform their design and operation is of paramount importance to achieving ecosystem-based management of transboundary fish stocks.

One way to gain a more nuanced interpretation of such institutions is through the degree of formality embedded in the attained agreements. The most formal, and prominent, arrangements involve bilateral or multilateral treaties signed by the heads of state, which convey binding commitments with full international legal status. On the contrary, tacit agreements possibly represent the most informal institutional type, which are akin to "unspoken rules" that are implied or inferred rather than directly stated (Lipson, 1991). In between are diverse forms that include verbal or written nonbinding declarations, memoranda of understanding, joint action plans, and agreed minutes. The three shared fisheries under discussion in this chapter have also shown varied levels of formality in the way the respective governance institutions are organized. Table 7.1 summarizes the institutional features that highlight this result.

The cases of the Pacific salmon and the Great Lakes fisheries both feature a highly formalized bilateral institutional setup, with the establishment of the Pacific Salmon Treaty and the Convention on the Great Lakes Fisheries, respectively, as well as the two binational commissions (PSC and GLFC). Together, they create binding expectations and official pledges to compliance. Further, the formal institutions involved in governing Pacific salmon can be considered somewhat more developed than the Great Lakes apparatus, since the geographically designated panels are given the responsibility to make regulatory recommendations that directly contribute to the development of fishery plans, while the mandate of GLFC is limited to, though no less important, information exchange and joint scientific

Table 7.1
Institutional Features of U.S.-Canadian Binational Fishery Governance

	Binational Fishery Network		
Institutional Features	**Pacific Salmon**	**Great Lakes**	**Gulf of Maine-Georges Bank Groundfishery**
Main target fish species	Chinook, sockeye, coho, pink, chum	Yellow perch, white perch, rainbow smelt, walleye, cisco, lake whitefish, lake trout, and chubs	Cod, haddock, yellowtail flounder
International legal frameworks	UN Convention on the Law of the Sea (1982)	None	UN Convention on the Law of the Sea (1982)
Binational agreements and legal frameworks	Fraser River Convention (1930); Pacific Salmon Treaty (1985)	Convention on Great Lakes Fisheries (1954)	U.S.-Canadian Fisheries Enforcement Agreement (1990)
Formal binational organizations	Pacific Salmon Commission	Great Lakes Fishery Commission	None
Key binational committees	Standing Committee; Technical Committee; "Geographical" Panel	Lake Committee; Council of Lake Committees	Transboundary Resources Steering Committee; TRAC; TMGC
Integration of scientific assessment	Stock and biological information from both governments are analyzed and reviewed by technical committees and panels, forming basis for FMPs to be approved and implemented by the governments	Scientific data is collected, analyzed, and interpreted by field-level biologists of technical committees who then report the findings to lake committees to inform management actions	TRAC prepares, conducts, and reviews stock assessment analyses and communicates results to TMGC who then provide nonbinding recommendations to the governments on the status of the resources and likely consequences of policy choices

Regulatory apparatus	PSC makes coordinated recommendations to U.S. and Canadian federal governments who each provide funding and regulatory oversight to state, provincial, aboriginal/tribal, and federal agencies to manage their deferred areas	No binational regulatory apparatus, with U.S. state and tribal governments and Canada-Ontario all having separate regulatory authority in their jurisdictional waters	TMGC's sharing allocation agreement for cod, haddock, and yellowtail flounder relies on domestic regulatory implementation of the two countries
Inclusion	U.S. and Canadian federal regulatory agencies, state and provincial agencies, aboriginal/intertribal organizations, industry representatives	U.S. and Canadian federal, state, and provincial management agencies, aboriginal/intertribal authorities	U.S. and Canadian scientists and managers representing federal regulatory agencies, industry representatives, fisher associations, New England Fishery Management Council
Informal relationships	Robust and long-lived; Facilitated through the committee and panel system	Robust; Facilitated through the committee system, coordinated research, and the implementation of a Joint Strategic Plan for Management of Great Lakes Fisheries (1981/1997)	Robust despite absence of formal binational structures, and facilitated through the bilateral informal committee system

Abbreviations: FMP, fishery management plan; PSC, Pacific Salmon Commission; TMGC, Transboundary Management Guidance Committee; TRAC, Transboundary Resources Assessment Committee.

research on Great Lakes fish stocks and sea lamprey. Moreover, the Fraser River Panel of the PSC is equipped with an advanced task of making in-season harvest regulations, a unique decision-making power given to a binational committee. The institutional agreements that guide the groundfisheries in Georges Bank in the Gulf of Maine are the least formal kind of the three, as neither treaty nor a joint management body has been established with the current structure of the steering committee remaining strictly advisory (see Table 7.1).

While the degree of formality in the institutional arrangements varies, what appears to be common in all three fisheries is the underlying functioning of informal mechanisms that supports and lubricates the implementation of the formal structure. In all three cases, as shown in Table 7.1, the science integration process, and especially the review of management recommendations, occurs through various committees that have inclusive membership among government and industry representatives. Emphasis is on creating and sustaining informal relationships through frequent interactions, casual exchange of information, relationship building, and awareness of each other, which are often cited as the key components to creating an effective fisheries regime. These elements are what build the normative and morally governed obligations as well as the shared cultural understandings and common "ways of doing things" that foster reciprocity and cooperation among transnational actors who otherwise may have little compelling incentive to engage in a cooperative behavior (Müller, 2004; Scott, 2008). In addition, there is a long macro-history of amicable relations between Canada and the United States. As two neighbors who have worked together closely on many strategic, economic, and environmental issues, a broader basis for establishing and sustaining strong informal institutions likely exist for these shared fisheries as well.

Informal networks among states and transnational actors are, in fact, not rare and peripheral (in the U.S.-Canadian context, see Gonzalez, Chapter 12). The scale and the diversity of such arrangements indicate that they are an important feature of world politics as well as transboundary environmental systems (Lipson, 1991; Lloret, 2013). Lipson (1991) argues that "informality is best understood as a device for minimizing the impediments to cooperation" (p. 500). We further claim that it is in fact essential to enabling cooperation. We tend to think that it is always present, albeit at times latent and not well understood. On the one hand, verbal agreements between parties offer greater flexibility, privacy, and speed of implementation than formally signed documents, but they may be considered less reliable or easily abandoned (Lipson, 1991). On the other hand, social norms and other tacit cultural understandings that promote collective action can be slow to build, resistant to change, and exhibit considerable inertia (North, 1990; Roland, 2004). Despite such a wide range of possibilities, informal institutions would prove advantageous when the rate of change of resource conditions are faster than the rate at which formal institutions can adapt (Lloret, 2013) and when transaction costs of amassing information and of engaging in political renegotiation appear too large. Informal institutions can thus be particularly relied upon to deal with uncertain events and to overcome crises. From our three fishery cases, we can identify that informal interactions are structured and reinforced through networks, which are institutional channels through which ideas and practices are transmitted and emulated among like-minded individuals. Hence, they facilitate embeddedness and social capital in the way the agencies engage in collaboration with one another (Owen-Smith & Powell, 2008). As the significance of these topics remains relatively underdeveloped, informality in institutional arrangements likely requires further research attention in the hope of improving the transboundary governance of shared fisheries and other environmental resources.

CONCLUSION

The substantial economic value and precarious ecological robustness of U.S.-Canadian shared fisheries ensure that their binational governance will remain an ongoing challenge. National sovereignty adds a layer of complexity to an already delicate balance of transboundary coordination. Nevertheless, the management of these fisheries is in large part a "technocratic" issue of scientific integration and bureaucratic decision making. As we have illustrated using three examples, transboundary fisheries governance occurs through collaborative networks of civil servants, industry representatives, and other professionals interacting through formal and informal channels. These fisheries and associated networks exhibit substantial variation in their socioeconomic meaning and composition (i.e., commercial or recreational), the biology of the fish and the ecological characteristics of the system, and the existence of context-specific organizations.

Yet they also exhibit important and instructive similarities. All three fishery collaborative networks are comprised of robust informal links among members, facilitating the exchange of information about problems and potential responses. These links take time to develop and are enabled by multilateral initiatives such as task forces, as well as many casual forums, including ad hoc working groups, phone calls, and drinks after work. Their existence and significance in the institutional processes suggest that, in "commons" problems like wildlife and biodiversity, and perhaps also with upstream-downstream "directional" problems like pollution, scholarly and technocratic investigations into how policy is made should take informality into account. Despite state sovereignty, national and international legal and regulatory regimes, and binational commissions, a substantial amount of the cooperative decision making for managing North American ecosystems is undertaken by career civil servants and other professionals with long-standing relationships operating through interagency, trans-national—and largely informal—networks.

ACKNOWLEDGMENT

This work was supported by the Social Science and Humanities Research Council of Canada [SSHRC grant number 435-2014-0970].

NOTES

1. Because steelhead and cutthroat are generally not caught in ocean fisheries, transboundary capture and management has focused on the five species of Pacific Salmon—chinook, sockeye, coho, pink, and chum.
2. The 1990 Fisheries Enforcement Agreement stipulates that Canada and the United States each enacts domestic regulations making it illegal for its nationals to fish in the waters of the other country, such that boundary infractions violate not just the laws of the foreign country, but also those of the own country.
3. Generally, U.S. management policy has focused on input controls restricting the intensity of fishing effort through area closures, gear specifications, days at sea allocations, and minimum size of fish caught. This is in contrast to the Canadian approach, which is mainly based on output controls that limit the amount of fish caught through the use of total allowable catches (TACs) and quotas for each species (see Herbert, 1995).

REFERENCES

Abel, D. (2014, November 10). Gulf of Maine fishermen face 6-month cod ban. *The Boston Globe*. Retrieved from: http://www.bostonglobe.com/metro/2014/11/10/federal-fishing-officials-ban-cod-fishing-gulf-maine-for-six-months/iD5F3K4AMJFWmwxuO3acKI/story.html

Acheson, J. M. (2006). Institutional failure in resource management. *Annual Review of Anthropology*, *35*, 117–134.

Agranoff, R., & McGuire, M. (2001). Big questions in public network management research. *Journal of Public Administration Research and Theory*, *11*(3), 295–326.

Allan, J. D., Abell, R., Hogan, Z., Revenga, C., Taylor, B. W., Welcomme, R. L., & Winemiller, K. (2005). Overfishing of inland waters. *BioScience*, *55*(12), 1041–1051.

Ames, E. P. (2004). Atlantic cod stock structure in the Gulf of Maine. *Fisheries*, *29*(1), 10–28.

Barkin, S. (2006). The Pacific salmon dispute and Canada-U.S. environmental relations. In P. Le Prestre & P. Stoett (Eds.), *Bilateral ecopolitics: Continuity and change in Canadian-American environmental relations* (pp. 197–210). Aldershot, UK: Ashgate.

Beddington, J. R., Agnew, D. J., & Clark, C. W. (2007). Current problems in the management of marine fisheries. *Science*, *316*(5832), 1713–1716.

Bedford Institute of Oceanography (2015a). Canada-U.S. transboundary resources steering committee. Retrieved from http://www.bio.gc.ca/info/intercol/sc-cd/index-en.php

Bedford Institute of Oceanography (2015b). International collaborations. Retrieved from http://www.bio.gc.ca/info/intercol/index-en.php

Brenden, T. O., Brown, R. W., Ebener, M. P., Reid, K., & Newcomb, T. J. (2013). Great Lakes commercial fisheries: Historical overview and prognoses for the future. In W. W. Taylor, A. J. Lynch, & N. J. Leonard (Eds.), *Great Lakes fisheries policy and management* (pp. 339–397). East Lansing, MI: Michigan State University Press.

Chuenpagdee, R., & Song, A. M. (2012). Institutional thinking in fisheries governance: Broadening perspectives. *Current Opinion in Environmental Sustainability*, *4*, 309–315.

Cochrane, K. L. (2000). Reconciling sustainability, economic efficiency and equity in fisheries: The one that got away? *Fish and Fisheries*, *1*(1), 3–21.

Cook, B. (2005). Lobster boat diplomacy: The Canada-US grey zone. *Marine Policy*, *29*(5), 385–390.

Cullis-Suzuki, S., & Pauly, D. (2010). Failing the high seas: A global evaluation of regional fisheries management organizations. *Marine Policy*, *34*(5), 1036–1042.

Fetterolf, C. M. (1980). Why a Great Lakes Fishery Commission and why a Sea Lamprey International Symposium? *Canadian Journal of Fisheries and Aquatic Science*, *37*(11), 1588–1593.

Ficke, A. D., Myrick, C. A., & Hansen, L. J. (2007). Potential impacts of global climate change on freshwater fisheries. *Reviews in Fish Biology and Fisheries*, *17*(4), 581–613.

Fisheries and Oceans Canada. (2012, April 24). Harper government commits to the responsible protection and conservation of Canada's fisheries [Press release]. Retrieved from http://www.dfo-mpo.gc.ca/media/npress-communique/2012/hq-ac12-eng.htm

Fisheries and Oceans Canada. (2015). Changes to the Fisheries Act. Retrieved from http://www.dfo-mpo.gc.ca/pnw-ppe/changes-changements/index-eng.html

Gaden, M., Goddard, C., & Read, J. (2013). Multi-jurisdictional management of the shared Great Lakes Fishery: Transcending conflict and diffuse political authority. In W. W. Taylor, A. J. Lynch, & N. J. Leonard (Eds.), *Great Lakes fisheries policy and management* (pp. 305–337). East Lansing, MI: Michigan State University Press.

Gaden, M., Krueger, C., Goddard, C., & Barnhart, G. (2008). A Joint Strategic Plan for Management of Great Lakes fisheries: A cooperative regime in a multi-jurisdictional setting. *Aquatic Ecosystem Health & Management*, *11*(1), 50–60.

Healy, R. G., VanNijnatten, D., & López-Vallejo, M. (2014). *Environmental policy in North America: Approaches, capacity, and the management of transboundary issues*. Toronto, ON: University of Toronto Press.

Herbert, G. J. (1995). Fisheries relations in the Gulf of Maine implications of an arbitrated maritime boundary. *Marine Policy*, *19*(4), 301–316.

Hudson, J. C., & Ziegler, S. S. (2014). Environment, culture, and the Great Lakes fisheries. *Geographical Review*, *104*(4), 391–413.

Imperial, M. T. (2005). Using collaboration as a governance strategy: Lessons from six watershed management programs. *Administration & Society*, *37*(3), 281–320.

Isset, K. R., Mergel, I. A., LeRoux, K., Mischen, P. A., & Rethemeyer, R. K. (2011). Networks in public administration scholarship: Understanding where we are and where we need to go [Supplement 1]. *Journal of Public Administration Research and Theory*, *21*, i157–i173.

Jentoft, S. (2004). Institutions in fisheries: What they are, what they do, and how they change. *Marine Policy*, *28*(2), 137–149.

Jentoft, S., & Chuenpagdee, R. (2009). Fisheries and coastal governance as a wicked problem. *Marine Policy*, *33*(4), 553–560.

Jinnah, S. (2014). *Post-treaty politics: Secretariat influence in global environmental governance*. Cambridge, MA: MIT Press.

Lapointe, G. (2013). *State of the Gulf of Maine Report: Commercial fisheries*. The Gulf of Maine Council on the Marine Environment.

Retrieved from http://www.gulfofmaine.org/2/wp-content/uploads/2014/03/commercial-fisheries-theme-paper-webversion.pdf

Layzer, J. A. (2011). *The environmental case: Translating value into policy* (3rd ed.). Washington, DC: CQ Press.

Leonard, N. J., Taylor, W. W., Goddard, C. I., Frank, K. A., Krause, A. E., & Schechter, M. G. (2011). Information flow within the social network structure of a Joint Strategic Plan for Management of Great Lakes Fisheries. *North American Journal of Fisheries Management*, *31*(4), 629–655.

Lipson, C. (1991). Why are some international agreements informal? *International Organization*, *45*(4), 495–538.

Lloret, A. (2013). Informal agreements in transboundary water resources. In A. Dinar & A. Rapoport (Eds.), *Analyzing global environmental issues* (pp. 170–185). New York, NY: Routledge.

McConnell, M. L. (2010). Observations on compliance and enforcement and regional fisheries institutions: Overcoming the limitations of the Law of the Sea. In D. A. Russell & D. L. VanderZwaag (Eds.), *Recasting transboundary fisheries management arrangements in light of sustainable principles* (pp. 71–98). Leiden, the Netherlands: Martinus Nijhoff Publishers.

McCrimmon, D. A., Jr. (2002). Sustainable fisheries management in the Great Lakes: Scientific and operational challenges. *Lakes & Reservoirs: Research and Management*, *7*(3), 241–254.

McDorman, T. L. (2009). Canada-United States cooperative approaches to shared marine fishery resources: Territorial subversion. *Michigan Journal of International Law*, *30*, 665–687.

McRae, D. (2010). The Pacific Salmon Commission. In D. A. Russell & D. L. VanderZwaag (Eds.), *Recasting transboundary fisheries management arrangements in light of sustainable principles* (pp. 101–113). Leiden, the Netherlands: Martinus Nijhoff Publishers.

Meltzer, E. (1994). Global overview of straddling and highly migratory fish stocks: The nonsustainable nature of high seas fisheries. *Ocean Development & International Law*, *25*(3), 255–344.

Mora, C., Myers, R. A., Coll, M., Libralato, S., Pitcher, T.J., Sumaila, R.U., . . . Worm, B. (2009). Management effectiveness of the world's marine fisheries. *PLOS Biology*, *7*(6), e1000131. doi:10.1371/journal.pbio.1000131

Müller, H. (2004). Arguing, bargaining and all that: Communicative action, rationalist theory and the logic of appropriateness in international relations. *European Journal of International Relations*, *10*(3), 395–435.

Munro, G. R., McDorman, T., & McKelvey, R. (1998). Transboundary fishery resources and the Canada United States Pacific Salmon Treaty. *Canadian-American Public Policy*, *33*, 1–43.

Myers, R. A., & Worm, B. (2003). Rapid worldwide depletion of predatory fish communities. *Nature*, *423*(6937), 280–283.

National Marine Fisheries Service. (n.d.). Regional fishery management councils. Retrieved from http://www.nmfs.noaa.gov/sfa/management/councils/

National Marine Fisheries Service. (2014, August 1). Statement regarding new information showing continued decline of Gulf of Maine cod stock [Press release]. Retrieved from http://www.nefsc.noaa.gov/press_release/pr2014/other/MA1402/

North, D. C. (1990). *Institutions, institutional change and economic performance*. Cambridge, UK: Cambridge University Press.

Owen-Smith, J., & Powell, W. W. (2008). Networks and institutions. In R. Greenwood, C. Oliver, K. Sahlin, & R. Suddaby (Eds.), *The Sage handbook of organizational institutionalism* (pp. 596–623). London, UK: Sage.

Pacific Salmon Commission. (2008). New bilateral agreement [Press release]. Retrieved from http://www.psc.org/pubs/AnnexIV/AnnexIVPressRelease22May08.pdf

Pacific Salmon Commission. (2016a). Commission meetings. Retrieved from: http://www.psc.org/meetings/

Pacific Salmon Commission. (2016b). Fraser River Panel. Retrieved from http://www.psc.org/about-us/structure/panels/fraser-river/

Pauly, D., Christensen, V., Guénette, S., Pitcher, T. J., Sumaila U. R., Walters, C. J., . . . Zeller, D. (2002). Towards sustainability in world fisheries. *Nature*, *418*(6898), 689–695.

Postel, S., & Carpenter, S. R. 1997. Freshwater ecosystem services. In G. Daily (Ed.), *Nature's services* (pp. 195–214). Washington, DC: Island Press.

Pudden, E. J., & VanderZwaag, D. (2010). Canada-United States bilateral fisheries management in the Gulf of Maine: Struggling towards sustainability. In D. A. Russell & D. L. VanderZwaag (Eds.), *Recasting transboundary fisheries management arrangements in light of sustainable principles* (pp. 177–207). Leiden, the Netherlands: Martinus Nijhoff Publishers.

Roland, G. (2004). Understanding institutional change: Fast-moving and slow-moving institutions. *Studies in Comparative International Development*, *38*(4), 109–131.

Russell, D. A., & VanderZwaag, D. L. (Eds.). (2010). *Recasting transboundary fisheries management arrangements in light of sustainable principles*. Leiden, the Netherlands: Martinus Nijhoff Publishers.

Ryder, R. A., & Orendorff, J. A. (1999). Embracing biodiversity in the Great Lakes ecosystem. In W. W. Taylor & C. P. Ferreri (Eds.), *Great Lakes fisheries policy and management* (pp. 113–143). East Lansing, MI: Michigan State University Press.

Scott, W. R. (2008). *Institutions and organizations: Ideas and interests* (3rd ed.). Los Angeles, CA: Sage Publications.

Southwick Associates. (2013). *Sportfishing in America: An economic force for conservation*. Alexandria, VA: American Sportfishing Association.

Sumaila, U. R., Alder, J., & Keith, H. (2006). Global scope and economics of illegal fishing. *Marine Policy*, *30*(6), 696–703.

Temby, O. (2015). The limits of transnational environmental network governance in North America. *Global Environmental Politics*, *15*(3), 176–183.

Temby, O., Rastogi, A., Sandall, J., Cooksey, R., & Hickey, G. M. (2015). Interagency trust and communication in the transboundary governance of Pacific salmon fisheries. *Review of Policy Research*, *32*(1), 79–99.

U.S. Fish and Wildlife Service. (2011). *Great Lakes Fish and Wildlife Restoration Act of 2006: Progress 1990–2010*. Washington, DC: USFWS Region 3 Fisheries Program. Retrieved from http://www.fws.gov/midwest/fisheries/glfwra-grants/Congress-report-1990-2010.pdf

Walker, B., Barrett, S., Polasky, S., Galaz, V., Folke, C., Engstrom, G., . . . de Zeeuw, A. (2009). Looming global-scale failures and missing institutions. *Science*, *325*(5946), 1345–1346.

Watson, R., & Pauly, D. (2001). Systematic distortions in world fisheries catch trends. *Nature*, *414*(6863), 534–536.

Welcomme, R. L., Cowx, I. G., Coates, D., Béné, C., Funge-Smith, S., Halls, A., & Lorenzen, K. (2010). Inland capture fisheries. *Philosophical Transactions of the Royal Society B: Biological Sciences*, *365*(1554), 2881–2896.

Wolf, A. T., Natharius, J. A., Danielson, J. J., Ward, B. S., & Pender, J. K. (1999). International river basins of the world. *International Journal of Water Resources Development*, *15*(4), 387–427.

EIGHT

Continental Counter-Invasion

Invasive Species Management in North America

DEBORA VANNIJNATTEN AND PETER STOETT

INTRODUCTION

Few threats to environmental security are as pernicious as the introduction of alien invasive species, widely considered to be the second greatest threat to biodiversity after habitat destruction (Lodge et al., 2006; Millenium Ecosystem Assessment Board, 2005).[1] Calls for coordinated action have come from the now-defunct Global Invasive Species Program (GISP), the Subsidiary Body on Scientific, Technical and Technological Advice to the Convention on Biological Diversity (SBSTTA-CBD), and the Invasive Species Specialist Group of the International Union for the Conservation of Nature (ISSG-IUCN).[2] North America is considered to be "extremely vulnerable" to the introduction of invasive species due to the highly interdependent economies and transportation systems of the three countries, as well as cross-border ecosystems that offer ready pathways for invasion, such as mountain ranges, deserts, freshwater lakes and rivers, and shared coastlines (Commission for Environmental Cooperation [CEC], 2008). Indeed, invasive species are one of the key drivers of native species extinction in North America, reflecting the impact of increased competition for food, space, or reproductive sites, and the introduction of parasites and disease (CEC, 2008, p. 32).

Invasions on the continent range from the microbial level to large animals. The spread of the Zika virus into Miami from South America, and the invasion of the Florida Everglades by discarded massive Burmese pythons and other snakes are but two high-profile examples. However, it can be argued that the most pernicious and costly invasions are of aquatic and plant species, which have combined to reshape the landscape of North America and will likely have an even more pronounced impact as climate change progresses. Given the sheer breadth of hydrological and terrestrial connections across the continent, and the complexity of the invasive species management (ISM) challenge, a wide spectrum of transboundary cooperation is required to effectively address this problem—from science, monitoring and information systems, to prioritizing and decision making, through to implementation and enforcement.

One of the central themes of this volume is the effective establishment of transnational networks of governance and expertise in emerging issues that affect the viability of North American ecosystems. This chapter examines the shared governance architecture with respect to prevention and early detection of invasive species. First, we map out the institutional elements as well as the national and transnational networks operating in ISM prevention and early detection, with a view to understanding the manner in which they interact and the intensity of their interactions. Second, we assess the degree to which these institutions and networks contribute to transboundary governance capacity, specifically, the capacity to prevent new introductions through the closing of invasion pathways and risk assessment protocols, establish monitoring and surveillance infrastructure, and coordinate activities in these areas across jurisdictions. We focus largely on ISM efforts related to aquatic species in the U.S.-Canadian context, but also briefly discuss the developing continental network on invasive plants. (Indeed there is much overlap here since many of the most problematic invasive plants, such as hydrilla and hyacinth, are themselves aquatic.)

A series of arguments is developed. The first is that the interactions between networks and institutions in the prevention and early detection architecture for invasive species might be characterized as recursive and iterative in nature. The interwebbing of overlapping policy (primarily transgovernmental) networks as well as research and information networks have created a mesh of connections that overlay a wide range of agency actors, scientific communities, and the nongovernmental sector, drawing them into research activities, coordinated policy activities, and even advocacy vis-à-vis their own governments. These network activities have been implicated in placing prevention and early detection on government agendas as policy priorities (and keeping them there), as well as fostering the development of a clearer set of objectives and firm mandates under (existing) formal transboundary agreements. Despite setbacks, both Canada and the United States have made notable progress towards national ISM strategies, and in the case of invasive plants, a continent-wide organization—under international guidelines—assists in the coordination of ISM, especially with respect to prevention. Perhaps the most significant threat to transboundary network and institution activities on both aquatic and plant invasive species, however, is the dwindling of federal and state or provincial resources. This is likely to have a detrimental impact, particularly on more informal transnational networks serving critical functions associated with disseminating scientific knowledge and building policy consensus.

INVASIVE SPECIES AS A TRANSBOUNDARY GOVERNANCE CAPACITY CHALLENGE

As an issue area, invasive species can be framed by multiple, politically charged themes, such as national security, human health, economic resilience, climate change, and others (see Stoett, 2010); regardless, they are a severe threat to ecological integrity and human prosperity.[3]

Aquatic invasive species are defined by U.S. legislation as "a nonindigenous species that threatens the diversity or abundance of native species or the ecological stability of infested waters, or commercial, agricultural, aquacultural or recreational activities dependent on such waters " (Nonindigenous Aquatic Nuisance Prevention and Control Act of 1990, 2004, section 1003). A high number of aquatic invasive species have established themselves in North America: more than 180 in the Great Lakes Basin (Ontario Ministry of Natural Resources, 2013); at least 94 with critical impact in the Rio Bravo/Laguna Madre Ecological Region (Mendoza et al., 2011, p. 1); and approximately 64 in the Gulf of Maine Region (Gulf of Maine Council, 2010, p. 1). Familiar culprits include the zebra and quagga mussels, the round goby, the sea lamprey (see Chapter 7 in this volume), the dreaded Asian carps, the alewife, the lionfish, and many others.[4] Pathways of invasion include ship ballast water, aquaculture, recreational activities (including stocking for sportfishing), aquarium releases, live food and bait, biological controls, and even ecological restoration efforts.

Similarly, invasive plants have a profound impact on local ecology (Luken & Thieret, 1997). Often the result of careless or ill-informed ornamental landscaping, they have found their way here through various trade routes, incidental releases of seeds, and purposeful introductions for agriculture and horticulture. Well-known invasive plants in North America include various forms of kudzu, knotweed, giant hogweed, dalmation toadlax, English holly, gorse, the common water hyacinth, hydrilla, and, perhaps most commonly, purple loosestrife. The latter has a fascinating history. It was brought to North America from Europe when early, wind-powered ships used native European soil as ballast. However, we need not evoke Asia or Europe, or even South America, to discuss the invasive plant problem in North America. Many invasive plants have covered an intracontinental range, spreading throughout the continent, moving from east to west or north to south or vice versa. For example, several of the state-listed noxious weeds in New Mexico, such as the black henbane, scotch thistle, and poison hemlock, originated in Canada.[5] Some plants are not just invasive in themselves; they (and plant and timber products) are also vectors for the spread of invasive insects (such as the emerald ash borer, listed as one of the top 10 invasive species by the North American Invasive Species Network [NAISN]) and agricultural pests. Even the transport of seeds is a great challenge. Indeed, 7% of all pests seized at U.S. ports of entry and border crossings between 1984 and 2000 were "plant propogative material" (McCullough, Work, Cavey, Liebhold, & Marshall, 2006). Changes in species ranges due to climatic variations are also an important factor, since this will have knock-off effects on pollinators, migratory species, forest biodiversity, and other crucial ecosystem services.

Taken together, then, aquatic and plant invasions pose serious, ongoing threats to agricultural production, economic development, food security, biodiversity, and other integral aspects of North American life. Though the costs of inaction are steep, the requirements for successfully addressing the invasive species problem are also considerable.[6] The "three-stage hierarchical approach" to ISM is viewed as the international gold standard and places very high expectations on governments, both in terms of their domestic policy activities and also their ability to work together. The hierarchy involves the following:

1. The prevention of new invasions as the overriding priority.
2. Early detection and rapid response (commonly known as EDRR; i.e., the identification of biological invasions as soon as possible, and the immediate eradication, where possible, of new infestations).
3. Management/containment of established populations of nonnative species such that their impact is mitigated. This includes the sustainable use of invasive species.

Given that invasive species are practically impossible to eradicate once established, it is critical to prevent the introduction of new invasive species into ecosystems in the first place (White House Council on Environmental Quality, 2010, p. 22). To achieve this aim, we need to determine and cut off the pathways (or vectors) of invasion and we also need assessment programs to evaluate candidate species that would be invasive should they arrive (e.g., from rivers in the Baltic region, or the Asian horticultural trade), so as to reduce risk. This requires mechanisms to ensure, for example, that the international shipping industry manages its ballast water appropriately, that the aquaculture, pet, and horticulture industries guard against intentional and unintentional "releases," and that border controls and inspections are enhanced. Further, the activities of users need to be regulated in very specific ways to minimize the risk of new introductions of invasive species (e.g., via ballast water or seeds imported for horticulture). A range of risk assessment, surveillance, and monitoring programs need to be put in place as well as mechanisms for direct and timely information sharing. Science-based risk assessment of species and pathways of introduction can provide early warning of potential threats.

These tasks require a multifaceted architecture for cooperation across borders that facilitates policy consensus and common action on all these fronts, as well as the sharing and coordinated deployment of resources. The key roles of institutions and networks in coordinating behavior, reducing transaction costs, and encouraging commitment to a specific enterprise (Buchanan & Keohane, 2006, p. 1) have been examined extensively by those studying the design of common pool resource management (e.g., Ostrom, 1990), international environmental governance (e.g., Biermann, Pattberg, & Zelli, 2010), socioecological systems (Berkes, Colding, & Folke, 2003), and water governance (VanNijnatten, Johns, Bryk-Friedman, & Krantzberg, 2016).[7]

Similarly, we focus here on institutions and networks that operate in a transboundary context, and in particular their capacity to foster functionally intense interactions, learn and adapt to new knowledge and changing conditions, and coordinate activities across governments and a range of policy actors in ways that support longer-term relationships (VanNijnatten et al., 2016; VanNijnatten & Craik, 2013, p. 10). Institutions are understood here as sets of *rules* shaping or constraining the behavior of actors, while networks are sets of *relations* that form structures that may also constrain or enable actors (Hafner-Burton, Kahler, & Montgomery, 2009, p. 560). In our analysis, we are particularly interested in the ways in which agency officials, civil society, and experts are linked through channels of information exchange, discussion, and diffusion. The point of studying networks is to identify patterns of relationships that might serve as "hubs, cliques, or brokers" of interest and can impact decision making (Hafner-Burton et al., 2009, p. 560).[8]

The functional intensity of transboundary institutions serves as an indicator of the extent to which institutions and networks are engaged in deeper forms of collaboration that require greater engagement and commitment from state and nonstate actors. VanNijnatten (2006) measures the

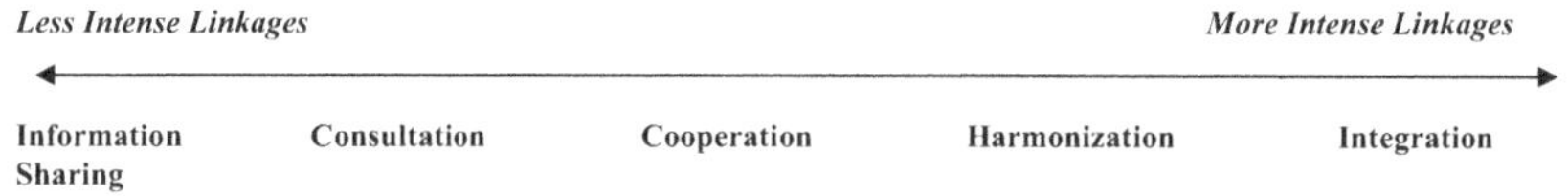

FIGURE 8.1 Functional Intensity Spectrum (VanNijnatten, 2006).

functional intensity of transboundary institutions on a spectrum ranging from less intense linkages, such as information sharing and consultation, to more intense activities, such as cooperation, harmonization, and even integration (Figure 8.1). This indicator is intended to uncover the aims and nature of the transboundary institutions and networks that operate on ISM. Given the focus on prevention and detection, the whole range of shared activities is required—information sharing, joint development and adoption of risk-assessment protocols, joint development and operation of monitoring and surveillance frameworks, and, in some cases, the harmonization of regulations (e.g., ballast water practices and the regulation of the ornamental horticulture trade).

Another key indicator of transboundary capacity, particularly in a context where scientific knowledge is new or is rapidly evolving (certainly the case for invasive biology), is the degree to which institutions and networks are capable of responding to changing conditions and new knowledge (e.g., Berkes et al., 2003). The objective here is to encourage policy learning, or what Kemp and Weehuizen (2005, p. 1) refer to as a conscious "change in thinking" about a problem and its associated policy, as well as offering opportunities for sharing "lessons learned." Out of information exchange and dialogue, and the learning process that follows, it is hoped that transboundary institutions and networks can facilitate consensus on actions to be taken, yet be nimble enough to reevaluate that consensus when science provides new insights.

Moreover, there is a great deal of decentralization, diversity, and pluralism within and across issue-specific domains in global environmental governance (e.g., Ostrom 2009a, 2009b; Stoett, 2012), and the ISM architecture is North America is no exception. Recent critiques in the policy capacity literature argue that there needs to be a greater focus on what we refer to here as "coordinative capacity," whether across government or across conventional boundaries and functional definitions of policies. In the international relations literature, the degree of coordination across multiple institutions and networks operating on (aspects of) the same issue is seen as a key variable that describes the potential of governance arrangements to achieve a common purpose (e.g., Biermann et al., 2010). VanNijnatten and Craik (2013, p. 10) note that this indicator can be investigated empirically through a focus on "points of interaction . . . across governance levels and scales, between governments and private actors, and across policy fields" as well as analyzing the degree to which these exchanges are mutually reinforcing.

The remainder of this chapter maps out some of the transboundary institutions and networks operating in ISM in North America, in both the aquatic and plant cases. It then applies the three indicators of institutional and network strength—functional intensity, learning, and coordinative capacity—to provide initial reflections on how the continental architecture contributes to the prevention and detection of invasive species. We adopt a "broad-brush" approach here, highlighting the most salient features of what is actually a very complex, multiscalar ISM governance architecture.

Institutions, Networks, and the Transboundary Governance of ISM in North America

The ISM architecture in North America is an interconnected system of institutions and networks that overlap in their foci and activities and can be tracked from the basin-level upwards to the regional level and then back down again. In the case of aquatic invasives, for example, actions are being undertaken across the continent and on both coasts. We focus primarily on the Great Lakes Basin, with some of the most established cooperative mechanisms in place, but also make reference to continental-level mechanisms as a somewhat newer locus for cooperative AIS activity.

Some of the earliest actions in the North American context to address aquatic species invasions were taken bilaterally between Canada and the United States in the Great Lakes Basin. In 1954, the Convention on Great Lakes Fisheries between The United States of America and Canada was put in place for the purpose of minimizing and eradicating the Atlantic sea lamprey, which had invaded the Great Lakes Basin and was implicated in the precipitous decline of several native fish species (see Chapter 7). The convention established a joint Great Lakes Fisheries Commission to undertake research on the affected fisheries and the invaders, recommend actions that might be taken on the basis of that research, and to formulate a plan for eradication of the lamprey (Convention on Great Lakes Fisheries between The United States of America and Canada, 1954, article IV). Surprisingly, the 1978 binational Great Lakes Water Quality Agreement did not address invasive species, and the 1985 revisions only included this problem in a cursory way, referring to the need to undertake research to determine the threat of AIS from ballast water and their impacts on other species and habitat (Great Lakes Echo, 2010).[9] The revisions did not specifically deal with prevention, control, and management efforts.

In 1988, in a letter to the two federal governments, the Great Lakes Fisheries Commission called attention to the serious threat to native fisheries by nonnative species carried into the basin in the ballast water of ocean-going ships, and recommended that the governments limit future introductions via this vector of invasion (Ridenour, 1988). This call to action was seconded by the binational International Joint Commission (IJC), established under the 1909 Boundary Waters Treaty, which also sent letters to both governments noting the need for immediate action on ballast water management. The Canadian Coast Guard responded in 1989 by introducing voluntary guidelines for the exchange of ballast water at sea. In 1990, the United States passed the Non-indigenous Aquatic Nuisance Prevention and Control Act, which mandated requirements preventing the discharge of ballast water in Great Lakes ports (Doelle, 2001, pp. 6–7).

Significantly, in 1991, the Great Lakes Commission—yet another transboundary entity, established to articulate and coordinate the interests of states and provinces around the basin—created the Great Lakes Panel on Aquatic Nuisance Species. The panel's mandate was "to coordinate the development of education, research and policy to prevent new aquatic invasive species from entering the Great Lakes Basin, and to control and mitigate those AIS populations already established" (Great Lakes Commission, 2013).[10] It aims to advise government policy makers, coordinate their policy responses across territorial boundaries, and educate policy actors and the broader public. Work by the Great Lakes Panel on Aquatic Nuisance Species (GLPANS) in the 1990s emphasized the need to create a stronger framework in the basin to prevent the introduction of new exotic species.

In 1996, the Clinton administration passed the National Invasive Species Act and ballast water discharge provisions became more stringent, with exchange required at sea (the Canadian ballast water requirements remained voluntary). However, a growing chorus of voices in transgovernmental and scientific networks was contributing to an emerging consensus that ballast exchange at sea was not sufficient to eradicate exotics in ballast water. Instead, it was argued that a biologically meaningful ballast effluent standard, with proper enforcement, was necessary (Council of Great Lakes Fishery Agencies, 2000).

In 2000, the problem of aquatic invasive species arrived on the agenda of the North American Commission for Environmental Cooperation, with an acknowledgment by the regional body that "North American ecosystems are being silently overrun by potentially devastating alien invasive species" (CEC, 2000, p. 43). The CEC proposed a "comprehensive approach to this trinational problem," through an evaluation of major pathways for biological invasion and formulating "carefully targeted" measures to eliminate future introductions in four "unique North American aquatic ecoregions": the Pacific Coast, the Gulf of Mexico, the Atlantic Coast, and the Great Lakes. Over 2001–2003, the CEC's Aquatic Invasive Species project commenced, with the organization hosting three meetings on preventing AIS introductions by "closing pathways" between the three countries, and gathering and sharing relevant information (CEC, 2003, p. 13). To guide these activities, a Trinational Aquatic Alien Invasive Species Working Group (TAAISWG) was created, composed of representatives from basin-level networks and domestic agencies, including Canada's Department of Fisheries and Oceans, several federal agencies in Mexico, and the interagency National Invasive Species Council in the United States. The CEC's work was also intended to complement the IJC's work in this area (CEC, 2000, p. 51).

Meanwhile, the International Association for Great Lakes Research (IAGLR), a "member-run professional association" made up of researchers studying the Great Lakes and its watersheds, released a "science translation" report in 2002, entitled Research and Management Priorities for Aquatic Nuisance Species in the Great Lakes, which characterized the aquatic invasive species threat as "one of the greatest risks to the health and productivity of our coastal marine ecosystems and the Great Lakes" (IAGLR, 2002, p. 1). The report advocated for a major increase in federal funding devoted to invasive species, in particular technologies and management strategies for ballast water treatment, interdiction of foreign vessels and the establishment of information, and risk assessment systems to track and identify future invaders. The report also indicated that governments needed to devote more attention to other vectors of invasion, such as aquaculture, the bait industry, and the aquarium industry.

In its communications and its subcommittee mandates into the 2000s, the GLPANS also continued to emphasize the need for coordinated prevention, rapid response, and surveillance measures. To kick start these efforts, the panel released research documents highlighting the key role of ballast water in the transport of invasive species into the basin, as well as a priority list of work that needed to be done to investigate different methods for ballast water effluent management (GLPANS, 2007, 2008). An overarching focus was on the development and application of risk assessment protocols, and the better management of information around the basin. At the regional level, the CEC also highlighted the need for "regional guidelines for assessing risks posed by aquatic species in selected trade-related pathways" (Bulas Montoro, 2004) and set about reviewing several different risk assessment techniques, settling on one approach originally developed by the Americans. The resulting CEC Risk Assessment Guidelines were then tested by all three countries, each choosing species perceived to be domestic threats (CEC, 2009, p.vii).[11]

It might be argued that the work of these transgovernmental and scientific networks prepared the ground for more ambitious efforts to combat the invasive species problem under the revised 2012 Great Lakes Water Quality Agreement (GLWQA). The IJC sets out several priorities in its biennial reports (now triennial, since the 2012 revision) to guide the work of its boards and working groups, under the terms of the agreement. In its 2004 biennial report, the commission urged the two governments "to issue a standing reference to the Commission to coordinate prevention measures to help halt this invasion (of aquatic species) to the Great Lakes" (IJC, 2004, p. vi). Heavy emphasis was placed on ballast water management, with the report making specific recommendations to the two governments to finalize national, mandatory, harmonized provisions. Although the reference was rejected by the two governments, some of the specific recommendations were accepted. Interestingly, the review of the GLWQA, conducted over 2004–2007 in preparation for negotiations on a revised agreement, did not suggest AIS-specific components of a bilateral regime, though it indicated the creation of a separate annex for invasive species was warranted.[12] Indeed, AIS was noted as one of the three most pressing issues, along with climate change and impacts from urbanization, that the agreement was ill-prepared to address (IJC, 2006).

In the 2012 revision of the GLWQA, the new Annex 6 dealing with aquatic invasive species represented a set of new policy and programmatic commitments, with the insertion of new language directing the Canadian and U.S. governments to prevent the introduction of invasive species, control and reduce the spread of existing AIS, and eradicate currently existing AIS within the basin (GLWQA, 2012, annex 6). The three-stage hierarchical approach has thus been incorporated into the formal basin regime, and there are process mechanisms under the agreement that encourage implementation.[13] The new binational regime in Annex 6 of the agreement directs the two national governments to adopt a "prevention-based approach, informed by risk assessments" in terms of developing measures to eliminate new AIS introductions, and to prioritize scientific evidence (GLWQA, 2012, annex 6). More concretely, within the first three years of the agreement, the parties must:

a. develop species watch lists;
b. identify priority locations for surveillance;
c. develop monitoring protocols for surveillance;

d. establish protocols for sharing information;
e. identify new AIS; and
f. coordinate effective and timely domestic and, where necessary, binational response actions to prevent the establishment of newly detected AIS (EDRR).

The parties are to report on their progress in achieving these goals every three years, and the first report was completed in fall of 2016. The report documents the considerable efforts made to put in place organizational structures and processes to facilitate implementation—particularly of the new annexes—that involve the participation not only of the two federal governments but also a host of governments at other levels, indigenous peoples, and other stakeholders. An Annex 6 Subcommittee on Aquatic Invasive Species was created in 2013 under the co-leadership of the United States Fish and Wildlife Service and Fisheries and Oceans Canada. The AIS Subcommittee works in close cooperation with GLPANS, the Great Lakes Commission and other existing networks. The AIS Subcommittee has been actively pursuing the objectives set out in Annex 6. Notably, an EDRR initiative that includes shared monitoring, surveillance, and information-sharing mechanisms as well as rapid response protocolshas been developed for the Great Lakes and road tested on Asian carp species and the aquatic plant species hydrilla (United States & Canada, 2016, pp. 60–64).

In addition to its work investigating pathways of invasion and how they might be "closed" as well as formulating risk assessment guidelines, both of which were intended to be used by policy makers in various locales across the continent, the CEC has also taken a targeted, more local approach to the application of these tools. A parallel effort to combine conservation and invasive species programming has been put in place under the CEC's Biodiversity and Conservation Working Group. In 2000, the working group organized a workshop in which 14 regions of prime importance for focused North American attention were identified, based on levels of threat to biological and ecological functions (Mendoza et al., 2011, p. 4); these included the Great Lakes/St. Lawrence Lowlands, the Gulf of Maine, and the Rio Bravo/Laguna Madre Delta Corridor. A subsequent effort was then made to specifically evaluate the threat of invasive species on each of the 14 regions (Burgiel & March, 2008), wherein the general tools and guidelines could be applied. One ecological region that emerged as a "crucial hotspot" was the Rio Bravo/Laguna Madre Delta Corridor on the Gulf of Mexico, which straddles the states of Louisiana and Texas in the United States and the state of Tamaulipas in Mexico. The CEC has initiated a more thorough study of this ecological region, with the aim of combining its conservation and invasive species program goals in this locale (Mendoza et al., 2011).

Invasive plant management appears to be better coordinated continentally (as opposed to at a cross-border or basin level), perhaps because it is not as complex a jurisdiction as shared water resources, but also because an international convention provides an overarching framework for regional cooperation. The International Plant Protection Convention, governed by the Commission on Phytosanitary Measures and hosted by the Food and Agricultural Organization (FAO) in Rome, provides a global forum for discussions and dissemination of information on invasive plant species, as do several other less formal data-sharing networks. However, regional collaboration is essential to counter plant invasions, and the convention calls explicitly for the creation of National Plant Protection Organizations (NPPOs) as well as regional bodies. The North American Plant Protection Organization (NAPPO) is perhaps the most advanced regional organization in this area (though, unsurprisingly, the European Union has an even more complex and integrated policy landscape on invasive species in general). NAPPO is funded through the three country NPPOs and meets in October every year to discuss and determine which plant species should be regulated for trade purposes. It has a mandate to promote trade, not just curtail it; it is not immune to the influence of industry, but maintains a reputation for decision making based on scientifically valid evidence, and contributes to the International Standards for Phytosanitary Measures accepted by the FAO and World Trade Organization. Invasive species are a priority of the NAPPO, though it deals with many other issue areas as well, such as biotechnology, the citrus industry, and electronic identification. Another connection with the FAO is the regional North American Forest Commission to which all three countries belong. Their Forest Insects and Disease Working Group gives technical advice to the NAPPO on matters related to forest pathology.

Equally important, perhaps, is that the horticulture industry has taken great pains to organize and professionalize around the invasive plants issue. For example, the North American Invasive Species Management Association is essentially an industry association that seeks to arrive at widely implemented standards on, among other things, weed-free forage and gravel. There is even a designated certification program for managers of invasive plants, which is often replicated at the state level; for example, the University of Rhode Island offers an Invasive Plant Management Certification Program. There are innumerable examples across the United States of voluntary codes and standards being implemented on various levels pertaining to plant species in ornamental horticulture; indeed, this could be used as a widely accepted example of industrial self-regulation. Combined with hundreds of research institutes across the continent and citizens' groups engaged in local detection and eradication campaigns, this industry-driven activity contributes to an impressive informal network buttressed by government departments in all three North American countries. However, this network remains heavily U.S.-weighted, and it needs to expand further into Mexico and Canada to have a truly continental effect, especially as climate change increases and decreases plant and tree ranges in the far south and north.

After what has been a period of relative inactivity on the part of the CEC with respect to AIS, it looked as if the continental ISM network might get additional attention and support. At the North American Leaders' Summit in June of 2016, U.S. president Obama, Canadian prime minister Trudeau, and Mexican president Nieto endorsed a wide-ranging and surprisingly detailed "Leaders' Statement on a North American Climate, Clean Energy, and Environment Partnership" (Prime Minister of Canada, 2016). While the statement focused primarily on low-carbon economy initiatives, the leaders also pledged to "strengthen cooperation on invasive alien species" on a continental scale, including establishing a trilateral working group. The working group was to be tasked with first undertaking a survey of existing transboundary AIS initiatives, after which a "high level joint Strategy and Action Plan" will be developed (Prime Minister of Canada, 2016). The statement was silent, however, on whether the focus is to be aquatic or plant invasive species, so one might assume that both will receive attention. However, with the election of Donald Trump as president and an administration that is both anti-environmental and uninterested in transboundary environmental cooperation, this initiative is very likely in limbo for the next several years.

Institutional Indicators of Transboundary Governance Capacity

It would appear, then, that policy (primarily transgovernmental) and scientific networks have been able to scope out the urgent nature of invasive species as a transboundary problem, identify those policy actions that are likely to prove most effective in preventing invasions, and put in place supportive tools that governments can use to coordinate their efforts. In both the aquatic and plant invasion cases, nongovernmental scientific research has proven instrumental.[14] In the case of Great Lakes aquatic invasives, one might argue that these efforts have resulted in concrete changes to the formal transboundary regime: policy and research networks were instrumental in creating and propagating a narrative about the immediacy and seriousness of the invasive species problem, and building consensus about the need for governments and users of the basin to take action (see Chapter 7). Moreover, the action advocated by networks such as GLPANS and the TAAISWG was quite specific in terms of *what*, exactly, should be done (i.e., prioritization of specific vectors of invasion and endorsement of a particular risk assessment process). In the Great Lakes, this fed into discussions about what should be done at the binational level by the IJC under the Biennial Priorities Process and the renegotiation of the GLWQA sometime later. It is perhaps not surprising, then, that the Annex 6 subcommittee under the revised 2012 GLWQA was able to reach agreement on an EEDR framework so quickly, building as it does on a range of existing and linked initiatives.

While this network architecture did not bind governments, policy actors, or basin users, it appears to have been instrumental in cultivating relationships across the science–policy divide and creating a set of self-enforcing norms encouraging a specific kind of action, much as can be seen in the proliferation of voluntary codes pertaining to invasive plants in the horticulture industry. The compliance mechanisms in place under the revised Annex 6 on invasive species are somewhat stronger, relying on progress reporting and accountability measures. Reporting on progress in fulfilling specific objectives and mandates is a well-established enforcement mechanism in the Great Lakes environmental governance regime, as it provides high public visibility in terms of political and public expectations.

The "functional intensity" of transboundary institutions serves as a broader indicator of the extent to which institutions and networks are engaged in deeper forms of collaboration. The governance framework described here exhibits high functional intensity across both its informal and formal elements. Early transboundary efforts under the GLPANS and the CEC's aquatic invasive species project seemed to "leapfrog" past the least functionally intense stages (i.e., information sharing and consultation) in favor of cooperation and in some cases harmonization—activities focused on working together to create shared programs with clear objectives, with the aim of bringing about a compatibility of actions across jurisdictions. In this respect, it might be argued that the relatively high level of functional intensity in newly created networks can be attributed, in the Great Lakes case, to the fact that these networks were created at the initiative of well-established transboundary institutions in the basin, and to significant efforts made on the U.S. side in the late 1990s to early 2000s to achieve interagency coordination and harmonization on invasive species through the National Invasive Species Council, among others. The binational regime being established under Annex 6 of the GLWQA is harmonization, stopping just short of establishing an integrated regime but creating the bases for consistency of goals and interoperability of programs.

One potentially significant observation in this particular case is that the overlapping nature of the basin network structures, binational institutions, and continental initiatives on ISM builds some level of stability into the governance framework. Secondary evidence from examining membership lists and anecdotal information from interviews suggests that interagency and intercommunity linkages cut across the different networks, from the basin to the binational and continental levels, and serve to support the transboundary architecture. This may help to create a degree of consistency of knowledge, effort, and message over time. On the other hand, one might sound a note of caution about "institutional congestion" (e.g., Jinnah, 2014; Najam, Papa, & Taiyab, 2007), whereby there are many mechanisms focused on managing invasive species, both within jurisdictions and across them, and the task of coordination is immense. This dynamic requires additional study, however. In the case of AIS, the new Annex 6 Subcommittee may act as the "point of convergence" for the many networks operating in this area.

After the 2008 recession, the fiscal situation of both national and subnational governments seemed to have a detrimental impact on transboundary interactions on invasives. Almost every document emanating from the networks and institutions over 2009–2014 noted that budget cuts were threatening the very foundation of their projects. Because most of the mechanisms profiled here are funded out of discretionary agency envelopes, which are themselves subject to jurisdiction-specific idiosyncratic cuts, it was difficult for them to continue the full range of activities they have undertaken over previous decades (GLPANS, 2013, p. 4). In a 2009 letter to federal officials, the GLPANS noted that, "the Panel has seen its federal funding diminish progressively over time to the point where it has become difficult to convene meetings and execute our mandate under federal statute" (GLPANS, 2009). Several AIS databases, for example, were discontinued. In 2011, the Canadian government disbanded its Invasive Alien Species Partnership Program, which matched local funding for specific projects aimed at identifying and publicizing aquatic and terrestrial invasive species. The sum saved was paltry (not even $10 million had been invested in the program from 2005 to 2011) compared to the costs of counterinvasion, or even the single Asian carp prevention program.[15] The very real risk here is that when cuts are replicated across the national and subnational jurisdictions that support the transboundary governance regime, both horizontally and vertically, this erodes the material capacity of the regime; through a death by a thousand cuts, as it were.

Most recently, the funding picture appears mixed. In the United States, the March and July 2016 announcements for projects being funded by the Great Lakes Restoration Initiative were overwhelmingly oriented towards invasives initiatives (U.S. Environmental Protection Agency, 2016). Both New York and Michigan provide programming and grants for early detection, spread prevention, and EDRR. In Canada, the Canadian Aquatic Invasive Species Network, an aquatic invasive species research program based at the University of Windsor closed due to a lack of federal government support, yet federal funding continues to support the new Aquatic Invasive Species Regulations and the Invasive Species Centre, and the 2014 Canada-Ontario Agreement on Great Lakes Water Quality and Ecosystem Health has been renewed (Treasury Board of Canada Secretariat, 2015). What appears clear is that funding for ISM is fragmented across agencies at different levels of governance and across agencies and nongovernmental organizations. Significantly, allocations are temporary, with most projects in the three- to five-year range. This makes it difficult to support networks over the long term. With the new Trump administration and their desire to defund and deregulate many environmental functions, it remains to be seen whether funding envelopes for Great Lakes initiatives will survive the coming years.

CONCLUSION

This chapter tracked some of the more high-profile formal and informal components of the aquatic invasive species transboundary governance architecture in North America, particularly (though not exclusively) with reference to the Great Lakes Basin; and looked briefly at efforts to limit the spread of invasive plants across the continent. Here, networks have operated in a more informal but functionally intense manner, through deliberation, persuasion, and consensus building, to articulate a widely accepted narrative about the nature and urgency of the invasive species problem, and the specific actions that should be taken to address it. This narrative has been key to building transboundary governance capacity on invasive species prevention and early detection, by diffusing new knowledge on invasives, fostering dialogue and policy consensus, and coordinating the disparate activities of governments in this area. Although additional research needs to be carried out, overlapping network memberships, drawing the same agencies and organizations into discussions at multiple levels of interaction, have been important for integration. The resilience of this architecture will certainly be tested in the current fiscal and budgetary context.

However, given their critical role, transnational expert networks could use better development. Climate change is already having a profound effect on species distribution in North America and it will exacerbate the problem of biological invasions. Similarly, there is a widespread movement towards the use of biological controls for invasives, and other initiatives to use invasive species as biofuel or food. These can be an efficient and nontoxic approach to extant problems, but can also lead to disaster if not implemented with proper information and care. The need for cross-border scientific and policy coordination has never been so obvious, and even the engagement of citizen science is vital if we are to tackle the problem across the continent. As in many spheres of environmental policy, invasive plant and aquatic species are too dangerous to be left to governments alone.

ACKNOWLEDGMENTS

Debora VanNijnatten would like to thank the Social Sciences and Humanities Research Council of Canada, as the research in this chapter was conducted with funding from a Partnership Development Grant associated with the Great Lakes Policy Research Initiative. Peter Stoett thanks Fulbright Canada and the Woodrow Wilson International Center for Scholars in Washington, DC, for funding.

NOTES

1. The IUCN concurs and adds that, on small islands, bioinvasion is "indisputably the first" greatest threat to biodiversity. See http://www.iucn.org/about/union/secretariat/offices/iucnmed/iucn_med_programme/species/invasive_species/.
2. Though the GISP (1997–2010) was, by an unfortunate confluence of events, cut off in its infancy, other international networks have emerged as the dominant transnational mode of information exchange, in particular the Global Invasive Alien Species Information Partnership and the Biodiversity Indicators Partnership, both of which derived their mandates from Article 8(h) of the CBD and in particular Target 9 of the 2011–2020 Strategic Plan for Biodiversity (known as Aichi Target 9). These networks cut across governments, international organizations, nongovernmental organizations, and universities.
3. There are opportunities to harvest IAS for benefit, be it for food security or bioenergy production, or other uses. The overwhelming evidence, however, suggests they are best conceived as a threat.

4. The North American Invasive Species Network (NAISN) includes four subspecies of Asian carp in its list of North America's "top 10" invasive species: grass, silver, bighead, and black. It also includes the lionfish, hydrilla (an invasive aquatic plant), and both the zebra and the quagga mussels. See http://www.naisn.org/TopTenSpeciesListwith links.pdf.
5. See http://plants.usda.gov/java/noxious?rptType=State&statefips=35.
6. In addition to the hundreds of millions of dollars it has already committed, it is estimated that the U.S. government will spend more than $15 billion to prevent the spread of the infamous Asian carp into Lake Michigan and the other Great Lakes. Even though Canada is not adjacent to Lake Michigan, the Canadian government has committed to spending more than C$15 million on related prevention, early warning, response, and management activities over the next five years.
7. See also *Review of Policy Research* 2015 special issue on North American environmental governance (edited by Temby & Stoett).
8. Interestingly, the NAFTA-CEC–supported North American Invasive Species Network uses a similar typology for its members: hubs (regional or international organizations and agencies), nodes (government agencies and networks), and affiliates (individuals who are interested as experts or stakeholders). The network has compiled a list of hundreds of organizations associated with invasive species management in all three countries (see http://www.naisn.org/documents /compendium%20for%20website_links.pdf).
9. These provisions can be found in the 1987 version of the Great Lakes Water Quality Agreement in Annex 6, 1(b), and Annex 17, 2(i).
10. The panel is a unique network, given that it is empowered under the Nonindigenous Aquatic Nuisance Prevention and Control Act of 1990, but operates in a binational capacity with representation from national, state, and provincial governments as well as regional agencies, user groups, local communities, tribal/aboriginal authorities, commercial interests, and the university/research community.
11. Meanwhile, the Trilateral Committee for Wildlife and Ecosystem Conservation and Management, established in 1996, has not adopted invasive species as one its primary concerns, to the dismay of some observers.
12. Here, it is important to bear in mind that reviewers were directed to focus on the strengths and limitations of the existing agreement, not to be prescriptive (G. Krantzberg, McMaster University, personal communication, May 12, 2016).
13. It is important to note, however, that actual compliance with provisions is left up to the parties to the agreement. This is hardly surprising

given the binational character of the agreement. Canada's recent efforts to establish a new national regulatory structure for AIS (as called for in Smith, Bazely, & Yan, 2014) are an indication of success on this front, though some Canadians argue it follows on the heels of a weakened fisheries act. See the proposed regulations at www.dfo-mpo.g..ca/science/enviro/ais-eae/consultations-eng.asp.

14. Margaret (Peg) Brady, NOAA Ocean and Coastal Council Acting Deputy of the Ecosystems Goal Team and NOAA's senior policy liaison to the U.S. National Invasive Species Council, especially praised the efforts of the Canadian Aquatic Invasive Species Network (personal communication, April 2012).
15. See https://ec.gc.ca/eee-ias/default.asp?lang=En&n=A49893BC-1.

REFERENCES

Berkes, F., Colding, J., & Folke, C. (2003). *Navigating social-ecological systems: Building resilience for complexity and change*. Cambridge, UK: Cambridge University Press.

Biermann, F., Pattberg, P., & Zelli, F. (Eds.). (2010). *Global climate governance beyond 2012: Architecture, agency and adaptation*. Cambridge, UK: Cambridge University Press.

Buchanan, A., & Keohane, R. O. (2006). The legitimacy of global governance institutions. *Ethics & International Affairs*, *20*(4), 405–437.

Bulas Montoro, J. M. (2004, June 8). Letter from CEC secretariat staff member to CEC Joint Pubic Advisory Committee chair Donna Tingley. Retrieved from http://www.cec.org/fr/sites/default/files/documents/jpac_advice_council/1561_Council-response-03-06_en.pdf

Burgiel, S., & March, I. (2008). *Project report to the Commission for Environmental Cooperation. Phase 1: Invasive species assessment of the CEC's priority conservation regions*. CEC: Montreal, QC.

Commission for Environmental Cooperation. (2000). *North American agenda for action 2001–2003: Conservation of biodiversity*. Retrieved from http://www.cec.org/Storage/32/2379_OperationalPlan01-03_en.pdf

Commission for Environmental Cooperation. (2003). *Closing the pathways of aquatic invasive species across North America: Overview and resource guide*. Montreal, QC: Author. Retrieved from http://www3.cec.org/islandora/en/item/2068-closing-pathways-aquatic-invasive-species-across-north-america-en.pdf

Commission for Environmental Cooperation. (2008). *North American mosaic: An overview of key environmental issues*. Montreal, QC:

Author. Retrieved from http://www3.cec.org/islandora/en/item/2349-north-american-mosaic-overview-key-environmental-issues-en.pdf

Commission for Environmental Cooperation. (2009). *Trinational risk assessment guidelines for aquatic alien invasive species.* Montreal, QC: Author. Retrieved from http://www3.cec.org/islandora/en/item/2379-trinational-risk-assessment-guidelines-aquatic-alien-invasive-species-en.pdf

Convention on Great Lakes Fisheries between The United States of America and Canada. (1954). Retrieved from http://www.glfc.org/pubs/conv.htm

Council of Great Lakes Fishery Agencies (2000). Reference on ballast water management or what do Great Lakes agencies want? [Draft]. Retrieved from http://www.glfc.org/boardcomm/cglfa/refballast.htm

Doelle, M. (2001). *Legal and policy responses to invasive species* [Background paper for the Commission for Environmental Cooperation]. Montreal, QC: Commission for Environmental Cooperation. Retrieved from http://www3.cec.org/islandora/en/item/2067-legal-and-policy-responses-invasives-species-en.pdf

Great Lakes Echo. (2010, June 11). Great Lakes water quality agreement: Aquatic invasive species. *Great Lakes Echo.* Retrieved from http://greatlakesecho.org/2010/06/11/great-lakes-water-quality-agreement-aquatic-invasive-species/

Great Lakes Panel on Aquatic Nuisance Species. (2007). *Introduction for the Great Lakes panel priority invasive species list, Research Coordination Committee* [Author's copy]. Ann Arbor, MI: Author.

Great Lakes Panel on Aquatic Nuisance Species. (2008, February 22). Re: Urgent need for effective federal regulations to prevent the discharge of organisms from vessels declaring ballast and no ballast on board [Letter to Gary Frazer and Timothy R.E. Keeney Co-Chairs, ANS Task Force (G-17J)]. Retrieved from http://projects.glc.org/ans/documents/08-02-22-GLPBWRectoANSTF-Final.pdf

Great Lakes Panel on Aquatic Nuisance Species. (2009, August 19). Re: Great Lakes Restoration Initiative [Letter to USEPA Great Lakes National Program Office (G-17J)]. Retrieved from http://www.glc.org/ans/documents/09-08-19-Comm-Priorities%20Dissemination-Cover-GLRI-Final-Sub.pdf

Great Lakes Panel on Aquatic Nuisance Species. (2013). Meeting agenda of the Great Lakes Panel on Aquatic Nuisance Species May 7–8, 2013 [Author's copy].

Great Lakes Water Quality Agreement, U.S.-Canada. (2012). Retrieved from https://binational.net//wp-content/uploads/2014/05/1094_Canada-USA-GLWQA-_e.pdf

Gulf of Maine Council on the Marine Environment. (2010). *Marine invasive species: State of the Gulf of Maine report*. Retrieved from http://www.gulfofmaine.org/state-of-the-gulf/docs/marine-invasive-species.pdf

Hafner-Burton, E. M., Kahler, M., & Montgomery, A. H. (2009). Network analysis for international relations. *International Organization*, *63*(3), 559–592.

International Association for Great Lakes Research. (2002). *Research and management priorities for aquatic invasive species in the Great Lakes*. Retrieved from http://www.iaglr.org/scipolicy/ais/ais_iaglr02.pdf

International Joint Commission. (2004). *Twelfth biennial report on Great Lakes water quality*. Retrieved from https://www.nrc.gov/docs/ML0703/ML070390585.pdf

International Joint Commission. (2006). *A Guide to the Great Lakes Water Quality Agreement: Background for the 2006 governmental review*. Retrieved from http://www.ijc.org/files/publications/ID1625.pdf

Jinnah, S. (2014). *Post-treaty politics: Secretariat influence in global environmental governance*. Cambridge, MA: MIT Press.

Kemp, R., & Weehuizen, R. (2005). Policy learning, what does it mean and how can we study it? Oslo: NIFU Step. Retrieved from https://brage.bibsys.no/xmlui/bitstream/handle/11250/226561/d15policylearning.pdf?sequence=1&isAllowed=y

Lodge, D. M., Williams, S., MacIsaac, H. J., Hayes, K. R., Leung, B., Reichard, S., . . . McMichael, A. (2006). Biological invasions: Recommendations for U.S. policy and management. *Ecological Applications*, *16*(6), 2035–2054.

Luken, J., and Thieret, J. (Eds.). (1997). *Assessment and management of plant invasions*. New York, NY: Springer.

McCullough, D. G., Work, T. T., Cavey, J. F., Liebhold, A. M., & Marshall, D. (2006). Interceptions of nonindigenous plant pests at US ports of entry and border crossings over a 17-year period. *Biological Invasions*, *8*(4), 611–630.

Mendoza, R., Arreaga, N., Hernandez, J., Segovia, V., Jasso, I., & Perez, D. (2011). *Aquatic invasive species in the Rio Bravo/Laguna Verde ecological region* (Background Paper 2011-02). Montreal, QC: Commission for Environmental Cooperation. Retrieved from http://www3.cec.org/islandora/en/item/10259-aquatic-invasive-species-in-rio-bravolaguna-madre-ecological-region-en.pdf

Millenium Ecosystem Assessment Board. (2005). *Ecosystems and human well-being: Current state and trends, volume 1*. Washington, DC: Island Press. Retrieved from http://www.millenniumassessment.org/en/Condition.html#download

Najam, A., Papa, M., & Taiyab, N. (2007, April 5). *Key challenges to global environmental governance*. Winnipeg, MB: International Institute for Sustainable Development. Retrieved from http://www.eoearth.org/view/article/153013/

Nonindigenous Aquatic Nuisance Prevention and Control Act of 1990 (subsequently reauthorized as the National Invasive Species Act of 1996), 16 U.S.C. § 4701. (2004). Retrieved from https://www.epw.senate.gov/envlaws/nanpca90.pdf

Ontario Ministry of Natural Resource. (2013). Aquatic invasive species. Retrieved from http://www.mnr.gov.on.ca/en/Business/Biodiversity/2ColumnSubPage/STDPROD_068689.html

Ostrom, E. (1990). *Governing the commons: The evolution of institutions for collective action*. Cambridge, UK: Cambridge University Press.

Ostrom, E. (2009a). A general framework for analyzing sustainability in socio-ecological systems. *Science*, *325*(5939), 419–422.

Ostrom, E. (2009b). *A polycentric approach for coping with climate change* (Working paper 5095). Report prepared for the World Development Report 2010 Core Team, Development and Economics Research Group, World Bank, Washington, DC. Retrieved from http://www19.iadb.org/intal/intalcdi/pe/2009/04268.pdf

Prime Minister of Canada. (2016, June 29). *Leaders' statement on a North American climate, clean energy and environment partnership*. Retrieved from http://pm.gc.ca/eng/news/2016/06/29/leaders-statement-north-american-climate-clean-energy-and-environment-partnership

Ridenour, J. M. (1988, August 4). Letter to U.S. Secretary of State George Schultz. Retrieved from http://www.ijc.org/php/publications/pdf/ID2.pdf

Smith, A., Bazely, D., & Yan, N. (2014). Are legislative frameworks in Canada and Ontario up to the task of addressing invasive alien species? *Biological Invasions*, *16*(7), 1325–1344.

Stoett, P. (2010). Framing bioinvasion: Biodiversity, climate change, security, trade, and global governance. *Global Governance: A Review of Multilateralism and International Organizations*, *16*(1), 103–120.

Stoett, P. (2012). *Global ecopolitics: Crisis, governance, and justice*. Toronto, ON: University of Toronto Press.

Treasury Board of Canada Secretariat. (2015). *Horizontal initiative: Great Lakes Basin ecosystem initiative*. Retrieved from https://www.tbs-sct.gc.ca/hidb-bdih/plan-eng.aspx?Org=0&Hi=30&Pl=656

United States & Canada. (2016). *2016 progress report of the parties: Pursuant to the Canada-United States Water Quality Agreement*. Retrieved from https://binational.net/wp-content/uploads/2016/09/PRP-160927-EN.pdf

U.S. Environmental Protection Agency. (2016). *Great Lakes restoration initiative*. Retrieved from https://www.epa.gov/great-lakes-funding/great-lakes-restoration-initiative-glri

VanNijnatten, D., & Craik, N. (2013). Designing integration: The system of climate change governance in North America. In N. Craik, I. Studer, & D. VanNijnatten (Eds.), *Climate change policy in North America: Designing integration in a regional system* (pp. 5–34). Toronto, ON: University of Toronto Press.

VanNijnatten, D., Johns, C., Bryk-Friedman, K., & Krantzberg, G. (2016). Assessing adaptive transboundary governance capacity in the Great Lakes Basin. *International Journal of Water Governance*, *1*(1), 7–32.

VanNijnatten, D. L. (2006). Towards cross-border environmental policy spaces in North America: Province-state linkages on the Canada-U.S. border [Special issue]. *AmeriQuests: The Journal of the Center for the Americas*, *3*(1).

White House Council on Environmental Quality. (2010, February 10). *Great Lakes restoration initiative action plan FY 2010–FY2014*. Retrieved from http://greatlakesrestoration.us/pdfs/glri_actionplan.pdf

NINE

Transnational Networks and Transboundary Water Governance in the Colorado River Delta

ANDREA K. GERLAK

INTRODUCTION

On May 14, 2014, the Colorado River reconnected with the ocean, an event that has not happened regularly for the past 50 years. It was the result of the delivery of a "pulse flow," running from two months in the spring of 2014, meant to mimic the spring floods that historically inundated the Colorado River Delta. National Geographic followed the flow of the river as it was released just below the Morelos Dam at the U.S.-Mexican border and made its way to the Gulf of California (Pitt, 2014). National Public Radio also chased the river, recording the voices of children, many of whom had never seen the river flow, splashing and playing in the water (Robbins, 2014). Robert Redford dramatized the story of the pulse flow in a short video aptly named *Renewal* (Raise the River, 2014).

The pulse flow experiment is part of the new era of binational cooperation between the United States and Mexico, stemming from Minute 319 to the 1944 treaty governing transboundary waters between the United States and Mexico. Under Minute 319, the two countries—along with a transnational network of actors—agreed to provide new flows of water to the riparian corridor and its delta (International Boundary and Water Commission [IBWC], 2012).[1] Notably, it marks the first time the two nations have delivered water to the delta to promote ecosystem restoration (IBWC, 2014). The agreement itself reflects a broader evolution in cooperation between the two countries to preserve the environment, save water, identify new water supplies, and offer greater flexibility in water deliveries to Mexico (Dibble, 2011; Lovett, 2012).

For many, the reunion of the river and the sea was long overdue. Today, less than 1% of the Colorado River's flow reaches the delta and no regular flow reaches the Gulf of California. Water that originally reached the delta has been diverted to cities and for agriculture (Zamora-Arroyo & Flessa, 2009, p. 24). Despite this, the delta remains a vibrant ecosystem. The delta's remnant patches, fed largely by accidental releases of river water, agricultural return flow, seepage, treated effluent, or other unintentional flows, provide habitat for migratory birds and endangered fish species (Pitt, Hinojosa-Huerta, & Carrillo-Guerrero, 2010, p. 4; Zamora-Arroyo et al., 2005, p. 34). In Mexico, the delta wetlands provide habitat for birds that are federally protected as endangered in the United States (Jenkins, 2007).

A transnational network has been emerging over the past decade to challenge what is seen by many as a more traditional, bureaucratic, centralized, and secretive management style of the International Boundary and Water Commission (IBWC), the joint commission that overseas all international boundaries, rivers, and streams covered by the treaties and conventions to which the United States and Mexico are parties.[2] This transnational network of actors operating to restore the Colorado River Delta can be seen as one of many environmental and conservation networks that have emerged along the U.S.-Mexican border in the past two decades. Laird-Benner and Ingram (2011) have mapped a larger network of border actors who have been active in the region in the past several decades, fueled by a strong positive narrative around love of place. Efforts to restore the delta and promote binational relations have resulted in some significant restoration, helping to generate a "delta in repair" (Gerlak, Zamora-Arroyo, & Kahler, 2013).

This chapter seeks to explore the role of the transnational Delta Restoration Network in the governance of the Colorado River Delta. It examines the shape and form of the network and its evolution over time. Specifically, we are keenly interested in the networks' governance functions and the extent to which these functions steer governance in relation to the mission and workings of the IBWC. We are interested in how the network interacts with this international institution that manages and regulates transboundary waters between the United States and Mexico, and how the network shapes the contours of transboundary governance in the Colorado River Delta.

We proceed as follows. First, we examine the governance functions of transnational networks. Next, we turn to a historical background of the IBWC and an outline of its modern challenges. We rely on primary documents, secondary literature, and interviews with knowledgeable actors to trace the emergence and evolution of the transnational network, highlighting different key stages, activities, and developments. Our findings suggest that rule setting is key to the shift towards more participatory and science-based governance that we uncover in governance of the Colorado River Delta. We conclude with a discussion of the broader implications for the role of transnational networks in transboundary water governance.

TRANSNATIONAL NETWORKS AND GOVERNANCE: INFORMATION SHARING, CAPACITY BUILDING, AND RULE SETTING

Transnational networks mobilize information, knowledge, and values with the objective of integrating new conceptions of environmental phenomena into everyday worldviews and practices (Lipschutz, 1997, p. 443). They shape governance by sharing information, building or enhancing capacity, implementing policies, and setting rules (Andonova, Betsill, & Bulkeley, 2009). Transnational networks may be seen as sites for the governance of global environmental issues, as arenas through which problems are shaped, defined, and contested, and in which resources are controlled and compliance is sought (Betsill & Bulkeley, 2004, p. 490).

The importance of networks is often seen in their ability to exchange knowledge and information and to forge norms about the nature and terms of particular issues (Betsill & Bulkeley, 2004; Conca, 2006). Beyond information-sharing and capacity-building functions, transnational networks steer governance through rule setting and implementation (Andonova et al., 2009; Bäckstrand, 2008, p. 87; Slaughter, 2004). Networks of environmental NGOs may serve as policy "teachers" or "exporters" of policy lessons, promoting learning through workshops and training sessions, and widening and reforming deliberation processes (Bomberg, 2007).

Integrating and coordinating information is thought to be a vital component of multilevel governance in border regions today (Blatter, 2001; Stein & Turkewitsch, 2010). Networks enable government agencies and international institutions to share and integrate specialized knowledge and develop institutional capacity to address emerging problems in modern governance (Stoett & Temby, 2015). Collaborative networks are utilized by governments to respond to complex natural resource issues where knowledge is highly specialized and fragmented (Temby, Rastogi, Sandall, Cooksey, & Hickey, 2015). They offer a cost-efficient way for governments to tap into that knowledge reservoir (Breitmeier, 2008). This reliance on the utility of networks by international institutions managing transboundary resources suggests that environmental governance may be becoming more participatory and open to diverse knowledge and expertise (Stoett & Temby, 2015).

THE IBWC AND TRANSNATIONAL NETWORK GOVERNANCE OF THE COLORADO RIVER DELTA

Historical Background and New Challenges

The Colorado River Delta is where the Colorado River meets the Gulf of California (see Figure 9.1). Water serving the delta arriving through the Colorado River mainstem and in the San Luis groundwater zone east of Yuma is under the oversight of the IBWC, the joint commission that oversees all international boundaries, rivers, and streams covered by the treaties and conventions to which the United States and Mexico are parties. The origins of the commission can be traced to the Convention of 1889 between the United States and Mexico, designed to resolve differences between the two countries related to the Rio Grande/Rio Bravo and Colorado Rivers, both of which form segments of the international boundary.

In 1944, the two countries entered into a treaty on "Utilization of Waters of the Colorado and Tijuana Rivers and of the Rio Grande." The treaty requires that the United States annually provide Mexico with 1.5 million acre-feet of Colorado River water, representing about 10% of the river's average flow. Under the 1944 treaty, the IBWC's duties expanded to include oversight allocation of treaty water resources, hydropower operations on the Rio Grande, and flood control along the Rio Grande and Colorado Rivers. Since 1973, the IBWC has held authority over groundwater and international salinity and pollution problems. When the IBWC exercises its rule-making power under the treaty, it must record its decisions in the form of minutes. There are more than 300 minutes to the treaty that serve as binding agreements once approved by both governments.

The IBWC's mission has been evolving as new actors and constituencies demand more environmentally sensitive, timely, and fiscally responsible boundary and water services in an atmosphere of binational cooperation and in a manner responsive to public concerns (Valdés-Casillas et al., 1998). Yet, the IBWC has been criticized for being secretive (Hayton, 1993; Sanchez, 1993) and maintaining monopolistic control over border resources data acquisition (Ingram & White, 1993, p. 155; Mumme, 2001, p. 122). Historically, it has limited its focus to problems of water supply and quality along the border, leaving issues of environmental protection

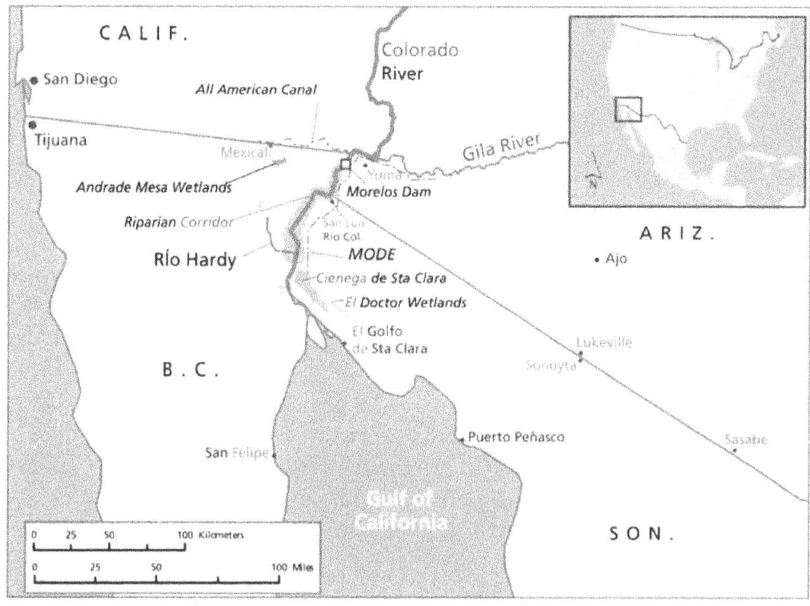

FIGURE 9.1 Map of the Colorado River Delta (Zamora-Arroyo & Flessa, 2009).

to the jurisdiction of other Mexican and U.S. agencies (Luecke et al., 1999, p. 34). It has been criticized for its inability to protect vulnerable ecological resources and to respond effectively to stakeholder concerns in water management (Glennon & Culp, 2002). Some argue that the national sections lack the capability and the prestige necessary to negotiate solutions to these complex border water disputes (Kelly & Szekely, 2004, p. 13). In the past decade, the IBWC has "heightened their public relations profile in an effort to improve their civic image" (Mumme, 2005, p. 509).

Today, the IBWC faces a good many challenges. Demographic growth and chronic water shortages have ushered in new demands on the treaty system. Economic asymmetry and social inequality also characterize the border region and pose challenges for the IBWC (Sanchez-Rodriguez & Mumme, 2013, p. 153). Over-allocation of Colorado River water is a major challenge threatening environmental solutions to the delta (Umoff, 2008, p. 92). Finally, climate variability stresses binational cooperation. Climate change estimates suggest that the Southwest is warming more quickly than the global average in most places, and because of low winter precipitation and warm, dry, windy spring seasons, snow pack and runoff to the Colorado River are decreasing (Karl, Melillo, & Peterson, 2009, pp. 51, 129). The recent U.S. Bureau of Reclamation's Colorado River Basin Water Supply and Demand Study (2012) projects climate change could further reduce total flows in the Colorado River by 9% or more in the next half-century.

Emergence of a Transnational Network

After a series of wet years brought back some wetland areas in the delta in the 1980s and 1990s, a collection of scientists, environmental organizations, public officials, and private business leaders began to take a renewed interest in this ecosystem and the possibility of restoration (Cohen, Henges-Jeck, & Castillo-Moreno, 2001; Luecke et al., 1999; Nagler, Glenn, Hursh, Curtis, & Huete, 2005; Zamora-Arroyo, Hinojosa-Huerta, Santiago, Brott, & Culp, 2008). These early efforts sought to assess threats to the ecosystems of the delta and upper gulf, and to identify opportunities for protecting and enhancing these resources. A group of researchers led by Dr. Carlos Valdés-Casillas, then director of Centro de Conservación de Recursos Naturales (CECARENA), and Professor Edward Glenn of the University of Arizona's Environmental Research Laboratory began to assess vegetation distribution, presence of wildlife, hydrology, and water quality in the delta and quickly became convinced of its potential for restoration (Marcos & Cornelius, 2004). The conservation organizations Pronatura Sonora of San Luis Río Colorado, Sonora, Mexico, and the Sonoran Institute in Tucson, Arizona, then initiated a joint community outreach program.[3]

By the late 1990s, large U.S.-based philanthropic organizations, such as the Ford Foundation and the Charles Stewart Mott Foundation, came to support a series of annual meetings on the border environment aimed at capacity building (Liverman, Varady, Chavez, & Sanchez, 1999, p. 629). Environmental NGOs had been active on both sides of the border for several decades, developing agendas and shaping environmental policy (Liverman et al., 1999). The playing field came to be crowded around delta conservation and restoration. The Environmental Defense Fund, Sierra Club, Ducks Unlimited, Nature Conservancy, Conservation International, American Rivers, Defenders of Wildlife, the Sonoran Institute, the Pacific Institute, Intercultural Center for the Study of Desert and Oceans, the Southwest Center for Biodiversity, and Pronatura were all pursing interests in the region (Luecke et al., 1999, p. 10).

These organizations offered a variety of plans to restore the delta, including a litigation strategy from the Defenders of Wildlife to push the United States to address river management downstream from federal dams and to consider habitat in Mexico as a suitable site for habitat loss mitigation (Varady, Hankins, Kaus, Young, & Merideth, 2001). Secretary of the Interior Bruce Babbitt convened a meeting in Washington, DC, in 1999 to bring together actors from the U.S. side of the border to discuss delta restoration. Even the IBWC got into the delta spirit. Minute 306 of the United States–Mexico Treaty for the Utilization of Waters of the Colorado and Tijuana Rivers and of the Río Grande, signed between the United States and Mexico in 2000, states that the two countries have an interest in environmental issues in the delta and cooperation is necessary.[4] This minute marks the beginning of a formal governmental recognition of environmental values in the delta. The IBWC was being discussed as an appropriate forum, and the "most viable institution" to promote conservation in the delta region (Varady et al., 2001, p. 206). Many possible roles were outlined for the IBWC in terms of managing existing flows for the benefit of delta ecosystems, establishing market mechanisms and funding sources for delta preservation, and conducting research and implementing restoration projects (Luecke et al., 1999).

Yet, the IBWC did not move to organize or facilitate binational cooperation. Rather, in the absence of IBWC leadership, a binational session organized by the Sonoran Institute brought scientists, water managers, and local resource users together for the first time to analyze information about the delta in an interdisciplinary manner (Zamora-Arroya et al., 2005). Scientific research from the previous two decades was relied upon as well as traditional knowledge provided by representatives of the local community and the Cucapa indigenous tribe. The workshop helped to produce a report identifying conservation priorities in the delta, titled *Conservation Priorities in the Colorado River Delta, Mexico and the U.S.* The report provided an opportunity for the large transnational network to demonstrate to federal and state stakeholders the scientific research that was underway in the region. In the absence of a formal framework to guide the activities of the various organizations working in the delta, the report served as a "common guide for moving forward in the delta" (Zamora-Arroyo et al., 2008, p. 874). It offered a "shared map" for network actors (P. Culp, personal communication, November 1, 2013).

Network Evolution and Change

Around the same time that network actors were developing a shared map of conservation priorities in the delta, there was a growing recognition that the larger environmental community strategy of litigation and forced solutions from a regulatory perspective was not going to work. The

Defenders of Wildlife lawsuit and efforts to influence the National Environmental Policy Act (NEPA) process under the 2001 Surplus Guidelines were coming to be seen as failed efforts (P. Culp, personal communication, November 1, 2013). With the failed litigation strategy, many groups, like Defenders of Wildlife and the Sierra Club, disengaged from the larger network. This made space for a different conversation. A smaller set of NGOs began talking about how they could build an international consensus and create collaborative paths to manage resource scarcity in the basin.

By 2005, a deliberately constructed core network emerged. Composed of NGOs active in the region for the past several decades and characterized by dedicated field staff and delta restoration programs, several NGOs that had been part of the larger transnational network coalesced into a core network. Core network members included the two local NGOs, Pronatura and the Sonoran Institute, along with the national environmental NGOs, the Environmental Defense Fund (EDF) and Nature Conservancy. These network actors came to understand that the larger network approach of pursuing independent strategies was not working. Rather, a common objective and more holistic approach were necessary. According to Jennifer Pitt, a long-time scientist with the EDF, a strategy or "theory of victory" was beginning to crystallize and unify the core network (personal communication, November 1, 2013). The theory involved engaging water users and managers for a new way to do business. At the heart of this new approach was the recognition that environmental flows would not be enough to get decision makers to the table. The new theory called for a voluntary binational process between the United States and Mexico in which environmental flows would play a key, but not isolated, role.

In terms of division of responsibility, network actors relied on historic strengths and expertise. The expertise of Pronatura and Sonoran Institute could be found in their community building and restoration work and their ability to perform joint projects, share funding, and complement each other's efforts. The EDF brought a strong policy dimension to the table with ideas for strategies that might be acceptable to state and federal water managers on the U.S. side of the border. The Nature Conservancy offered technical capacity and expertise for monitoring.

Network actors continued to perform governance functions associated with information sharing and capacity building. Science was seen as key to learning about the condition of the system, its benefits and how the system is responding to particular actions (O. Hinojosa-Huerta, personal communication, October 25, 2013). University-based research centers on both sides of the border have been a historically important source of studies providing credible, scientific data documenting delta conditions (Luecke et al., 1999, p. 37). When network actors began to recognize that in order to restore the Colorado River Delta successfully, it was critical that riverine and estuarine restoration efforts be complementary, they called attention to the need for research on the delta's estuary, its water needs, and opportunities for restoration. In 2005, a new collaborative initiative developed to address this research need. The Research Coordination Network for the Lower Colorado River Delta (RCN-CRD), a National Science Foundation–funded effort, comprised of natural scientists, social scientists, humanists, and legal scholars that facilitates interdisciplinary, interinstitutional, and binational research on the Colorado River Delta of the United States and Mexico, facilitated the initial phases of this collaboration.

Enhancing public participation was also an objective of the network. The EDF continued its work to encourage public participation in policy and management decisions and recommending coordination among the various involved organizations to ensure that efforts were not duplicated (Luecke et al., 1999). For Pronatura and the Sonoran Institute, public participation focused primarily on local stakeholders living in the delta region. When they initiated community-based restoration activities in the delta along the Hardy River, a 16-mile-long tributary stream to the Colorado River that is an important and permanent water source for the delta, on-the-ground projects involved partnerships with local stakeholders and recreational tourist camp owners to restore habitat (Hinojosa-Huerta et al., 2005).

The first opportunity to demonstrate this new strategy emerged in 2005 with the development of Surplus Guidelines, spurred by the multiyear drought, decreasing system storage, and growing demands for Colorado River water. With the drought as new opportunity, network actors worked deliberately on the guidelines and presented the Secretary of the Interior with a proposal for Colorado River drought management establishing a voluntary, compensated water conservation program that minimizes the likelihood of large, uncompensated water shortages. The Conservation before Shortage policy proposal was based on the principle that shortage criteria should maximize the reliability and predictability of water deliveries on the Colorado River by introducing increased flexibility into the management of river resources when shortage conditions are imminent (EDF, 2005). It proposed an approach to the management of shortages in the Lower Colorado through the implementation of a tiered conservation program that is tied to the surface elevation of Lake Mead.

Network actors would come to work with U.S. Bureau of Reclamation modelers to evaluate and fine tune policy alternatives. Invited to draft one of the two alternatives in the environmental impact statements for the federal NEPA process, network actors presented a conceptual paper,

Taking ICS to Mexico. The paper identified the potential benefits associated with widening the scope of the policies developed through the seven basin states' agreement to allow Mexico's participation in multiyear water storage and release activities in Lake Mead, both as a means of shortage mitigation and as a means of improving flexibility in water management and providing for the restoration of pulse flows to the delta ecosystem (Zamora-Arroyo et al., 2008, p. 881). The proposal developed widespread support within the basin states as a means of improving binational water management. All seven states signed a letter stating that the concept of reservoir mechanisms was important and that further dialogue with Mexico was needed. Some of these ideas were later built into the so-called preferred alternatives adopted by the U.S. Bureau of Reclamation, and in the United States, federal agencies began to study additional storage for the United States and Mexico, demonstrating real policy change on the U.S. side of the border.

Ultimately, participation in the Surplus Guidelines process was a strategic step for the newly coalesced network. It reflected the emerging "theory of victory" that recognized a binational agreement would not coalesce around the delta. If the network had any hope for future binational agreements, however, Mexico would need to be integrated into the larger framework. A reservoir storage mechanism would also be chiefly important to create a base flow for the delta. Network actors would later receive the Partners in Conservation Award from the U.S. Department of the Interior for their contributions to improving water management of the Colorado River system through the development of Conservation before Shortage proposals and other ideas, which were evaluated by the U.S. Bureau of Reclamation in developing new rules for managing the Colorado River under drought conditions (EDF, 2009).

A Heightened Binational Process

Network actors subsequently worked with water management agencies in Arizona, Nevada, and California and key experts in Mexico to initiate an informal dialogue about opportunities for direct cooperation between state, federal, and local stakeholders in the United States and Mexico to advance various municipal, agricultural, and environmental objectives. The enthusiasm associated with this initial, informal dialogue was such that it was expanded and folded into a new binational process. With the Joint Declaration of U.S. and Mexico to Discuss Joint Cooperative Actions Related to the Colorado River, which was signed by U.S. Department of the Interior Secretary Dirk Kempthorne and Mexican Ambassador Arturo

Sarukhan in 2007, the United States and Mexico recognized the IBWC as the "appropriate organization" to expedite discussions to further Colorado River Delta cooperation.

Although working with and engaging local communities was always part of the strategy of the network, especially exemplified in the work by Pronatura and the Sonoran Institute, the idea of public participation was broadening as network NGOs pressed to participate in more formal planning for the delta. NGOs were officially incorporated for the first time in 2008 when a binational "core group" of stakeholders was established to consider water conservation and augmentation measures in the lower Colorado River Basin. Because network actors played such a central role in leading earlier informal discussions, NGO representatives were appointed to both the U.S. and Mexican core groups organized under the direction of the IBWC (Zamora-Arroyo et al., 2008, p. 881).

This stakeholder process was formalized in 2010 with Minute 317 to the treaty: A Conceptual Framework for US-Mexico Discussions on Colorado River Cooperative Actions. Minute 317 stipulates that the commission shall

> explore opportunities for bi-national cooperative projects that minimize the impacts of potential Colorado River shortage conditions; generate additional volumes of water using new water sources by investing in infrastructure such as desalinization facilities; conserve water through investments in a variety of current and potential uses; and envision the possibility of permitting Mexico to use United States infrastructure to store water.

The Commissioners agreed to establish a binational Consultative Council under Minute 317, composed of representatives of the commission along with the respective federal governments and the basin states, to facilitate consideration of the legal, administrative, and policy matters associated with these issues. It was intentionally established as a forum to exclude NGOs.

Meanwhile, network actors continued to perform governance functions around information sharing and capacity building. Through this interdisciplinary and collaborative process, network actors began to focus on the need to secure water for a permanent flow for the delta. As part of these efforts, network actors worked with decision makers on the Mexican side of the border to develop and implement a strategy for bringing effluent from the newly completed Las Arenitas wastewater treatment plant to the Hardy River. Along the way, network actors built relationships with environmental and tourism ministry officials, which helped to garner support from other state agencies, including the State Water Commission and the Governor of Baja California (Zamora-Arroyo et al., 2008). The State of Baja California, with the concurrence of the National Water Commission, signed an agreement in 2007 with the Mexican NGOs involved in the process, formally dedicating a flow of at least 12,300 acre-feet of treated water for the Hardy River. The agreement was the first of its kind in Mexico (Zamora-Arroyo et al., 2008, p. 878). The treated effluent helps to reduce the salinity of the water and maintain water levels, thus enhancing habitat in several existing restoration sites in tourist areas. As part of the agreement, the Ecological Association of Hardy-Colorado River Users, Pronatura, and the Sonoran Institute committed to monitor water quality and ecological conditions in the Hardy River and of the effluent.

In 2008, the Colorado River Delta Water Trust was created to acquire rights and deliver water for habitat restoration in the delta. This effort was led by Pronatura and the Sonoran Institute, supported by private foundations from the United States and Mexico, and made possible through collaboration with government agencies, including CONAGUA, the National Institute of Ecology, and the Secretary of Environment and Natural Resources in Mexico, as well as the U.S. Department of the Interior's Fish and Wildlife Service (Zamora-Arroyo et al., 2008, p. 876). With guidance of a technical committee formed by network actors, the trust has been acquiring permanent water rights to maintain and restore the necessary flows for the conservation of the delta. But then network members came to recognize that the delta needed more permanent and regular baseline flow and not just periodic pulse flow to support and enhance thousands of acres of riparian and marsh habitat. Efforts were needed beyond the water trust to target upstream infrastructure, such as reservoirs and dams on the Colorado River (O. Hinojosa-Huerta, personal communication, October 25, 2013). A heightened binational process would be necessary to get the delta the water it so desperately needed.

Cooperative efforts continued in 2010, when after a series of negotiations between the two countries in consultation with network actors, the United States and Mexico signed Minute 316. Under the accord, the countries agreed to operate the Yuma desalting plant at one-third capacity for one year. The United States sought to operate the Yuma desalting plant, in an effort to ensure it could continue to meet Mexico's allocation of Colorado River water in the face of significant shortages. To ensure flows to the Ciénega de Santa Clara, one of the largest and most biologically rich wetland areas in the delta, the 30,000 acre-feet of water lost in the plant's operation would be replaced by the United States, Mexico, and environmental NGOs. The Ciénega, threatened by reduced flows and increased salinity by the plant's operations, supports large populations of endangered desert pupfish and Yuma clapper rails.

Under the plan, the United States would provide 10,000 acre-feet from groundwater sources; Mexico would provide 10,000 acre-feet of water by leasing water rights; and NGOs would provide 10,000 acre-feet by leasing water rights. A collaborative monitoring program, established among the University of Arizona, the Sonoran Institute, Pronatura, the Universidad Autónoma de Baja California, and the Upper Gulf of California and Colorado River Biosphere Reserve, was established to study the effect of the desalting plant on the Ciénega and its overall health.

In a landmark agreement, the United States and Mexico agreed to a new five-year water sharing agreement in November 2012 that would bring new water to the Colorado River Delta. Under Minute 319 to the 1944 Water Treaty, the United States, Mexico, and network actors agreed to provide some 158,088 acre-feet of water, including 52,696 acre-feet as base flows, to the riparian corridor and its delta. Minute 319 helped to launch a larger stakeholder binational process. To implement the agreement, the United States and Mexico decided to pursue a small team strategy. As a result, 12 small teams were formed under IBWC/CILA. For example, the Environmental Flows Small Team convened a group of agency representatives and researchers from both the United States and Mexico in 2013 to help develop a flow plan and a hydrograph. Network actors were active in this process, leading many small groups and helping to support implementation of Minute 319. Ultimately, the minute represents a strategy of packaging and linking a whole bunch of issues together and not just environmental flows in isolation (J. Pitt, personal communication, November 1, 2013). It offers something for everyone. As an important gesture to the United States, Mexico agrees to take shortages as the water users do in the lower Colorado River Basin. Similarly, with the minute, water users and agencies in the United States recognize that restoration of the delta is important to Mexico. Interestingly, Minute 319 ties long-term shortages to restoration and opens the possibility for water exchanges.

In recent years, the core network has been further united around implementation of Minute 319. To help reach the US$10 million goal for water and restoration commitments, network actors helped form the Raise the River Campaign, a collaboration between Sonoran Institute, Pronatura, the EDF, the Redford Center, the Nature Conservancy, and the National Fish and Wildlife Foundation (NFWF). According to the campaign, "Raisetheriver.org sees a day when the Colorado River once again flows into the Gulf of California, and the delta is brought back to life. By raising awareness, money and, ultimately the water level of the river, we will restore the wetlands and reconnect the river with the Gulf" (Raise the River, 2013, p. 1). The Redford Center initiated the partnership following the production of *Watershed*, a documentary about the Colorado River system released in 2012. The NFWF and the Nature Conservancy participate in a fundraising role and the Nature Conservancy also works to raise funds and provide expertise on the small teams. U.S.-based Packard and Walton Foundations also support the work. According to Francisco Zamora-Arroyo of the Sonoran Institute, the new partnership is a natural fit (personal communication, October 24, 2013). The Redford Center's approach of creating awareness, solutions, and acting meshes well with the network's long-term strategy and approach. Generating scientific knowledge and information sharing remains a central network goal in the implementation of Minute 319. To maintain interest in environmental flows, there is a need to demonstrate the benefits of such flows. This requires a substantial monitoring effort to look at the pulse flows as it occurs and to observe changes in landscape and hydrology (J. Pitt, personal communication, November 1, 2013). In this way, environmental flows to the delta remain central to the network's strategy and theory of victory.

DISCUSSION: SHIFTING TOWARDS GREATER PARTICIPATORY, SCIENCE-BASED GOVERNANCE IN THE COLORADO RIVER DELTA

The story of the transnational network operating around restoration of the Colorado River Delta is the story of the development and growth of a network. It is also the story of the subsequent shrinking and coalescence of the network. As the litigation strategy of the larger initial network failed, many actors abandoned the network. A few groups that had occupied the core of the larger network worked to reshape and reconstitute the network.

The goals established by this core network reflected members' interests and experiences working in the delta. As our discussion of the development and evolution of the networks reveals, these goals include conducting scientific research, restoring habitat, securing water, and enhancing public participation. These goals match up well against the network's strategies and larger governance functions. For example, network strategies to enhance public participation through local stakeholder participation in restoration projects along with more formal NGO representation in binational process illustrates capacity-building and rule-setting governance functions (see Table 9.1).

In performing these governance functions, network members rely on larger nested networks. Connections to these more peripheral networks

Table 9.1
Network Goals, Strategies, and Related Governance Functions

Goals	Strategies	Related Governance Functions
Conducting scientific research	Reports and articles; Monitoring; Establishing priorities	Information sharing
Restoring habitat	Habitat restoration projects	Information sharing; Capacity building
Securing water	Water Trust	Capacity building
Enhancing public participation	Local stakeholder participation in restoration projects; Formal NGO representation in binational process	Capacity building; Rule setting

serve to heighten engagement and joint dialogue, and help to maintain and grow the network by building trust and creating new bonds (O. Hinojosa-Huerta, personal communication, October 25, 2013). For example, network actors from Pronatura and the Sonoran Institute rely on a more local network in the Mexicali Valley related to restoration. The more nationally oriented groups of the EDF and TNC rely on a more U.S.-based network around broader Colorado River conservation and management issues. Network actors rely on these groups for a broader understanding of river policy and politics. But these groups also support the network by helping to communicate the larger message of the Colorado River as an iconic river with great environmental and recreational value (J. Pitt, personal communication, November 1, 2013).

In our analysis, we find that the governance functions are evolving with the network performing more information-sharing functions initially in terms of conducting scientific research and restoring habitat. These goals and strategies may be seen as information-sharing functions. Information is the main resource that is channeled to steer constituents towards network goals. Knowledge-generating and norm diffusion roles are key to the network. Some of these efforts, particularly about establishing restoration projects, also help to build capacity, which the network increasingly develops as it forms the Water Trust and works to enhance public participation. For the network, building capacity helps to enable action. As earlier research on network governance has indicated, as process entangled with negotiation over rights and responsibilities and struggles over the nature of the problem and its appropriate solutions, capacity building becomes a critical means through which governing is accomplished (Andonova et al., 2009, p. 64). As one network actor noted, building agency capacity is necessary to help steer agencies to allow for and permit water conservation within the broader context of environmental policy (F. Zamora-Arroyo, personal communication, October 24, 2013).

As the network pushed for greater stakeholder and public participation in formal binational processes, the network moved into rule-setting functions. Through rule setting, networks contribute to governance by validating norms, creating new norms, and establishing rules intended to guide and constrain constituents (Andonova et al., 2009; Kalfagianni & Pattberg, 2011). Through persuasion and dialogue that characterizes communicative actions, the network helps steer governance (Risse, 2004). We observe this shift at both the national and binational level in terms of governance.

At the national level, the network has offered proactive alternatives to environmental issues, thereby establishing a more positive dialogue with the government agencies. This dialogue has made it possible to explore the creative use of Mexican environmental regulations to develop a framework for the restoration of the Colorado River Delta (Zamora-Arroyo et al., 2008, p. 877). One example of this can be found in network actors' efforts in Mexico to help influence, and then benefit from, a change in national water law so "environmental uses" can be a use in Mexico under its recently amended National Water Law. In the past five years, network actors have been working with the National Water Commission in Mexico (Comisión Nacional del Agua [CONAGUA]) to make wetland restoration a priority. New institutional arrangements have resulted from these efforts. For example, the newly created Specialized Working Group on Wetlands was established as part of the Watershed Council (organized by CONAGUA) and under Mexico's National Water Law (O. Hinojosa-Huerta, personal communication, November 6, 2013).

In the binational context, through rule-setting governance functions, the network has helped steer the IBWC. Initially, in the absence of leadership, and with the IBWC not managing emerging conflicts well (e.g., Surplus Guidelines, consultations around the lining of the All American Canal), the transnational network emerged and filled the vacuum by convening actors, studying and developing priorities, and managing on-the-ground restoration projects. This is not to say that the network alone is responsible for the shift at the IBWC. Rather, the network benefited from timely changes underway at the IBWC, including a more open and responsive leadership with Carlos Marin's appointment to the U.S. IBWC in 2006, and then subsequently Roberto Salmon in 2007, following the death of both the U.S. and Mexican heads of the IBWC in a plane crash in 2007 (Mumme & Little, 2010).

When the binational process heightened in the mid-2000s, the IBWC seized upon the opportunity. The binational process offered a new role for the commission whereby it could escape the geopolitical dynamic that has historically curtailed its behavior. CILA Commissioner Roberto Salman called the delta a priority in 2013 (F. Zamora-Arroyo, personal communication, October 24, 2013). There is a public recognition by the IBWC that the network has been important in helping the United States and Mexico manage the water and improve the environment (F. Zamora-Arroyo, personal communication, October 24, 2013). Some network actors argue that the IBWC has grown to absorb environmental responsibility and believe in the importance of restoration of the delta (O. Hinojosa-Huerta, personal communication, October 25, 2013). The IBWC's present engagement in on-the-ground restoration projects in the delta is a powerful signal of this new direction.

This change in priority is also accompanied by a shift in the rules around participation. The dialogue has broadened to move beyond conversations between actors in Washington, DC, and Mexico City alone. Today, the network has a real seat at the table and an active role in supporting implementation of Minute 319. In part, the network has benefited from a shift in approach by the U.S. government away from the position that the Secretary of the Interior is the "water master" who dictates water operations and management along the Colorado River. Rather, at the national level, the United States is looking for stakeholders to help solve problems. It is also organizing behaviors of the relevant organizations in a manner that is most effective, which allows for a stronger and more active role for the IBWC in transboundary water governance.

This shift towards great participatory and science-based governance can be seen in the recent delivery of a "pulse flow," running for two months in the spring of 2014, which was meant to mimic the spring floods that historically inundated the Colorado River Delta. The event was historic. It reconnected the Colorado River with the ocean, an event that has not happened regularly for the past 50 years. As some students of the event noted, the "pulse flow re-created a river-scape and became a place to gather, recreate, remember and hope" (Bark, Robinson, & Flessa, 2016, p. 171). As a component of Minute 319, brokered by the IBWC, the water release was part of a pilot project to provide water for the environment. It marks the first time the two nations have delivered water to the delta to promote ecosystem restoration (IBWC, 2014). Flows for the delta were part of a larger package of issues that reflect the commitment of both countries to address water shortage in the Colorado River Basin. Experts contributed to more than three years of intensive negotiation, which culminated in the creation of the agreement to make the pulse flow a reality (Cohen & Gleick, 2012).

The intention of the pulse flow was to document its hydrologic and biologic effects; scientists were even uncertain that the water would reconnect with the gulf. Through a collaborative process, the Minute 319 Science Team is studying the pulse flow to better understand its benefits and impacts and to plan for future pulse flow events. The "core" of this group is composed of veterans of the earlier National Science Foundation (NSF)–supported Research Coordination Network on the Colorado River Delta. The progress report of the binational Environmental Flows Team (2014) indicates increases in green vegetation along the route wetted by the flow and in the wider area of the riverbanks (Earth Observatory, 2014).

Despite these shifts, we find that some issues remain off the table and continue to be resisted by the IBWC. Most notable is the issue of groundwater. Although there have been some notable efforts through a binational technical work group to integrate data and establish formal timetables, the IBWC has not effectively integrated groundwater data in a meaningful way to shape or influence policy (Ingram, 2000, p. 187; Szekely, 1993, p. 36), and a race to the bottom has resulted (Mumme, 2000, pp. 83–84). Groundwater remains a "taboo" subject for binational talks (de la Parra, Van Schoik, & Patron-Soberano, 2013, p. 139).[5]

Steve Mumme, a scholar of transboundary water management, has critically argued that narrow conversations of water swaps have been occurring in the Consultative Council, rather than difficult but needed dialogue about the overall water availability or commitment to long-term technical understanding of the delta's water needs (personal communication, May 1, 2013). Indeed it is too soon to know if these recent developments can further translate environmental values and priorities into other areas of border water management (Mumme, 2016b) or if they will substantially alter the treaty regime's approach to water management (Mumme, 2016a, p. 36).

CONCLUSION

In this chapter, we explored how networks of actors have been operating collaboratively to shift transboundary water governance in the Colorado River Delta region to be more participatory and science-based. We traced the emergence and evolution of the transnational network, highlighting different key stages, activities, and developments. Our discussion draws upon findings from international relations literature on transnational networks as well as collaborative governance literature in public policy research.

We have found that the transnational network around the delta performs a variety of governance functions, including information-sharing, capacity-building, and rule-setting functions. Our case study suggests that rule setting, along with deliberate activities and strategies that aim to reshape who participates and how participation occurs, is key to more participatory and science-based governance. In this way, the network has performed more traditional roles in knowledge creation and monitoring but also more "hard" governance in terms of shaping new processes for binational cooperation and implementing minutes to the treaty that governs the delta. The new forums that are being created and new management actions and behaviors collectively demonstrate this shift in governance.

These findings provide a platform for future research around transnational networks and governance functions. More research is necessary to unpack the role of governance functions in other types of networks to better understand how the nature of the issue itself matters or how a different formula of network actors (e.g., less NGO-based) that includes private sector actors plays out. Next steps might include more empirical research to understand how different forms of network governance interact and steers other international institutions in other cross-border or more multinational contexts. One direction for future scholarship would be to study how peripheral networks interact with more core transnational networks to shape learning across networks.

NOTES

1. This includes some 158,088 acre-feet of water, including 52,696 acre-feet as base flows, to the riparian corridor and its delta.
2. Except the 21-mile stretch between the northern and southern international boundaries, the delta is largely under Mexican jurisdiction, split between Sonora and Baja California states and the federal government.
3. See Pronatura at http://www.pronatura.org.mx/ and Sonoran Institute at http://www.sonoraninstitute.org/.
4. Interestingly, the Minute was negotiated under the authority of the 1970 boundary treaty and not the 1944 treaty, because linking it to the 1944 water treaty proved too controversial at the time.
5. According to de la Parra et al. (2013),

> The reticence by both governments to engage in a discussion on joint groundwater management is most evident in the Imperial-Mexicali valleys, where the All-American Canal incident of 2006 left several scars that neither federal government nor the State of California would care to touch. For U.S. entities, the concern appears to be the wetland habitat that has sprouted down-gradient from the agricultural fields in the Imperial Valley, within Mexican territory, due to the infiltration of irrigation water over decades. For Mexico, the concern is how to rein in private agricultural wells that are not fully regulated. In any event, groundwater can be euphemistically deemed as an area of opportunity for both countries within joint water management. (pp. 139–140)

REFERENCES

Andonova, L. B., Bestill, M. M., & Bulkeley, H. (2009). Transnational climate governance. *Global Environmental Politics*, *9*(2), 52–73.

Bäckstrand, K. (2008). Accountability of networked climate governance: The rise of transnational climate partnerships. *Global Environmental Politics*, *8*(3), 74–102.

Bark, R. H., Robinson, C. J., & Flessa, K. W. 2016. Tracking cultural ecosystem services: Water chasing the Colorado River restoration pulse flow. *Ecological Economics*, *127*, 165–172.

Betsill, M. M., & Bulkeley, H. (2004). Transnational networks and global environmental governance: The cities for climate protection program. *International Studies Quarterly*, *48*(2), 471–493.

Blatter, J. (2001). Debordering the world of states: Towards a multi-level system in Europe and a multi-polity system in North America? Insights from border regions. *European Journal of International Relations*, *7*(2), 175–209.

Bomberg, E. (2007). Policy learning in an enlarged European Union: Environmental NGOs and new policy instruments. *Journal of European Public Policy*, *14*(2), 248–268.

Breitmeier, H. (2008). *The legitimacy of international regimes*. Farnham, UK: Ashgate Publishers.

Cohen, M., & Gleick, P. H. (2012, November 20). An historic step toward saving the Colorado River and Delta. *Huffington Post*. Retrieved from: http://www.huffingtonpost.com/peter-h-gleick/an-historic-step-toward-sb 2167513.html

Cohen, M. J., Henges-Jeck, C., & Castillo-Moreno, G. (2001). Preliminary water balance for the Colorado River Delta, 1992–1998. *Journal of Arid Environments*, *49*(1), 35–48.

Conca, K. (2006). *Governing water: Contentious transnational politics and global institution building*. Cambridge, MA: MIT Press.

de la Parra, C. A., Van Schoik, R., & Patron-Soberano, K. (2013). The state of sustainability and the evolving challenges of managing the U.S.-Mexico border environment. In Wilson, C. E., & Lee, E. (Eds.), *The state of the border report: A comprehensive analysis of the U.S--Mexico border* (pp. 122–149). Washington, DC: Wilson Center.

Dibble, S. (2011, February 6). U.S.-Mexico boost collaboration on Colorado River. *San Diego Union-Tribune*, p. A1. Retrieved from http://www.signonsandiego.com/news/2011/feb/06/us-mexico-boosting-collaboration-colorado-river

Earth Observatory. (2014). A pulse of new life on the Colorado River. Retrieved from http://earthobservatory.nasa.gov/IOTD/view.php?id=84904&utm_source=Circle+of+Blue+WaterNews+%26+Alerts&utm_campaign=ae89a98f08-Federal-Water-Tap-RSS_EMAIL_CAMPAIGN&utm_medium=email&utm_term=0_c1265b6ed7-ae89a98f08-250654650

Environmental Defense Fund. (2005, July 18). Leading conservation groups offer shortage proposal for Colorado River "conservation before shortage" proposal emphasizes short-term conservation to avoid abrupt disruptions in water deliveries. Retrieved from http://www.edf.org/news/leading-conservation-groups-offer-shortage-proposal-colorado-river

Environmental Defense Fund. (2009, May 7). Environmental defense fund honored with Department of Interior Partners in Conservation award. edf.org. Retrieved from http://www.edf.org/news/environmental-defense-fund-honored-department-interior-partners-conservation-award

Environmental Flows Team. (2014, December 4). Minute 319 Colorado River Delta environmental flows monitoring: Initial progress report. Retrieved from http://www.circleofblue.org/waternews/wp-content/uploads/2014/12/Reclamation_Min319Monitoring.pdf?utm_source=Circle+of+Blue+WaterNews+%26+Alerts&utm_campaign=ae89a98f08-Federal-Water-Tap-RSS_EMAIL_CAMPAIGN&utm_medium=email&utm_term=0_c1265b6ed7-ae89a98f08-250654650

Gerlak, A. K., Zamora-Arroyo, F., & Kahler, H. P. (2013). A delta in repair: Restoration, binational cooperation, and the future of the Colorado River Delta. *Environment: Science and Policy for Sustainable Development*, 55(3), 29–40.

Glennon, R. J., & Culp, P. W. (2002). The last green lagoon: How and why the Bush administration should save the Colorado River Delta. *Ecology Law Quarterly*, *28*, 903–992.

Hayton, R. D. (1993). The matter of public participation. *Natural Resources Journal*, *33*(2), 275–282.

Hinojosa-Huerta, O., Briggs, M., Carrillo-Guerrero, Y., Glenn, E. P., Lara-Flores, M., & Román-Rodríguez, M. (2005). *Community-based restoration of desert wetlands: The case of the Colorado River Delta* (PSW-GTR-191). Washington, DC: USDA Forest Service.

Ingram, H. (2000). Transboundary groundwater on the U.S.-Mexico border: Is the glass half full, half empty, or even on the table? *Natural Resources Journal*, *40*, 185–188.

Ingram, H., & White, D. R. (1993). International boundary and water commission: An institutional mismatch for resolving transboundary water problems. *Natural Resources Journal*, *33*(1), 153–176.

International Boundary and Water Commission. (2012, November 20). United States and Mexico, commission signs Colorado River agreement [Press release]. Washington, DC: Author. Retrieved from http://www.ibwc.state.gov/Files/Press_Release_112012.pdf

International Boundary and Water Commission. (2014, May 16). Colorado River reconnects with the sea following historic release of water for the environment [Press release]. Washington, DC: Author. Retrieved from http://www.ibwc.gov/Files/Press_Release_051614.pdf

Jenkins, M. (2007, February 5). The efficiency paradox. *High Country News*.

Kalfagianni A., & Pattberg P. (2011). *The effectiveness of transnational rule-setting organisations in global sustainability politics: An analytical framework* (Global Governance Working Paper No 43). Amsterdam, the Netherlands: The Global Governance Project.

Karl, T. R., Melillo, M., & Peterson, T. C. (Eds.). (2009). *Global climate change impacts in the United States*. New York, NY: Cambridge University Press.

Karvonen, A. (2011). Politics of urban runoff: Nature, technology, and the sustainable city. Cambridge, MA: MIT Press.

Kelly, M., & Szekely, A. (2004). *Modernizing the International Boundary and Water Commission* (Policy Paper No. 1). Berkeley, CA: University of California, Center for Latin American Studies.

Laird-Benner, W., & Ingram, H. (2011). Sonoran desert network weavers: Surprising environmental successes on the U.S./Mexico border. *Environment: Science and Policy for Sustainable Development*, *53*(1), 6–16.

Lipschutz, R. (1997). Networks of knowledge and practice: Global civil society and protection of the global environment. In L. A. Brooks &

S. D. VanDeveer (Eds.), *Saving the seas: Values, scientists, and international governance* (pp. 427–468). College Park, MD: Maryland Sea Grant College.

Liverman, D. M., Varady, R. G. Chavez, O., & Sanchez, R. (1999). Environmental issues along the United States-Mexico border: Drivers of change and responses to citizens and institutions. *Annual Review of Energy and Environment*, *24*(1), 607–643.

Lovett, I. (2012, November 20). U.S. and Mexico sign a deal on sharing the Colorado River. *New York Times*.

Luecke, D. F., Pitt, J., Congdon, C., Glenn, E., Valdés-Casillas, C., & Briggs, M. (1999). *A delta once more: Restoring riparian and wetland habitat in the Colorado River Delta*. Washington, DC: Environmental Defense Publications.

Marcos, J., & Cornelius, S. (2004). Mapping the organizational landscape in the Colorado River Delta: The big picture on binational collaboration. *Southwest Hydrology*, (January/February), 22–24.

Mumme, S. (2000). Minute 242 and beyond, challenges and opportunities for managing transboundary groundwater on the Mexico-U.S. border. *Natural Resources Journal*, *40*, 341–378.

Mumme, S. P. (2001). The US-Mexico International Boundary and Water Commission in the sustainable development era. *IBRU Boundary and Security Bulletin*, *9*(2), 117–125.

Mumme, S. P. (2005). The International Boundary and Water Commission under fire: Policy prospective for the 21st century. *The Journal of Environment & Development*, *14*(4), 507–524.

Mumme, S. P. (2016a). Enhancing the U.S.-Mexico treaty regime on transboundary rivers: Minutes 317–319 and the elusive environmental minute. *The Journal of Water Law*, *25*(1), 27–37.

Mumme, S. P. (2016b). Scarcity and power in US–Mexico transboundary water governance: Has the architecture changed since NAFTA? *Globalizations*, *13*(6), 702–718.

Mumme, S. P., & Little, D. J. (2010). Leadership, politics, and administrative reform at the United States Section of the International Boundary and Water Commission, United States and Mexico. *Social Science Journal*, *47*(2), 252–270.

Nagler, P. L., Glenn, E. P., Hursh, K. Curtis, C., & Huete, A. (2005). Vegetation mapping for change detection on an arid zone river. *Environmental Monitoring & Assessment*, *109*(1–3), 255–274.

Pitt, J. (2014, April 21). Nature responds to Colorado River Delta pulse flow. *National Geographic*. Retrieved from http://newswatch.nationalgeographic.com/2014/04/21/nature-responds-to-colorado-river-delta-pulse-flow/

Pitt, J., Hinojosa-Huerta, O., & Carrillo-Guerrero, Y. (2010). Getting ahead of a water crisis: Binational collaboration in the Colorado River Basin. Retrieved from http://www.atl.org.mx/coloquio/images/stories/curricula/Osvel%20Hinojosa-Jennifer%20Pitt%20ponencia%20ingl%C3%A9s.pdf

Raise the River. (2013). *Restoring the Colorado River Delta: Restoration opportunity guide*. National Fish and Wildlife Federation, Sonoran Institute, Environmental Defense Fund, Pronatura, The Nature Conservancy, and Redford Center.

Raise the River. (2014). Renewal: A reborn Colorado River once again finds her path to the sea. Retrieved from http://raisetheriver.org/stories/

Risse, T. (2004). Global governance and communicative action. *Government and Opposition*, *39*(2), 288–313.

Robbins, T. (2014, April 4). Waters will flood part of Colorado River, for just a few weeks. *National Public Radio*. Retrieved from http://www.npr.org/2014/04/04/298732484/waters-will-flood-part-of-colorado-river-for-just-a-few-weeks?utm_source=Circle+of+Blue+WaterNews+%26+Alerts&utm_campaign=695b9e44fa-RSS_EMAIL_CAMPAIGN&utm_medium=email&utm_term=0_c1265b6ed7-695b9e44fa-250654650

Sanchez, R. (1993). Public participation and the IBWC: Challenges and options. *Natural Resources Journal*, *33*(2), 283–298.

Sanchez-Rodriguez, R., & Mumme, S. P. (2013). Protecting the environment? In P. H. Smith & A. Selee (Eds.). *Mexico and United States: The politics of partnership* (pp. 139–159). Boulder, CO: Lynne Reiner Press.

Slaughter, A. M. (2004). *A new world order*. Princeton, NJ: Princeton University Press.

Stein, M., & Turkewitsch, L. (2010). Multi-level governance in Canadian and American intergovernmental relations. In H. Enderlein, S. Walti, & M. Zurn (Eds.), *Handbook on multilevel governance* (pp. 184–202). Cheltenham, UK: Edward Elger.

Stoett, P., & Temby, O. (2015). Bilateral and trilateral natural resource and biodiversity governance in North America: Organizations, networks, and inclusion. *Review of Policy Research*, *32*(1): 1–18.

Szekely, A. (1993). How to accommodate an uncertain future into institutional responsiveness and planning: The case of Mexico and the United States. *Natural Resources Journal*, *33*(2), 397–404.

Temby, O., Rastogi, R., Sandall, J., Cooksey, R., & Hickey, G. M. (2015). Interagency trust and communication in the transboundary governance of Pacific salmon fisheries. *Review of Policy Research*, *32*(1): 79–99.

Umoff, A. A. (2008). An analysis of the 1944 U.S.-Mexico water treaty: Its past, present, and future. *Environs: U.C. Davis School of Law Environmental Law and Policy Journal*, *32*(1), 69–98.

U.S. Bureau of Reclamation. (2012). *The Colorado River Basin water supply and demand study: Study report*. Washington, DC: U.S. Department of the Interior, Bureau of Reclamation.

Valdés-Casillas, C., Hinajosa-Huerta, O., Muñoz-Viveroz, M., Zamora-Arroyo, F., Carrillo-Guerrero, Y., Delgado-Garcia, S., . . . Luecke, D. (1998). *Information database and local outreach program for the restoration of the hardy river wetlands, lower Colorado River Delta, Baja California and Sonora, Mexico* [A report to the North American Wetlands Council]. Retrieved from http://www.sci.sdsu.edu/salton/InfoDatabaseRioHardy.html

Varady, R. G., Hankins, K. B., Kaus, A., Young, E., & Merideth, R. (2001). . . . to the Sea of Cortes: Nature, water, culture and livelihood in the lower Colorado River Basin and Delta: An overview of issues, policies, and approaches to environmental restoration. *Journal of Arid Environments*, *49*, 195–209.

Zamora-Arroyo, F., & Flessa, K. W. (2009). Nature's fair share: Finding and allocating water for the Colorado River Delta. In L. L. Hoffman, E. D. McGovern, R. G. Varady & K. W. Flessa (Eds.), *Conservation of shared environments: Learning from the United States and Mexico* (pp. 23–38). Tucson, AZ: The University of Arizona Press.

Zamora-Arroyo, F., Hinojosa-Huerta, O., Santiago, E., Brott, E., & Culp, P. (2008). Collaboration in Mexico: Renewed hope for the Colorado River Delta. *Nevada Law Journal*, *8*, 871–889.

Zamora-Arroyo, F., Pitt, J., Cornelius, S., Glenn, E., Hinojosa-Huerta, O., Moreno, M., . . . Parra, I. (2005). *Conservation priorities in the Colorado River Delta, Mexico and the United States*. Prepared by the Sonoran Institute, Environmental Defense, University of Arizona, Pronatura Noroeste Dirección de Conservación Sonora, Centro de Investigación.

TEN

Environmentalists, Natural Resources, and the Fence on the Mexico Boundary

STEPHEN P. MUMME AND CHRISTOPHER BROWN

INTRODUCTION

On May 11, 2005, President George W. Bush signed an inaptly named piece of legislation, the Real ID Act of 2005, into law (PL109-13). With a stroke of the presidential pen, important achievements in environmental protection along the U.S.-Mexican border were thrust into jeopardy. Among the outcomes of the act was the ability to build almost unlimited border security infrastructure completely outside of the existing regime of state and federal environmental policy that had long existed to protect environmental quality and natural resources. "The Fence" (which, in various places along the border, actually consists of a triple fence and a complex system of roads) was built almost wholly outside of the National Environmental Policy Act (NEPA), the California Coastal Act of 1976, the federal Coastal Zone Management Act, and an assortment of other regulatory instruments, with major impacts on flora, fauna, and a range of hydrologic processes. Remarkably, aside from a small set of local environmental activists, Bill H.R. 1268, passed into law with scarcely a peep from national environmental groups or border-level organizations outside the San Diego area. This was not for lack of serious concern once the deed was done. The truth is that environmental groups were preoccupied with other battles. In this case, they were outflanked by a clever maneuver in the House Rules Committee and stymied politically by arguments for homeland—read border—security. The U.S.-Mexican border environment is the worse for it.

Why did this occur, what does it mean, and has the environmental community been able to mend this breach and gain greater influence in border security as it impacts environmental values in the border area? From a political science perspective, we might attribute this policy outcome to the well-known pattern of punctuated equilibrium, a situation in which an opposition political coalition adroitly maneuvers to switch consideration of a policy matter to another, more favorable, congressional committee or committees in Congress (Baumgartner & Jones, 1991, pp. 1046–1051). This presumes, however, that the issue in question—border environmental protection—was dominated by a defined policy subsystem and contested by competing policy coalitions. However, this assumption is questionable. Marshaling border-level environmental concern in Washington, DC, is difficult, as it requires alliances with well-established national environmental advocacy groups. In the run-up to the North American Free Trade Agreement (NAFTA) in the early 1990s, such alliances were forged (Hoggenboom, 1998, 151–153). Environmental mobilization and transnational activism grew rapidly in the border region. By the mid-2000s, however, the institutionalization of environmental activism through new agencies such as the Border Environment Cooperation Commission (BECC) and the North American Development Bank (NADB), combined with diminished public funding for environmental initiatives, contributed to a slackening of environmental mobilization along the border (Cohen, 2003, p. 55; Mumme, 2014, p. 414) and diminished the level of attention paid to border environmental issues in the Beltway. Moreover, the venues for environmental policy in the U.S. Congress are multiple and dispersed (Rosenbaum, 2002, pp. 66–67), which complicates any argument for a clear-cut venue shift related to border environmental policy. These complications have been exacerbated by the reduced focus of the federal government on border environmental issues in light of the hypersecuritization of border policy that we have seen since the 9/11 attacks (Good Neighbor Environmental Board [GNEB], 2007). A better explanation is that groups supporting environmental improvement on the U.S.-Mexican border were simply sidestepped by a much stronger coalition favoring immigration restriction and border security. In other words, the battle between pro-environment and pro-security coalitions at the border was never directly engaged. Environmentalists, whose border-specific concerns were poorly consolidated and given effect through fragmented venues in Congress, had little opportunity to join the argument and were thus easily vanquished by this classic act of legislative legerdemain. With the sharp insertion of security into practically every aspect of border environmental cooperation since 2005, it is reasonable to ask whether environmentalists have begun to bridge this policy gap in the hope of influencing the debate over border security and its environmental impacts.

THE POLITICS OF THE REAL ID ACT OF 2005

The compelling problem of U.S. national security since the fatal events of September 11, 2001, unquestionably poses a serious challenge to other domestic and international policy commitments. The U.S.-Mexican border, which as a front-line region receives a disproportionate share of national security attention, has taken much of the brunt of this shift in national priorities. Considerable effort and expense has been put into reinforcing border security and containing migration along the 1,967-mile international boundary between Mexico and the United States. One of the policy causalities is environmental protection.

To appreciate this, one has to set recent developments against the backdrop of the strengthening of environmental protection along the border in the 1990s. The NAFTA initiative mobilized environmental concern with border conditions to an unprecedented degree, resulting in a range of new environmental programs and institutions and the strengthening of older ones. After 1993, the binational program for environmental protection, Border XXI, and the linked agencies for border environmental infrastructure development, the BECC and NADB, produced an infusion of investments in environmental protection in the border region.

The federal retreat from U.S. investment in binational environmental cooperation was already underway when the events of 9/11 occurred. Program financing was on the decline. When U.S. and Mexican environmental agencies announced the program successor to the Border XXI Program, their new Border 2012 Program placed greater weight on state and local participation in policy development (USEPA, 2003). This was not a bad thing in itself, but it signaled less federal financial support. It was followed by a ratcheting down of U.S. commitment to the Border Environmental Infrastructure Fund (BEIF), which is operationally housed at NADB and the primary vehicle for subsidizing investments in BECC-certified environmental projects (dos Santos, 2004; GNEB, 2005). Binational relations generally suffered from U.S. neglect of Mexican concerns due to the U.S.' single-minded effort to ramp up national security (Starr, 2004). A thorny dispute over Mexico's treaty water obligations on the Rio Grande also proved a diplomatic irritant.

It was in this state of frayed U.S.-Mexican relations and diminished attention to the border environment that the Real ID Act arises. Responding to the alarmist rhetoric of the so-called War on Terror, immigration restrictionists in Congress, buoyed by populist demonstrations and vigilantism along the border, intensified their efforts to tighten enforcement of immigration law. They drew on the 1996 Illegal Immigration and Immigrant Responsibility Act (IIRIRA) that authorized the U.S. Attorney General to construct roads and fences in the vicinity of the U.S.-Mexican border to thwart illegal immigration (Section 102 (a)), including a 14-mile triple barrier fence at San Diego (Section 102 (b)). IIRIRA's Section 102 (c) allowed the attorney general to waive both the 1973 Endangered Species Act and NEPA (Nunez-Neto & Vina, 2005, p. 3). In 2002, the newly established Department of Homeland Security (DHS) assumed authority over border enforcement through its operational agency, the Bureau of Customs and Border Protection (CBP). When CBP moved to build the final 3.5 miles of the fence at San Diego, it was stymied by environmental lawsuits and a California Coastal Commission review.

Politically, the immigration debate intensified due to the rising numbers of undocumented aliens residing in the United States after IIRIRA (Camarota, 2005). In 2002, the Mexican government stepped up efforts to issue its external identification card, the *matricula consular*, in an effort to provide Mexican migrants a mechanism for accessing drivers' licenses, health, and financial services.[1] These matricula cards, issued by Mexican consulates nationwide, were controversial. They attracted the attention of prominent congressional restrictionists like Colorado Congressman Tom Tancredo, who challenged their verifiability and duplicability.

Shortly after the 108th Congress reconvened in February 2004, the Bush administration introduced a major legislative proposal for comprehensive immigration reform predicated on a substantial new guest worker provision coupled with an expedited pathway to citizenship for legally resident aliens (White House, 2004). The president's proposal got a lukewarm reception in Congress. James Sensenbrenner of Wisconsin, the chairman of the House Judiciary Committee, made known he would sponsor an effort to rein in use of the matricula document nationwide to strengthen national security and border enforcement. This initiative was controversial for several reasons, not the least of which was its clear intrusion on state prerogative to set the terms for issuance of drivers' licenses and other credentials for access to state and state-administered federal services. Even so, the measure was written into an omnibus intelligence reform bill in 2004. The immigration provisions of the intelligence bill were removed by the Senate (Dlouhy, 2005b, p. 402).

Sensenbrenner and other restrictionists were also concerned with what they perceived as the slow pace of implementing certain provisions of the 1996 IIRIRA, including fence construction at San Diego. The fencing project had gone forward except for a 3.5-mile span that threatened the sustainability of the Tijuana River estuary, a major coastal protected zone abutting the border immediately south of San Diego (Stern, 2005a, p. 443). Even after the creation of the DHS, resistance by ecological preservationists and environmental groups had held up further development.

The debate over the president's proposed guest worker policy and the matriculas and how to deal with them continued through the spring and summer of 2004, and was politicized further by the pending general election that November. In Arizona, a highly restrictive state initiative, the Arizona Taxpayer and Citizen Protection Act, or Proposition 200, was placed on the ballot. It required proof of citizenship to access state services (State of Arizona, 2004) and passed and became law in 2005.

In this politically charged climate, Sensenbrenner persuaded Republican house leaders to attach his anti-matricula bill to the first guaranteed-to-pass legislation in the 109th Congress, a supplemental appropriations bill funding the war in Iraq. Shortly after HR 418—the anti-matricula bill dubbed the Real ID Act of 2005—was introduced, it was amended by the House Judiciary Committee in February 2005 to incorporate a remarkably broad provision, ostensibly for purposes of hastening construction of the Tijuana River section of the San Diego border fence (Dlouhy, 2005a, p. 442). This provision exempted the DHS from all domestic legislation that might conceivably hinder it from building security infrastructure along the entire U.S. border with Canada and Mexico, not just the San Diego region.

Specifically, the bill's language provided that the Secretary of Homeland Security shall have "the authority to waive, and shall waive, all laws," that he or she "determines necessary to ensure expeditious construction of the barriers and roads" along the international borders of the United States (Dlouhy, 2005a, p. 442). As noted by *Congressional Quarterly* analysts at the time, this language meant the only thing standing between the DHS and a fence-building project was the secretary's determination and the appropriations process. The draconian provision trumped all federal, state, tribal, and municipal law, utterly exempting the DHS from either the environmental impact statement process or any other public disclosure required by NEPA, even in the planning process.

This remarkable measure did not proceed unchallenged. When HR 418 was appended to the Iraq War supplemental, HR 1268, senators amended the section to add a provision for federal court review on constitutional grounds (Dlouhy, 2005c). As amended, passed, and signed into law on May 11, 2005, the legislation read:

(1) In general. Notwithstanding any other provision of law, the Secretary of Homeland Security shall have the authority to waive all legal requirements such Secretary, in such Secretary's sole discretion, determines necessary to ensure expeditious construction of barriers and roads under this section. Any such decision by the Secretary shall be effective upon being published in the Federal Register.

(2) Federal court review.

(A) In general. The district courts of the United States shall have exclusive jurisdiction to hear all causes or claims arising from any action undertaken, or any decision made, by the Secretary of Homeland Security pursuant to paragraph (1). A cause of action or claim may only be brought alleging a violation of the Constitution of the United States. The court shall not have jurisdiction to hear any claim not specified in this subparagraph.

The remarkable aspect of this legislative history is that despite these unprecedented provisions—the Congressional Research Service attested it found no other instance of a law ever that permitted a federal agency to so completely and unilaterally avoid the requirements of other federal statutes (Dlouhy, 2005a, p. 443)—these became law in the absence of any serious public debate or congressional discussion of their environmental implications or impacts. Moreover, no environmental group inside the Beltway appeared to testify against the bill or could be found mentioned in the congressional record questioning the bill. At the time Real ID was under discussion, only one national environmental organization, the Wilderness Society, even reported on the Homeland Security provisions of HR 418/HR 1268 (Wilderness Society, 2005). Virtually every other "big ten environmental group," including such heavyweights as the National Wildlife Federation, Sierra Club, Natural Resources Defense Council, Defenders of Wildlife, Audubon, and Environmental Defense, was silent.[2] Adding force to this assessment, it is worth noting that a review of the committee hearings for the Senate Foreign Affairs Committee, the House International Relations Committee, and the House Committee on Homeland Security for 2005 through April 2006 found that none of them focused on the environmental implications of homeland security or border security or involved any environmental witnesses or testimony or submitted statements by environmental organizations.[3] In other words, in the legislative arenas dealing with border security, where it mattered most, environmentalists were entirely absent from the debate. Our further review of environment-related committee hearings and debate in the 109th Congress found no reference to the environmental impact of HR 418 or any other immigration legislation. In sum, immigration restrictionists and border hawks in the House and the Senate simply avoided engaging the issue in any relevant security committees or any of the historic committees and subcommittees tasked with federal environmental concerns (a list of these committees is found in Rosenbaum, 2002, pp. 68–69).

The policy effect of the Real ID Act is certainly comprehensive. Not only does it confer on the Secretary of Homeland Security the ability to construct roads, barriers, or fencing at will along the border contingent on congressional funding, it means that any binational environmental project or program that affects or might be affected by such infrastructure needs to have DHS approval to proceed. For the first time in U.S. history, environmental concerns could be dismissed at will at the discretion of a single agency.[4]

THE REAL ID AND SECURE FENCE ACTS: ENVIRONMENTAL IMPACTS AT THE BORDER

Upon its enactment, congressional restrictionists immediately sought funding for as much as 700 miles of border fencing divided in at least five segments in the so-called Sensenbrenner bill, HR-4437, which passed the House in December 2005 (U.S. House of Representatives, 2005). With minor modifications, this initiative became law as the Secure Fence Act of 2006. A review of the impacts of fence construction in general and in select areas highlights the long-term impact of the Real ID and Secure Fence Acts on the long-term viability of the border environment.

While the degree of adverse impact hinges on the type of infrastructure actually constructed, there is little doubt that construction and traffic worsen air quality in all boundary-adjacent areas where roads are built. Conventional fences impede or prevent wildlife flows and their construction may well impact endangered or threatened species. Fences, even permeable fences or a series of posts, disrupt watersheds and runoff, altering patterns of percolation and absorption, changing patterns of germination and seed dispersal, and altering natural habitat. In early 2007, when the project began, none of this had been examined in depth, nor were any binational teams or studies established to investigate this impact. By 2009, several such projects were underway, but many experts thought these were too late in coming to mitigate the fence's adverse effects. Doyle (2014) notes that fence as constructed in the Organ Pipe

Cactus National Monument acted as a literal dam that resulted in spill erosion and loss of riparian habitat.

Conservation Challenges

To better appreciate the far-reaching impacts of tactical security infrastructure on the border region, it is useful to consider what is at stake. The security structures authorized by the Secure Fence Act are situated in or cut across vital ecosystems and conservation zones along the U.S.-Mexican and U.S.-Canadian border, presenting numerous conservation challenges.

The U.S.-Mexican boundary, for example, runs 1,952 miles from coast to coast and bisects numerous distinctive ecological zones, including two of North America's biodiversity "hot spots"—the California Floristic Province near the Pacific Coast and the Madrean Pine-Oak Woodlands associated with the Sonoran and Chihuahuan desert zones. The California Floristic Province alone contains an estimated 3,488 species of vegetation, 61% of which is endemic to the region (Reimann, 2007, p. 105). The boundary either abuts or passes near 37 federal protected areas in the United States and 7 in Mexico (U.S. Geological Survey [USGS], 2006), most of which are directly intended to protect and conserve wildlife and habitat and represent billions of dollars of conservation investment between the two nations, with antecedents that extend back more than half a century.

The fence and other security-based physical structures threaten this rich endowment of natural resources in many ways. Ecosystem specialists and wildlife biologists associate physical barriers with altered interaction between flora and fauna and modifications of water flows sustaining natural habitats. Among the principal impacts on natural flora are: fragmentation of plant communities, the introduction of invasive and exotic species, soil erosion and compaction, altered zones of seed dispersal, pollination, and propagation, altered plant communities due to modified hydrology, and microclimate variations (Peters, 2007, p. 96). Impacts on fauna include edge effects of fragmentation, barriers to species dispersion and migration, interrupted genetic exchange, proliferation of noxious fauna, light pollution hazards for nocturnal fauna, and stressors arising from noise pollution associated with construction, surveillance, vehicular and human traffic, and other security-related disturbances (Moya, 2007, pp. 65–66). Koleff et al. (2007, p. 131) argue that the U.S. border fence, "will generate further ecosystem fragmentation and will bring about significant deterioration of plant and animal communities, preventing free movement of wildlife populations between the United States and Mexico by eliminating biological corridors and ecosystems, which would place their long term conservation in a critical state."[5]

Securitization has also complicated policy coordination and binational initiatives for environmental cooperation. The elevation of security policy in U.S. national and regional planning has been rapidly pursued with less consideration for policy integration and environmental practice than many environmental researchers and scientists and environmental advocacy groups deem to be acceptable. It has also been done unilaterally, bypassing many existing binational and trinational agencies and programs with conservation mandates. Since 2005, the DHS Secretary has invoked the Real ID Act to waive federal and state environmental law on five different occasions, suspending as many as 30 different laws in the process.[6] While the DHS has consulted with affected agencies and other stakeholders, its consultations have been criticized as ad hoc, out-sourced, unresponsive, and laced with conflict and disagreement among the affected domestic parties (Eriksson & Taylor, 2009, pp. 3–5).

A total of 13 major federal protected zones lie along the international boundary and this list does not include all private or state government reserves (USGS, 2006). As many as 450 rare or endemic species, and 85 threatened or endangered species may be found along the international boundary, many inhabiting these protected areas (Ingram, 1998, p. 5). In addition to problems outlined here, with respect to the Tijuana estuary, any fence built along the Arizona border or the Rio Grande should be assumed to have adverse environmental consequences, particularly when accompanied by roads, stadium lights, remote sensing monitoring systems, helicopter landing pads, and other security infrastructure. The Center for Biological Diversity notes, for instance, that Sonoran pronghorn antelope numbers are already declining; fewer than 300 may be found on either side of the border (Center for Biological Diversity, 2006). Species like the masked bobwhite quail are now being reintroduced on the Arizona border (Mensah, 2010), and such programs will be threatened if not eliminated by these border security measures.

Along the Rio Grande, a vast, interconnected network of wildlife habitats comprise the Lower Rio Grande Valley National Wildlife Refuge, home to 1,100 plants, 287 butterfly species, and nearly 900 vertebrates including 465 types of birds. The U.S. Fish and Wildlife Service describes the refuge as one of the most biologically diverse wildlife corridors in the continental United States (Brown, 1998). These habitat zones span the international boundary and are sure to be impaired by the fencing project.

Another protected area worthy of some additional exploration is the San Pedro Riparian National Conservation Area (SPRNCA), a 57,000-acre riparian area designated as a federally protected zone in 1988. SPRNCA is home to more than 350 species of mammals, reptiles, amphibians, and birds, and Doyle (2014) notes that impacts of the border fence in the region include restrictions on wildlife movement that threaten the viability of wildlife populations. In fact, plans to develop a conservation plan for the jaguar (*Panthera onca*) were dropped in 2008 by the U.S. Department of the Interior due to limited populations in the United States; critics of the fence argue it plays a major role in limiting movement of jaguars north of the U.S.-Mexican border (Herbert, 2010). The effectiveness of the fence in regard to limiting the movement of humans is examined by McCallum, Rowcliffe, and Cuthill (2014), who note "the intermittent fencing present in this part of the world does affect some native species, but does not necessarily restrict the movement of humans (including illegal migrants), who may negatively impact native species" (p. 1).

Border fencing not only impacts protected zones but also scars and disrupts reserved tribal lands. Of the 27 Native American tribes inhabiting the border region (GNEB, 2005, p. 8), four have lands directly abutting the international boundary. Tribal leaders wish to preserve the environmental, ecological, and historic endowments of their domains and do not wish to see national security achieved disproportionately at their expense. These tribes share cross-border cultural ties with Mexican sister communities that depend on a common ecological endowment bisected by the international line. Perhaps the most evident case of this dynamic is that of the Tohono O'odham Nation, which is literally bisected by the international border. Despite guarantees in the Gadsden Purchase that free movement of tribal members is guaranteed, the border fence and related enforcement actions by CBP officials makes cross-border movement of tribal members impossible, with severely negative impacts on subsistence and religious practices of the Tohono O'odham and their overall cultural survival (Levin, 2017; Witman, 2011).

In sum, fencing on the scale now entrusted to the DHS seriously impacts the border environment, related preservationist concerns, institutional and bilateral affairs, and the cultural fabric of the communities that exist along the border. Most environmentalists agree that the environmental progress realized at the border over the past three decades should not be surrendered or compromised in a panicked rush. Nor should these values be set aside or otherwise disarticulated from security discussions in the nation's capital and statehouses. It is vital, then, that border environmental policy and environmental policy writ large have a seat at the table when infrastructural changes of the current magnitude, following the November 2016 election, are under discussion. Unfortunately, this has not yet happened.

ENVIRONMENTAL RESPONSE AND MOBILIZATION

While it is fair to say that many environmentalists were appalled at the ill-considered rush to build tactical security infrastructure at the border in 2005–2006, it is equally fair to say they responded too late to seriously affect the border fence project or mitigate its damaging effects. As noted previously, the environmental lobby was bypassed in the legislative treatment of the Real ID and the Secure Fence Acts. In their aftermath, environmentalists mounted what might be described as a partial mobilization against the fence. This response included (1) legal challenge of specific DHS administrative actions including waivers under the Real ID Act; (2) legislative initiatives in Congress; and (3) regional and binational coalition building and mobilization to opposed fence construction in specific localities along the border. On the whole, however, this fragmented effort failed to gain political traction even after Barack Obama took office. A short review tells the story.

Legal Challenge

At this point, both the national and border environmental communities have yet to fashion a broad-gauged coalition to challenge these draconian securitization initiatives, yet piecemeal efforts did take place in various places along the border. In the summer of 2007, after construction began along the Arizona-Sonora border, Defenders of Wildlife and the Sierra Club filed a temporary restraining order halting work on the fence at the southern reach of the San Pedro River National Conservation Area. The order was granted by federal district court. In October 2007, U.S. Secretary of Homeland Security Michael Chertoff responded by exercising his waiver authority. In May 2008, the environmentalists' petition was amended in light of Chertoff's further waiver of environmental rules for the entire 470 miles reach of the Arizona boundary and 22 miles along the Rio Grande cutting through the Lower Rio Grande Wildlife Refuge in Hidalgo County (Archibold, 2008). In June 2008, the U.S. Supreme Court refused to hear the environmentalists' appeal, and construction resumed in the riparian zone.

In May 2008, after Chertoff—in the face of resistance by conservation groups, municipal leaders and property owners—waived environmental statutes for the Lower Rio Grande Valley, a further lawsuit was filed opposing construction of the fence in the lower Rio Grande section of the international border. In this case environmentalists joined with the Texas Border Coalition, an advocacy group for Texas border counties and towns, in filing the suit, which focused almost entirely on property rights. The lawsuit was subsequently dismissed in federal district court. In sum, legal challenges to DHS waiver authority and administrative decisions have failed to arrest construction of the fence or affect its design and configuration.

Legislative Challenge

As contracts were let for fence construction in early 2007, environmentalists led by Defenders of Wildlife[7] and the Center for Biological Diversity, with somewhat tepid support from other national environmental groups and more passionate support from numerous state and local groups along the border, finally began to lobby Congress for mitigation action. The first fruits of this effort were realized when Arizona Congressman Raul Grijalva introduced H.R. 2593, the *Borderlands Conservation and Security Act*, in June 2007 (Hurowitz, 2007). This bill, with 49 congressional sponsors, sought to amend the Real ID and Secure Fence Acts to rescind the DHS secretary's waiver authority, grant DHS discretion as to where to locate fencing, and require DHS consultation with land management and natural resource agencies regarding environmental impact on public lands. The bill, however, was practically dead on arrival in the House Resources Committee, and excepting one subcommittee hearing in Brownsville (Kamp, 2008), and some press coverage, received little discussion on Capitol Hill. It may, however, have had the effect of prodding other national environmental organizations, notably the Sierra Club, to embrace opposition to the border fence (Hurowitz, 2007).

Otherwise, the 110th Congress was as vacant of environmental testimony and debate on the environmental effects of the fence as its predecessor. Virtually no discussion can be found on the topic in any of the relevant committees, from foreign relations and homeland security to those dealing with environment and natural resources. In 2009, with democrats at the helm of the 111th Congress, the prospects should have been better. Congressman Grijalva reintroduced the bill in slightly modified form as H.R. 2076, renamed the Border Security and Responsibility Act. This time, ironically, it had even fewer congressional sponsors, though environmental organizations were quick to line up in support. Still, like its predecessor, it was stillborn with little discussion outside the border region.

The 112th and 113th congresses proved as inhospitable to the fence-environment issue as their predecessors, with just one hearing focused on environmental regulations and border security, a joint subcommittee hearing of the House Committee on Oversight and Government Reform's Subcommittee on National Security, Homeland Defense, and Foreign Operations and the House Natural Resources Committee's Subcommittee on National Parks, Forest and Public Lands with agency witnesses from the departments of the interior and agriculture but not a single voice from the environmental community (U.S. House of Representatives, 2011c). The hearing saw various border security hawks scold DHS/CPB officials for trying to accommodate the concerns of other agencies on public lands (Burr, 2011, A13). Two anti-environment bills, a bill To provide U.S. Customs and Border Protection with access to Federal lands . . . (H.R. 1922) and a proposed National Security and Federal Lands Protection Act (H.R. 1505), were introduced in 2011, the latter with language giving the DHS overriding authority over all federal lands within 100 miles of the boundary (Adams, 2011; U.S. House of Representatives, 2011b, 2011c). These bills, opposed by the Obama administration, eventually died. A further effort on the part of Congressman Grijalva, the Border Security and Responsibility Act of 2013 (H.R. 547) died in the house with no co-sponsors (U.S. House of Representatives, 2013).

In sum, as the Obama administration confronted a hostile House of Representatives after the fall 2010 midterm election, the best that could be said of environmentalists with respect to the border security question was that they had made a modest effort to affect the congressional agenda. Yet they remained locked out of key legislative venues, even committees and subcommittees where they arguably had congressional allies. They could only lobby and hope for executive resistance to further congressional initiatives to weaken environmental enforcement at the border.

Environmental Mobilization

If there is a bright spot in the picture of environmental activism on the border fence it is most certainly the concerted and sustained efforts of border state and local environmental organizations and allied partners to resist it. As early as 2006, immediately following passage of the Secure Fence Act, concerned individuals and environmental organizations raised the alarm as to its potentially damaging effects. These concerns were sufficiently compelling to gain the attention of the EPA's border environment advisory board, the GNEB, comprised of local, state, and federal stakeholders in environmental protection on the U.S. side of the border. The GNEB mentioned the problem in its 9th annual report (GNEB, 2006) and expanded on its concerns in 2007 in its 10th report, which called for enhanced cooperation between security and environmental protection agencies (GNEB, 2007).

By mid-2007, at least two state chapters of the Sierra Club (Arizona and Texas) had formally declared their opposition. At about the same time a coalition of environmental groups and local activists coalesced into the No Border Wall (NBW) Coalition and began partnering with the Texas Border Coalition and private landowners to press their case with the DHS and state and congressional allies. In September 2007, the NBW coalition staged a Hands-across-the-Rio protest followed by a "Pachanga in the Park" in Brownsville and protests in other border cities from Texas to California.

As the DHS began revealing its plans for border fencing and commenced condemnation proceedings, the NBW coalition gained other allies. Some labor unions expressed sympathy—the Southwest Workers Union hosted a No Border Wall strategy conference in San Antonio in March 2008. Individuals affiliated with NBW, notably the head of University of Texas at Brownsville's nursing department, Eloise Tamez, staged protests that drew national media attention. Most Texas border city mayors joined the fray, as did some of their colleagues in other border cities. Even Texas government departments, notably Texas Parks and Wildlife, came out unofficially against the fence. Other academic and scholarly associations of conservationists and wildlife biologists joined the critique. In the fall of 2007, an international meeting in Mexico sponsored by the Mexican government's environmental ministry with an array of U.S. and Mexican scholars participating lambasted the fence project, claiming violations of international law. At the University of Texas, law school faculty and students built a case against the fence on human rights and environmental grounds, offering legal counsel to aggrieved property owners, filing Freedom of Information Requests with the DHS, and raising the issue at the international level with the Organization of American States. In December 2007, El Paso conservationist Judy Ackerman drew considerable press when she was arrested for protesting construction in the Rio Bosque, a local wildlife refuge along the boundary just east of the city (Patterson, 2008).

Such voices, naturally, were opposed by a vociferous coalition of anti-immigration restrictionists and often drowned out by the clamor for border security and immigration control. Even so, the protests had some effect, placing the DHS in the spotlight. Fence criticism, profiled in major newspapers across the country and featured on PBS's *NOW with David Brancaccio*, fueled more unfavorable attention.[8] As early as April 2008, DHS unwrapped its new environmental stewardship program, declaring its intention to consider environmental impacts as it proceeded, though not conceding its final authority on environmental and cultural issues related to tactical security infrastructure and gaining "operational control" of the border (DHS, 2006). By February 2009, the *Wall Street Journal* reported that environmental protest was seriously delaying construction of the Rio Grande segment of the border fence (Simon, 2009). In April, Janet Napolitano, the newly appointed secretary of the DHS and former governor of Arizona, signaled it would place a moratorium on new fence construction in the Rio Grande Valley while it reconsidered border security requirements. Napolitano followed this measure with the appointment of a new 20-member Southwest Border Task Force to advise the DHS on border security policy. While the group included a few known critics of the fence, not a single environmentalist could be found on the list.

While construction of the fence stalled at roughly 670 miles of various forms of obstacles ranging from triple thick pedestrian fences to Normandy barriers and bollards, with US$50 million extended for environmental mitigation in the fall of 2009, it was clear that the Obama administration was reluctant to confront the Secure Fence Act's questionable mandate. The frustration was evident at the GNEB, which directed a blistering letter to the White House in December 2009 and followed up with a range of mitigation suggestions in its 2010 report (Ganster, 2009; GNEB, 2010). Among other points, the GNEB's 2009 letter advised Obama to:

- Require that all border security infrastructure projects fully comply with the National Environmental Policy Act (NEPA) as well as other laws including environmental, historic, and archeological preservation laws.
- Work with Congress to amend the REAL ID Act of 2005 to remove the provisions allowing the Secretary of Homeland Security to waive legal requirements.
- Fully incorporate adequate review, public participation, and scientific analysis into the design and implementation of all border security infrastructure projects.
- Facilitate review by the International Boundary and Water Commission (UIBWC) of projects that may cause deflection or obstruction of the normal flow of the river or their flood flows, ensuring continued compliance with the 1970 Boundary Treaty between the U.S. and Mexico and other international agreements.
- Systematically monitor the entire fence and supporting infrastructure for effects resulting from its construction and develop actions to modify, redesign, or mitigate the negative outcomes realized or anticipated by the existing construction. (Ganster, 2009)

Little has changed to alter this equation. In 2010 the DHS, responding in part to the GNEB's criticism, authorized Customs and Border Protection to spend US$50 million on environmental mitigation. The DHS also agreed to develop a monitoring protocol to assess the environmental impact of the border fence (Sutley, 2010, 2011), work on improving stakeholder engagement in the design and implementation of select tactical security infrastructure on the boundary, and coordinate better with other federal and state agencies on environmental matters—and otherwise agreed to take further suggestions under advisement. The DHS also terminated funding for the ill-conceived "virtual fence" along the border—not on environmental grounds but because of repeated technical failures. As noted earlier, the 2010 transfer of political power to Republican hands in the U.S. House of Representatives made it even more difficult to push through mitigating legislation amending or reversing the deleterious effects of the Real ID Act and the Secure Fence Act. The situation has recently worsened. The 2014 midterm election produced Republican majorities in both the U.S. House and Senate that are unlikely to change course on either environmental issues related to the fence or the underlying immigration and security issues that we argue were the preconditions to both the Real ID and Secure Fence Acts. A rather strange alignment in the outcome of congressional inability or unwillingness to act on any meaningful immigration reform (put simply, nothing in the way of immigration reform has come from the last four sessions of Congress) has occurred with the ongoing presidential campaign. In 2015, Donald Trump made fence building a centerpiece of his bid for the Republican Party's presidential nomination, boasting he would make Mexico finance the wall to the tune of "tens of billions of dollars" (Chuck, 2015). Once elected he proceeded to make good on his promise, signing an executive order on January 2017 ordering the DHS secretary to construct the wall (White House, 2017) despite evidence that a majority of Americans opposed the measure (Gorman, 2017).

ENVIRONMENTALISTS, NATURAL RESOURCES, AND BORDER SECURITY: THE CHALLENGE AHEAD

The remarkable end-run by the immigration restriction and border security coalition at the expense of the border environment is unprecedented and historic. It is, to quote Peter Douglas, executive director of the California Coastal Commission, "a monument to the politics of fear" (Broder, 2005). It reflects the successful policy conflation of antiterrorist rhetoric and immigration restriction expressed as a need for heightened border enforcement, particularly the interdiction of unauthorized human transit across the international boundary. It is hard to see how it might be reversed or modified short of a constitutional challenge, itself unlikely, or congressional reassessment, also unlikely in the current climate of national security and migration concerns.

At this point both the national and border environmental communities have yet to fashion a broad-gauged coalition to challenge these draconian securitization initiatives. What is evident is that environmental advocacy organizations interested in border environmental protection and binational cooperation cannot follow the normal pathways of policy influence where border security is concerned. Several assumptions should guide environmental efforts to regain their footing on border environmental affairs in the new ambit of national security and nativist fears.

First, environmentalists must learn to speak the language of comprehensive approaches to migration. Comprehensive approaches look beyond border enforcement to the causes of emigration to the United States and entertain the option of dealing with migration as a development problem, which opens the door to considering immigration in a regional, North American, sustainable development framework. Approaching security and immigration in this comprehensive and regional frame offers a long-term, enduring solution to the underlying problem of migration and affords an opportunity to look at environmental protection as an integral part of an overall solution for North American development and security (Pastor, 2005, 2011).

Second, as recent GNEB reports and comment letters imply, environmentalists must aggressively insert themselves into the policy debate over infrastructure. They must be prepared to review and recommend alternative designs for fencing and other proposed infrastructure and bring these to the attention of the DHS and its related agencies and to congressional committees. They should insist on being represented on a panel of experts to review the utility and effectiveness of border security infrastructure proposed by DHS officials.

Third, they must mobilize and demand that national security at the border incorporate consideration of environmental and social values (civil liberties). They must make common cause with other social interests adversely affected by the securitization coalitions now dominating border policy. Environmental organizations in the Beltway and along the border should clamor for a hearing on substantive environmental committees in Congress, both the House and the Senate.

Fourth, they must focus greater attention on the current array of border programs and institutions. They should insist that Border 2012 establish a policy forum for discussions of securitization policy and its environmental and public health effects on border areas and communities. Security discussions in the context of Border 2012 have until now largely centered on the border-wide working groups tasked with emergency preparedness and response. This is clearly insufficient in the current policy environment.

Fifth, environmentalists and citizens at large must continue to use such legal and political mechanisms as may be available to challenge destructive projects advanced by security interests and immigration restrictionists. While the Real ID Act certainly endows the DHS with extraordinary power in the matter of border infrastructure development, it has yet to be tested fully in the courts. Even its advocates concede that if the DHS were to indiscriminately override all other concerns on the U.S. and Canada borders, the public reaction might well force the government to reconsider and revise this legislation.

NOTES

1. Mexico's Secretariat of Foreign Relations has issued matricula cards since 1871 (Secretaria de Relaciones Exteriores, 2004).
2. The Sierra Club had joined a lawsuit in 2004 against extension of the border fence at San Diego with several local and California state-level environmental organizations. Both the Wilderness Society and Defenders of Wildlife publicly criticized the Real ID Act after its passage. After Michael Chertoff invoked the Real ID Act's authority in September 2005, Defenders' attorney Brian Segee denounced the decision as an "enormous and unnecessary precedent" (Yahoo News, 2005).
3. Hearings were surveyed for these committees using a Lexis/Nexis congressional search of all committee hearings. Scheduled witnesses for all committee hearings for 2005–2006 are listed—these were reviewed by Stephen Mumme. The only testimony that mentioned the environment at the border was by Inspector General of Homeland Security Richard Skinner in December 2005, well after the Real ID Act became law. Skinner's remarks centered on the remaining administrative encumbrance for Homeland Security initiatives arising from environmental legislation (Skinner, 2005, p. 6).
4. It should be noted that there is a precedent for waiving the requirements of U.S. domestic law on diplomatic grounds at the border. Historically, the IBWC was exempted from the application of the U.S. Clean Water Act and the U.S. Clean Air Act in developing diplomatic solutions to border water and sanitation problems along the U.S.-Mexican border.

5. Doyle (2014) notes that DHS can both provide for needed security infrastructure on the U.S.-Mexican border and lessen environmental impacts if it studies the impacts of planned fencing projects as part of the design process and shares results of these studies with communities in the areas where fencing is planned.
6. The first such waiver was to complete triple-barrier fencing along a 14-mile stretch of boundary at San Ysidro at the western end of the international boundary; the second, also in 2005, to proceed with fencing 120 miles of Arizona-Sonora boundary abutting the Goldwater National Gunnery Range; the third, in 2007, to authorize fencing along the San Pedro National Conservation Area; the fourth, in the spring of 2008, to proceed with fencing along the lower Rio Grande River below Laredo, Texas; and fifth, also in 2008, to proceed through the Otay Mountain Wilderness (Archibold, 2008).
7. Defenders of Wildlife published a lengthy report in March 2006 that was highly critical of the border fence along the Sonoran Desert section of the international boundary (Segee & Neeley, 2006).
8. Independent film producers got in the act by 2008, with three films, *The Fence*, *The Wall*, and *Wild v. Wall*, this latter film released by the Sierra Club in 2010. Defenders of Wildlife also produced a video critical of the border fence.

REFERENCES

Abel, A. (2002, March 28). *The Monterrey commitments*. Americas Program Feature. Silver City, NM: Interhemispheric Resource Center. Retrieved from http://intrabecc.cocef.org/programs/intranetnotasperiodico/uploadedFiles/Mont.pdf

Adams, J. S. (2011, September 26). Border bill would expand Homeland Security powers. *USA Today*. Retrieved from http://usatoday30.usatoday.com/news/nation/story/2011-09-26/homeland-security-federal-lands-bill/50561694/1

Archibold, R. (2008, April 2). Government issues waiver for fencing along border. *New York Times*, p. A18.

Baumgartner, F. R., & Jones. B. D. (1991). Agenda dynamics and policy subsystems. *Journal of Politics*, *53*(4), 1044–1074.

Broder, J. (2005, July 4). With Congress's blessing, a border fence may finally push through to the sea. *New York Times*. Retrieved from http://www.nytimes.com/2005/07/04/us/with-congresss-blessing-a-border-fence-may-finally-push-through-to-the.html?_r=0

Brown, N. C. (1998). *Endangered Species Bulletin*. Lower Rio Grande Valley National Wildlife Refuge. Retrieved from https://www.highbeam.com/doc/1G1-54023110.html

Burr, T. (2011, April 16). Chaffetz uses grisly images to stress point. *Salt Lake Tribune*, p. A13.

Camarota, S. A. (2005). *Immigrants at mid-decade: A snapshot of America's foreign-born population in 2005*. Washington, DC: Center for Immigration Studies.

Center for Biological Diversity. (2006). *Borderlands and boundary waters*. Retrieved from http://www.biologicaldiversity.org/swcbd/programs

Chuck, E. (2015, July 23). Donald Trump's border wall would cost billions, experts say. *NBC News*. Retrieved from http://www.nbcnews.com/news/us-news/trumps-border-wall-would-cost-billions-n396551

Cohen, M. A. (2003). Rise and fall of environmental NGOs along the Mexico-U.S. border. In B. Hogenboom, M. A. Cohen, & E. Antal (Eds.), *Cross-border activism and its limits* (pp. 41–59). Amsterdam, the Netherlands: Centre for Latin American Research and Documentation.

Dlouhy, J. A. (2005a, January 31). Immigration fight looms. *CQ Weekly*, pp. 246

Dlouhy, J. A. (2005b, February 14). Lawmakers spar over asylum. *CQ Weekly*, pp. 402–403.

Dlouhy, J. A. (2005c, February 21). Critics blanch at dodging laws to build border wall. *CQ Weekly*, pp. 442–443.

dos Santos, P. (2004). [Letter to the president, vice-president, speaker of the U.S.-House of Representatives.] In Good Neighbor Environmental Board, *Children's environmental health* (7th annual report; EPA 130-R-04-001) (pp. 31–33). Washington, DC: Environmental Protection Agency.

Doyle, P. (2014). Unintended consequences: The environmental impacts of border fencing and immigration reform. *Arizona Journal of Environmental Law and Policy*, *3*, 1047–1051.

Eriksson, L., & Taylor, M. (2009). *The environmental impacts of the border wall between Texas and Mexico*. Unpublished manuscript. University of Texas, Austin, Texas.

Ganster, P. (2009, December 2). [Letter to President Barack Obama.] In Good Neighbor Environmental Board. (2010). *A blueprint for action on the U.S.-Mexico Border, 13th report to the President and Congress of the United States* (EPA 130-R-10-001) (pp. 67–72). Washington, DC: Environmental Protection Agency. Retrieved from https://www.epa.gov/sites/production/files/documents/eng_gneb_13th_report_final.pdf

Good Neighbor Environmental Board. (2005). *Water resources management on the U.S.-Mexico border, 8th report to the President and Congress of the United States* (EPA 130-R-05-001). Washington, DC: Environmental Protection Agency.

Good Neighbor Environmental Board. (2006). *Air quality and transportation & cultural and natural resources, 9th report to the president and congress of the United States* (EPA 130-R-06-002). Washington, DC: Environmental Protection Agency.

Good Neighbor Environmental Board. (2007). *Environmental protection and border security on the U.S.-Mexico Border, 10th report to the president and congress of the United States* (EPA 130-R-07-003). Washington, DC: Environmental Protection Agency.

Good Neighbor Environmental Board. (2010). *A blueprint for action on the U.S.-Mexico Border, 13th report to the president and congress of the United States* (EPA 130-R-10-001). Washington, DC: Environmental Protection Agency.

Gorman, M. (2017, February 2). Poll finds majority disapprove of president Trump's executive orders. *Newsweek.* Retrieved from http://www.newsweek.com/trump-executive-orders-majority-disapproval-poll-551873

Hebert, H. J. (2010, January 18). U.S. jaguar plan spoiled by border fence, critics say. *National Geographic News.* Retrieved from http://news.nationalgeographic.com/news/2008/01/080118-AP-jaguars.html

Hogenboom, B. (1998). *Mexico and the NAFTA environment debate.* Utrect, the Netherlands: International Books.

Hurowitz, G. (2007, October 16). Why environmental groups have been slow to fight the borderwall. *Grist.* Retrieved from http://grist.org/article/hurowitz/

Ingram, H. (1998, June 3–6). Planning for natural disaster: Unsustainable development of the U.S./Mexico border. In *Cross-border waters: Fragile treasures for the 21st century, proceedings of the 9th U.S./Mexico Border States Conference on Recreation, Parks, and Wildlife,* sponsored by the U.S. Department of Agriculture, U.S. Forest Service, Rocky Mountain Research Station (pp. 3–13). Tucson, Arizona.

Kamp, D. (2008, April 13). Politicians condemn waivers for border fence. *Nogales International,* p. A1.

Koleff, P., Lira-Noriega, A., Urquiza, T., & Morales, E. (2007). Priorities for biodiversity conservation in Mexico's northern border. In A. Cordova & C. A. de la Parra (Eds.), *A barrier to our shared environment: The border fence between the United States and Mexico* (129–142). Tijuana, Mexico: Colegio de la Frontera Norte.

Levin, S. (2017, January 26). "Over my dead body": tribe aims to block Trump's border wall on Arizona land. *The Guardian*. Retrieved from https://www.theguardian.com/us-news/2017/jan/26/donald-trump-border-wall-tohono-oodham-arizona-tribe

McCallum, J. M., Rowcliffe, J. M., & Cuthill, I. C. (2014). Conservation on international boundaries: The impact of security barriers in four protected areas in Arizona, USA. *PloS One*, *9*(4), e93679.

Mensah, K. (2010). Masked bobwhite quail reintroduction ahead of schedule. *Arizona Highways*. Retrieved from https://arizonahighways.files.wordpress.com/2010/05/the-ambitious-masked-bobwhite-quail-re.pdf

Moya, H. (2007). Possible impacts of border fence construction and operation on fauna. In A. Cordova & C. A. de la Parra (Eds.). *A barrier to our shared environment: The border fence between the United States and Mexico* (65–76). Tijuana, Mexico: Colegio de la Frontera Norte.

Mumme, S. P. (2014). Trade and environmental protection along the U.S.-Mexico border. *Global Society*, *28*(4), pp. 398–418.

Nunez-Neto, B., & Vina, S. R. (2005). *Border security: Fences along the U.S. international border* (CRS Order Code RS22026). Washington, DC: Congressional Research Service.

Pastor, R. A. (2005, June 9). *A North American community approach to security* (testimony invited by the Subcommittee on the Western Hemisphere, U.S. Senate Foreign Relations Committee).

Pastor, R. A. (2011). *The North American idea*. Oxford, UK: Oxford University Press.

Patterson, K. (2008, December 29). Will the border wall stand? *Newspaper Tree*. Retrieved from http://newpapertree.com/features/3245

Peters, E. (2007). Possible impacts of border fence construction and operation on flora. In A. Cordova & C.A. de la Parra (Eds.), *A barrier to our shared environment: The border fence between the United States and Mexico* (95–104). Tijuana, Mexico: Colegio de la Frontera Norte.

Riemann, H. (2007). Ecological risks involved in the construction of the border fence. In A. Cordova & C.A. de la Parra (Eds.), *A barrier to our shared environment: The border fence between the United States and Mexico* (105–114). Tijuana, Mexico: Colegio de la Frontera Norte.

Rosenbaum, W. R. (2002). *Environmental politics and policy* (5th ed.). Washington, DC: CQ Press.

Secretaria de Relaciones Exteriores. (2004). *Most frequently asked questions about the matricula consular*. Mexico, DF: Instituto de Mexicanos en el Exterior.

Segee, B. P., & Neely, J. L. (2006). *On the line: The impacts of immigration policy on wildlife and habitat in the Arizona borderlands*. Washington, DC: Defenders of Wildlife.

Simon, J. (2009, February 4). Border-fence project hits snag. *Wall Street Journal*. Retrieved from https://www.wsj.com/articles/SB123370523066745559

Skinner, R. L. (2005, December 16). *Statement before the subcommittee on management, integration, and oversight, to the Committee on Homeland Security, U.S. House of Representatives, 109th Congress* [Author's copy].

Starr, P. K. (2004). U.S.-Mexican relations. *CSIS Hemisphere Focus*, *12*(2).

State of Arizona. (2004). Arizona Taxpayer and Citizen Protection Act [Proposition 200].

Stern, S. (2005a, February 21). Birds and bulldozers. *CQ Weekly*, p. 443.

Sutley, N. H. (2010, April 21). [Council on Environmental Quality letter to Paul Ganster, Chair, Good Neighbor Environment Board.] In Good Neighbor Environmental Board, *A blueprint for action on the U.S.-Mexico border. 13th report to the President and Congress of the United States* (EPA 130-R-10-001). Washington, DC: Environmental Protection Agency.

Sutley, N. H. (2011, February 11). [Council on Environmental Quality letter to Paul Ganster, Chair, Good Neighbor Environment Board.] Retrieved from https://www.epa.gov/sites/production/files/documents/ceq_response_020711.pdf

U.S. Department of Homeland Security. (2006). Environmental planning program. DHS Directives System (MD Number 023-01). Retrieved from https://dau.gdit.com/aqn201a/pdfs/MD023-01_Environmental_Planning_Program.pdf

U.S. Environmental Protection Agency. (2003). *Border 2012: U.S.-Mexico environmental program* (EPA-160-R-03-001). Washington, DC: Environmental Protection Agency.

U.S. Geological Survey. (2006). Homepage for the USGS U.S.-Mexico border field coordinating committee. Retrieved from http://www.cerc.usgs.gov/fcc/

U.S. House of Representatives. (2005). Border Protection, Antiterrorism, and Illegal Immigration Control Act of 2005, H.R. 4437.

U.S. House of Representatives. (2011a). *The border: Are environmental laws and regulations impeding security and harming the environment? Joint hearing before the Committee on Oversight and Government Reform, Subcommittee on National Security, Homeland Defense, and Foreign Operations and Committee on Natural Resources, Subcommittee on National Parks, Forest and Public Lands.*

U.S. House of Representatives. (2011b). National Security and Federal Lands Protection Act, H.R. 1505.

U.S. House of Representatives. (2011b). *To provide U.S. customs and border protection with access to federal lands to carry out certain security activities in the southwest border region, and for other purposes*, H.R. 1922.

U.S. House of Representatives. (2013). Border Security and Responsibility Act, H.R. 547.

White House. (2004, January 7). Remarks by President George W. Bush on immigration policy. Office of the Press Secretary. Retrieved from http://georgewbush-whitehouse.archives.gov/news/releases/2004/01/20040107-3.html

White House. (2017, January 25). *Executive order: Border security and immigration enforcement improvements*. Retrieved from https://www.whitehouse.gov/the-press-office/2017/01/25/executive-order-border-security-and-immigration-enforcement-improvements

Wilderness Society. (2005). *Tip sheet: Border fight*. Washington, DC: The Wilderness Society. Retrieved from http://www.wilderness.org/NewsRoom/TipSheets/20050415.cfm

Witman, L. (2011, August 10). Tohono O'odham Nation confronts widening border fence. *San Francisco Examiner*. Retrieved from http://www.examiner.com/article/tohono-o-odham-nation-confronts-widening-border-fence

Yahoo News. (2005, September 15). Federal authority trumps environmental concerns. Retrieved from http://news.yahoo.com/s/kgtv/200509/lo_kgtv/2938522

PART III

ENERGY AND CLIMATE CHANGE MITIGATION

ELEVEN

The Canadian Oil Sands Policy-Planning Network

GEORGE A. GONZALEZ

INTRODUCTION

The Canadian oil (or tar) sands are at the center of a debate over U.S. energy policy. The oil sands, located in the province of Alberta, are a high carbon substitute for crude oil. The continued development of the oil sands (i.e., bitumen) portends substantially higher levels of atmospheric carbon dioxide ("Tar Sands," 2011). The specific focus of the debate over the Canadian oil sands was the Keystone XL pipeline, which would connect Alberta to a petroleum-refining infrastructure in Texas (Davenport, 2015a). The pipeline would have presumably accelerated the extraction of the oil sands (Kaufman, 2015).

The need for greater petroleum production from the oil sands is the result of high petroleum demand in the North American (especially U.S.) market, and broad concerns about existing supplies of conventional crude (Deffeyes, 2001; Kurczy, 2010; Yergin, 2011). While the Canadian oil sands have been in the news of late, this source of petroleum has been part of North American oil strategy since the 1950s. Understanding the oil sands as part of Canadian-U.S. energy thinking necessitates the identification of the economic elite-led policy-planning network through which corporate North America formulates policy ideas and political consensus (Gonzalez, 2016; Klassen, 2014; Sklair, 2001). With regard to Canadian oil in general, this resource has, broadly speaking, served America's political and economic needs (Clarkson & Mildenberger, 2011; Pratt, 2001). This is in part due to the priority given the export market by Canada's prime oil-bearing province—Alberta (Bow, 2009, Chapter 5; Clarkson, 1982, pp. 36–42; Rennie 2004).

Prior to the North American oil industry's incorporation of the oil sands in its strategy for the energy future, the oil sands (as a way to encourage regional economic activity) were promoted by the Alberta regional growth coalition as early as the 1910s. Thus, the development of the oil sands is consistent with economic elite theory, and a subtheory of this approach: local growth machine theory.

I begin my analysis by outlining economic elite theory. In the following section, I discuss how the provincial government of Alberta sought to encourage the development of the tar sands. Then I proceed to outline how in the 1950s and 1960s, in the context of the Cold War and the precipitous growth of U.S. oil and gasoline consumption, the Canadian oil sands came to be viewed as strategic asset. This reasoning culminated with Sun Oil Company's initiation of significant petroleum production from the tar sands in the early 1960s. The oil shocks of the 1970s reinforced the view that unconventional petroleum, like the oil sands, is a strategic asset that can be used to meet U.S. energy demand.

ECONOMIC ELITE THEORY

Advocates of economic elite theory hold that the nation's economic elite is the dominant political force in U.S. society (Barrow, 2016; Hay, Lister, & Marsh, 2006, Chapter 2; Miliband, 1969; Wetherly, Barrow, & Burnham, 2008). Clyde Barrow (1993) points out that "typically, members of the capitalist class [or the economic elite] are identified as those persons who manage [major] corporations and/or own those corporations." He adds that this group composes no more than 0.5% to 1.0% of the total U.S. population (p. 17).[1] This group as a whole is the upper class and the upper echelon of the corporate or business community. The wealth possessed by the economic elite allows them to exercise a high level of influence over the state and to accumulate greater amounts of other valuable resources (Barrow, 1993, p. 16), such as social status (Krugman, 2014b), deference (Confessore, 2014), publicity (Hulse & Parker, 2014), prestige (Collins, 2014), organization (Confessore, 2013; Koch Party, 2014), campaign finances (Kuhner, 2014; Lichtblau, 2015; Mutch, 2014), lobbying power (McIntire, 2012), political access (Parker, 2015), and both legal (Barkan, 2013; Lewis, 2014) and scientific expertise (Lipton, 2014). Economic elites develop policy goals and political consensus through policy-planning networks (Domhoff, 2013).

Recent investigative journalism has identified part of the economic elite-led policy network centered on the politics and policies of the Canadian oil sands. Writing for the web-based *Canadian Dimension*, journalist Macdonald Stainsby (2011) argues that through the guise of philanthropy economic elites are manipulating the political activity of groups opposed to the development of the oil sands. Stainsby focuses his analysis on the North American Oil Sands Coalition (NATSC). This coalition includes a number of groups who convey opposition to petroleum production from the oil sands: The Pembina Institute, Environmental Defense Canada, ForestEthics, World Wildlife Fund (Canada), The Sierra Club of Canada (and associated regional chapters), Eco Justice, the Canadian Boreal Initiative, and "perhaps most important to note" Greenpeace Canada. The NATSC receives virtually all of its financing from economic elite-led foundations. Stainsby emphasizes the role of the Pew Charitable Trusts, which "was soilted with a multi-billion dollar grant from Sunoco [Sun Oil Company] and today their board of directors is more than 50 percent tied to Sunoco, either through the Pew family or executive work with the oil giant." Other foundations that donate through the Tides Foundation ("a sort of clearing house for other philanthropists and foundations") to the NATSC are: the Rockefeller Brothers Fund, the Ford Foundation, and the Hewlett Foundation.

Stainsby holds that economic elite funding of and participation in groups that are in ostensive opposition to extracting the Canadian oil sands represents an effort at "co-opting environmentalism," whereby environmental groups could be prompted into an "Oil Sands Partnership Agreement that only marginally mitigates the environmental damage from developing the oil sands." Mark Dowie (1995) argues that the co-opting of environmentalism (i.e., environmental groups) in the U.S. context began in earnest during the 1980s under the Reagan administration.

Worse still is the prospect of "symbolic inclusion" (Cahn, 1995; Dryzek, 1996). Arguably, the participation of environmental groups in such organizations as the NATSC, and any environmental agreements or legislation intended to mitigate environmental damage from extracting oil sands, are potentially symbolic. In other words, in practice the production of petroleum from the oil sands goes ahead full throttle, in spite of any agreement with environmental groups or laws on paper. In such a case, agreements or laws are symbols intended to pacify public opinion on environmental concerns (Gonzalez, 2016, Chapter 6).

Another approach to analyzing the participation of economic elites in organizations that object to the development of the oil sands is as a *policy planning network*. Hence, apart from potentially managing environmental groups or public opinion, economic elites may get involved with those in opposition to the oil sands to gain greater insight into and understanding of the environmental issues surrounding this energy source. Opposition groups muster arguments and science in critiquing the oil sands, thereby educating economic elites (and others) on the environmental and economic perils surrounding the oil sands (Johnson, 2014). It is noteworthy that recently the province of British Columbia advised against the proposed Enbridge Northern Gateway pipeline.[2] The pipeline was planned in case the proposed Keystone XL pipeline was rejected—as indeed it was by the Obama administration (although the succeeding Trump administration recently did authorize the pipeline; Baker & Davenport, 2017). In arguing against building the pipeline from the Alberta oil sands to British Columbia, the provincial government drew on the environmental critiques offered by opposition groups (Austen, 2013).

The failure to build the Enbridge pipeline, and even Keystone XL, may not slow down Canadian oil sands production. While a great deal was made politically about the recently rejected Keystone XL pipeline project (Davenport, 2015a), it may be the case that it is shaping up to be more symbol than substance (Edelman, 1988; Nocera, 2015). This is because beyond the Keystone XL project there is an active effort to develop the infrastructure necessary to produce oil from the Canadian tar sands full throttle (Kaufman, 2015). Apart from the Keystone project, this effort is flying below the political radar. Newly proposed pipelines, and the expansion of existing pipelines, will "enable oil sands production to climb by more than 25 percent in the next decade even if the Keystone pipeline is ultimately blocked" (Krauss & Austen, 2014). Additionally, the United States is authorizing the development of a robust set of railroad links between itself and the Canadian oil sands (Krauss, 2013a, 2013b). In responding to the announced rejection of the Keystone XL pipeline, Christine Tezak, an energy market analyst at ClearView Energy Partners (a Washington firm), explained that "From a market perspective, the industry can find a different way to move that oil. How long it takes is just a result of oil prices. If prices go up, companies will get the oil out" (as quoted in Davenport, 2015c). "In terms of distribution and what people will pay, Keystone doesn't really mean much," said Tom Kloza, global head of energy analysis at Oil Price Information Service (as quoted in Krauss, 2015b). It is noteworthy that oil exports from Canada (including oil sands dilbit [diluted bitumen]) to the United States have already increased to 3.8 million barrels per day from 2.5 million barrels in 2008, while imports from OPEC countries have significantly declined (Krauss, 2015b).

Nevertheless, the United States did make significant gestures indicating that the Keystone XL pipeline would be constructed. This includes the building of part of the planned pipeline (Elbein, 2012) and a 2014 report by the U.S. Department of State, in which it was argued that the Keystone XL pipeline (projected to carry 830,000 barrels of oil) would create minimal environmental risks. This would primarily assume that the Canadian tar sands would be extracted regardless of whether or not the Keystone XL pipeline is constructed.[3] As noted earlier, the developing of the Canadian oil sands will significantly add to the carbon content in the atmosphere. Even the writers of the state department report who favor the Keystone XL pipeline noted that producing oil from the oil sands creates 17% more carbon dioxide than conventional petroleum (Davenport, 2014, A1; also see Broder, 2013; "Oil Sands and the Carbon Numbers," 2011). According to the most recent data, production from the oil sands (in 2014) was at 2.3 million barrels per day (Alberta Energy, 2017).

Another major environmental risk associated with the oil sands is spillage. Liquefied bitumen is highly toxic and notoriously difficult to clean up (Fitzsimmons, 2010; Sassoon, 2012). It is the fear of dilbit spillage that caused British Columbia to advise against its proposed pipeline. This fear is the reason that the Obama administration in 2011 rejected the initial Keystone XL pipeline route (Broder & Frosch, 2011). Had the U.S. government authorized the building of Keystone XL under President Obama (in spite of the grave environmental risks associated with expanding oil sands production), it would have been in part the result of the fact that the oil industry (and corporate North America) has conceptualized the oil sands as a viable alternative to conventional oil. As already alluded to, this reasoning is evident as early as the 1950s in the business-led and financed policy-planning network. What has been explicitly elided in this corporate reasoning is conservation (i.e., directly reducing energy use) in North America as an energy strategy.

But before the Canadian oil sands came fully into the sights of major oil companies, the tar sands was promoted by the Alberta regional government. The research and ideation developed by the provincial government set the stage for major production of the oil sands that began in the 1960s.

THE RESEARCH COUNCIL OF ALBERTA

Among North American subnational governments (i.e., Canadian provinces and U.S. states), the government of Alberta has historically been among the most aggressive in seeking to forward the economic fortunes of its region. Subgovernments in the North American West limited themselves to providing the legal, political, and physical infrastructure (e.g., roads, ports, schools) needed to attract capital investment and a labor force (Moehring, 2004), whereas Alberta adopted a more direct role in fostering local and regional economic activity. Edmonton subsidized various sectors of the economy, including ranching, farming, and manufacturing (Klassen, 1999).

Drawing on local growth machine theory (noted in the introduction of this chapter), it appears that Edmonton's promotion of local and regional economic growth is driven by the local growth coalition. A regional or local growth coalition is composed of economic interests and economic elites who benefit from economic growth in a specific locality or region. The core groups of local growth coalitions are large landholders and land developers (i.e., real estate interests). Other important members of such coalitions include banks, utilities, regional media outlets, and law firms that specialize in real estate transactions. Local growth coalitions seek to attract investment and economic activity to their specific locality. Large land owners and land developers benefit from increased investment and economic activity in their specific area because such increases usually translate into greater demand for land and built facilities, and, hence, increased prices for such land and facilities. Other members of local growth coalitions benefit from local economic growth because such growth generally expands the local consumer base. Particularly central to the economic development of the North American West were railroads, which promoted local and regional growth in an effort to create and expand traffic on their lines (Orsi, 2007; Otter, 1997).

In order to achieve the economic benefits derived from increased economic growth, local growth coalitions strive to create a political and physical milieu that attracts investment, tourism, and other forms of economic activity to their locality (Logan & Molotch, 2007). In *The Politics of Air Pollution* (2005), I have shown how local economic interests led the way in shaping the legal and regulatory rules needed to abate urban air pollution in the U.S. context. Local growth coalitions take these actions because excessive localized air pollution (smoke, smog) is perceived as a threat to the regional economy. Owen Temby (2013) demonstrates that these same interests successfully pursued a similar outcome in Canada, specifically in Toronto (also see Temby & O'Connor, 2015). In addition, local economic interests led the way in deploying the engineering needed to manage water pollution (Gonzalez, 2013b). Again, local growth coalitions take these actions because poorly managed (and excessive) localized water pollution (raw sewage, waterborne toxins) is a threat to the regional economy.

Consistent with economic elite theory, local growth coalitions are able to have their desire for local growth dominate the local and regional political agenda because its members possess the political resources of wealth and income (Orr & Johnson, 2008; Stone, 1989). Historian A. A. Den Otter (1982), for instance, outlines how the wealthy Galt family in the late 19th century played a substantial role in shaping the growth strategies of southern Alberta and its economic links with Montana. As a result, local and state governments pursue local economic growth (Eisinger, 1988), often at the expense of other values (Harvey, 1985).

Starting in the 1910s the Alberta government directly promoted the oil sands. The promotion of the oil sands by the Alberta government was seemingly prompted by the construction of a railroad line to Fort McMurray in 1909. This remote destination is in the heart of oil sands country in the northern part of the province (Breen, 1993, p. 441; Klassen, 1999, p. 74; Schneider, 1989, Chapter 10 and pp. 317–318). Hence, the Alberta growth machine was at the center of a policy-planning network focused on the oil sands.

The province championed the oil sands in significant part through the Research Council of Alberta, housed in the University of Alberta. Walter H. Johns, one-time president of the university, notes that the Research Council of Alberta was established in 1911–1912, and was "of such great service to the province"—overseeing "staff involvement in several of the professional faculties in research directed to the interests of Alberta. . . . This was especially true of the Faculties of Agriculture and Engineering, but covered other fields as well, such as Geology and Chemistry" (p. 41). The council's name initially was the Scientific and Industrial Research Council of Alberta, and it was "the first provincial research organization of its kind in Canada" (Chastko, 2004, p. 13).

Until the 1950s the oil industry had little interest in the Alberta oil sands. Paul Chastko (2004), who has documented the history and politics of the Canadian tar sands, notes the engineering challenge in extracting petroleum from the oil sands. Chastko explains that "tar sands oil does not flow like lubricating oils. It is very viscous at the best of times, prompting one observer to compare extracting oil from the sand to removing honey from a bowl of sugar" (p. 6). Through the Alberta Research Council the provincial government financed the research and promotional efforts of Karl Clark. Johns (1981) notes that Clark was "appointed by the government . . . to investigate the Athabasca bituminous sands" (p. 82). Chastko notes of work by government researchers like that of Clark on the oil sands that "government-sponsored research clearly found a receptive audience as commercial projects simply expanded on paths of inquiry blazed by government researchers" (p. 22).

Alberta's policies towards the oil sands did create political friction and political opposition within the Alberta petroleum industry. This is because Alberta's oil production is "stranded." In other words, oil extracted in

Alberta is limited to reaching central and western North America. (Eastern Canada is supplied by international oil producers; Austen 2013b.) Thus, Alberta's oil producers have a limited market that is susceptible to overproduction and glutting. This "weakness" was exacerbated with major oil finds in the province in the post-World War II period (Fossum, 1997; Plotnick, 1964), and by an oil import quota instituted by the United States in the 1950s (Bohi & Russell, 1978; Yergin, 1991). To help manage this situation Alberta empowered a Conservation Board to cap and prorate (i.e., allocate) regional petroleum production (Breen, 1993). Therefore, production from the oil sands would add petroleum to a market that was adequately serviced by conventional crude. Worse still, in situations where oil prices were low, tar sands would likely displace conventional petroleum. This is because oil sands extraction is labor- and capital-intensive, and thus production would continue even in a low price environment in order to retain skilled labor and defray the heavy cost of equipment (Austen, 2016). Therefore, when in the mid-1950s the Great Canadian Oil Sands put in a proposal before the Conservation Board to produce 20,000 barrels per day of petroleum from the oil sands, the Canadian Petroleum Association formed a special committee to "prepare a vigorous brief protesting the applicant's submission" (as quoted in Breen, 1993, p. 446).

Nevertheless, during much of the 20th century the provincial government "would direct the oil sands effort" (Chastko, 2004, p. 63). This effort included financing demonstration projects and private sector ventures.

THE CANADIAN OIL SANDS AS A STRATEGIC ASSET

In the context of growing and high levels of U.S. consumption of gasoline in the post-World War II period (Duffield, 2008), the Canadian oil sands became part of the North American system of petroleum production.[4] As early as 1951, the tar sands was identified as a resource in the context of the Cold War—one that can be drawn upon if North American access to international oil supplies falters. Significantly, the Sun Oil firm took up producing petroleum from the oil sands as part of a long-term plan. In the aftermath of the 1973 oil shock, economic elite policy discussion groups identified synthetic oil as a response to any shortfalls in global petroleum supplies. Oil from oil sands (and other unconventional petroleum) is referred to as synthetic oil.

In 1951 the first conference on the oil sands was held in Alberta. Chastko (2004) describes the conference as follows: "Senior oil company executives, officials from various levels of government, and a score of scientists gathered at the University of Alberta to hear and discuss papers on a variety of oil sands-related topics." A theme that was proffered at the conference was "the importance of the oil sands for the security of the North American continent." More specifically, "If North America lost access to cheap offshore imports, the oil sands could serve as an effective backstop" (pp. 89, 90). Among the firms represented at the oil sands conference were Sun Oil, Imperial Oil, Gulf Oil, Union Oil Company of California, and Shell Oil (Oil Sands Project, 1951, pp. 367–371). The provincial Minister of Mines and Minerals entered an official government policy statement into the conference record. In his speech to the conference, the Minister made a point of highlighting this aspect of the statement: "The following policy has been adopted to encourage immediate development to meet the ever-increasing demand for petroleum products and to offset the effect of the uncertainty of supply else in the world . . . *and to further the security of this continent*" (Tanner, 1951, p. 175, emphasis in original). The minister noted in his conference speech that "it is important that we carry out a good program of development of our natural resources in the interest of security" (Tanner, 1951, p. 177).

During the early 1960s the Sun Oil Company initiated the major commercial development of the Canadian tar sands—the first company to do so. In undertaking the production of petroleum from the oil sands the Sun Oil Company did not do so for profit—at least not in the near to medium term. Chastko (2004) holds that it is "difficult to explain Sun Oil's involvement as part of a sound business strategy." He goes on to point out that "in fact, sound business practices might have argued against the company's involvement with the oil sands. . . . Synthetic crude production meant high fixed costs for production. . . . The likelihood of Sun recouping its initial investment in the near future seemed remote." Chastko concludes: "Clearly, something other than a concern for the corporate bottom line was the determining factor in Sun's involvement with the oil sands" (p. 111). Arthur M. Johnson (1983), a historian of the Sun Oil Company notes that by the early 1970s the company "invested $300 million and lost $70 million" on the tar sands project (p. 161). In doing so, the Sun Oil firm "made significant contributions to the research and development of oil sands operations" (Chastko, 2004, p. 190).

Indeed, the Sun Oil Company was linked to the Alberta's oil sands policy-planning network. J. Howard Pew, the company's longtime chief executive, was a friend of Ernest Manning (Chastko, 2004, p. 112; Johnson, 1983, p. 129), who was the prime minister of Alberta for 25 years. Manning was from the politically conservative Social Credit

Party (Finkel, 1989). Nevertheless, Manning, as prime minister, championed the oil sands (Chastko, 2004, pp. 63–67).

Johnson (1983) reports that shaping Pew's reasoning in pursuing the oil in the tar sands was the idea that "consumption of petroleum was outrunning the discovery of reserves and that by the mid-1980s, in the absence of some countervailing development, there could be a serious worldwide crude-oil shortage" (p. 130). In the 1970s there was global oil shortage, and economic elite-led policy discussion groups did identify synthetic crude as an answer to this shortfall.

The Oil Shocks of the 1970s and Beyond

In 1973 the Persian Gulf region of the Middle East took on particular importance for the Western allies. What came into relief in 1973 is that the region contained the key supplies of petroleum for the Western world. The petroleum-bearing countries of the region are Iran, Iraq, Kuwait, Saudi Arabia, United Arab Emirates, and Qatar, with Iran, Iraq, Kuwait, and Saudi Arabia being the primary producing countries for the world's oil market. The Persian Gulf nations today possess the majority of the world's known petroleum reserves—Saudi Arabia alone is estimated to hold 20% to 25% of the world's proven reserves of petroleum (Calder, 2012).

The Persian Gulf's strategic importance is in significant part the result of U.S. oil policies. This is particularly apparent on the demand side. As U.S. cities became more and more sprawled (Beauregard, 2006), and as a result more automobile dependent (Kenworthy, 2008; Kenworthy & Laube, 1999), U.S. oil consumption steadily climbed (Duffield, 2008).

The United States responded militarily to its apparent dependency. U.S. policy makers used the country's superior political and military position to ensure that Persian Gulf oil remained in the U.S. sphere of influence, and that the region's petroleum sufficiently flowed (Yetiv, 2011).

This emphasis on the supply-side to deal with the United States' energy problems of the 1970s is reflected in two reports put out by the Twentieth Century Fund (now the Century Fund). This organization is a foundation that, in the 1950s and 1960s, sponsored studies on the natural resource needs of the United States' expanding economy (e.g., Barach, 1964; Carskadon & Soule, 1957; Dewhurst, 1955). The Twentieth Century Fund created two policy-planning groups in the early 1970s composed largely of economic elites who put forward proposals to deal with the U.S. petroleum situation. One task force, convened in 1973, was titled "The Twentieth Century Fund Task Force on United States Energy Policy." On this task force was a director and senior vice president of Exxon; a vice chairman of the board of the American Electric Power Company; Walter J. Levy (a consultant to most major oil firms) ("As Oil Consultant," 1969); a vice chairman of the board of Texas Commerce Bancshares (a major Texas bank) (Buenger & Pratt, 1986, p. 299); and the chairman of the board of Carbomin International Corporation (an international mining firm). The other task force, formed in 1974, was known as the Twentieth Century Fund Task Force on the International Oil Crisis. Walter J. Levy and the executives from Carbomin and Texas Commerce Bancshares also served on this task force. Also on this Twentieth Century Fund task force was the chairman of the board from Atlantic Richfield (an oil firm), a managing director from Dillon, Read & Co. (a leading New York investment management firm), the chairman of the board from the Louis Dreyfus Corporation (an investment management firm), the chairman and president of The First National Bank of Chicago, and a consultant to Wells Fargo Bank (a major California bank). Also on these task forces were academics (mostly economists) from Princeton, Harvard, MIT, and the University of Virginia, as well as the presidents of Resources for the Future (which was on the two task forces) and the Carnegie Institution (only on the energy policy group)—both of which are economic elite-led research institutes (Twentieth Century Fund Task Force, 1975, pp. vii–viii; Twentieth Century Fund Task Force, 1977, pp. xi–xii; Winks, 1997, pp. 44, 196).

In the wake of the 1973 oil shortage and the Organization of Petroleum Exporting Countries (OPEC) seeking to maintain high oil prices, both of the Twentieth Century Fund's task forces advised that the United States should strive to develop sources of oil and energy outside of the OPEC countries. This would serve to reduce the strategic positioning of OPEC countries over petroleum and petroleum prices. OPEC includes all the Persian Gulf oil producers, plus Algeria, Angola, Gabon, Libya, Nigeria, Venezuela, and Indonesia. The Twentieth Century Fund's task force on the international oil crisis (1975) advised that "the best remedy for the problems caused by the increased price of oil [brought about by OPEC members] would be, simply, to lower the price" of petroleum. "The Task Force believes that this remedy should be sought through reliance on market forces" (p. 9). The task force goes on to explain in its report that "*the most effective means of exerting market pressure will be to accelerate exploration for crude and develop producing capacity from*" areas outside of OPEC (p. 9, emphasis in original). The task force on U.S. energy policy (1977) averred:

> *That it is essential that the nation take firm and forceful action to implement a comprehensive near-term energy program*

> *designed to assure greater availability of domestic supplies of oil and other sources of energy.* (p. 5, emphasis in original)

The authors of this task force report went on to explain:

> Our present dependence on OPEC cannot be eliminated, but it can—and should—be lessened, thus reducing the competition for OPEC supplies and consequently the political and economic power of the cartel. While we cannot achieve independence, a lessening of our dependence can make a disruption of supplies or a more aggressive price policy on the part of OPEC much less likely. (p. 5)

Therefore, the key recommendations put forward by these policy-planning groups, made up in large part of economic elites, in light of U.S. oil dependency on OPEC countries was to expand the supply of available energy free from OPEC control, and not necessarily to reduce energy consumption.

Particularly noteworthy for a discussion centered on the Canadian oil sands is the fact that the Twentieth Century Fund's task force on "United States Energy Policy" in 1977 "*recommed[ed] an extensive program of government-supported research and development for new energy sources.*" The task force specifically pointed to oil shale and synthetic oil/gasoline (derived from coal). It also advised government funding "to develop the more exotic alternative energy sources" (24–25, emphasis in original).

Just prior to the oil shock of (October) 1973, Walter J. Levy—who served on both of the Twentieth Fund energy task forces—released a report on the Canadian oil sands. Levy's report (dated February 1973) was titled *Emerging North American Oil Balances: Considerations Relevant to a Tar Sands Development Policy* (W. J. Levy Consultants Corp., 1973). While this report predates the oil shock of the early 1970s, Levy was nevertheless writing during a time when the United States was running an oil deficit that could only be expected to increase. Moreover, the political instability of the Persian Gulf region did give policy makers cause to worry. As such, Levy opined that "looking ahead, the picture is one of rapidly increasing prices for increasingly insecure foreign oil supplies." Levy adds that "it is not only that foreign producing areas are insecure, but the rising proportion of U.S. oil supplies that must be drawn from these sources makes the problem that much greater" (W. J. Levy Consultants Corp., 1973, p. iv).

Tellingly, Levy elides conservation as an answer to America's energy dilemma of the early 1970s, and instead focuses entirely on arguing for the development of energy sources that could be developed within North

America to reduce U.S. oil vulnerability. He wrote: "In the short run, there is relatively little the United States can do to mitigate potential supply problems, aside from measures to stockpile larger inventories of oil" (W. J. Levy Consultants Corp., 1973, p. iv). With no anticipated effort to curb consumption, Levy foresaw that "the future demand of the United States for secure sources of oil is so large that the United States will look to all potentially available North American resources in due course" (p. vi). Consistent with Levy's supply side energy reasoning (bias), he argued for "longer run" "policies directed at providing incentives for development of North American resources—conventional oil and gas, synthetics [i.e., oil from coal; oil shale; and tar sands], and nuclear power" (p. iv). Levy went on to aver that among the various sources of synthetic oil in North America that Canada's "tar sands would appear to hold out the potential at least of development of larger volumes of production at an earlier date and with somewhat less uncertainty than either U.S. oil shale or coal liquefaction" (p. vi).

The onset of the 21st century witnessed a new energy shock of sorts—as oil prices spiked at US$147 a barrel in 2008. Following 2008, petroleum prices on the world market did tend to persist at around US$100 a barrel (i.e., historic highs) (Reed, 2015). With concerns about oil prices and, more broadly, about available supplies of petroleum, the Council on Foreign Relations (CFR) sponsored a study on the Canadian tar sands, *The Canadian Oil Sands: Energy Security vs. Climate Change* (Levi, 2009). The advisory committee overseeing this study included officials from the oil behemoths Exxon Mobil and Chevron (Coll, 2013; Yergin, 1991, 2011). Also on this committee was Tara Billingsley, who at the time was a staff member at the Energy and Natural Resources Committee of the U.S. Senate. John Deutch, CIA director under the Clinton administration (Mazzetti, 2013, p. 16; Weiner, 1995), served on this advisory committee, as did individuals representing the Natural Resources Defense Council, the Pew Center on Global Climate Change, and the World Resources Institute. Steven Mufson, who regularly reports on energy issues for the *Washington Post*, was also on the advisory committee. In addition to Exxon Mobil and Chevron, private firms represented on this committee included PIRA Energy Group, ARC Financial Corp., and Louis Capital Markets (Levi, 2009, p. 45).

In the Foreword to the Canadian oil sands report, the president of the CFR summarizes its recommendations. The summary identifies tar sands production as bolstering America's energy security and notes that the "security benefits" of the oil sands "cannot be ignored." The CFR president goes on to explain that "the report's recommendations focus on policies that would provide incentives to cut the emissions generated in producing each barrel of crude from the oil sands, but in a way that is careful to avoid directly discouraging increased production" (Haas, 2009, p. vii).

CONCLUSION

With historically high oil prices (Krauss, 2015a) and broad concerns about global petroleum supplies, the Canadian oil sands serve to address the relatively strong worldwide demand for energy. This demand is led by the United States and its massively sprawled (and gasoline dependent) urban zones (Gonzalez, 2009, 2012, 2013a, 2016). Prior to the North American energy industry conceptualizing the oil sands as a backup to conventional petroleum supplies, there existed a regional policy-planning network focused on the oil sands. This network involved the Alberta provincial government and, more specifically, the Research Council of Alberta. The regional growth coalition's political support for oil sands development was a key component in maintaining the technical momentum underlying the tar sands throughout the early part of the 20th century. Ultimately, the Sun Oil Company, headed by J. Howard Pew, picked up the oil sands as a major commercial project, and its money-losing efforts helped sustain the technical and engineering milieu surrounding the oil sands. Today, ongoing development of dilbit transport links (pipelines and railroad lines) to northern Alberta (the Obama administration rejection of Keystone XL notwithstanding) would be the fruition of the century-long work of the Canadian oil sands policy-planning network. Unfortunately, these transport links may very well push the global warming phenomenon past the point of no return.

NOTES

1. Barrow (1993) explains that "corporations emerged as the dominant economic institutions in capitalist societies by the end of the nineteenth century." He goes on to note that as early as the late 1920s "the bulk of U.S. economic activity, whether measured in terms of assets, profits, employment, investment, market shares, or research and development, was concentrated in the fifty largest financial institutions and five hundred largest nonfinancial corporations" (p. 17). Also see Cohen (2015).

   Political Scientists Jeffrey A. Winters and Benjamin I. Page (2009), hold that "it is now appropriate to . . . think about the possibility of *extreme* political inequality, involving great political influence by a very small number of extremely wealthy individuals." They go on to add that "we argue that it is useful to think about the U.S. political system in terms of oligarchy" (p. 744; emphasis in original). Also see Dewan and Gebeloff (2012), Frank (2014), Krugman (2011, 2014a), Leonhardt (2014), and Winters (2011).

2. Despite the opposition of the provincial government, the Northern Gateway Oil pipeline has been approved by the Canadian national government. While this pipeline is seemingly going forward, the company building it must meet 209 conditions, and "none of them are viewed as insurmountable" (Austen, 2014).
3. A recent U.S. Environmental Protection Agency report held that with lower oil prices, pipelines like the proposed but rejected Keystone XL may be needed to transport Canadian oil sands crude, as moving petroleum via railroad is more expensive (Davenport, 2015b).
4. Between 1946 and 1953, U.S. gasoline usage went from 30 billion gallons annually to 49 billion, amounting to a yearly growth rate of slightly over 7.2%. In 1958 U.S. gasoline consumption exceeded 59 billion gallons (American Petroleum Institute, 1959, pp. 246–247).

REFERENCES

Alberta Energy. (2017). Oil sands: Facts and statistics. Retrieved from http://www.energy.alberta.ca/OilSands/791.asp

American Petroleum Institute. (1959). *Petroleum facts and figures: Centennial edition*. New York, NY: American Petroleum Institute.

As oil consultant, he's without like or equal. (1969, July 27). *New York Times*, sec. 3, p. 3.

Austen, I. (2013a, June 1). British Columbia opposes planned oil sands pipeline. *New York Times*, p. B3.

Austen, I. (2013b, August 2). TransCanada plans pipeline to East Coast. *New York Times*, p. B3.

Austen, I. (2014, June 18). Despite protests, Canada approves Northern Gateway Oil pipeline. *New York Times*, p. B2.

Austen, I. (2016, May 5). Canadian wildfires curtail oil sands production. *New York Times*. Retrieved from https://www.nytimes.com/2016/05/06/world/americas/canadian-wildfires-curtail-oil-sands-production.html

Baker, P., & Davenport, C. (2017, January 25). President revives two oil pipelines thwarted under Obama. *New York Times*, p. A1.

Barach, A. B. (1964). *USA and its economic future: A Twentieth Century Fund survey*. New York, NY: Macmillan.

Barkan, J. (2013). *Corporate sovereignty: Law and government under capitalism*. Minneapolis, MN: University of Minnesota Press.

Barrow, C. W. (1993). *Critical theories of the state*. Madison, WI: University of Wisconsin Press.

Barrow, C. W. (2016). *Toward a critical theory of states: The Poulantzas-Miliband debate after globalization.* Albany, NY: State University of New York Press.

Beauregard, R. A. (2006). *When America became suburban.* Minneapolis, MN: University of Minnesota Press.

Bohi, D., & Russell, M. (1978). *Limiting oil imports.* Baltimore, MD: Johns Hopkins University Press.

Bow, B. (2009). *The politics of linkage: Power, interdependence, and ideas in Canada-US relations.* Vancouver, BC: UBC Press.

Breen, D. H. (1993). *Alberta's petroleum industry and the conservation board.* Edmonton, AB: University of Alberta Press.

Broder, J. M. (2013, March 2). Report may ease path for new pipeline. *New York Times*, p. A9.

Broder, J. M., & Frosch, D. (2011, November 11). U.S. review expected to delay oil pipeline past the election. *New York Times*, p. A1.

Buenger, W. L., & Pratt, J. A. (1986). *But also good business: Texas commerce banks and the financing of Houston and Texas, 1886–1986.* College Station, TX: Texas A&M University Press.

Cahn, M. A. (1995). *Environmental deceptions: The tension between liberalism and environmental policymaking in the United States.* Albany, NY: State University of New York Press.

Calder, K. E. (2012). *The new continentalism: Energy and twenty-first-century Eurasian geopolitics.* New Haven, CT: Yale University Press.

Carskadon, T. R., & Soule, G. H. (1957). *USA in new dimensions: The measure and promise of America's resources, a Twentieth Century Fund survey.* New York, NY: Macmillan.

Chastko, P. (2004). *Developing Alberta's oil sands: From Karl Clark to Kyoto.* Calgary, AB: University of Calgary Press.

Clarkson, S. (1982). *Canada and the Reagan challenge.* Toronto, ON: Lorimer.

Clarkson, S., & Mildenberger, M. (2011). *Dependent America?: How Canada and Mexico construct US power.* Toronto, ON: University of Toronto Press.

Cohen, P. (2015, January 19). Study finds global wealth is flowing to the richest. *New York Times*, p. B6.

Coll, S. (2013). *Private empire: ExxonMobil and American power.* New York, NY: Penguin.

Collins, G. (2014, March 6). Billion dollar babies. *New York Times*, p. A29.

Confessore, N. (2013, November 27). New rules would rein in nonprofits' political role. *New York Times*, p. A1.

Confessore, N. (2014, March 2). Big-money donors demand larger say in party strategy. *New York Times*, p. A1.

Davenport, C. (2014, February 1). Federal report removes hurdle for oil pipeline. *New York Times*, p. A1.

Davenport, C. (2015a, January 21). Rare moment of consensus for senate on Keystone pipeline. *New York Times*, p. A13.

Davenport, C. (2015b, February 4). E. P. A. says pipeline could spur emissions. *New York Times*, p. A16.

Davenport, C. (2015c, November 7). President rejects Keystone pipeline, invoking climate. *New York Times*, p. A17.

Deffeyes, K. S. (2001). *Hubbert's peak: The impending world oil shortage*. Princeton, NJ: Princeton University Press.

Dewan, S., & Gebeloff, R. (2012, January 15). One percent, many variations. *New York Times*, p. A1.

Dewhurst, F. (1955). *America's needs and resources: A new survey*. New York, NY: Twentieth Century Fund.

Domhoff, G. W. (2013). *Who rules America?* (7th ed.). New York, NY: McGraw-Hill.

Dowie, M. (1995). *Losing ground: American environmentalism at the close of the twentieth century*. Cambridge, MA: MIT Press.

Dryzek, J. S. (1996). Political inclusion and the dynamics of democratization. *American Political Science Review*, *90*(1): 475–487.

Duffield, J. S. (2008). *Over a barrel: The costs of U.S. foreign oil dependence*. Stanford, CA: Stanford University Press.

Edelman, M. (1988). *Constructing the political spectacle*. Chicago, IL: University of Chicago Press.

Eisinger, P. K. (1988). *The rise of the entrepreneurial state: State and local economic development policy in the United States*. Madison, WI: University of Wisconsin Press.

Elbein, S. (2012, November 24). Pipeline protest draws pepper spray from deputies. *New York Times*, p. A13.

Finkel, A. (1989). *The social credit phenomena in Alberta*. Toronto, ON: University of Toronto Press.

Fitzsimmons, E. G. (2010, July 30). Regulators warned company on pipeline corrosion. *New York Times*, p. A15.

Fossum, J. E. (1997). *Oil, the state, and federalism: The rise and demise of petro-Canada as a statist impulse*. Toronto, ON: University of Toronto Press.

Frank, R. (2014, November 16). Another widening gap: The haves vs. the have-mores. *New York Times*, p. BU4.

Gonzalez, G. A. (2005). *The politics of air pollution: Urban growth, ecological modernization, and symbolic inclusion*. Albany, NY: State University of New York Press.

Gonzalez, G. A. (2009). *Urban sprawl, global warming, and the empire of capital*. Albany, NY: State University of New York Press.

Gonzalez, G. A. (2012). *Energy and empire: The politics of nuclear and solar power in the United States*. Albany, NY: State University of New York Press.

Gonzalez, G. A. (2013a). *Energy and the politics of the North Atlantic*. Albany, NY: State University of New York Press.

Gonzalez, G. A. (2013b). The U.S. politics of water pollution policy: Urban growth, ecological modernization, and the vending of technology. *Capitalism Nature Socialism*, *24*(4), 105–121.

Gonzalez, G. A. (2016). *American empire and the Canadian oil sands*. New York, NY: Palgrave Macmillan.

Haas, R. N. (2009). Foreword. In *The Canadian oil sands: Energy security vs. climate change*. New York, NY: Council on Foreign Relations.

Harvey, D. (1985). *The urbanization of capital: Studies in the history and theory of capitalist urbanization*. Baltimore, MD: Johns Hopkins University Press.

Hay, C., Lister, M., & Marsh, D. (Eds.). (2006). *The state: Theories and issues*. New York, NY: Palgrave Macmillan.

Hulse C., & Parker, A. (2014, March 21). Koch group, spending freely, hones attack on government. *New York Times*, p. A1.

Johns, W. H. (1981). *A history of the University of Alberta: 1908–1969*. Edmonton, AB: University of Alberta Press.

Johnson, A. M. (1983). *The challenge of change: The Sun Oil Company, 1945–1977*. Columbus, OH: Ohio State University Press.

Johnson, K. (2014, December 28). Race to build on river could block Pacific oil route. *New York Times*, p. A20.

Kaufman, D. (2015, January 17). The other pipeline you should worry about. *New York Times*, p. A17.

Kenworthy, J. R. (2008). Energy use and CO_2 production in the urban passenger transport systems of 84 international cities: Findings and policy implications. In P. Droege (Ed.), *Urban energy transition from fossil fuels to renewable power* (pp. 211–236). Amsterdam, the Netherlands: Elsevier.

Kenworthy, J. R., & Laube, F. B., with Newman, P., Barter, P., Raad, T., Poboon, C., & Guia, B., Jr. (1999). *An international sourcebook of automobile dependence in cities 1960–1990*. Boulder, CO: University Press of Colorado.

Klassen, H. C. (1999). *A business history of Alberta*. Calgary, AB: University of Calgary Press.

Klassen, J. (2014). *Joining empire: The political economy of the new Canadian foreign policy*. Toronto, ON: University of Toronto Press.

Koch Party. (2014, January 26). *New York Times*, p. SR14.

Krauss, C. (2013a, October 31). Looking for a way around Keystone XL, Canadian oil hits the rails. *New York Times*, p. B1.

Krauss, C. (2013b, November 22). Working around Keystone XL, Suncor Energy steps up oil production in Canada. *New York Times*, p. B3.

Krauss, C. (2015a, January 13). Oil prices: What's behind the drop? *New York Times*, p. B4.

Krauss, C. (2015b, November 7). Pipeline plan was begun amid dim U.S. forecasts. *New York Times*, p. A12.

Krauss, C., & Austen, I. (2014, May 13). Rocky road for Canadian oil. *New York Times*, p. B1.

Krugman, P. (2011, November 4). Oligarchy, American style. *New York Times,* p. A31.

Krugman, P. (2014a, January 20). The undeserving rich. *New York Times*, p. A17.

Krugman, P. (2014b, January 27). Paranoia of the plutocrats. *New York Times*, p. A19.

Kuhner, T. (2014). *Capitalism v. democracy: Money in politics and the free market constitution*. Palo Alto, CA: Stanford University Press.

Kurczy, S. (2010, November 11). International energy agency says "peak oil" has hit. *Christian Science Monitor*. Retrieved from http://www.csmonitor.com/World/Global-Issues/2010/1111/International-Energy-Agency-says-peak-oil-has-hit.-Crisis-averted

Leonhardt, D. (2014, May 4). All for the 1%, 1% for all. *New York Times*, p. MM23.

Levi, M. A. 2009. *The Canadian oil sands: Energy security vs. climate change*. New York, NY: Council on Foreign Relations.

Lewis, E. L. (2014, October 5). Who are "we the people"? *New York Times*, p. SR1.

Lichtblau, E. (2015, May 3). Paralyzed F. E. C. can't do its job, chairwoman says. *New York Times*, p. A1.

Lipton, E. (2014, February 10). Fight over wage illustrates web of industry ties. *New York Times*, p. A1.

Logan, J. R., & Molotch, H. L. (2007 [1987]). *Urban fortunes: The political economy of place*. Berkeley, CA: University of California Press.

Mazzetti, M. (2013). *The way of the knife: The CIA, a secret army, and a war at the ends of the earth*. New York, NY: Penguin.

McIntire, M. (2012, April 22). Nonprofit acts as a stealth business lobbyist. *New York Times*, p. A1.

Miliband, R. (1969). *The state in capitalist society*. New York, NY: Basic Books.

Moehring, E. P. (2004). *Urbanism and empire in the far west, 1840–1890.* Reno, NV: University of Nevada Press.

Mutch, R. E. (2014). *Buying the vote: A history of campaign finance reform.* New York, NY: Oxford University Press.

Nocera, J. (2015, January 17). The Keystone XL illusion. *New York Times*, p. A17.

Oil sands and the carbon numbers. (2011, August 22). *New York Times*, p. A18.

Oil Sands Project. (1951). *Proceedings: Athabasca Oil Sands Conference.* Edmonton, AB: Shnitka, King's Printer.

Orr, M., & Johnson, V. C. (Eds.). (2008). *Power in the city: Clarence Stone and the politics of inequity.* Lawrence, KS: University Press of Kansas.

Orsi, R. J. (2007). *Sunset limited: The Southern Pacific Railroad and the development of the American West, 1850–1930.* Berkeley, CA: University of California Press.

Otter, D. A. A. (1982). *Civilizing the West: The Galts and the development of western Canada.* Edmonton, AB: University Press of Alberta.

Otter, D. A. A. (1997). *The philosophy of railways: The transcontinental railway idea in British North America.* Toronto, ON: University of Toronto Press.

Parker, A. (2015, January 21). "Koch primary" tests hopefuls in the G. O. P. *New York Times*, p. A1.

Plotnick, A. R. (1964). *Petroleum: Canadian markets and United States foreign trade policy.* Seattle, WA: University of Washington Press.

Pratt, L. (2001). *Energy: Free trade and the price we paid.* Edmonton, ON: Parkland Institute.

Reed, S. (2015, March 17). Prices fall to 6-year low for U.S. oil. *New York Times*, p. B1.

Rennie, B. J. (Ed.). (2014). *Alberta premiers of the twentieth century.* Regina, SK: University of Regina.

Sassoon, D. (2012, August 21). Crude, dirty and dangerous. *New York Times*, p. A19.

Schneider, E. (1989). *Ribbons of steel: The story of the northern Alberta railways.* Calgary, AB: Detselig Enterprises.

Sklair, L. (2001). *The transnational capitalist class.* Malden, MA: Blackwell.

Stainsby, M. (2011, August 1). A tar sands partnership agreement in the making? *Canadian Dimension.* Retrieved from http://canadiandimension.com/articles/4070/

Stone, C. N. 1989. *Regime politics: Governing Atlanta, 1946–1988.* Lawrence, KS: University Press of Kansas.

Tanner, N. E. (1951). Government policy regarding oil-sands leases and royalties. In *Proceedings: Athabasca Oil Sands Conference*. Edmonton, AB: Shnitka, King's Printer.

Tar sands and the carbon numbers. (2011, August 22). *New York Times*, p. A18.

Temby, O. (2013). Trouble in Smogville: The politics of Toronto's air pollution during the 1950s. *Journal of Urban History*, *39*(4), 669–689.

Temby, O., & O'Connor, R. (2015). Property, technology, and environmental policy: The politics of acid rain in Ontario, 1978–1985. *Journal of Policy History*, *27*(4), 636–669.

Twentieth Century Fund Task Force on the International Oil Crisis. (1975). *Paying for energy*. New York, NY: McGraw-Hill.

Twentieth Century Fund Task Force on United States Energy Policy. (1977). *Providing for energy*. New York, NY: McGraw-Hill.

Weiner, T. (1995, March 11). Man in the news: John Mark Deutch; reluctant helmsman for a troubled agency. *New York Times*. Retrieved from http://www.nytimes.com/1995/03/11/us/man-in-the-news-john-mark-deutch-reluctant-helmsman-for-a-troubled-agency.html

Wetherly, P., Barrow, C. W., & Burnham, P. (Eds.). (2008). *Class, power and the state in capitalist society: Essays on Ralph Miliband*. New York, NY: Palgrave MacMillan.

Winks, R. W. (1997). *Laurence S. Rockefeller: Catalyst for conservation*. Washington, DC: Island Press.

Winters, J. A. (2011). *Oligarchy*. New York, NY: Cambridge University Press.

Winters, J. A., & Page, B. I. (2009). Oligarchy in the United States. *Perspectives on Politics*, 7(4), 731–751.

W. J. Levy Consultants Corp. (1973). *Emerging North American oil balances: Considerations relevant to a tar sands development policy*. New York, NY: Author.

Yergin, D. (1991). *The prize: The epic quest for oil, money, and power*. New York, NY: Simon & Schuster.

Yergin, D. (2011). *The quest: Energy, security, and the remaking of the modern world*. New York, NY: Penguin.

Yetiv, S. A. (2011). *Explaining foreign policy: U.S. decision-making in the Gulf Wars*. Baltimore, MD: Johns Hopkins University Press.

TWELVE

U.S.-Mexican Energy Relations

Clean-Energy Integration Falling Behind?

MARCELA LÓPEZ-VALLEJO

INTRODUCTION

North America (Canada, United States, and Mexico) is a prime example of a region moving towards energy integration, based heavily on an already well-established fossil fuels trade. Oil, gas, coal and, recently, nonconventional fuels will continue to fulfill the energy needs of the region. However, integration is fragmented into two bilateral energy relationships: that of the United States with Canada, and that of the United States with Mexico. Canadians and Americans share the closest energy relationship in the world. Canada is the major supplier of energy to the United States (including crude oil, refined petroleum products, electricity, coal, uranium, etc.) representing almost 90% of energy exports. In this context, the United States has become an exporting power in the last five years, when the shale revolution and new perforation technologies (e.g., fracking) boomed (Aguilera & Radetzki, 2015; U.S. Energy Information Administration, 2016).

The intensity of this bilateral integration, through infrastructure connections and the trade of oil, gas, and fossil-fuel electricity, is also present in the U.S.-Mexican relationship (Petraeus, Zoellick, & O'Neil, 2014). However, it contrasts in the disparity of capacities resulting in an evident technological dependence of Mexico, where the country exports crude oil to the United States and then imports it back in the form of refined petroleum products. In addition, the technological gap between both countries is growing fast. For example, even though in 2012 Mexico discovered several rich oil wells in deep waters and shale fields, the capacity to drill them is minimal. In 2012, the United States drilled 9,100 shale wells and 137 deep-water oil wells, but Mexico drilled only 3 shale wells and 6 deep-water wells (Baker Institute for Public Policy, 2013, p. 4; Petróleos Mexicanos, 2013).

To try to address this technological gap, to overcome the decrease of the Cantarell basin, and to look for new markets based on Mexico's energy potential, structural energy reforms were put in place in 2013 and 2014. The Mexican Energy Reform (MER) opened the energy sector to the market, dismantling the two monopolist companies (PEMEX for oil and gas and Comisión Federal de Electricidad [CFE] for electricity), and established new forms of contracting for other companies (Mexican or foreign, public or private) that previously were forbidden by the Constitution. In this context, the U.S. Congress ratified the Agreement between the United States of America and the United Mexican States Concerning Transboundary Hydrocarbon Reservoirs in the Gulf of Mexico (also called the Transboundary Agreement, or TBA).[1] This agreement calls for equal distribution of the oil and gas located at the border of both countries in the Gulf of Mexico, to avoid one country's companies from drilling the other country's resources (U.S. Congress, 2012, p. 10). The MER and the TBA show that both countries are willing to help along the integration of their fossil fuel sectors through bilateral cooperation and business mechanisms.

Nonetheless, there is another type of energy relationship between Mexico and the United States, one that has not performed as well: integration of clean-energy sources and technologies. Historically, relations between Mexico and the United States have included these types of energies. Since the 1970s, renewable bilateral programs or bilateral joint commissions for climate change have been put in place (Wood, 2010). The North American Agreement for Environmental Cooperation and the North American Energy Working Group, both formed in the 1990s, tried to encourage regional and bilateral collaboration. Several bilateral initiatives at the federal level regarding clean or renewable energy were enabled in the first decade of the 21st century. The Bilateral Framework on Clean Energy and Climate Change (or CEBA) in 2009 served as the basis for several task forces, notably the U.S.-Mexican Cross-border Electricity Task Force (CETAF), which has been in operation since 2010, and the Clean-Energy and Climate Policy Task Force (CECPOTAF), launched in 2015. The U. S. Agency for International Development (USAID) provides support to CEBA through some of its programs, such as the Mexico's Global Climate Change Program and the Low Emissions Development Program. More recently, in 2016 some advances were made through a memorandum of understanding between Canada, the United States, and Mexico, which addressed energy and climate-change collaboration. This document was reinforced with specific commitments resulting from the North American Leader's Summit (NALS), hosted by Canadian Prime Minister Justin Trudeau in June 2016 (Prime Minister of Canada, 2016).

The framework to operate these commitments in both countries encouraged decarbonization paths. Mexico enacted the very last piece of the MER, the Energy Transition Law (ETL), in December 2015. The ETL addresses clean-energy deployment through energy efficiency, green certificates, and new operation rules for the electricity markets (Diario Oficial de la Federación, 2015). The ETL gave operative basis to climate-change goals established in the Climate Change General Law of 2012. In the United States, the Clean Power Plan (CPP) of 2014 allows for reducing carbon pollution from power plants in terms of efficiency with a transition from coal to natural gas and renewables (U.S. Environmental Protection Agency, 2015). In recent years, both countries individually advanced towards clean-energy development, yet no comprehensive integration program was put in place. Integration of electricity markets is still incipient and mainly performs in border states.

This two-track energy relationship—one for fossils represented by TBA and the fossil part of the MER (F-MER), and the other for clean energy by CEBA, the clean part of the MER (C-MER) and the CPP—appears to run in different directions with regard to bilateral energy integration and environmental aspects. The TBA and the F-MER have an environmental component to palliate fossil activities' impacts a posteriori; however, the treatment of environmental protection and sustainability in these two mechanisms relies on different approaches. The TBA asks Mexico to standardize environmental norms with the United States, promoting inspections by both parties; the F-MER is immersed in a series of overlapping national environmental laws and standards, which the newly created National Agency for Industrial Safety and Environmental Protection for the Hydrocarbon Sector (ANSIPA, for its name in Spanish) must address. On the other hand, CEBA deals with a variety of energy sources that claim to be clean but are classified differently by each country. The C-MER includes renewables and nuclear energy, whereas the CPP also includes renewables but focuses on technologies such as carbon capture and storage or energy efficiency standards.

The guiding argument of this chapter is that, with the leadership of the United States in the region's energy transition, the prevailing bilateral energy relationship facilitated change and adaptation for Mexico's policy framework in a fossil-oriented approach (exemplified by the TBA and the F-MER) to deepen fossil fuel integration. Based only on cooperation instruments and attraction of clean-energy investment, the bilateral clean-energy integration was addressed only tangentially, leaving environmental protection behind and subject to interpretation by both countries. Clean-energy integration means that the energy sectors of both countries are or will be willing to develop clean-energy sources, converters, carriers, and services in interconnected and standardized forms. In this regard, there seems to be two different types, intensities, and rhythms of the U.S.-Mexican bilateral energy integration. This situation divorces comprehensive bilateral energy governance from compliance with emissions reduction and environmental protection in the region. It also speaks of the minimal attention that the clean-energy sector has received in the integration processes of fossil-producer countries.

This chapter is divided into three sections. As the object of bilateral energy integration, it is important to define what clean energy means, so the first section presents a brief discussion about what sources are considered clean energy and to what degree they are environmentally friendly. The second section puts forth the recent bilateral clean-energy mechanisms that speak of cooperation and some sort of incipient attempt at integration; the CEBA (with its two task forces, CETAF and CECPOTAF), some of USAID's environmental programs, and the NALS are explored. The third section analyzes to what extent the Mexican Energy Reform contributes to bilateral clean-energy integration. Finally, the conclusions discuss how energy relations between the United States and Mexico perform in different types, intensities, and rhythms, avoiding a regional and comprehensive governance scheme that includes environmental protection.

HOW ENVIRONMENTALLY FRIENDLY ARE CLEAN-ENERGY SOURCES IN THE BILATERAL RELATIONSHIP?

The first problem of U.S.-Mexican environmental cooperation (linked with the energy integration) is conceptual. What kinds of energy sources are environmentally friendly? How "clean" are the energies being objected to bilateral trade? There are different categorizations of "clean energies" in both countries. Some of them include hydropower or nuclear energy, some of them only take into account renewables, others include biofuels, and others prefer "less dirty" versions of coal, oil, or synthetic fuels. For example, the U.S. Department of Energy supports clean coal technology as an environmentally friendly type of energy, which sharply reduces air emissions and other pollutants from coal-burning power plants (U.S. Department of Energy, 2014). A middle-ground position is taken by the

U.S. Environmental Protection Agency, which includes clean-energy supply options such as highly efficient combined heat and power[2] and green power generated by renewable energy sources (U.S. Environmental Protection Agency, 2014a). In contrast, the Florida Renewable Energy Association notes that "unfortunately, it has become increasingly necessary to define this term [clean energy] unequivocally due to the persistent attempts of industry representatives for non-renewable and environmentally hazardous energy sources to co-opt the term for the purpose of presenting these non-clean sources in a better, more acceptable light" (Florida Renewable Energy Association, 2014). This is a case in which the definition of clean energy rests on the level of carbon intensity. For example, the U.S. Clean Energy Standard Act of 2012 establishes that clean energy includes sources that generate electricity with a carbon intensity lower than 0.82 metric tons per megawatt-hour (such as clean coal), as well as efficiency-improving elements in the nuclear or hydropower sources (U.S. Senate, 2012).

In Mexico the situation is very similar. When the Secretariat of Energy (SENER) talks about renewables, it includes wind, solar, geothermal, hydroelectric, and waste-to-management sources, as well as nuclear energy (Secretaría de Energía, 2012b, 2013a).[3] The Secretariat of Environment and Natural Resources (SEMARNAT) even includes combined-cycle gas turbines, fracking processes, and clean coal as a "less dirty" industries that will become clean-energy sources in the near future and will address climate change and sustainability (Enciso, 2014). (It is important to note that the discussions for the ETL were driven by this debate.) At the end of the day, "less dirty" standards were included for hydrogen, carbon capture and storage, and co-generation. These criteria are different for the United States and Mexico. For example, co-generation efficiency varies among generation capacities in México and, in the United States, a general criteria is applied to all cases (Diario Oficial de la Federación, 2015; Secretaría de Energía, 2012b).

As the energy relationship in terms of clean sources is not standardized, this chapter only focuses on renewable sources and how their bilateral integration has been left behind. Table 12.1 summarizes the types of renewable energy sources established by Mexican SENER, their CO_2 emissions, and their environmental impacts as established by the U.S. Environmental Protection Agency. As shown in Table 12.1, almost all types of renewable energy account for some environmental impacts. However, to achieve the label of "clean," the focus needs to be put in the complete cycle of production-consumption and waste (water pollution, greenhouse gas [GHG] emissions, etc.), as well as on social impacts such as land-use change. In this sense, clean energies should (1) produce the minimal

Table 12.1
Clean Energy Sources and Their Environmental Impacts

Clean Energy Sources	Fuel	CO_2 Emissions (pounds of CO_2 per million BTU)	Other Impacts (water use, solid waste, land use)
	Biomass	Biomass power plants emit nitrogen oxides and a small amount of sulfur dioxide. CO_2 produced causes no net increase in the atmosphere considering it is part of the natural cycle.	The boilers burning the biomass need water for steam production and for cooling. Water can be re-used. Biomass power plants have pollutant build-up in the water used. The burning of biomass creates a solid waste called ash. Biomass grown for fuel purposes and biomass power plants require large areas of land.
	Landfill gas	Burning landfill gas produces nitrogen oxides emissions as well as trace amounts of toxic materials. The carbon dioxide released from burning landfill gas is considered to be a part of the natural carbon cycle of the earth. Burning landfill gas prevents the release of methane	Engines or combustion turbines that burn landfill gas to produce energy typically require negligible amounts of water. Landfill gas technologies do not produce any substantial amount of solid waste while creating electricity.
	Municipal solid waste (MSW)	Burning MSW produces nitrogen oxides and sulfur dioxide as well as trace amounts of toxic pollutants, such as mercury compounds and dioxins. The average air emission rates in the United States are 3,685 lbs/MWh of carbon dioxide, 1.2 lbs/MWh of sulfur dioxide, and 6.7 lbs/MWh of nitrogen oxides.	Power plants that burn MSW typically require an amount of water per unit of electricity generated, similar to fuel power plants. MSW power plants discharge used water. Pollutants build up in the water used in the power plant boiler and cooling system. The cooling water is considerably warmer when it is discharged than when it was taken in.

(continued)

Table 12.1 (*continued*)

Clean Energy Sources	Fuel	CO_2 Emissions (pounds of CO_2 per million BTU)	Other Impacts (water use, solid waste, land use)
Renewables and Permanently Available Sources	Solar (photovoltaic)	Negligible	The production of photovoltaic wafers creates very small amounts of hazardous materials that must be handled properly to avert risk to the environment or to people.
	Solar (thermal)	Negligible	Solar-thermal technologies may tap local water resources if the liquid that is being heated to create steam is water. In this case, the water can be re-used. Solar-thermal technologies may require a significant amount of land.
	Eolic	Negligible	Wind turbines in areas with little rainfall may require the use of a small amount of water. Land around wind turbines can be used for other purposes, such as the grazing of cattle or farming. Bird and bat mortality has been an issue at some wind farms.
	Geothermal	Negligible	For geothermal plants that rely on hot, dry rocks for energy, water from local resources is needed to extract the energy. —Geothermal power plants can possibly cause groundwater contamination when drilling wells and extracting hot water or steam. —Geothermal power plants typically require the use of less land than fossil fuel power plants.

	Hydroelectric	Negligible	Dams can greatly affect the flow of rivers, altering ecosystems and affecting the wildlife and people who depend on those waters. Assessment of the environmental impacts of a specific hydropower facility requires case-by-case review.
Nuclear	Uranium	Nuclear power plants do not emit carbon dioxide, sulfur dioxide, or nitrogen oxides as part of the power generation process. However, fossil fuel emissions are associated with the uranium mining and uranium enrichment process as well as the transport of the uranium fuel to and from the nuclear plant.	Nuclear power plants use large quantities of water for steam production and for cooling. Heavy metals and salts build up in the water used in all power plant systems, including nuclear ones. Nuclear power plants sometimes discharge small amounts of tritium and other radioactive elements. Spent fuel is stored at the nuclear plants at which it is generated.

Source: Based on data from U.S. Environmental Protection Agency (2014b); Union of Concerned Scientists (2014).

impact possible to the environment, (2) manage waste in ways that do not impact the environment, (3) avoid land-use change (deforestation mainly), and (4) guarantee sustainability and decarbonization. If we take into account these criteria, clean energy would exclude all fossil fuels and forms of "less dirty" versions of conventional fuels, nonconventional fuels, nuclear energy, and some types of renewable energy such as hydroelectricity. As a result, not many types of energies would be left to fulfill the "clean" criteria. Due to the high costs associated with this scenario, the combination of both renewables and clean-energy standards appears to be the only short-term solution the United States and Mexico have found. In addition, pressure from industrial lobbies is strong and economic growth is supported by a high demand of energy for production-consumption. This was the perspective of the C-MER and the CPP. To switch from cooperation schemes to a bilateral integration, Mexico and the United States would have to "clean up" the fossil-fuel relationship by introducing other sources and policies into their energy mixes with the goal of harmonizing standards and dealing with integrated environmental policies. For this aim, some advances have been made between the United States and Mexico, as well as at the North American regional level.

CEBA, TASK FORCES, AND NALS: CLEANING UP THE BILATERAL ENERGY RELATIONSHIP

The conceptual ambiguity about what qualifies as clean energy is evidenced in the U.S.-Mexican cooperation schemes in which different definitions complicate integration. As acknowledged by some analysts, the interest of the United States in cooperating with Mexico has been based on boosting renewable energies in Mexico to integrate this cleaner source into their grids to meet social environmental concerns and some states' clean-energy or renewable portfolios, especially those of California (Healy, VanNijnatten, & López-Vallejo, 2014; Rabe, 2013). Facing the lack of a comprehensive federal law on climate change in the United States, the support of local diversification strategies to address climate change had to be present (López-Vallejo, 2014). From the Mexican side, in 2008, the Congress passed the Law for the Beneficial Use of Renewable Energies and the Finance of the Energy Transition (LAERFTE, for its name in Spanish), which established the goals for achieving a renewable portfolio of 35% to 2024. This law was accompanied by the General Law on Biofuels and Security (Diario Oficial de la Federación, 2008). LAEFTE provided the basis for promoting bilateral agreements negotiated at the federal level to fill part of the gap in clean-energy cooperation. This would be the case with the U.S.-Mexican CEBA of 2009. CEBA works with some USAID programs, such as Mexico's Global Climate Change Program and the Low Emissions Development Program. In the words of Eleanor Fox, the Energy and Natural Resources Officer of the U.S. Department of State in 2013, the goal of this cooperation scheme is to create governance mechanisms between different actors "to exchange information on energy and climate issues, and to work on regulations and programs to encourage energy conservation and the use of renewables" (Fox, 2013). According to the White House, the CEBA goals are:

- to establish a mechanism for political and technical cooperation and information exchange, especially in renewable energy, energy efficiency, adaptation, market mechanisms, forestry and land use, green jobs, low carbon energy technology development and capacity building, and
- to build upon cooperation in the border region promoting efforts to reduce greenhouse gas emissions, to adapt to the local impacts of climate change in the region, as well as to strengthen the reliability and flow of cross border electricity grids and by facilitating the ability of neighboring border states to work together to strengthen energy trade. (White House, 2009)

Although the CEBA opens the door to other low-carbon energy technologies in practical terms, the focus has been limited to renewables (specifically wind projects), energy efficiency (especially on cross-border smart-grid transmission), and GHG monitoring (Garrison, 2010; Rowlands, 2013). In this regard, some important activities had been registered since the enactment of this agreement. For example, in CEBA's bilateral meeting of 2010, the emphasis was put on low-carbon development, climate change (UN Climate Fund), renewable energy, and technological development (Secretaría de Relaciones Exteriores, 2010a, 2010b). That same year, task forces under this framework were put to work. The U.S.-Mexican Cross-border Electricity Task Force (CETAF) started operations with the goal of promoting the renewables' market in both countries. It involved industry, stakeholders, and local governments led by representatives of both federal governments. This initiative goes further and tries to identify and remove obstacles to transboundary trade in renewable energy and electricity projects, specifically regarding different standards, lack of investment, leaks and inefficiency in electricity transmission, as well as promotion of smart grids (Secretaría de Energía,

2012a, 2014a). Optimism took over with the successful consolidation of exports of wind energy from Baja California in Mexico to the state of California in 2010 and the establishment of six specific working groups: (1) land use and environmental planning, (2) market planning, (3) electricity planning, (4) financing and cost recovery, (5) information, (6) operational issues (Wood, 2010).

Some other strategies were included in the 2011 meeting:

- Coordination of minimum appliance standards and discussion of Mexican appliance labeling efforts similar to U.S. programs
- Cooperation on wind energy through the memorandum of understanding between the U.S. Department of Energy's National Renewable Energy Laboratory and Mexico's Electricity Research Institute
- Analysis of electricity system maturity and identification of strategies to implement smart-grid technologies
- Cooperation on energy efficiency in the hemisphere under the Energy and Climate Partnership of the Americas and globally with the major economies through the Clean Energy Ministerial process
- Completion of an atlas of carbon sources and sinks, together with Canada, for North America in 2012, and potential opportunities for expanded collaboration in carbon capture and storage
- Development of Mexico's "Clean Transport" program. (Embassy of the United States in Mexico, 2011)

However, when implementation arrived, results were not as expected. An analysis by the Wilson Center establishes that in 2012 "there [was] insufficient capacity in cross-border transmission lines, and a seeming lack of political will on the part of the federal governments in the United States and Mexico to move forward with an agenda to address the problem. A largely stagnant bilateral dialogue on the issue, through the Cross-Border Electricity Task Force, has failed to produce meaningful results and requires a new injection of energy to reboot its efforts" (Wood, 2012, p. 7).

Little progress was registered in the 2012 meeting where the discussions took another direction and focused on exchange of experiences for "sustainable regulation of non-conventional gas" (Secretaría de Energía, 2012c). However, for the 2013 reunion, both countries went back to the original path and talked about standards, energy-efficiency mechanisms, renewables, and climate change strategies (Secretaría de Medio Ambiente y Recursos Naturales, 2013).

Prior to the enactment of the Mexican ETL in December 2015, the United States and Mexico launched a new bilateral CECPOTAF. As mentioned in the Joint Statement on U.S.-Mexican Climate Policy Cooperation (White House, 2015), this interagency task force would be chaired by Secretaries of Energy and Environment in both countries, hold meetings, and participate in the Clean Energy Ministerial Process (the last two meetings were held in Mexico and in the United States). The result of this bilateral task force is still uncertain; however, the joint participation at the last two multilateral ministerial meetings for clean energy and efficiency has been successful in addressed topics such as efficient lighting, low-carbon power systems, clean-energy access policies, and cooperation and exchange of knowledge about low-carbon policies through a Clean-Energy Solutions Center (International Energy Agency, 2015, 2016).

The USAID's programs have also promoted clean-energy collaboration with Mexico. Specifically, the USAID/Mexico's Global Climate Change Program aims to help Mexico reduce emissions from deforestation and forest degradation (REDD). This program also included some countries in Central America. USAID also helped Mexico to implement the Low Emissions Development Program (LED), which established a strong national monitoring, reporting, and verification system GHG. This five-year USAID strategy granted $70 million and was consistent with CEBA's original goals plus the addition of REDD mechanisms (Ribando, Ratner, Villareal, & Hagerty, 2014). However, this program has an audit mechanism by which USAID reviews fulfillment of goals by all partners. Unfortunately, the general comments since the 2011 audit have evidenced failure. For example, according to their first-year work plans, 77 activities for LED and 105 activities for REDD were required to be implemented from October 2011 to September 2012. However, both sets of activities were late, implementing only 61 activities of LED and 31 out of 105 of the REDD mechanism to October 2012. According to USAID, "key activities, such as setting up the grants component, supporting the creation of the financial structure for a national REDD system, and supporting the development of a monitoring, reporting, and verification system for GHG, had not started or were significantly behind schedule" (U.S. Agency for International Development, 2013). It is important to note that this has been the result of numerous problems with the partners of the U.S. Government in this program—Nature Conservancy and Tetra Tech, Inc.—and, to a lesser extent, the Mexican authorities.

Despite these results, in May 2014 USAID and the Secretariat of Energy (SENER) signed three agreements that reestablished trust in both governments to continue cooperation. The first was with SENER; the

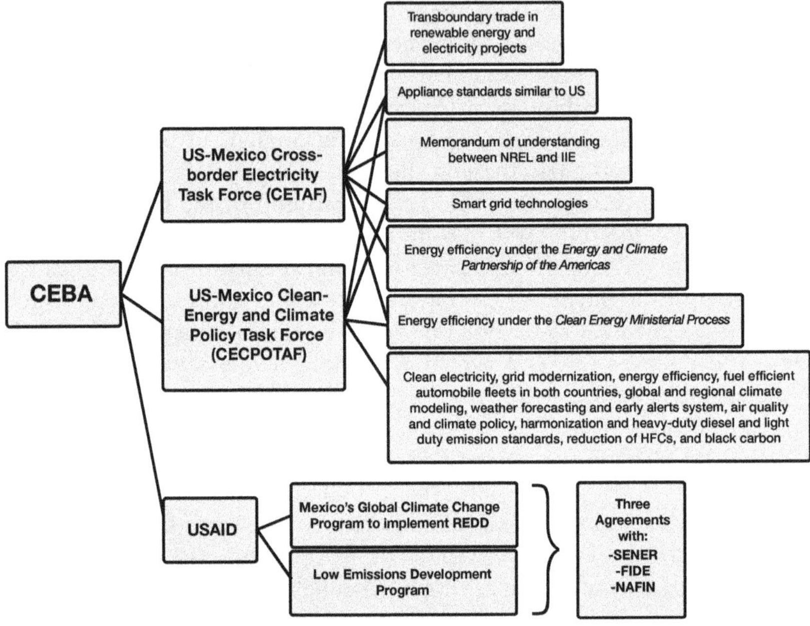

FIGURE 12.1 Bilateral Programs and Initiatives under CEBA (Author's elaboration).

second was with the Electricity Savings Fund (FIDE, for its name in Spanish), an efficiency trust fund; and the third was with National Financing (NAFIN, in Spanish), a financial institution that administers cooperation funds, especially to promote green credits for medium and small companies (Secretaría de Energía, 2014c). Figure 12.1 summarizes the bilateral programs currently working under the CEBA framework.

Although not expressed in specific programs, the North American Leader's Summit of 2016 gave political support to these bilateral mechanisms. Among the most important agreements regarding the energy–climate link, were to reach a regional goal of 50% of clean-energy power generation by 2025 and to address short-life climate pollutants such as black carbon, hydrofluorocarbons, and methane (Prime Minister of Canada, 2016).

Far from integration, in general, bilateral cooperation regarding clean energy emphasized energy efficiency (climate-friendly technologies and smart grids), some standardization (especially in the transportation area), and renewable projects (underscoring wind and solar). Results have been quite limited as compared to the original goals of CEBA and the two supporting instruments (USAID's programs and the two task forces) The Mexican Energy Reform provides a different context within which these agreements will operate, however, environmental gaps and challenges are still to be addressed. In this context of market openness, the newly created CECPOTAF and the commitments of NALS may advance further cooperation by establishing comprehensive harmonized standards. This route may lead to clean-energy integration in the long run.

BILATERAL CLEAN-ENERGY TRADE AND THE MEXICAN ENERGY REFORM

In Mexico, reforms to restructure the energy sector were sent to Congress by President Enrique Peña Nieto in 2013, following a trend towards energy openness that began in the 1990s. After several months of debate, Congress (and local congresses) approved the energy reform on December 21, 2013, which allowed for the enactment of a package of energy-related laws (Diario Oficial de la Federación, 2013a; Gobierno de la República, 2013, Appendix 1). The debate continued during the first semester of 2014, when the so-called secondary laws, or operative rulings, were discussed and enacted. In general, the reform and its secondary laws opened the possibility for private and international companies to enter into exploration and extraction of oil and gas, as well as to produce energy for electricity, areas in which both national energy companies had fallen short.[4]

The reform package included clean energy to produce electricity. Some institutions were put in place and others acquired certain responsibilities. Institutions such as the National Center of Energy Control (CENACE, as in Spanish), the Secretariat of Energy (SENER), and the Regulatory Commission for Energy (CRE, in Spanish) are vital actors in this new electricity scheme. According to Article 16 of the newly created Law for the Electricity Industry (LIE, for its name in Spanish), CENACE will operate the electricity market and grant open and nondiscriminatory access to both the Mexican CFE and private and foreign providers. The CRE is now in charge of regulating and granting permissions for power generation and establishes prices for CFE transmission and distribution of electricity (Diario Oficial de la Federación, 2014a). In 2012, The General Law on Climate Change was enacted in 2012 with the goal of reducing greenhouse gases to 20% by 2020, 30% by 2030, and 50% by 2050 (Diario Oficial de la Federación, 2012). Clean-energy development is the key to achieving these goals. With the Energy Reform, the Special Program for the Development of Renewable Energies, based on the LAERFTE, was designed by SENER to address climate change as well as to try to reboost the market (Centro de Investigación y Desarrollo, 2013; Secretaría de Energía, 2014b). Although this program addressed an important operative capacity of the sector, it fell short in goals and definitions. As Jesús Antonio del Río, president of the Institute of Renewable Energies of UNAM notes, this program's goals are very modest, especially with regard to solar and wind sources (Canales, 2014).

LAERFTE was substituted by the ETL in 2015. Together with the ETL and the new rulings for the operation of the electricity market, the LIE opened the door for two possible electricity providers: CFE and independent producers (big and small, Mexican or foreign). These providers can sell the energy to CFE directly, or use it for self-consumption, co-generation, and trade. Contracts are only granted to regulators who promote the use of clean-energy sources and clean technologies (Diario Oficial de la Federación, 2013b, 2014a). Through minimum quotas of clean energy and clean technologies, as well as clean-energy certificates for providers, the Mexican climate goals established in 2012 climate-change law are on course to be fulfilled (Diario Oficial de la Federación, 2012; PricewaterhouseCoopers, 2014).

In a bilateral scheme, CEBA and USAID's programs intend to support clean electricity trade. However, in practical terms this trade is performed at cross-border scales in fragmented vertical transnational markets (Sovacool & Ridortsov, 2013). This is the case for the interconnection between some of the Northern Mexican States, such as Baja California (specifically the cities of Tijuana, Mexicali, and La Rosita) and their counterparts in California (San Diego, Miguel, and Imperial Valley) in the framework of the Western Electricity Coordinating Council (WECC).

Although renewable generation in Mexico accounts for wind, geothermal, solar, and hydro, most of the electricity traded to the United States comes from wind and geothermal sources. The wind park of La Rumorosa is the most important source, with an installed capacity of 258 megawatts (Secretaría de Economía, 2013; Triolo, 2015). In this trade relationship, several projects will benefit from the Mexican Energy Reform. For example, in the area of Sierra de Juárez, U.S. companies such as Intergen and IEnova are building 47 turbines to produce 155 megawatts to be exported to California (IEnova, 2014). In this sense, Mexican clean energy is aiding the U.S. partners to meet their energy-efficiency and climate-change goals, as well as their renewable portfolios. The goals of the CETAF seem to be supported by this energy trade and the opening of the electricity generation in the Mexican Energy Reform. This context is intended to boost the clean-energy market by attracting U.S. investment to solve some of the infrastructure limitations, such as building cross-border transmission lines (to date, the transmission capacity from Baja California to California is only 800 megawatts). In fact, after the reform, the scenario for the wind energy bilateral market was perceived to be very attractive to U.S. companies. This sector was to become "the leading renewable energy sector for U.S. exports. This is consistent with an oversupply of wind turbine manufacturing capacity and demonstrates the growing reliance on exports for the sector" (U.S. Department of Commerce, 2014). Nonetheless, in March 2016, the first Mexican long-term wholesale electricity auction took place and the results partially confirm this assertion. All projects granted were to develop renewable energy with wind and solar sources; yet out of the 11 awards granted, only one was for the U.S. company SunPower Corporation through its Mexican subsidiary (Centro Nacional de Control de Energía, 2016). No other U.S. company was awarded and no wind project was granted to U.S. participants. As analyst Steven Chu suggests, this auction indicates that the real prices of renewables in the United States must be lower to be competitive (McMahon, 2016). The wind project and the other solar projects were granted to companies from Italy, Spain, India, and China at prices around US4 cents per kilowatt hour (Centro Nacional de Control de Energía, 2016). Nonetheless, wind and solar sources have a great potential for electricity cross-border trade and market integration due to the history of success with regional electricity integration through cross-border markets.

Geothermal sources are also important in the U.S.-Mexican trade. To date, the Mexican geothermal sector has a capacity of electricity export of 645 megawatts to the United States. The Mexican Energy Reform put special attention to this area of opportunity by enacting the Law of Geothermal and National Waters. Mexico is the fourth most important producer worldwide, with an installed capacity of 839 megawatts (Arellano, Manuel, Bazán, & Ortiz, 2011; Secretaría de Energía, 2015b). The main goal of this law is to give dynamism to the exports of clean electricity to the United States, given that most of the current and potential projects are in Baja California, in the area of Cerro Prieto.[5] This law opens the sector to private investment (foreign or domestic), but grants the possibility of concessions for all the water used in the generation of electricity, either geothermal water or other type of water. This means that this resource will be in hands of private investors, causing scarcity and environmental damage, as explained in Table 12.1. In addition, the prices of electricity from the Cerro Prieto geothermal plant are unequal. On the Mexican side, the price of electricity is 770% higher than what California consumers pay for this imported electricity (Esquivel, 2014).[6] This seems to indicate that the Mexican geothermal subsector is subsidizing California consumers.

In wind, solar, and geothermal energy trade the Mexican Energy Reform created incentives to intensify the bilateral relationship. Before the reform, the commercialization was exclusively in the hands of CFE; with the reform, CFE will have to compete with private companies in Mexico or outside the country for the final consumer preferences. It is expected that this competition can effectively lower the prices of electricity, but without detailed scrutiny and control by the regulators (CENACE, SENER, and CRE), it can be dangerous and can result in situations like the California electricity disaster some years ago, in which private generators together saturated the transmission network to charge more or to threaten shortages (Aristegui Noticias, 2014). In other words, this can result in the creation of "electricity" cartels manipulating the prices and the quantity of electricity sold to the public. The Mexican Energy Reform failed to address this topic with regard to cross-border integrated electricity markets.

The energy reform tried to compensate this situation with other kind of incentives. It mandated the creation of fiscal mechanisms to address environment. Green fiscal credits, clean-energy certificates, a carbon tax, and a carbon market platform work as an integral system. Green fiscal credits will be given to those companies willing to invest in renewables and clean technologies. The ETL, for its part, gave basis to the Clean Energy Certificates (CEC) mechanism, where SENER establishes a minimum percentage of clean-energy generation to generators or distributors. If they cannot comply with the goals, they compensate by buying CECs. If generators or distributors fail to accomplish this, they are fined (Alarcón, 2014; Diario Oficial de la Federación, 2014b). CENACE will establish the price of CECs and operate the market. This instrument operates with an obligatory approach in which the clean-energy participants are forced to comply with the law through this market rather than through courts. In other words, participants who do not comply with the law have a market option before paying a fine established by the CRE (Diario Oficial de la Federación, 2014b). It is worth noting that the national agency, ANSIPA, will not take part of the monitoring and sanctioning of violations regarding the clean-energy sector. The judicial organism PROFEPA (for its name in Spanish) will perform these duties under very limited institutional capacities. What will happen when a company decides not to pay the fine, does not generate clean energy as agreed, or decides to close the business and leave the facilities? In this sense, the answers are still unclear, but perhaps then the cases will be taken to the courts (De Régules, 2015).

The carbon tax was originally mandated by the General Law for Climate Change of 2012 but was not activated until after the reform was passed. Prices were established in a range between US$3.00 and US$4.00

per ton of CO_2. Taxpayers have two options: They can pay the tax and trust that it will be used for adaptation and mitigation of public projects or can pay it through the nascent MexiCO2 carbon market (MexiCO2, 2014). The latter option is generally chosen by companies listed in the Mexican Stock Exchange. The carbon allowances can only be purchased from the 231 projects already registered under the Clean Development Mechanism (CDM) of the Kyoto Protocol located in Mexico, which represents about 8.8 million green allowances or 1.4% of the Mexican national emissions. However, almost all CDM projects account for energy efficiency and not for developing clean-energy sources. The projects range from renewable development to technology change, carbon capture, prevention of energy leaks, waste management, REDD mechanisms, efficiency in demand and distribution/transmission, and development a wind park (Balderas, 2014).

All these incentives to develop clean-energy projects work separately and are not linked to each other. For example, the MexiCO2 carbon market is not linked to the clean-energy certificates, yet there is no relationship between the carbon tax and the fiscal green credits. Needless to say, these instruments are not linked to the bilateral clean-energy scheme with the United States (or with the border states). These instruments need to coordinate with those of Mexico's NAFTA partners, the United States and Canada, especially with their transregional carbon markets and state/provincial energy portfolio standards (Brown & Sovacool, 2011; López-Vallejo, 2014). This scenario, where there are different ways to participate in the clean-energy projects, might encourage cherry-picking practices with different methodologies, prices, and approaches to clean energy, which does not help in building a solid U.S.-Mexican clean-energy relationship.

CONCLUSION: TYPES, INTENSITIES, AND RHYTHMS OF U.S.-MEXICAN ENERGY INTEGRATION

In view of the clean-energy cooperation schemes, the multiple environmental instruments in the bilateral relationship and the adding up of the not-yet-solved environmental gaps and challenges of the Mexican Energy Reform, what is the trend for the energy integration between the United States and Mexico? Is integration of clean-energy sources in the same path as the fossil-fuel sector? Does bilateral cooperation address environmental impacts, or is it only focused on "cleaning up the relationship" through developing cooperation mechanisms to help strengthen specific markets? This last section discusses the twofold energy relationship, concluding that there are different types, intensities, and rhythms of the bilateral agenda.

Different Types of Energy Relationships

Bilateral energy relationships can be divided into two types. The fossil component is consolidated through the TBA of 2012 and aided by the F-MER. Without a doubt, fossil-fuel exploration and exploitation will attract U.S. investment. In the other energy relationship, clean energy has not proven to be successful for bilateral integration goals due the different approaches in the type of resources to be included in the energy mixes, the diversity and unlinked mechanisms (if market led or state driven), and the different levels of cooperation (state, cross-border, or federal). The Mexican Energy Reform offers a complicated context, as well. As the Mexican Center for Environmental Law mentions, the MER opens the door to "less dirty" energies, such as nonconventional fuels (Centro Mexicano de Derecho Ambiental, 2014). For example, combined-cycle gas turbines, nuclear, shale gas, and clean coal are considered by Mexican Secretary of Environment (SEMARNAT, in Spanish) to be sources that would not have serious impacts on the environment; in other words, they are considered "semi-friendly" with the environment. This seems contradictory when trying to fulfill two different goals with the same energy sources: (1) to increase oil and gas production to meet local and trading demands and (2) to reach the environmental goals by including clean energy in the mix.

The discussion about fuel production-consumption versus environmental protection has been solved in the bilateral relationship (and in the Mexican Energy Reform) by supporting policies, agreements, and reforms under an "efficiency" approach, sometimes forgetting about sustainability (which encourages the rational consumption of resources with the capacity to replenish them just as it were before our use). Of course, this concept calls for decreasing consumption in the long run. Efficiency is not an ambitious concept. Its only appeal is that it saves resources in the short run based on costs and productivity, in other words to encourage "green growth," where economic growth is fundamental, but with less environmental damage because of efficiency, cleaner energy sources, and management of disasters (Jacobs, 2013; Wood, 2013). Ideally, these efficiency elements accumulate over time.

Different types of energy relationships are also evidenced when acknowledging that the Energy Reform opened the door to "green washing," in which Mexico imports gas to generate electricity for domestic consumption and exports a certain amount of electricity from clean sources to the United States. In this sense, the neighboring U.S. states transfer environmental externalities across the border. This "clean maquiladora" effect may prevent Mexico from meeting its renewable portfolio and climate change goals, and it may avoid clean-energy integration as well.

Different Rhythms of Energy Relations

The bilateral clean-energy instruments have had ups and downs. When the CEBA was enacted, inertia allowed time for institutions to cooperate and create programs for funding. However, when the implementation phase arrived, nothing seemed to work, which caused projects to stagnate. Curiously enough, the Mexican Energy Reform recovered the trust of both bilateral parties and boosted clean-energy cooperation through the ETL. However, the environmental gaps and challenges of this reform will make it difficult to operate as a basis for bilateral integration, especially when policy overlap is present. In contrast, the fossil-fuel sector is moving forward very quickly. The original calendar proposed for the different rounds to offer energy fossil-fuel projects in auctions was planned to start in September 2014 and go on until the end on 2016. However, the Mexican Congress decided to accelerate the process and started as soon as the operative rulings were enacted in the first week of August 2014, presenting a very tight new calendar. Mexican authorities wanted to attract investment as soon as possible and take advantage of the TBA in the Gulf of Mexico. Some U.S. companies participated in the different phases of Round 1 winning contracts, especially for phase 1.4 for deep-water projects.

A last element to evidence the twofold rhythm of the energy bilateral relationship is the different stage in which both sectors perform. The clean-energy relationship is based on few and specific cooperation mechanisms that face several problems. The best working initiatives have performed at local levels, where neighboring cities or states agree upon clean-energy trading schemes. In contrast, fossil-fuel relations (oil and gas) have been referred to as the essence of the energy integration, with no real need to account with additional bilateral mechanisms. Yet the TBA offered the confirmation of the solidity of this integration. These two approaches (cooperation and integration) seem to show the current stages of the energy relationship for both types of sources.

Different Intensities of Energy Relations

The size of the fossil-fuel bilateral market is huge as compared to clean energy. Energy carriers, converters, and services have been working to facilitate trade. The only challenge to this trade relationship is to adjust quickly to new and more abundant resources at low and uncertain prices (e.g., shale gas). In contrast, clean energy, either its direct consumption or for electricity production, requires infrastructure that is not working properly and is not available in Mexico. For example, clean energy needs special carriers (e.g., energy storage by batteries, flywheels, compressed air and pumping technologies), converters (e.g., catalyst converters or smart grids), and services (e.g., incentives to investment, transfer of technology, diversification of suppliers or price schemes) to operate. It would be useless to commercialize an electric vehicle if power comes from fossils or there are no stations to connect and recharge batteries on streets and highways.

Despite these obstacles, some clean-energy sources have developed unexpectedly well due to their rapid fall in cost. A Bloomberg New Energy Finance report suggests that investment in clean technologies reached US$1.3 billion in the first half of 2014, compared to US$1.6 billion in 2013. The report indicates that global investment worldwide in these sources grew in 2015 to nearly six times as compared to 2004, establishing a new record of one-third of one trillion dollars, despite cheap oil and an increase in solar technologies. For Mexico, investments in 2015 reached US$4.2 billion, up by 114%, and the United States invested $56 billion, up by 8% as compared to 2015. This represents the highest investment since 2011 stimulus policies for the sector (Bloomberg New Energy Finance, 2016).

In this context, the fossil-fuel relationship between the United States and Mexico is intensifying and the clean-energy sector has been developed individually by each country, leaving integration aside. A series of factors explain this. For Mexico, fossil fuels historically have supported the country's public spending. In addition, there is very low institutional capacity to manage the clean-energy sector; this has been an obstacle to integrating local communities into renewable projects.[7] Another reason is that the lack of technical capacity has not allowed the sector to grow (e.g., there is a lack of transmission capacity) (Huacuz, 2013).[8] And the leak of electricity in the distribution network represents losses of more than 18%, which is two times the OECD average (PricewaterhouseCoopers, 2014). These technical limitations create uncertainty, inhibiting the development of an integrated clean-energy market for electricity generation. In addition, there is a failure to effectively link business and research centers, as well as very low public budgets. This result is that technology for big projects is generally imported from other countries, such as the United States, or borrowed through international organizations such as the World Bank or the United Nations (Huacuz, 2013).

To sum up, the different types, intensities, and rhythms of the bilateral energy relationship seem to speak of an important fossil-fuel integration (aided by the Mexican reform) while leaving behind clean-energy integration. Consolidation of fossil-fuel markets and relations is expected to increase and strengthen. However, to meet environmental targets governments are including clean energy in their energy portfolios and are trying to create new cross-border clean-energy markets. The establishment of a clear agenda for talks on bilateral cooperation has started, yet no plans for integration are in sight.

NOTES

1. This TBA was negotiated to give continuity to a series of agreements created since the 1970s, especially the 2000 Treaty on the Continental Shelf. With the enactment of the Bipartisan Budget Act of 2013 (P.L. 113-67), signed by President Obama on December 26, 2013, the U.S. Congress approved the agreement and prepared for its implementation. For a detailed discussion about the road to its approval in the U.S. Congress, see Hagerty (2014).
2. Combined Heat and Power processes can be applied to both renewable and fossil fuels. The specific technologies employed and the efficiencies they achieve will vary, but in every situation this technology offers the capability to make more efficient and effective use of valuable primary energy resources. For further information see Combined Heat & Power Association (2014).
3. Although once working, nuclear plants emit no CO_2 emissions, its residues are toxic and any spill would cause irreparable environmental impacts. See both National Energy Strategies drafted by the Mexican Secretariat of Energy under the Calderón and Peña administrations.
4. Some experts mention that reforms since Vicente Fox have "disguised" the new hiring models under the name of "multiple service contracts," to let foreign companies explore and exploit Mexican reserves in concession schemes. For a deeper discussion and a critical approach, see Manzo (2009).
5. However, geothermal exploitation has its environmental perils. As a report by Greenpeace mentions, the danger of induced seismicity, land collapse and land pollution, the big amounts of water use, the lack of waste-water management, or the constant fluxes of sulfuric gas to the atmosphere can reduce the promised sustainability. See Greenpeace México (2014).
6. This information was obtained by a request to the business sector of Baja California and the Universidad Autónoma del Estado de Baja California Federal Institute of Access to Information (IFAI, in Spanish).
7. This was the case of the wind park built in La Ventosa, Oaxaca, where the communities fought against the project when it started some years ago.

8. For example, although the publication of the National Inventory of Renewable Energy Sources (INER) is an important advance, there are some technical limitations regarding inconsistent methodologies. This also happens with the National Atlas of geographical feasibility for renewable energy sources to develop. See Secretaría de Energía (2015a, 2015b).

REFERENCES

Aguilera, Roberto F., & Radetzki, M. (2015). *The price of oil*. Cambridge, UK: Cambridge University Press.

Alarcón, J. (2014). ¿Para qué sirven los Certificados de Energía Limpia que propone la reforma energética? Mexico City, DF: Elephant Publishing. Retrieved from http://www.animalpolitico.com/blogueros-neoliberal-nel-liberal/2014/05/21/para-que-sirven-los-certificados-de-energia-limpia-que-propone-la-reforma-energetica/

Arellano, V. C., Bazán, G., & Ortiz, G. (2011, March–April). México cuenta con recursos geotérmicos abundantes y ampliamente distribuidos en el territorio. *Energía a Debate*. Retrieved from http://energiaadebate.com/las-bondades-de-la-geotermia/

Aristegui Noticias. (2014). La energética, una reforma muy radical: La CFE va a morir [Interview with Miriam Grunstein]. Retrieved from http://aristeguinoticias.com/0705/mexico/la-energetica-una-reforma-muy-radical-la-cfe-va-a-morir-especialista-en-cnn/

Baker Institute for Public Policy. (2013). Mexico's energy reform—Powering the future. Houston, TX: Baker Institute for Public Policy. Retrieved from http://bakerinstitute.org/media/files/Research/ff4bf622/MC-Pub-MexicoReforms2-112613.pdf

Balderas, A. (2014). El carbon tax y el mercado de carbono en México. Milenio.com. Retrieved from http://www.milenio.com/firmas/arturo_balderas_torres/carbon-tax-mercado-carbono-Mexico_18_231756900.html

Bloomberg New Energy Finance. (2016). Clean energy defies fossil fuel price crash to attract record $329BN global investment in 2015. Bloomberg New Energy Finance. Retrieved from: http://about.bnef.com/press-releases/clean-energy-defies-fossil-fuel-price-crash-to-attract-record-329bn-global-investment-in-2015/

Brown, M. A., & Sovacool, B. K. (2011). *Climate change and global energy security: Technology and policy options*. Cambridge, MA: MIT Press.

Canales, G. (2014). El sueño dorado de la energía solar.*¿Cómo Ves? Revista de Divulgación Científica de la UNAM*, *17*(193), 16–18.

Centro de Investigación y Desarrollo, A. C. (2013). Renovando el futuro energético de México: Diagnóstico y propuestas para impulsar el desarrollo de las energías renovables del país. Mexico City: Author. Retrieved from http://cidac.org/esp/uploads/1/Renovando_el_futuro_energe__tico-100913.pdf

Centro Mexicano de Derecho Ambiental. (2014). Postura ante la Reforma Energética. Mexico City, DF: Author. Retrieved from http://www.cemda.org.mx/postura-ante-la-reforma-energetica/

Centro Nacional de Control de Energía. (2016). Concluyó la evaluación de las ofertas económicas de la Primera Subasta Eléctrica de Largo Plazo. Mexico City, CDMX: Author. Retrieved from http://www.cenace.gob.mx/Docs/MercadoOperacion/Subastas/31%20Comunicado%20Subasta%20v2016%2003%2030.pdf

Combined Heat & Power Association. (2014). What is CHP? London, UK: Author. Retrieved from http://www.chpa.co.uk/what-is-chp_15.html

Comisión Reguladora de Energía. (2011). Resolución Núm. RES/003/2011 por la que la Comisión Reguladora de Energía expide la metodología para el cálculo de la eficiencia de los sistemas de cogeneración de energía eléctrica y los criterios para determinar la cogeneración eficiente. Mexico City, DF: Author. Retrieved from http://www.cre.gob.mx/documento/3382.pdf

Comisión Reguladora de Energía. (2012). Resolución Núm. RES/291/2012 por la que la Comisión Reguladora de Energía expide las disposiciones generales para creditar sistemas de cogeneración como cogeneración eficiente. Mexico City, DF: Author. Retrieved from http://www.cre.gob.mx/documento/3383.pdf

De Régules, C. (2015). Entrevista: Ser garante de la seguridad de las personas y del ambiente, nuestra misión. *Energía a Debate*, *11*(67), 29–36.

Diario Oficial de la Federación. (2008). *Ley para el aprovechamiento de energías renovables y el financiamiento de la transición energética*. Mexico City, DF: Author. Retrieved from http://www.diputados.gob.mx/LeyesBiblio/ref/laerfte/LAERFTE_orig_28nov08.pdf

Diario Oficial de la Federación. (2012). *Ley General de Cambio Climático*. Mexico City, DF: Author. Retrieved from http://www.dof.gob.mx/nota_detalle_popup.php?codigo=5301093

Diario Oficial de la Federación. (2013a). *Decreto por el que se reforma y adicionan diversas disposiciones de la Constitución Política de los Estados Unidos Mexicanos, en Materia de Energía*. Mexico City,

DF: Author. Retrieved from http://www.dof.gob.mx/nota_detalle.php?codigo=5327463&fecha=20/12/2013

Diario Oficial de la Federación. (2013b). *Ley del Servicio Público de Energía Eléctrica*. Mexico City, DF: Author. Retrieved from http://dof.gob.mx/nota_detalle.php?codigo=5265363&fecha=24/08/2012

Diario Oficial de la Federación. (2014a). *Ley de la Industria Eléctrica*. Mexico City, DF: Author. Retrieved from http://dof.gob.mx/nota_detalle.php?codigo=5355986&fecha=11/08/2014

Diario Oficial de la Federación. (2014b). *Lineamientos que establecen los criterios para el otorgamiento de Certificados de Energías Limpias y los requisitos para su adquisición*. Mexico City, DF: Author. Retrieved from http://www.dof.gob.mx/nota_detalle.php?codigo=5366674&fecha=31/10/2014&print=true

Diario Oficial de la Federación. (2015). *Ley de Transición Energética*. Mexico City, DF: Author. Retrieved from http://dof.gob.mx/nota_detalle.php?codigo=5421295&fecha=24/12/2015

Embassy of the United States in Mexico. (2011). US-Mexico bilateral framework on clean energy and climate change. Mexico City, DF: Author. Retrieved from http://mexico.usembassy.gov/press-releases/ep110523-climate.html

Enciso, A. (2014). Las ventajas del gas natural rebasa los daños que causaría el fracking: SEMARNAT. Mexico City, DF: La Jornada. Retrieved from http://www.jornada.unam.mx/2014/08/20/politica/007n1pol

Esquivel, E. (2014). La Ley de Energía Geotérmica: negocio para grandes corporativos. Mexico City, DF: SDPnoticias. Retrieved from http://www.sdpnoticias.com/columnas/2014/07/23/la-ley-de-energia-geotermica-negocio-para-grandes-corporativos

Florida Renewable Energy Association. (2014). *Clean energy defined*. Miami, FL: Florida Renewable Energy Association. Retrieved from http://www.cleanenergyflorida.org/clean-energy-defined/

Fox, E. (2013). 60-second interview at the Mexican International Renewable Energy Congress 2013. London, UK: Green Power Conferences. Retrieved from http://www.greenpowerconferences.com/EF/?sSubSystem=Prospectus&sEventCode=MIREC2013&sSessionID=44072929246e44852ff0e95391d3a22f-15309314&sDocument=fox

Garrison, J. L. (2010). Clean energy & climate change opportunities assessment for USAID/Mexico. Rockville, MD: John L. Garrison Environment and Climate Change Consultant. Retrieved from https://www.climate-eval.org/sites/default/files/evaluations/300%20Clean%20Energy% 20%26%20Climate%20Change%20Opportunities%20Assessment%20for%20USAIDMexico.pdf

Gobierno de la República. (2013). *Reforma energética*. Mexico City, DF: Author. Retrieved from http://cdn.reformaenergetica.gob.mx/explicacion.pdf

Greenpeace México. (2014). Análisis del Contenido de las iniciativas presentadas por el Ejecutivo Federal en materia energética. Ley de Energía Geotérmica. Mexico City, DF: Author. Retrieved from http://m.greenpeace.org/mexico/Global/mexico/Docs/2014/renovables/Ana%CC%81lisis%20Ley%20de%20Energi%CC%81a%20Geote%CC%81rmica%20GPMx.pdf

Hagerty, C. L. (2014). Legislation to approve the U.S.-Mexico transboundary hydrocarbons agreement. Washington, DC: Congressional Research Service. Retrieved from http://fas.org/sgp/crs/row/R43610.pdf

Healy, R., vanNijnatten, D., & López-Vallejo, M. (2014). *Environmental policy in North America: Capacities, approaches and transboundary issue management in Canada, the United States and Mexico*. Toronto, ON: University of Toronto Press.

Huacuz, J. M. (2013, July–September). El inventario de las energías renovables en el marco de la transición energética en México. *Boletín IIE*. Mexico City, DF: Instituto de Investigaciones Eléctricas. Retrieved from http://www.iie.org.mx/boletin032013/divulga.pdf

IEnova. (2014). Energía Sierra Juárez. Baja California, MX: Author. Retrieved from http://ienova.com.mx/english/services-esj.html

International Energy Agency. (2015). Clean Energy Ministerial 6 (CEM6). Merida, YUC: Author. Retrieved from http://www.cleanenergyministerial.org/Events/CEM6

International Energy Agency. (2016). Clean Energy Ministerial 7 (CEM7). San Francisco, CA: Author. Retrieved from http://www.cleanenergyministerial.org/Events/CEM7

Jacobs, M. (2013). Green growth. In R. Falkner (Ed.), *The handbook of global climate and environment policy*. West Sussex, UK: Wiley-Blackwell.

López-Vallejo, M. (2014). *Reconfiguring global climate governance in North America: A transregional approach*. Surrey, UK: Ashgate.

Manzo, J. L. (2009). La privatización reciente de los hidrocarburos en México. In John Saxe Fernández (Ed.), *La Energía en México: Situación y alternativas*. Mexico City, CDMX: Universidad Nacional Autónoma de México.

McMahon, J. (2016, May 8). Steven Chu: Mexico's energy auction reveals true price of U.S. renewables. *Forbes*. Retrieved from http://www.forbes.com/sites/jeffmcmahon/2016/05/08/steven-chu-mexicos-energy-auction-reveals-true-price-of-u-s-renewables/#55aae12575d2

MexiCO2. (2014). Mercado de Carbono. Mexico City, DF: MexiCO2 Plataforma Mexicana de Carbono. Retrieved from http://www.mexico2.com.mx/medio-ambiente.php?id=9

Petraeus, D., Zoellick, R. B., & O'Neil, S. K. (2014). *Independent task force report no. 71: North American, time for a new focus.* Washington, DC: Council of Foreign Policy.

Petróleos Mexicanos. (2013). Anuario Estadístico 2013. Mexico City, DF: Author. Retrieved from http://www.pemex.com/acerca/informes_publicaciones/Documents/anuario_estadistico_2013/anuario-estadistico-2013_131014.pdf

PricewaterhouseCoopers. (2014). Reforma energética de México Implicaciones y oportunidades en el sistema eléctrico nacional. Mexico City, DF: Author. Retrieved from http://www.pwc.com/es_MX/mx/industrias/archivo/2014-01-implicaciones-reforma-energetica.pdf

Prime Minister of Canada. (2016). Leaders' statement on a North American climate, clean energy, and environment partnership. Retrieved from http://pm.gc.ca/eng/news/2016/06/29/leaders-statement-north-american-climate-clean-energy-and-environment-partnership

Rabe, B. (2013). Building on sub-federal climate strategies: The challenges of regionalism. In N. Craik, I. Studer, & D. VanNijnatten (Eds.), *Climate change policy in North America: Designing integration in a regional system* (pp. 71–107). Toronto, ON: University of Toronto Press.

Ribando, C., Ratner, M., Villareal, A., & Hagerty, C. L. 2014. *Mexico's oil and gas sector: Background, reform efforts, and implications for the United States.* Washington, DC: Congressional Research Service. Retrieved from http://fas.org/sgp/crs/row/R43313.pdf

Rowlands, I. (2013). Deploying the smart grid across borders in North America. In N. Craik, I. Studer, & D. VanNijnatten (Eds.), *Climate change policy in North America: Designing integration in a regional system* (pp. 132–156). Toronto, ON: University of Toronto Press.

Secretaría de Economía. (2013). Energías Renovables. Mexico City, DF: Author. Retrieved from http://mim.promexico.gob.mx/work/sites/mim/resources/LocalContent/42/2/130726_DS_Energias_Renovables_ES.pdf

Secretaría de Energía. (2012a). Avanza la conformación de grupos de trabajo para promover el mercado regional de energía renovable entre México y Estados Unidos. Mexico City, DF: Author. Retrieved from http://www.sener.gob.mx/portal/Default.aspx?id=2224

Secretaría de Energía. (2012b). *Estrategia Nacional de Energía 2012–2026.* Mexico City, DF: Author. Retrieved from http://www.sener.gob.mx/res/PE_y_DT/pub/2012/ENE_2012_2026.pdf

Secretaría de Energía. (2012c). México y Estados Unidos renuevan su compromiso con la promoción de las energías limpias y el combate al cambio climático. Mexico City, DF: Author. Retrieved from http://www.sener.gob.mx/portal/Default.aspx?id=2232

Secretaría de Energía. (2013a). *Estrategia Nacional de Energía 2013–2027*. Mexico City, DF: Author. Retrieved from http://www.sener.gob.mx/res/PE_y_DT/pub/2013/ENE_2013-2027.pdf

Secretaría de Energía. (2013b). Key elements of the energy reform. Mexico City, DF: Author. Retrieved from http://sener.gob.mx/res/prensa/KEY%20ELEMENTS%20OF%20THE%20ENERGY%20REFORM.pdf

Secretaría de Energía. (2014a). Firman México y Estados Unidos Memoranda de Entendimiento para apoyar implementación de energías limpias. Mexico City, DF: Author. Retrieved from http://www.sener.gob.mx/portal/Default.aspx?id=2859

Secretaría de Energía. (2014b). *Programa Especial para el Aprovechamiento de Energías Renovables*. Mexico City, DF: Author. Retrieved from http://www.dof.gob.mx/nota_detalle.php?codigo=5342501&fecha=28/04/2014

Secretaría de Energía. (2014c). *Prospectiva del Sector Eléctrico 2013–2017*. Mexico City, DF: Author. Retrieved from http://sener.gob.mx/res/PE_y_DT/pub/2013/Prospectiva_del_Sector_Electrico_2013-2027.pdf

Secretaría de Energía. (2015a). Atlas Nacional de Zonas Factibles para el Desarrollo de Energías Renovables. Mexico City, DF: Author. Retrieved from http://www.energia.gob.mx/portal/Default.aspx?id=2924

Secretaría de Energía. (2015b). Inventario Nacional de Energía Renovable. Mexico City, DF: Author. Retrieved from http://inere.energia.gob.mx/publica/version3.1/

Secretaría de Medio Ambiente y Recursos Naturales. (2013). Cuarta reunión del Marco Bilateral México-Estados Unidos sobre Energía Limpia y Cambio Climático. Mexico City, DF: Author. Retrieved from http://saladeprensa.semarnat.gob.mx/index.php/noticias/1024-cuarta-reunion-del-marco-bilateral-mexico-estados-unidos-sobre-energia-limpia-y-cambio-climatico

Secretaría de Relaciones Exteriores. (2010a). Avanza la conformación de grupos de trabajo para promover el mercado regional de energía renovable entre México y Estados Unidos. Mexico City, DF: Author. Retrieved from http://www.sener.gob.mx/portal/Default.aspx?id=2224

Secretaría de Relaciones Exteriores. (2010b). Third Meeting of the Mexico-United States Bilateral Framework on Clean Energy and Climate Change. Mexico City, DF: Author. Retrieved from http://www.sre.gob

.mx/en/index.php?option=com_content&view=article&id=1554:third-meeting-of-the-mexico-united-states-bilateral-framework-on-clean-energy-and-climate-change&catid=27:archives&Itemid=322

Sovacool, B., & Ridortsov, R. (2013). Energy governance in the United States. In A. Golthau, *The handbook of global energy policy*. West Sussex, UK: John Wiley & Sons Ltd.

Triolo, R. (2015). Integración eléctrica en la región fronteriza: Beneficios y barreras. *Energía a Debate*, 66. Retrieved from http://energiaadebate.com/integracion-electrica-en-la-region-fronteriza-beneficios-y-barreras/

U.S. Agency for International Development. (2013). Audit of USAID/Mexico's global climate change program. San Salvador, El Salvador: Author. Retrieved from http://oig.usaid.gov/sites/default/files/audit-reports/1-523-13-006-p.pdf

U.S. Congress. (2012). Oil, Mexico, and the Transboundary Agreement. Washington, DC: Author. Retrieved from http://www.foreign.senate.gov/imo/media/doc/77567.pdf

U.S. Department of Commerce. (2014). Renewable energy top markets for U.S. exports 2014–2015. Washington DC: Author. Retrieved from http://export.gov/build/groups/public/@eg_main/@reee/documents/webcontent/eg_main_070688.pdf

U.S. Department of Energy. (2014). Clean coal power initiative. Washington, DC: Department of Energy. Retrieved from http://energy.gov/fe/science-innovation/clean-coal-research/major-demonstrations/clean-coal-power-initiative

U.S. Energy Information Administration. (2014). Countries—Overview. Washington, DC: Author. Retrieved from http://www.eia.gov/countries/index.cfm?view=reserves

U.S. Energy Information Administration. (2016). Petroleum & other liquids. Washington, DC: Author. Retrieved from https://www.eia.gov/dnav/pet/pet_move_exp_dc_NUS-Z00_mbbl_m.htm

U.S. Environmental Protection Agency. (2015). Fact sheet: Clean power plan key changes and improvements. Washington, DC: Author. Retrieved from https://www.epa.gov/cleanpowerplan/fact-sheet-clean-power-plan-key-changes-and-improvements

U.S. Environmental Protection Agency. (2014a). Clean energy. Washington, DC: Author. Retrieved from http://www.epa.gov/cleanenergy/

U.S. Environmental Protection Agency. (2014b). How does electricity affect the environment? Washington, DC: Author. Retrieved from http://www.epa.gov/cleanenergy/energy-and-you/affect/

U.S. Senate. (2012). Bill END12149—The Clean Energy Standard Act of 2012. Washington DC: US Senate. 112th Congress. Retrieved from http://www.energy.senate.gov/public/index.cfm/files/serve?File_id=b3580f37-ec8c-4698-a635-3e19f9815b9a

White House. (2009). US-Mexico announce bilateral framework on clean energy and climate change. Washington, DC: Author. Retrieved from http://www.whitehouse.gov/the_press_office/US-Mexico-Announce-Bilateral-Framework-on-Clean-Energy-and-Climate-Change

White House. (2015). Joint statement on U.S.-Mexico climate policy cooperation. Washington, DC: Author. Retrieved from https://www.whitehouse.gov/the-press-office/2015/03/27/joint-statement-us-mexico-climate-policy-cooperation

Wood, D. (2010). *Environment, development and growth: U.S.-Mexico cooperation in renewable energies*. Washington, DC: Woodrow Wilson International Center for Scholars. Retrieved from http://www.wilsoncenter.org/sites/default/files/Renewable%20Energy%20report.pdf

Wood, D. (2012). *Re-energizing the border: Renewable energy, green jobs and border infrastructure*. Washington, DC: Woodrow Wilson International Center for Scholars. Retrieved from http://www.wilsoncenter.org/sites/default/files/RE_Energizing_Border_Wood.pdf

Wood, D. (2013). Growing potential for US-Mexico energy cooperation. Washington, DC: Woodrow Wilson International Center for Scholars. Retrieved from http://wilsoncenter.org/sites/default/files/wood_energy.pdf

APPENDIX

Table 12.2
Main Elements of the Mexican Energy Reform (2013–2014)

Criteria	With the Reform
Ownership of resources	100% Mexican, but payment to companies with production in some cases
Ownership of national companies	PEMEX and CFE 100% Mexican and public
Constitutional changes	Article 25: change form "State companies" to "State productive enterprises" Articles 27 and 28: Reform towards productive companies aided by private participation and banning of monopolies.

(*continued*)

Table 12.2 (*continued*)

Criteria	**With the Reform**
Contract models	Contracting models: • Multiple service • Shared profit • Shared production • Licenses • A combination of the four *Note:* Private persons are permitted to participate in power generation, marketing, transmission, and distribution under CFE and state regulation.
Institutions	National Center for Natural Gas Control (CENEGAS): gas Mexican Fund of Petroleum for Stabilization and Development National Center of Energy Control (CENACE): electricity National Agency for Industrial Safety and Environmental Protection for the Hydrocarbon Sector National Hydrocarbons Commission and Regulatory Energy Commission are strengthened by granting them legal personality, technical-management autonomy, and budgetary self-sufficiency.
Transparency mechanisms	All contracts with transparency clause Citizens can verify contracts and payments to companies External audits Union out of the board of directors, but with collective rights
Fiscal regime	Budgetary autonomy. PEMEX will only transfer as much as a 4.7% of its profits to the national budget.*

Source: Author's elaboration on information from Diario Oficial de la Federación (2013b); Gobierno de la República (2013); Secretaría de Energía (2013b).

* The Mexican Energy Reform was linked to the fiscal reform approved at the end of 2013. In order to transform PEMEX and CFE into "state productive enterprises," some fiscal arrangements had to be made. The fiscal law states that it will decrease the fiscal burden of PEMEX gradually and applicable to all new developments (and in some cases for old ones).

THIRTEEN

Fluid Relations

Hydro Developments, the International Joint Commission, and U.S.-Canadian Border Waters

DANIEL MACFARLANE

INTRODUCTION

Beginning in the late 19th century, a proliferation of hydrogenerating stations developed on both sides of the U.S.-Canadian border. These were among the earliest on the globe; there is debate about which example of North American hydro generation should be considered the first, as some measure by the first working generator and others by the first hydro plant or the first commercial generation. Electricity was being generated from water by the early 1880s in Canada—Chaudière Falls in Ottawa and Montmorency Falls outside Quebec City—and in the United States—Appleton, Wisconsin, and Grand Rapids, Michigan. By 1886 there were 45 water-powered electric plants in the United States and Canada combined.

By 1920, hydro represented 97% of the electricity produced in Canada and 20% in the United States. By the 1940s, it was still responsible for about 90% of the electricity generated in Canada and 40% in the United States. (Canadian Hydropower Association, 2008; Office of Energy Efficiency and Renewable Energy, n.d.). Though the ratio of hydro production to total electricity generation in the United States would decline over the course of the 20th century, the United States would remain one of the biggest hydro producers in the world. Contingent on which measurement one uses, in the 21st century Canada is behind only China in global hydro production, with the United States also in the top five.

Although the largest generating stations in Canada are now in northeastern Canada (i.e., Quebec, Newfoundland, and Labrador), for the first two-thirds of the 20th century most of Canada's largest hydroelectric generating stations were along the international border on the Columbia, St. Lawrence, and Niagara Rivers. Sites such as Niagara Falls attracted hydro development for obvious reasons, but technological restrictions (e.g., electric transmission technology) and population distribution were also prime considerations. Niagara Falls was the proving ground for the first successful long distance transmission on the continent, and then a leader in cross-border transmission lines (see Rowlands, Chapter 14).

The development of various hydrostations and water control schemes on border waters helped bring about the creation of the Boundary Waters Treaty in 1909. This joint U.S.-Canadian treaty (with the British technically handling the Canadian side) created the International Joint Commission (IJC), which first met in 1912. For a hydroelectric development to fall under the purview of the IJC, it must materially affect the levels or flows of a border water, for example, a river or lake that crosses or forms the border. This includes not only hydrostations themselves, but other engineering remedial works—e.g., dams, weirs, conduits, etc.—that impact water levels or regulate flows, such as from Lake Superior into the St. Mary's River, from Lake Erie into Lake Ontario via the Niagara River, and from Lake Ontario into the St. Lawrence River. Such developments require transnational approval via the IJC unless a separate U.S.-Canadian special agreement is put in place.

This chapter focuses on the construction of border hydroelectric developments since the formation of the IJC. Four different regional groupings of border hydrostations can be identified: (1) Great Lakes-St. Lawrence; (2) Pacific Northwest; (3) Maine-New Brunswick border; (4) Rainy River/Lake of the Woods (Figure 13.1). The largest stations, as well as those of medium size, are within the Great Lakes-St. Lawrence and Pacific Northwest systems, while the other two groupings are made up of relatively smaller stations.

These border hydrostations are of interest not only because they collectively reveal the historical roots and evolution of past policies, but also because they have direct relevance for understanding and conceptualizing contemporary Canadian federalism and U.S.-Canadian relations, particularly in the realms of energy policy, environmental governance, and the role of subnational governments. The processes that led to the construction of the border hydrostations entrenched provincial water rights, increased the role and importance of substate actors in bilateral relations, and expanded North American intergovernmentalism. The development of shared waters helped establish patterns that continue to frame Cana-

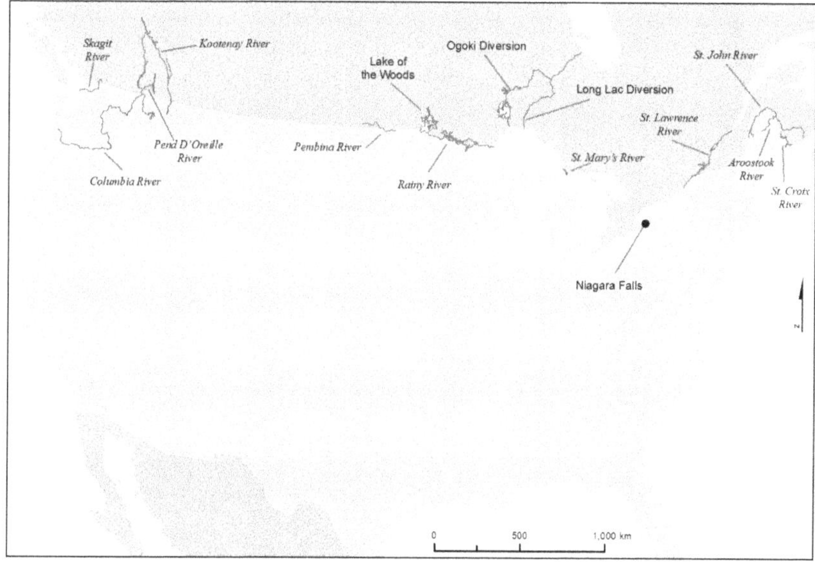

FIGURE 13.1 Border Waters Covered in This Chapter

dian environmental and energy domestic policies and relations with the United States on issues such as oil and gas, acid rain, water quality, and binational toxins.

Boundary stations played a key role in the evolution of the IJC, which remains the most important institutional manifestation of the various contemporary U.S.-Canadian transborder environmental governance regimes. The commission was integral to the creation of the hydro developments covered in this chapter; in turn, these hydrostations shaped the approach and character of the IJC. The development of border waters reveals, on the one hand, some of the IJC's historical limitations and flaws, serving as a cautionary tale about what policy makers can realistically expect out of the commission in the 21st century. On the other hand, this same history reveals the adaptability and anticipatory potential of the IJC, indicating it can have a constructive role to play in 21st-century environmental governance, particularly within the contextual uncertainty of climate change.

The history of border developments runs the gamut in terms of representing conflict and cooperation between Canada and the United States. The many small day-to-day transnational interactions, such as those predicated on shared waters, act as shock absorbers for the punctuated conflicts that periodically arise in U.S.-Canadian relations. At the same time, several of the large hydro developments were themselves punctuated conflicts that threatened the amicability of U.S.-Canadian relations. These conflicts also reveal that Canada's periodically confrontational approach to border hydroelectric developments was driven in part by cultural and ideational factors, represented by a unique form of Canadian "hydraulic nationalism." This study shows that these factors and nationalisms should be taken into account as conceptual tools for understanding Canada's contemporary approach to transborder environmental issues.

THE BOUNDARY WATERS TREATY AND THE INTERNATIONAL JOINT COMMISSION

Border boundary water issues such as the Chicago diversion (which takes water from Lake Michigan and sends it to the Mississippi River watershed), sharing the waters of the St. Mary and Milk Rivers in the western prairies, and dividing the hydroelectric generating capacity of Niagara Falls and the St. Lawrence River led to the creation of the International Waterways Commission (IWC) in 1903. In 1906 and 1907 the IWC made a series of recommendations that called on Canada and the United States to adopt principles of law governing uses of international waters along the boundary between, and to create an international body with authority to study and regulate the use of these waters. In the ensuing negotiations, Canadian negotiators wanted a powerful body, while American officials sought a weaker one; the eventual result was a compromise. The Boundary Waters Treaty was signed on January 11, 1909, by James Bryce, the British Ambassador to the United States, and by Elihu Root, the U.S. Secretary of State. Securing the agreement was a significant coup for Canada, since the much more powerful United States was agreeing to a commission within which the two countries were equal. Great Britain technically signed the treaty for Canada, though the Canadian government did much of the negotiating, and it was therefore an important nation-building step for Canada.

The Boundary Waters Treaty notably granted equal navigation access to the waters covered by the treaty, and regulations were adopted concerning water diversions and changes to water levels; essentially, any changes in the level of a border water required agreement through the IJC, a body created by the treaty (or a special agreement between the federal governments outside of the IJC). The treaty outlined an order of precedence for how border waters could be used:

1. Uses for domestic and sanitary purposes
2. Uses for navigation
3. Uses for power

However, no reference was made to industrial, recreational, or environmental uses, though these were incorporated over time. The treaty assigned the IJC four categories of function that the new body was expected to discharge, which are summarized in Table 13.1.

The treaty settled some specific border water disputes and created the IJC, which held its first meeting in Washington, DC, on January 10, 1912 (Boundary Waters Treaty, 1909). The treaty established the commission as a six-member body in which there is parity between Canada and the United States. Three commissioners are appointed by Order-in-Council (in fact by the Prime Minister of Canada) to the Canadian section, and three by the President of the United States with confirmation required by

Table 13.1
Expected Functions of the International Joint Commission

Type	**Articles of BWT**	**Function**
Administrative	Article V, VI	Directing the measurement and division of the waters of Niagara River and the St. Mary and Milk Rivers
Quasi-judicial	Articles III, IV, VIII	Passing upon applications for permission to use, divert, or obstruct treaty waters (commission approval with relevant conditions is typically given in an Order of Approval, which the Commission then monitors for compliance)
Investigative	Article IX	Examining and making recommendations on any differences arising along the common boundary (these investigations are called "references" and recommendations are nonbinding)
Arbitral	Article X	Making binding decisions with respect to any questions arising between the two countries; this function has never been used

Source: Adapted from Willoughby (1981).

Abbreviations: BWT, Boundary Waters Treaty.

the U.S. Senate. The IJC is not an arm of government and commissioners are technically independent from the government that appointed them. However, the IJC has historically been somewhat limited in its ability to go beyond the wishes of the two federal governments. The commission's reports are advisory, not binding, and it is difficult for the IJC to initiate investigation or consideration of environmental issues not referred to it. For various reasons, the Harmon Doctrine was included in the treaty, though it has been widely rejected. The doctrine essentially allows the upriver country to do what it wants with waters that cross the border (McCaffrey, 1996), which meant that the treaty effectively only applied to waters that formed the border, with the Great Lakes and St. Lawrence being the most prominent. To be fair, it is likely that the treaty and the IJC would never have been achieved if the treaty drafters had been more ambitious and included stronger enforcement capabilities.

The Boundary Waters Treaty has often been characterized as a pioneering piece of environmental management legislation. The treaty was also an initial step in the rapprochement that characterized Canadian-U.S. ecopolitics for most of the 20th century (Dorsey, 1998). The IJC is the key to the regime established by the 1909 treaty, and has often been portrayed as a model for bilateral cooperation. (For a sampling of the range of interpretations see the various contributions to Spencer, Kirton, & Nossal, 1981.) The IJC is a unique kind of international institution that combines interstate and supranational functions. As an adaptable governance form, it has evolved over time (as an organization and the way it has been used and approached) and increasingly has incorporated transnational policy networks, public feedback, and scientific/engineering expertise. It has succeeded in providing a framework and ground rules that have, for the most part, prevented or resolved bilateral disputes over boundary and transboundary waters for more than a century. It has been said that the philosophy of dispute-settlement and conflict-avoidance in the Boundary Waters Treaty was far more sophisticated than perhaps any comparable piece of bilateral machinery then existing in Western society. Even the use of the word "pollution" was novel at the time (Cohen, 1981, p. 108).

Nonetheless, an extended analysis of the IJC's first century of operation shows that its behavior, role, and function changed significantly over time. For its initial decades it was an elite form of water apportionment that favored industrial and government interests at the expense of environmental, recreation, and local interests. The IJC, rather than dissuading hydraulic engineering megaprojects, was in fact a chief proponent of them. Moreover, these water quantity issues reveal that the argument that the commission has always been a global model for transborder environmental governance is based on a partial myth; the history of the IJC is characterized by an initial half century of mixed results, followed by a period from the 1940s to the 1960s of partisan politics resulting in large-scale endeavors with dubious environmental impacts, followed by a period of more noticeable success up to about the 1990s (Clamen & Macfarlane, 2015). Indeed, water quantity references, often connected to hydroelectric developments, were the overarching concern of the commission for its first half century. Into the 1960s, the IJC was dominated by prevailing societal mind-sets about the need to engineer environmental resources for maximum production, Moreover, over its first half century of existence there were some cases in which the IJC did not operate efficiently, splitting along national lines and failing to make timely or effective recommendations. In the immediate post- World War II period, certain members of the IJC became increasingly partisan as the body pushed for water control mega-projects that entrenched unnatural water stage levels that have been ecologically detrimental.

Thus, the successes of the IJC and the concomitant high regard for it as an organization are more of a post-1950s development. For the first half of its existence the IJC was generally much more concerned with apportioning water resources and quantities. During the 1960s the commission became a leader in addressing Great Lakes water quality and pollution issues, building consensus, legitimacy, and governmental will by incorporating scientific and public opinion. In the process, IJC engineers were at the forefront of the growing realization that cyclical natural causes, rather than anthropogenic modifications, have been more responsible for fluctuating Great Lakes water levels. Furthermore, the IJC began recommending against further large-scale engineering solutions.

Both the originators and the first members of the IJC assumed that its quasi-judicial role would be much more important than its investigative role, and for three decades this assumption seemed correct (Willoughby, 1981). The IJC was initially reluctant to settle legal issues and establish precedents, but generally adopted pragmatic solutions. Of the 50 cases handled by the commission prior to 1944, 39 were applications for approval of specific works under the quasi-judicial power of article VIII and only 11 were references under article IX, the investigative function.

During the second half of the 20th century, the story was reversed—between 1944 and 1979, for example, there were 35 references and 20 applications (Willoughby, 1981). Between 1979 and 2012 there were 12 references and 3 applications although the IJC was very busy between 2000 and 2012 reviewing their Orders of Approval for Lake Superior and Lake Ontario. Immediately following World War II, the IJC approved major border hydroelectric developments, namely the megaprojects on the St. Lawrence, Niagara, and Columbia Rivers.

HUDSON'S BAY WATERSHED

The first few dockets that the IJC handled involved water bodies to the west of Lake Superior that, though they form the U.S.-Canadian border, ultimately flow to Hudson's Bay. The first two applications concerned Rainy River and Lake, and the third was a reference about Lake of the Woods regulation (IJC Dockets 1, 2, 3). The Canadian community of Fort Frances is located on the Rainy River—which separates Ontario from Minnesota—at its outlet from Rainy Lake, with the U.S. community of International Falls on the south side of the river (Figure 13.2). The Fort Frances generating station had been built on the Rainy River in 1909. This hydroelectric station shares a dam across the river with the U.S.-owned International Falls generating station. As a result of these hydrostations, the IJC was invoked to deal with the regulation of water levels. These Rainy Lake levels and outflows remained an ongoing concern for the IJC over its first half century, as there were a number of subsequent references, applications, and orders, including a 1938 convention (IJC Docket

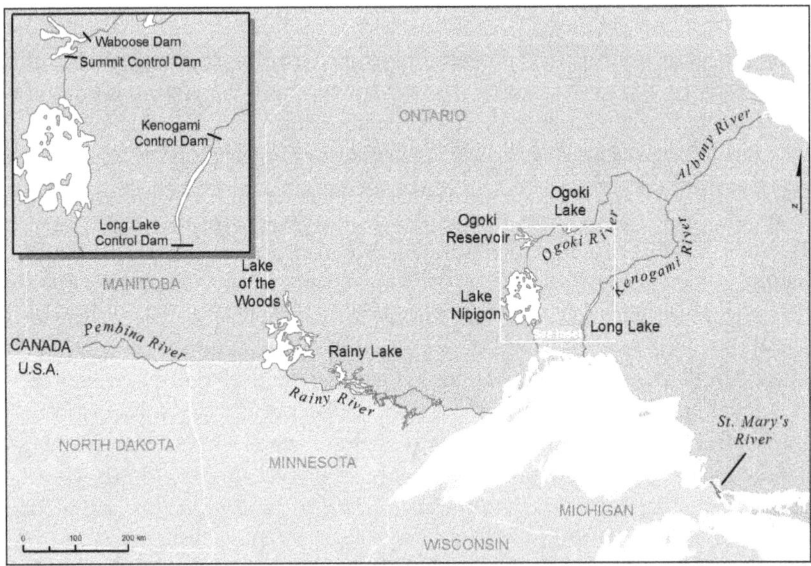

FIGURE 13.2 Hudson's Bay Watershed and Lake Superior Watershed Developments

50). The Fort Frances generating station was completely rebuilt in 1954 and produces 10 megawatts (MW) annually.

The Rainy River flows from Rainy Lake into Lake of the Woods, which is drained by the Winnipeg River. The Norman Dam was completed in the late 1890s, replacing an earlier dam on the Winnipeg River at the town of Kenora, Ontario, though it did not have the capacity to generate electricity until 1926. This dam is well north of the border, but it influences the outflow of the transborder Lake of the Woods. In the first instance of a "reference," the Canadian and U.S. governments referred levels of Lake of the Woods (which is divided between Minnesota, Ontario, and Manitoba) to the IJC in 1912. Negotiations between the Canadian federal government and the two provinces actually proved to be more protracted and fractious than did Canadian relations with the United States. Eventually a 1925 treaty (and a subsequent protocol) authorized the construction of regulating works and the creation of the International Lake of the Woods Board of Control to regulate outflows when lake levels failed to meet or exceed the prescribed lake levels (1056-1061.25 sea-level datum). The regulation of water stages was predicated on achieving an "advantageous" and "dependable flow" that took into account the various dominant interests—e.g., flood control, hydro production, municipal water, lake users (Benidickson, n.d.; Dreisziger, 1974).

GREAT LAKES-ST. LAWRENCE BASIN

The St. Marys River flows from Superior to Huron, bisecting the sister cities of Sault Ste. Marie, Michigan, and Sault Ste. Marie, Ontario. Various schemes to develop hydropower from the St. Marys River at Sault Ste. Marie resulted in the construction of several private hydrostations, particularly on the U.S. side of the river, by the early 20th century. However, these stations and plans to expand their electric production (e.g., in 1898 the Michigan Lake Superior Power Company sought to divert 32,000 cubic feet of water per second) impacted water levels in the St. Marys River, which had transborder implications, particularly for navigation (Dreisziger, 1981, p. 11). Consequently, hydroelectric production near Sault Ste. Marie was a factor in the push for the Boundary Waters Treaty and the IJC, and subsequent structures to control water flows for hydro production here did fall under the aegis of the IJC. In 1914 the commission approved the building of the binational Lake Superior Compensating Works (a 16-gated structure with 8 gates on each side of the international boundary), which directed water from the St. Marys River to the power plants. At the same time, the IJC established the first of its joint boards, the

Lake Superior Board of Control, to regulate water levels and flows of Lake Superior (IJC Dockets 6, 7, 8).[1] These works and the connected water regime were not politically or diplomatically controversial, and the establishment of work and a board to control the fluctuation of lake levels was a significant step for the IJC.

On both the Niagara and St. Lawrence Rivers, a number of private hydrostations had been built in the decade leading up to the conclusion of the Boundary Waters Treaty. Initial bilateral talks about a St. Lawrence deep waterway dated to the 1890s but it took more than half a century for an agreement (Macfarlane, 2014). This was both a hydroelectric (power dams) and navigation project (locks and canals). There were failed U.S.-Canadian St. Lawrence accords in 1932 and 1941, as special interests in the United States (e.g., railways, coal, east coast ports) helped block congressional assent. The 1941 St. Lawrence accord was actually an executive agreement that comprehensively covered transborder water projects in the Great Lakes-St. Lawrence Basin. In the immediate post–World War II years a variety of economic and defense factors brought further pressure to bear on a St. Lawrence seaway and power project: in particular, the ability of a deep waterway to transport the recently discovered iron ore deposits from the Ungava district in Labrador and northern Quebec to the steel mills of the Great Lakes.

Growing frustrated with U.S. inaction, Canada attempted to pursue an all-Canadian Seaway, but the United States blocked a solely Canadian waterway, which was deemed to be inimical to U.S. economic and security interests. In the early 1950s the IJC approved the plans for a transnational St. Lawrence power project and created the International St. Lawrence River Board of Control. (This was not the first time that the IJC had formed a board or investigation on a St. Lawrence issue, for example, a dam at Waddington, New York, and the Massena Power Canal attracted the IJC's attention around the time of the World War I). Then, through a 1954 bilateral U.S.-Canadian agreement, Canada reluctantly acquiesced in the construction of a joint seaway with the United States (Macfarlane, 2014).

The separate Ogoki-Long Lac diversions are often considered together because they use various regulating works and dams, featuring hydroelectric stations, to divert into Lake Superior water that originally drained north to the Hudson's Bay watershed. Together they are the largest diversion into the Great Lakes Basin, putting in about as much water as the Chicago diversion takes out. The Long Lac diversion, completed in 1941, connects the headwaters of the Kenogami River with the Aguasabon River, which naturally discharges into Lake Superior about 250 kilometers east of Thunder Bay, Ontario. The Ogoki diversion, completed in 1943, connects the upper portion of the Ogoki River to Lake Nipigon and from there flows into Lake Superior 96 kilometers east of Thunder Bay. These diversions were developed mainly to generate hydroelectric power at Niagara Falls power stations, since Ontario was permitted to use the extra volume of water these diversions added to the Great Lakes (local hydroelectric production as well as transportation of the pulpwood logs southward were also motivating factors).

Long Lac-Ogoki water continues to be utilized at Niagara Falls, itself another major water issue that had been included in the half century of St. Lawrence Seaway discussions and failed agreements (Macfarlane, 2013a, 2013b). Large-scale hydroelectric production and distribution had its birth at Niagara Falls in the late 19th century. By the 1920s, there were multiple water-power and hydrostations operating on both sides of Niagara. Water was diverted away from the Horseshoe and American Falls (the two main cataracts that make up Niagara Falls) to supply the various powerhouses. Before the end of the 19th century there were public concerns about the aesthetic impact of decreased water levels on the falls, as well as the industry that crowded the shoreline to take advantage of the water power.

Both the U.S. Burton Act (1906) and the Boundary Waters Treaty put restrictions on the amount of water that could be diverted away from the falls, as did the Boundary Waters Treaty. During the World War I the Niagara water diversion limits imposed by the United States via the Burton Act were lifted and all the water that could be utilized was made available for power diversion. The 1920 Federal Power Water Act moved the U.S. Niagara diversion limits to those set by the Boundary Waters Treaty, which would remain in effect until World War II. While some limitations were instituted on the volume of diversions between the two world wars, further expansion of hydro production facilities on both sides of the Niagara gorge took place, including the construction of lengthy diversion conduits. Canada and the United States accelerated their various undertakings, transnational boards, and studies aimed at maintaining or increasing power diversions without sacrificing the great cataract's scenic appeal.

Both countries signed the Niagara Convention and Protocol in 1929. However, this Niagara convention was not able to make it through the U.S. Senate. Subsequent engineering studies recommended remedial works to achieve a sufficiently distributed volume of flow, or at least the "impression of volume," which would create an unbroken crestline (Macfarlane, 2013a). After the failed 1932 and 1941 St. Lawrence agreements, during World War II the two countries agreed that the limits on the amount of water diverted at Niagara Falls for wartime needs could be temporarily increased. Subsequently, further withdrawals were allowed during the war, rising to a total diversion of 54,000 cubic feet squared (cfs) for Canada and 32,500 cfs for the United States. Canada and the United States agreed to split the cost of constructing a stone-filled weir—a submerged dam—above the falls, which would raise the water level in order to facilitate greater diversions without an apparent loss of scenic beauty.

The wartime Niagara diversions continued on an indefinite—and technically illegal—basis after the end of the World War II. The two countries separated the Niagara diversion issues from the repeatedly stalled St. Lawrence negotiations, and a Niagara Diversion Treaty was signed in 1950. This U.S.-Canadian treaty accord called for further remedial works, to be approved by the IJC, and virtually equalized water diversions while restricting the flow of water over Niagara Falls to no less than 100,000 cfs during daylight hours of what was deemed the tourist season (8:00 a.m. to 10:00 p.m. from April to mid-September, and from 8:00 a.m. to 8:00 p.m. during the fall), and no less than 50,000 cfs during the remainder of the year. This worked out to Canada and the United States together taking about three-quarters of the total flow over the falls outside of tourist hours (Macfarlane, 2013a).

A 1,550-foot control dam was built from the Canadian shore, parallel to and about 225 feet downstream from the weir built in the 1940s, featuring 13 sluices (5 more were soon added) equipped with control gates. The purpose of this structure was to control water levels and spread out the water both for appearance and because flows concentrated in certain places caused more erosion damage. The diverted water went to the hydroelectric stations downstream. The IJC's International Niagara Board of Control monitors operation of the control works by the power entities Ontario Power Generation and the New York Power Authority.

Excavation also took place along the flanks of Horseshoe Falls (64,000 cubic yards of rock on the Canadian flank and 24,000 cubic yards on the U.S. flank) in order to create a better distribution of flow and an unbroken crestline at all times (Macfarlane, 2013a). To compensate for erosion, crest fills (100 feet on the Canadian shore and 300 feet on the U.S. side) were undertaken, parts of which would be fenced and landscaped in order to provide prime public vantage points.

EAST COAST

Border hydroelectric developments on the east coast primarily involve waters that form or cross the Maine-New Brunswick border (Figure 13.3). The Milltown Dam on the St. Croix River was among the first hydro dams built in Canada, with its original construction dating to the 1880s. The St. Croix River forms the border between the two countries, but because

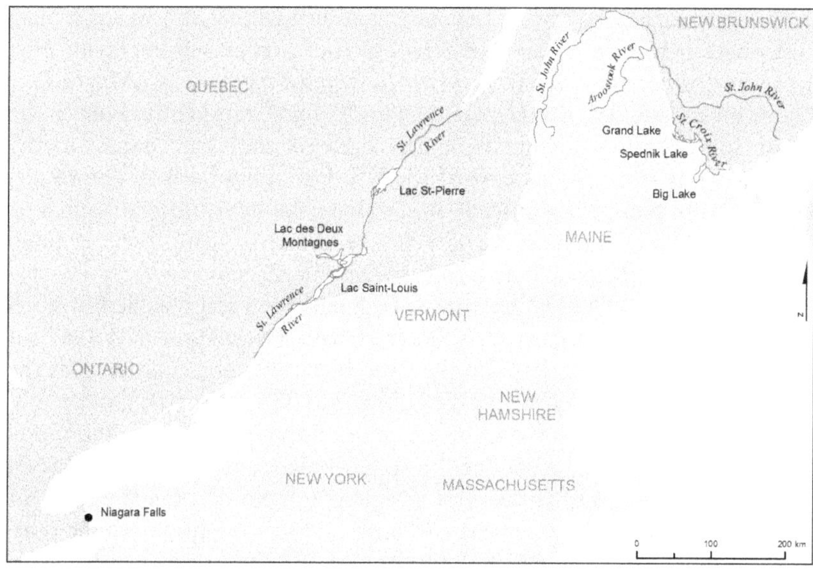

FIGURE 13.3 Niagara, St. Lawrence, and East Coast Developments

of its early date of completion this dam was not referred to the IJC. A 1918 application to build a powerhouse on the U.S. side was withdrawn, but a 1932 application to reconstruct the dam was approved by the IJC in 1934 (IJC Dockets 16 and 32). It should be noted that electricity is exported from this small dam across the river to the United States. Two other private dam structures that span the border in the St. Croix are subject to IJC orders of approval: the Vanceboro Dam and Grand Falls Dam. The latter received IJC approval in 1915 and then again in 1931, while the former predated the IJC but then received the commission's approval in 1965 when the company owning the dam applied to rebuild it (i.e., replace the timber structure with concrete) a few feet upstream (IJC Dockets 10, 11, 22, 28). The Vanceboro Dam operates primarily as a control structure, allowing power to be produced from the resulting reservoir at the Grand Falls and Milltown stations. In the 1960s the IJC approved its replacement by a larger dam (IJC Docket 80)

The Tinker Dam is on the Aroostook River just east and downstream of the Maine-New Brunswick border. The reservoir of this hydroelectric station, dating originally to the 1920s, extends across the international border. There are also control facilities and a powerhouse on this river in Maine, and the province and state collectively regulate the flow through "special agreements" that obviate the need for IJC approval. The Saint

John River forms the border between northern Maine and western New Brunswick before flowing entirely through the latter province, playing host to several other New Brunswick hydro developments (e.g., Mactaquac Dam) on its way down to the Bay of Fundy. The Grand Falls Dam on the Saint John River—distinct from the dam of the same name on the St. Croix—is situated just east of the U.S.-Canadian border. The resulting reservoir extended almost 30 miles along the international stretch of the St. John River, and because of a change of owners it was twice granted IJC approval in the mid-1920s (IJC Dockets 19, 22, 63).

The St. Croix Paper Company, which had been responsible for much of the previous development on the St. Croix River, applied in 1967 for permission to replace a dam on the river, but it was not built because the company did not accept the conditions of the IJC's order (IJC Docket 87). Various attempts at tidal hydroelectric development in Passamaquoddy Bay, an estuary that lies between the St. Croix River and the Bay of Fundy, also did not come to fruition (IJC Dockets 60 and 72). On the topic of developments that did not move forward, and moving briefly to the prairies, the Pembina River, which flows through Manitoba and North Dakota before debouching into the Red River, deserves mention. In 1962, in response to a reference, the IJC recommended a plan of cooperative development on the Pembina River for hydro development, which the two countries did not implement (IJC Docket 76).

PACIFIC NORTHWEST

The Pacific Northwest features a number of rivers that cross the U.S.-Canadian border, many of which are prime hydroelectric sites (Figure 13.4). The Columbia River, which is the fourth-largest river on the continent, has its headwaters in British Columbia, though the bulk of its watershed is in the United States. Schemes to harness it for flood control and hydroelectricity date back to the early 20th century. Prior to World War II the United States built many power stations on the Columbia and its tributaries, such as the massive Bonneville and Grand Coulee projects. But the full potential of the Columbia for U.S. electric development and flood control could only be unlocked if the upper parts of the river situated in Canada were also dammed to provide storage reservoirs. Canada was, for its part, eager to develop hydro facilities on the Columbia in its territory. Thus, in 1944 Canadian and U.S. authorities requested that the IJC determine "whether a greater use than is now being made of the waters of the Columbia River System would be feasible and advantageous" (IJC Dockets 42, 43, 44, 45, 47, 48, 49).

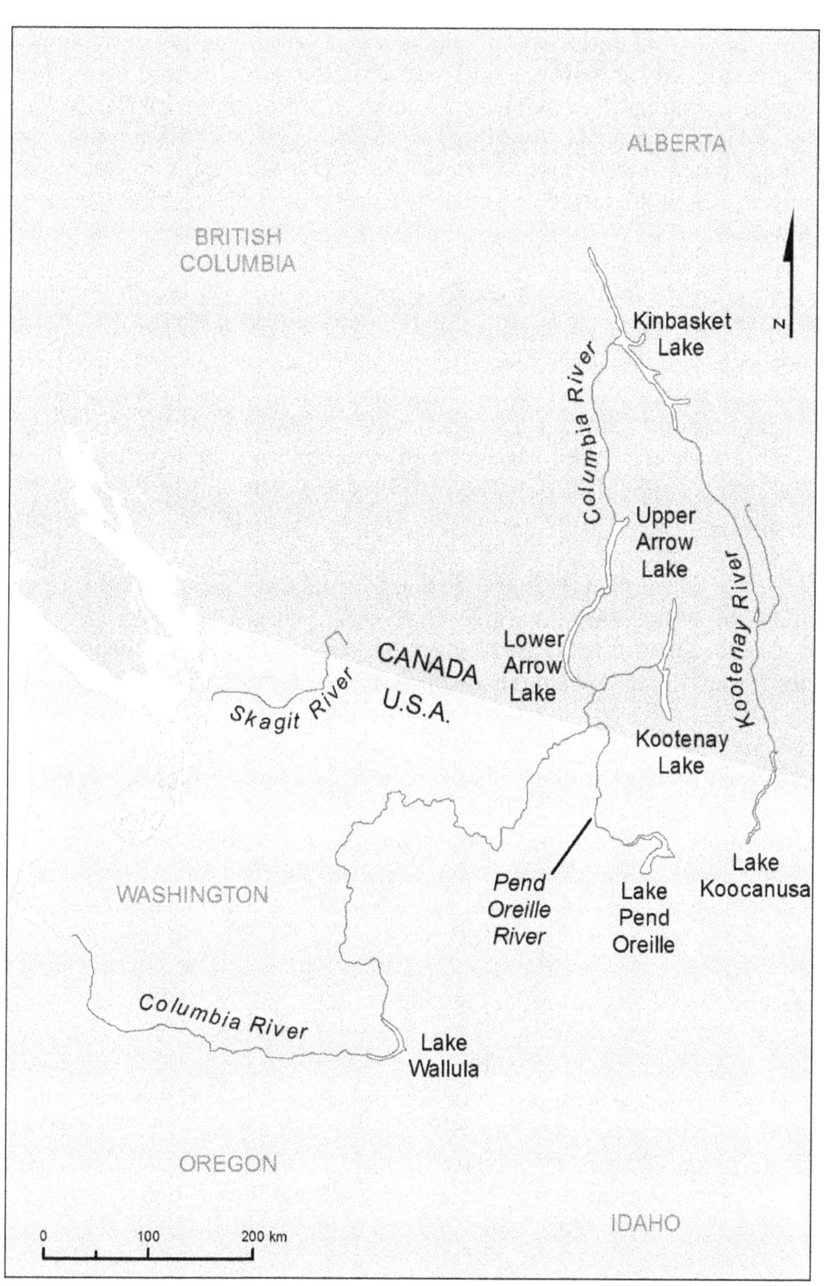

FIGURE 13.4 Pacific Northwest Developments

The IJC and both countries undertook engineering studies and plans that continued well into the 1950s. In 1954, the Social Credit Premier of British Columbia, W. A. C. Bennett, made an agreement with Kaiser Aluminum and Chemical Corporation of the United States to develop a large storage dam on the upper Columbia River. In return for a 50-year water license, British Columbia would receive 20% of the electricity generated downstream. The federal government, however, opposed this for a variety of reasons, including the fact that the Kaiser plan would interfere with ongoing IJC studies for the overall rationalization of the river. In 1955 the Liberal government of Canada, led by Prime Minister Louis St. Laurent, passed the International River Improvements Act, which stipulated that a federal license was necessary in order to dam an international river. Since the IJC had still not made a recommendation, the St. Laurent government entered into active negotiations about developing the Columbia with President Dwight D. Eisenhower and the U.S. government. After John Diefenbaker's Conservatives took power in Canada in 1957, negotiations accelerated.

The IJC adopted the principle that Canada could claim half the power and flood control benefits conferred on downstream U.S. interests by storage in Canada. After considering three different plans, the negotiators finally settled on a scheme that involved three dams in Canada, including a High Dam for the Arrow Lakes. In compensation for the Americans receiving these downstream benefits, Canada was to receive cash and half of the extra U.S. electricity that the control dams made possible. Based on these terms the Columbia River Treaty was signed in January 1961 and soon ratified by the United States. Three dams would be built in Canada (Duncan, Mica, and Keenleyside) as well as another (Libby) on the U.S. side of the transborder Kootenay River. The reservoir would extend upriver into Canada (IJC Docket 65). The Canadian dams benefited downstream U.S. power and flood control interests, but could generate electricity in their own right.

But it soon became apparent that Premier Bennett was opposed, not only because he was peeved about Ottawa's interference, but also because the treaty's terms would interfere with his "two rivers" scheme, which would simultaneously replumb the Columbia and Peace Rivers for hydro development. Bennett insisted on selling the power to U.S. entities. However, such sales contravened the long-established federal policy of allowing the export of electric power only on a nonpermanent basis.

Many Canadians were also opposed to the 1961 Columbia treaty, perceiving it as a capitulation to the United States. Critics complained that Canada received few benefits relative to the United States and argued that alternative development proposals would put less Canadian territory (such as the Arrow Lakes Valley) under water, would allow for more hydro generation in Canada, and would give Canada much greater control over the future use and diversion of Columbia waters. One of the most prominent and vociferous opponents of the treaty, General A. G. L. McNaughton, was the chairman of the Canadian Section of the International Joint Commission. He actively promoted an all-Canadian plan that would see the Kootenay River diverted into the Columbia in order to create greater water flows, which in turn would enable more hydro dams to be built entirely on the Canadian side before the river went into the United States. In fact, McNaughton's all-Canadian plan for the Columbia stemmed from his failure to achieve an all-Canadian St. Lawrence Seaway in the 1950s.

After winning the 1963 federal election, the new prime minister, Lester Pearson, proposed that the Columbia matter be settled by a protocol and exchange of notes, rather than a new treaty. The prime minister quickly moved to forge a federal-British Columbia agreement. Bennett was amenable now that the sale of long-term downstream benefits was on the table. An elaborate series of triangular negotiations between British Columbia and the Canadian and U.S. federal governments took up much of the remainder of 1963, dealing with sticking points such as downstream benefits and the creation of an integrated continental electric grid. The end result was the 1964 Columbia Protocol.

The protocol modified the 1961 Columbia River Treaty and governed its implementation. The revised terms included new procedures for the operation of flood control; reaffirmation and clarification of Canada's rights to make diversions for consumptive and other uses; and the increase in Canada's entitlement to downstream power benefits (Sanderson, 2012). The siting of the three Canadian dams remained unchanged. The United States would return to Canada half the power it generated that was made possible by the Canadian works, and Canada sold its downstream benefits for C$254 million over 30 years to a group of U.S. utilities, and then passed on these proceeds to British Columbia. In total, the treaty coordinates the operation of 14 dams on the Columbia mainstem as well as multiple dams on tributaries. Either country could terminate the treaty after 60 years with 10 years notice (making 2014 the earliest point at which either side could indicate plans to renegotiate or pull out).

The project is certainly not without its critics. Donald Waterfield labeled Pearson's handling of the Columbia and failure to renegotiate the 1961 treaty as a "pusillanimous surrender" and is joined by many others who see the Columbia projects as further evidence of U.S. imperialism towards Canadian natural resources (Waterfield, 1970, p. 116). Electricity from the Columbia served to further integrate the two countries' power grids, which nationalist detractors claim prevented the formation of a national Canadian grid (Mouat, 2012). Moreover, many scholars have revealed a range of negative ecological impacts, as infrastructure and thousands of people had to be relocated when their land was submerged under the new reservoirs.

The Libby Dam was installed on the Kootenay (Kootenai in United States) River as part of the Columbia River Treaty, and dams on other rivers in the northwest had transborder implications. Since the 1910s the City of Seattle had plans in the works for a High Ross Dam on the Skagit River, which starts in British Columbia before crossing into the State of Washington. Over the next half century, despite an informal agreement by British Columbia and approval from the IJC, a deal for compensation was not reached because the High Ross Dam would flood land in British Columbia. Instead, Seattle City and Light built a smaller Ross Dam on the U.S. side. Completed in 1953, this 540-foot-tall dam flooded 12,000 acres in Washington State and another 550 acres in British Columbia (IJC Docket 46; Van Huizen, 2013).

In 1967, British Columbia agreed to let Seattle raise the Ross Dam. This High Ross Dam would flood substantially more land on the Canadian side of the border. But in the wake of the 1967 agreement, environmental opposition from both sides of the border helped prevent the implementation of this agreement, which stretched into the 1980s. In 1984 the U.S.-Canadian Skagit River Treaty was signed. The agreement stipulated that, in exchange for not raising the Ross Dam, British Columbia would sell power produced in other areas, which included raising the Seven Mile Dam on the Pend D'Oreille River. Ironically, the Seven Mile Dam was a reversal of the Skagit controversy, as it involved a dam on the Canadian side flooding out land on the U.S. side (Van Huizen, 2013).

The Pend-D'Oreille River (Pend Oreille on the American side) is a tributary of the Columbia River. It begins in Idaho and then flows northwest into Washington State, joining the Columbia in southeastern British Columbia just north of the international border. There are five dams on the Pend D'Oreille—two in Canada and three in the United States. In addition to the Seven Mile Dam, another power structure on the Pend D'Oreille—the Waneta Dam—had previously received IJC consideration. This dam, built by Consolidated Mining and Smelting Company of Canada to aid its Trail Smelter complex, flooded a very small portion of land in the United States and received IJC approval in the 1950s (IJC Docket 66).

THE POLICY LEGACY OF BORDER HYDROELECTRICITY

The development of hydroelectricity on border waters has policy ramifications in several areas, both past and present: U.S.-Canadian environmental diplomacy (especially water and energy), cultural influences on foreign and environmental policy, the role of subnational governments and intergovernmentalism, and the evolution and importance of the IJC. These developments allow us to directly compare and contrast over a long period Canadian and American attitudes towards electricity, energy, technology, national identity, and the roles of the state and industry. On the one hand there were certainly many shared goals, approaches, and assumptions; on the other hand, hydroelectric development clearly had a different nation-building and nationalist capacity for Canadians. Constitutional and judicial—or "institutional"—variables were important, but it is clear that domestic ideational and cultural variables must be considered as casual factors in this resulting multilayered diplomacy (Hocking, 1993; Kukucha, 2008).

What can be termed "hydraulic nationalism" was readily apparent in many Canadian cases of border hydroelectric development, particularly in the Great Lakes-St. Lawrence Basin. These border waters play a more fundamental role in the Canadian national imagination than they do in American culture, for in Canada hydroelectricity is imbued with a distinct nationalist tint. To provide a more specific example, from a constructivist perspective the cultural perception of the St. Lawrence as "Canadian" underpinned the push for an all-Canadian Seaway. Various strains of Canadian nationalism—particularly geographic, environmental, and technological—coalesced to frame the St. Lawrence River as an exclusively "Canadian" resource and led to Ottawa's attempt to build a solely Canadian waterway. Furthermore, the St. John, Niagara, and Rainy Rivers—among others—are seen as "Canadian" rivers more than American. The Columbia is perhaps a unique exception because, although there are competing ideational claims to this water body, a strong case can be made that the Americans take a more possessive view of the river. Nonetheless, when the Canadian combination of national identity, rivers, and hydroelectricity are linked to perennial nationalist worries about sovereignty and resource colonization by the United States, even rivers with contested nationalism claims such as the Columbia are easily written into the Canadian pantheon. Thus, contemporary policy makers would be well advised to take heed of this Canadian nationalism. In particular, Canadians have a strong attachment to hydroelectric development as a way of exploiting what is widely considered the country's natural resources birthright.

Border hydroelectric developments have had a tremendous impact on Canadian electricity exports to the United States. Electricity sent across the border at Niagara played an especially influential role. The powerhouses built on the Canadian side of the Niagara gorge in the first decades of the 20th century were subsidiaries of U.S. companies, and the majority of the electricity produced at these plants was sent across the river to the United States. Indeed, much of the electricity was exported because there was little market for it in Canada at that point (Perlgut, 1978, p. 10). Several other cross-border interconnections followed, each involving the firm export of electricity from Canada to one isolated customer on the U.S. side (e.g., an 85-year export contract for 56 MW to Alcoa from a generating station on the St. Lawrence at Cedar Rapids, Quebec) (Perlgut, 1978, pp. 11–12). Under the Wilfred Laurier Liberals, the Canadian federal government adopted a laissez-faire approach to electricity exports, and by 1910 about one-third of Canada's electricity was being exported (Martin-Neilsen, 2009).

Many Canadians resented this state of affairs, however, and the desire to keep power and develop industry helped lead to the creation in 1906 of a provincial publicly owned power utility, the Hydro-Electric Power Commission of Ontario (HEPCO, or Ontario Hydro). This commission would begin with the distribution of electricity, but over the following decades Ontario Hydro subsequently acquired the aforementioned private Niagara generating station, built several of its own massive hydroelectric facilities along the Niagara River, and expanded the hydroelectric transmission network throughout Ontario (while still continuing exports to the United States). Ontario Hydro was also responsible for constructing the Canadian share of the St. Lawrence power works.

The same concerns that led to the creation of Ontario Hydro were also linked to the federal passage of the Exportation of Power and Fluids and Importation of Gas Act of 1907. This act required Canadian power exports to secure an annual license, gave the federal Parliament the authority to levy an export duty on hydroelectricity, disallowed hydro power from being sold at a lower price in the United States, and featured a recall clause that allowed exports to be quickly revoked if the power was required in Canada. The 1907 act would undergo minor modifications in 1925 and 1955, with the duty later abolished in 1963. South of the border, the U.S. president had the power to authorize the construction of border facilities that could be used to export electricity, but it was not until 1920 that the U.S. government was given the authority to license exports, when the Federal Power Act created the Federal Power Commission (FERC as of 1977).

Domestic Canadian opposition to electricity exports to the United States reached a fever pitch during World War I, resulting in what Karl

Froschauer has called the "repatriation crisis," which involved various studies into the nature of Canadian electrical development and exports, such as the Drayton Report (Froschauer, 1999). Internal opposition continued during the interwar period, but the federal government was reluctant to take any strong action because the country still depended on coal imported from the United States. In 1925, the Mackenzie King government enacted a minor duty on electricity sold across the border. According to Janet Martin-Neilsen this duty "was too low to have immediate repercussions on the ability of companies to export hydroelectric power," and

> it marked the beginning of a gradual change in the style of Canadian electricity exports. As the Canadian and American electricity grids became increasingly interconnected in the interwar years, electricity trade between the two countries changed from unidirectional firm power sales from Canada to the United States to interruptible power sales in both directions. (Martin-Neilsen, 2009, pp. 126–127)

Nonfirm (i.e., interruptible) power sales have dominated the Canadian-American electricity trade since World War II. Up to the 1960s, the majority of power exported from Canada to the United States was via Ontario, and St. Lawrence and Niagara power had played the leading role in shaping Ontario and the federal government's approach to electricity exports. These two megaprojects thus entrenched Canadian-U.S. energy relations and paved the way for the development of transborder electricity grids that proliferated beginning in the 1960s (as of 1975, there were 65 international interconnections, with a total transfer capability of over 6,000 MW) and the Canadian allowance of long-term firm power (as part of the Columbia River Treaty arrangements), as well as the petroleum and natural interconnections that would soon become prominent aspects of continental energy allocations (Perlgut, 1978, p. 11).

Control of natural resources, particularly hydroelectricity, has historically exerted a decentralizing effect on federal-provincial relations. The British North America Act was not clear about the federal government's ability to negotiate and implement international agreements in areas of provincial jurisdiction (though in the 1937 Labour case the courts had ruled that a treaty negotiated by the federal government did not automatically change laws in provincial jurisdiction). In the case of the St. Lawrence, this ambiguity was further exacerbated by a lack of clarity about hydropower on navigable rivers. The various Canada-Ontario accords concerning the waters of the St. Lawrence and Niagara represented a positive shift in federal-provincial cooperation and went a long way towards erasing the acrimony of the pre-1945 years. They also entrenched provincial claims to water rights on navigable streams, as well as patterns of both formal and informal intergovernmentalism that have had a salient impact on Canada's conduct in international relations. Moreover, the noticeable increase since the 1950s in active substate participation can be correlated to the outcomes of St. Lawrence negotiations (Paquin, 2010).

In the case of the St. Lawrence project, the Ontario and New York power authorities were direct and indirect shapers of policy not only at the high diplomatic level, but also at the local, borderlands, and technical levels. In the lead-up to the 1950 Niagara Treaty, the chairman of HEPCO, Robert Saunders, went to Washington to lobby for the project. This form of para- or provincial diplomacy came to involve an informal understanding with an American newspaper bureau official who advocated for HEPCO's point of view and provided information about opposition in the United States to the St. Lawrence development (author interview with Dennis Dack, May 2, 2011). This is one of the earliest such lobbying forays by a provincial representative, and thus can be seen as initiating a trend that would accelerate in subsequent decades.

Border hydroelectric developments profoundly influenced the evolution of the IJC, itself a key institution in the history of U.S.-Canadian relations. The IJC has moved from a bureaucratic to a post-bureaucratic model though it blends the two categories and certainly retains aspects of the bureaucratic model (Stoett & Temby, 2015). Likewise, the IJC has displayed elements of both a capacity-building and a regulatory institution: it solicits for public input, helps shape consensus, and collaborates widely, yet it has regulatory functions that involve a gatekeeper role in terms of approving project applications and handling references, and a role in implementation oversight. The IJC is also an example of "fragmented bilateralism" (Mumme & Duncan, 1997). However, the fact remains that without the consent of the Canadian and U.S. federal governments, the IJC has little legal and regulatory capacity, as it has no active enforcement mechanisms, though it can use its reputation and symbolic authority to influence environmental issues.

The IJC was the key bilateral environmental institution over the course of the 20th century and is commonly seen as a pioneering model of bilateral environmental cooperation, yet it has become increasingly marginalized in recent decades. For example, it has only minor roles in the Great Lakes Water Quality Agreements and the 1991 Air Quality Agreement, and has no official role under the 2008 Great Lakes-St. Lawrence River Basin Sustainable Water Resources Agreement. Nonetheless, as an organization the IJC remains important in terms of policy, symbolism, and "legitimacy building." The approach employed in this chapter ultimately aligns its interpretative matrix with the "rational-legal authority" approach stemming from the constructivist camp of International Relations theory (Barnett & Finnemore, 2004; Biermann & Siebenhuner, 2009). In line with this theory, the IJC has a great deal of autonomy; has developed its own bureaucratic culture and internal processes; and has gained a reputation among many for effectiveness, expertise, and impartiality because of these processes. As such, it currently wields symbolic and tangible power to frame scientific information with policy applicability, orient problems, and identity actors and solutions (often itself as the impartial repository of technocratic expertise).

Noting the IJC's failures and limitations vis-à-vis border hydrostations need not inevitably lead to the conclusion that the IJC's influence should be circumscribed. To the contrary, the IJC's history shows how flexible and adaptable it can be, and the fact that it emerged in the 1960s and 1970s as a champion of water and air quality, particularly in the Great Lakes Basin, demonstrates that the commission can be a vehicle for environmental protection rather than engineering ambition. Though the Boundary Waters Treaty's focus on the apportionment of water may be a bit outdated, the IJC has a demonstrated capacity for anticipatory policy. Given that climate change is likely to have significant impacts on border waters, even if the nature of these impacts remains debated (e.g., lower or higher levels on the Great Lakes), the IJC should remain relevant to policy makers and the two federal governments must be willing to utilize and work through the commission.

CONCLUSION

The Boundary Waters Treaty of 1909 established the IJC, and together the treaty and the commission have governed many hydrostations built along the U.S.-Canadian border during the 20th century. Four different regional groupings of border hydrostations have been identified: (1) Great Lakes-St. Lawrence; (2) Pacific Northwest; (3) Maine-New Brunswick border; and (4) Rainy River/Lake of the Woods. Collectively, these stations were key aspects of Canada's evolving environmental diplomacy with the United States over the last century. The largest and most significant were on the Columbia, St. Lawrence, and Niagara Rivers, and together these three have shaped U.S.-Canadian environmental relations and transborder policy.

Canada is of course notorious for its production and exportation of fossil fuels, and the evolution of the border hydro regime sheds light on current U.S.-Canadian resource and energy disputes, such as softwood lumber or the Keystone XL pipeline. Indeed, there are striking parallels between the negotiation of the St. Lawrence Seaway and Power Project and the Keystone XL project. Both are transborder energy conduits that the Canadian federal government indicated were of great national importance, but which the U.S. government has repeatedly stalled, influenced at least in part by various special interests (and ecological concerns in the case of the pipeline). In response, Canada threatened to go its own way and bypass the United States (i.e., the Northern Gateway project) and both the St. Lawrence and Keystone XL impasses have had negative repercussions for the tenor of U.S.-Canadian relations.

The present focus on fossil fuels, though warranted because of the impact of carbon emissions on climate change, also has the tendency to obscure the fact that Canada remains heavily reliant on hydroelectric production, both for domestic consumption and export to the United States. Border hydro developments established the parameters, technological momentum, and transborder relationships that continue to frame contemporary energy and environmental relations between Canada and the United States; thus, understanding many of the patterns of contemporary U.S.-Canadian environmental relations—and the oscillation between cooperation and conflict—requires heeding the history of developing hydroelectricity along the border. Electricity from the St. Lawrence, Niagara, and Columbia generating stations were, for example, the primary sources of electricity exported to the United States until the 1970s.

These projects must be part of policy discussions about Canada's energy future, including the role of hydroelectricity itself. As of 2014 the two countries party to the Columbia River Treaty have the option of renegotiating or pulling out of the treaty, and both the Canadian and U.S. governments are in the midst of considering how to modernize the pact and better account for ecological impacts and climate change. In a similar fashion, there is currently a strong push for changing the method of regulation for the upper St. Lawrence River and Lake Ontario. The existing method has been in place since the early 1960s and does not allow for natural water fluctuations and stage levels, which creates ecological impairments. The IJC advocates changing the method of regulation to the so-called Plan 2014, which would better balance environmental impacts with the needs of other users (IJC, 2014).

A number of the dams covered in this chapter are much smaller in physical size and amount of energy produced than those on the St. Lawrence, Niagara, and Columbia. Given the recent push in North America to remove dams because of their environmental impacts, such as blocking fish migration and spawning, the utility of many of these border dams must be questioned (DamNation, 2014; Stanley & Doyle, 2003). Though generally considered to be a "clean" form of energy production relative to other alternatives, it is becoming increasingly clear that large hydro reservoirs emit methane, which is a more potent greenhouse gas than carbon. In addition, hydro developments along the U.S.-Canadian border that create large reservoirs (i.e., not run-of-the river) have had uneven impacts; for example, groups with less political power such as The First Nations often bear the brunt of displacement. The lessons of these border developments and reservoirs are even more pertinent since it appears that the era of large-scale hydro developments and water diversions is not over, at least not in Canada, as huge hydrostations are under construction on the Peace River in British Columbia and at Muskrat Falls in Labrador, and there is a planned expansion of the hydro facilities on rivers in northern Quebec. The legacy of the hydrostations in this chapter should give contemporary policy makers pause when they consider hydroelectricity as a renewable energy source; indeed, wind and solar energy might well be more sustainable investments.

NOTE

1. Rule 1949 was adopted in 1951 to hold the level of Lake Superior between the limits of 602.1 and 603.6 as near as possible.

REFERENCES

Annin, P. (2006). *Great Lakes water wars.* Washington, DC: Island Press.

Barnett, M., & Finnemore, M. (2004). *Rules for the world: International organizations in global politics.* Ithaca, NY: Cornell University Press.

Benidickson, J. (n. d.) *Sunset country: Approaching the watershed.* Unpublished manuscript.

Biermann, F., & Siebenhuner, B. (Eds). (2009). *Managers of global change: The influence of international environmental bureacracies.* Boston, MA: MIT Press.

Boundary Waters Treaty. (1909, January 11). United States-Great Britain (for Canada), 36 Stat. 2448.

Canadian Hydropower Association. (2008). Hydropower in Canada: Past, present, and future. Retrieved from https://canadahydro.ca/reports reference/cha-reports-and-publications

Clamen, M., & Macfarlane, D. (2015). The International Joint Commission, water levels, and transboundary governance in the Great Lakes. *Review of Policy Research*, *32*(1), 40–59.

Cohen, M. (1981). The commission from the inside. In R. Spencer, J. Kirton, & K. R. Nossal (Eds.), *The International Joint Commission seventy years on* (pp. 106–123). Toronto, ON: University of Toronto Centre for International Studies.

DamNation. (2014). Dir. Ben Knight. Patagonia Pictures. DVD.

Dorsey, K. (1998). *The dawn of conservation diplomacy: U.S.-Canadian wildlife protection treaties in the Progressive Era*. Seattle, WA: University of Washington Press.

Dreisziger, N. F. (1974). The International Joint Commission of the United States and Canada, 1895–1920: A study in Canadian-American relations [Doctoral dissertation]. University of Toronto.

Dreisziger, N. F. (1981). Dreams and disappointments. In R. Spencer, J. Kirton, & K. R. Nossal (Eds.), *The International Joint Commission seventy years on* (pp. 8–23). Toronto, ON: University of Toronto Centre for International Studies.

Froschauer, K. (1999). *White gold: Hydroelectric power in Canada*. Vancouver, BC: University of British Columbia Press.

Hocking, B. (1993). *Localizing foreign policy: Non-central governments and multilayered diplomacy*. New York, NY: Macmillan.

International Joint Commission. (2014). *Lake Ontario-St. Lawrence River plan 2014*. Retrieved from: http://www.ijc.org/en_/Plan2014/home

Kukucha, C. (2008). *The provinces and Canadian foreign trade policy*. Vancouver, BC: University of British Columbia Press.

Macfarlane, D. (2013a). "A completely man-made and artificial cataract": The transnational manipulation of Niagara Falls. *Environmental History*, *18*(4), 759–784.

Macfarlane, D. (2013b). Creating a cataract: The transnational manipulation of Niagara Falls to the 1950s. In C. Coates, S. Bocking, K. Cruikshank, & A. Sandberg (Eds.), *Urban explorations: Environmental histories of the Toronto region* (pp. 251–267). Hamilton, ON: McMaster University, L. R. Wilson Institute for Canadian Studies.

Macfarlane, D. (2014). *Negotiating a river: Canada, the U.S., and the creation of the St. Lawrence Seaway*. Vancouver, BC: University of British Columbia Press.

Martin-Neilsen, J. (2009). South over the wires: Hydroelectricity exports from Canada, 1900–1925. *Water History*, *1*, 109–129.

McCaffrey, S. (1996). The Harmon Doctrine one hundred years later: Buried, not praised. *Natural Resources Journal*, *36*, 549–590.

Mouat, J. (2012). The Columbia Exchange: A Canadian perspective on the negotiation of the Columbia River treaty. In B. Cosens (Ed.), *Transnational river governance in the face of uncertainty* (pp. 14–42). Corvallis, OR: Oregon State University Press.

Mumme, S. P., & Duncan, P. (1997). The Commission for Environmental Cooperation and environmental management in the Americas. *Journal of Interamerican Studies and World Affairs*, *39*(4), 41–62.

Paquin, S. (2010). Federalism and compliance with international agreements: Belgium and Canada compared. *The Hague Journal of Diplomacy*, 5, 173–197.

Perlgut, M. (1978). *Electricity across the border: The U.S.-Canadian experience*. New York, NY: C. D. Howe Research Institute.

Sanderson, C. W. (2012). The Columbia River Treaty after 2024. In B. Cosens (Ed.), *The Columbia River Treaty revisited: Transboundary river governance in an age of uncertainty*. Corvallis, OR: Oregon State University Press.

Spencer, R., Kirton, J., & Nossal, K. R. (Eds.). (1981). *The International Joint Commission seventy years on*. Toronto, ON: University of Toronto Centre for International Studies.

Stanley, E. H., & Doyle, M. W. (2003). Trading off: The ecological effects of dam removal. *Frontiers in Ecology and the Environment*, *1*, 15–22. Retrieved from http://dx.doi.org/10.1890/1540-9295(2003)001[0015:TOTEEO]2.0.CO;2

Stoett, P., & Temby, O. (2015). Bilateral and trilateral natural resource and biodiversity governance in North America: Organizations, networks, and inclusion. *Review of Policy Research*, *32*(1), 1–18.

Van Huizen, P. (2013). Flooding the border: Development, politics, and environmental controversy in the Canadian-U.S. Skagit Valley [Doctoral dissertation]. University of British Columbia.

Waterfield, D. (1970). *Continental waterboy: The Columbia River controversy*. Toronto, ON: Clarke, Irwin.

Willoughby, W. (1981). Expectations and experience, 1909–1979. In R. Spencer, J. Kirton, & K. R. Nossal (Eds.), *The International Joint Commission seventy years on* (pp. 24–42). Toronto, ON: University of Toronto Centre for International Studies.

FOURTEEN

U.S.-Canadian Subnational Electricity Relations

Interests, Institutions, and Interactions

IAN H. ROWLANDS

INTRODUCTION

Energy issues have risen up North American agendas—in a variety of local, regional and international ways. Changes in both supply-side realities (in particular, the increased use of hydraulic fracking techniques to augment natural gas and other fossil fuel production), demand-side priorities (in particular, the continued urgency of climate change, as catalyzed by the recent reports of the Intergovernmental Panel on Climate Change), and possibilities (here, I am referring to the increased use of information and communications technologies to make the demand side more responsive and potentially "smarter") have given the "energy file" a greater sense of urgency and significance across the continent.

Of course, that is not to say that energy has not traditionally had international dimensions (including within North America). Globally, fossil fuels (oil, gas, and coal) collectively represent the world's second most-traded goods or services (behind chemicals), with their value just under US$2 trillion in 2014 (add petroleum products to the calculation and the value is around US$3 trillion; UN Conference on Trade and Development, 2015, p. 20). Continentally, moreover, energy has been a key part of relations between Canada and the United States for decades. Trade between the two countries predates the 1988 Free Trade Agreement, but was further catalyzed by that agreement and the subsequent North American Free Trade Agreement of 1994 (Battram & Lock, 1988; Hufbauer & Schott, 2005, pp. 395–440). But consideration of international energy issues, which are often closely tied to discussions of energy security, has usually focused on fossil fuels (and oil in particular).[1]

This chapter investigates a part of this agenda that does not get as much attention as issues of fossil fuel extraction and movement between countries; namely, electricity transmission between states and provinces. More specifically, it investigates relationships between subnational parts of Canada and the United States on electricity issues. It focuses on two different parts of this transborder frontier: Manitoba/Midwest and Québec/Northeast. There is a variety of actors in each of these situations, with different scale, reach, perspective, and interests. Locations exist whereby these actors engage with each other through informal means (e.g., media exchanges) as well as more formal mechanisms (e.g., regulatory hearings). Such interactions are sometimes characterized by conflict and the aforementioned differences clash when simultaneously brought to light. There can, however, be cooperation to determine whether there are mutual benefits from some kind of international electricity transmission between the two countries. This chapter reveals that conflict is more common than cooperation. To increase the chances of securing the latter, I will argue that the issue requires more comprehensive analysis that considers impacts across different sectors and scales. While not assuming that all international links of this kind would necessarily be advantageous, there could nevertheless still be outcomes with joint gains that should not be lost. Laying bare all of the challenges and opportunities would increase the odds of finding such wins.

SETTING THE CONTEXT: U.S.-CANADIAN ELECTRICITY RELATIONS

This section aims to set the context for a more focused investigation of the politics of transborder electricity cooperation by reviewing, briefly, the state of electricity systems in Canada and the United States, the extent to which they are currently connected, and the broader agenda associated with U.S.-Canadian electricity relations.

Electricity in Canada and the United States

Electricity systems in Canada and the United States are complex and operate at various scales. Canada is the world's sixth-largest generator of electricity (International Energy Agency [IEA], 2015, p. 27), with approximately 63% of the country's electricity production coming from its vast hydropower resources (Natural Resources Canada [NRCan], 2015, p. 78). Indeed, Canada is the world's second-largest generator of hydropower (IEA, 2015, p. 19). Fossil fuel and nuclear resources provide additional supply, with their shares approximately 21% and 13%, respectively (NRCan, 2015). While these are the country's total supply figures, it is also important to recognize that there are stark variations across the provinces. A number are hydro-dominated, such as Manitoba, Newfoundland and Labrador, and Quebec, each of whom have at least 95% of their supply portfolio sourced from hydropower (NRCan, 2015, p. 78). Others, such as Alberta, Nova Scotia, and Saskatchewan, are largely fossil based. Ontario is a relatively unique hybrid, with nuclear power as its largest contributor and other energy sources (particularly hydropower and fossil fuels) also making critical contributions (NRCan, 2015, p. 78).

A similar investigation of demand indicates that country-wide, industrial customers make the greatest demand on the power sector (39%) followed by residential and commercial customers (30% and 29%, respectively; NRCan, 2015, p. 86). Some provinces, however, have relatively inexpensive electricity, which they have used not only to attract energy-intensive industries, but also to encourage multiple end uses for electricity; accordingly, their share of industrial demand is relatively high as is their per capita residential consumption figure. Quebec is a prime example. The industrial share is 43%, which is above the national average, but per capita residential consumption is also quite high at 7,718 kWh/person (Statistics Canada, 2015). Alternatively, other provinces make more extensive use of natural gas, particularly for heating, and their share of residential demand is thus relatively low and their per capita residential consumption figure is also quite low. In Alberta, the share of total residential electricity consumption is 17% and the per capita residential consumption is 2,622 kWh/person (Statistics Canada, 2015).

Canada's energy systems and associated energy policies are dominated by provincial or territorial resources and governance structures. (The terms of the Canadian Constitution provide provinces with lead authority regarding "development, conservation and management of sites and facilities in the province for the generation and production of electrical energy" [Section 92A(1)].) Of course, outside entities exert influence (nationally and internationally), but the province or territory serves as the locus of decision making.

Turning to the United States, one can also review the supply, demand, and governance characteristics in a country that is the world's second-largest generator and user of electricity, as well as producer of greenhouse gas emissions (IEA, 2015, pp. 27, 48–57). In terms of supply, in 2015 coal and natural gas each contributed 33% to the country's electricity supply.

Other fuels that made at least a 5% contribution were nuclear power (20%), hydropower (6%), and wind (5%) (U.S. Energy Information Administration [EIA], 2016d). Again, there are important regional variations; for example, coal is particularly important in places like Kentucky and West Virginia whereas natural gas plays a leading role in states such as Florida and California (EIA, 2016c).

On the demand side, in 2014 the shares were as follows: residential, 37%; commercial, 36%; and industrial 27% (EIA, 2016b). In some jurisdictions, particularly in the South, prices are relatively low, which attracts industrial activity. Louisiana and Washington have the lowest industrial electricity prices—under five cents per kilowatt hour—as compared with more than 15 cents in Alaska and Hawaii (EIA, 2016a).

Finally, while state regulation is important in the United States (in the form of public utility commissions) and the federal government also has a regulatory role, particularly when international activities are involved, it is also important to note the role of independent system operators and regional transmission organizations. These groups include reliability councils, which comprise multi-stakeholders who work to improve the reliability of the bulk power system and exercise important influence in the development of U.S. electricity grids.

U.S.-Canadian Electricity Exchanges to Date

Canada and the United States have had electricity interchanges for more than a century. Indeed, this transnational electricity interconnection was the first of its kind in the world (Bahar and Sauvage, 2013, p. 44). During the past hundred years or so, they have grown in number and capacity. Currently they share more than three dozen major transmission interconnections. Every Canadian province that shares a land border with the United States has at least one such connection; Ontario has the most (17) and Quebec has the one with the highest voltage (765 kilovolts [kV]) (Canadian Electricity Association [CEA], 2013, p. 6). In 2014, Canada's National Energy Board reported that 58,555 gigawatt hours (GWh) of electricity was exported from Canada to the United States, at a value of C$2.930 billion, and 12,808 GWh was imported, at a value of C$604 million (National Energy Board, 2015a). The largest exchanges were as follows:

Quebec to Vermont	10,872 GWh
Quebec to New York	9,167 GWh
Washington to British Columbia	8,943 GWh
Manitoba to Minnesota/North Dakota	8,567 GWh

Ontario to New York	7,692 GWh
Ontario to Michigan	6,077 GWh
British Columbia to California	5,157 GWh
Quebec to Maine	2,293 GWh
New Brunswick to Maine	2,065 GWh

Source: National Energy Board (2015b, 2015c).

Calls for Greater U.S.-Canadian Electricity Exchanges

Currently, the discussion about greater interconnections between the two countries is receiving attention.[2] Consideration of international electricity linkages is emerging from both Canada and the United States.

On the Canadian side of the border, examples of such calls for greater electricity cooperation include McLaughlin and Page (2010); Goodman (2010), who calls for a "Canada-US Energy Trade Council" to provide a more formal mechanism to discuss North American energy security; the Canadian Electricity Association (2013, 2016); Burn (2014), who advocates for a "North American Framework on Energy and the Environment"; and Demerse (2016). On the U.S. side, voices include Biette and Finn (2013), who argue that "Canada and the United States should work together to upgrade and replace our aging transmission lines while also modifying our grid to take advantage of the new ways in which we produce our electricity" (p. 3). Ek and Fergusson (2014) note some of the potential benefits for the United States:

> Canadian sources of renewable power may have the potential to reduce the need to build new, long-distance transmission projects (which can take up to a decade or more to permit and construct) in the United States. For example, imports of hydropower from Québec into New England and New York, using new but relatively short power lines, have been suggested by the transmission system authorities in those regions as an alternative to building power lines to Midwestern wind farms. (p. 52)

And former U.S. energy secretary Steven Chu argues that the two countries "should work together on hydroelectric and wind energy and boost transmission infrastructure between the two countries" (Canadian Business, 2013).

Indeed, turning to the arguments that are advanced more generally regardless of which side of the border they come from—economics is often at the heart of the assertions. Baker, Sklokin, Coad, and Crawford (2011), for instance, maintain that "the market is of significant importance to both countries, with many economic benefits achieved due to this trade market" (p. 19). Explicitly noting price differentials in electricity across parts of the U.S.-Canadian border, the Energy Policy Institute of Canada (2012) observes that "this differential suggests there is significant potential economic benefit from increased electricity trade between provinces—in addition to the opportunity to increase exports to the American market" (p. 129). Antweiler (2014) extends that analysis, concluding that reciprocal "load smoothing provides an economically significant rationale for integrating North America's fragmented interconnections into a continental 'supergrid' " (p. 1).

Security is also often talked about—that is, how greater interconnections could serve to enhance reliability, affordability, defensibility, and whatever other characteristics the particular proponent associates with the term "security." For the United States, Canada is seen as a "valued and trusted neighbor to the north" (Blanchard & Jacobson, 2011–2012, p. 237), and thus one with whom it is (usually) acceptable to share an energy future. Terry (2012) also talks about "security reliability" in a continental sense, noting that, although greater interconnections can give rise to increased exposure (to terrorists, etc.), "North American energy security will be better served by a policy of energy interdependence" (p. 51).

Environmental gains are another potential benefit. Amor, Pineau, Gaudreault, and Samson (2011) made a detailed investigation into how increased electricity exchanges among those states and provinces in the northeastern part of the continent reduce net greenhouse gas emissions, with a particular emphasis on the potential offered by increased hydropower exports from Québec. Using real data from 2006 to 2008, they conclude that the net result was 20.6 megatonnes (Mt) of avoided emissions over this three-year period, which corresponds with more than 8% of Québec's annual emissions. They argue that adding life cycle emissions to the calculation increases reductions by 35%, to 27.9 Mt.

There is also the prospect of liberating greater use of renewables. Bahar and Sauvage (2013) argue that

> cross-border trade in electricity can thus enable countries to gain access to more flexible power plants (both conventional and renewable such as hydropower, geothermal, and biomass) located in a wider geographical area, which can then reduce the costs of balancing power stemming from increasing [renewable energy] penetration. To the extent that it does help dampen variability,

> increased trade could therefore allow greater penetration of intermittent renewable-energy power plants. (p. 7)

Less specifically, increased interactions on electricity issues across the border could support a range of other activities that would, in turn, generate their own benefits. As Globerman (2012) argues, more explicit efforts at bilateral cooperation in the area of scientific and technological innovation could help both countries substantially reduce "the use of carbon-based fuels in favor of renewable and greener sources of energy" (p. 475). It is important to think about how greater interconnections in one area could spawn innovation and increase productivity more broadly.

Barriers to Greater U.S.-Canadian Electricity Exchanges

The literature on international energy governance in general and U.S.-Canadian electricity relations in particular highlight the fact that it is not always easy to pursue international cooperative arrangement on energy issues. To set the context, Hughes and Lipscy (2013) highlight the basic building blocks required to analyze the "politics of energy," namely, "the interests of policy makers, business, and other socioeconomic actors; the role of domestic institutions in aggregating interests; and the goals and effectiveness of cooperation" (p. 458). They also argue that there are important differences across various fuel types. With energy being such a crucial driver of societal (including economic) well-being, world leaders often aim to minimize their need to secure energy resources through international relations.

Regarding U.S.-Canadian energy relations, Hale (2012) sets the broader context. He notes that the relationship is characterized by a multitude of connections (not only intergovernmental, but transnational more generally) and they are also nested within broader international policy streams. He notes that there are three dimensions to these transborder linkages: political-strategic, trade-commercial, and psychological-cultural dimensions. Moreover, there are many different actors at work: "extensive (if asymmetrical) and overlapping jurisdictions of state and provincial governments on energy and environmental issues add yet another dimension, reflected in both the institutionalization of cross-border regional networks and the efforts of provincial governments to project their interests and influence in the United States" (Hale, 2012, p. 305). In sum, it makes for a complex policy (and political) environment.

Gattinger (2012) is another observer who has focused on the U.S.-Canadian relationship in terms of energy. She draws attention to four key dimensions of energy policy making and reflects upon them in light of Canadian and U.S. government efforts to advance policy both domestically and bilaterally. These dimensions are markets, environment, security, and social acceptability. To meet joint needs, attention must be paid to all four.

Notwithstanding these kinds of challenges, there have been cooperative arrangements on electricity for more than a century. Moreover, formal institutional roots extend back decades. As noted by Terry (2012):

> A non-governmental organization known as the North American Electrical Reliability Council (NERC) was originally formed in 1968 to manage the overlapping electrical grids in North America. The U.S. National Energy Policy Act of 2005 called for the creation of a self-regulating Electric Reliability Organization, for which the NERC was ideally suited. Consequently, the Council was renamed the North American Electrical Reliability Corporation in 2006. The corporation has public and private representatives from the United States, Canada, and Mexico that consider continental issues. (p. 12)

Ek and Fergusson (2014) provide additional background on the NERC.

As noted earlier, free trade agreements during the past 30 years have also served as catalysts for greater transborder cooperation on electricity issues. McKinney (2008) notes that

> the interdependencies between the United States and Canadian energy industries have developed because of economic forces and policy decisions. Integration was certainly fostered by the domestic deregulation of the American and Canadian energy industries. The U.S.-Canadian free trade agreement, and its successor NAFTA, have also had some effect upon the integration of the energy industries. These agreements removed both tariff and non-tariff barriers to trade in energy products. (p. 8)

NAFTA spurred other trilateral initiatives, including the North American Energy Working Group within the Security and Prosperity Partnership. Additionally, there have been bilateral efforts. The Clean Energy Dialogue between Canada and the United States has been active since 2009 and has had bilateral electricity relations as part of its broader agenda. The good will emanating from the 2016 meeting among the leaders of Canada, Mexico, and the United States, which resulted in a commitment to develop a "North American Climate, Clean Energy, and Environment

Partnership," means that the continental level could also be a catalyst for activity going forward (Government of Canada, 2016).

THREE PROJECTS

Against this background, I take a deeper dive into the issue by looking at three projects in particular. I do not intend to suggest that there are no others worthy of mention. Some recently completed projects may offer important insight, particularly those that take innovative approaches to infrastructure. The recently completed Montana-Alberta Tie Line (operational as of 2013), a privately financed transmission line that is also Alberta's first electricity connection with the United States is a case in point (see, for example, Doucet, Kleit, & Firkirdanis, 2013). Others are in relatively early stages of development and therefore have less history upon which to reflect. One such example would be a proposal to lay a transmission line on the floor of Lake Erie to link Ontario and Pennsylvania, thus connecting Ontario's IESO system and this part of the U.S. PJM system. Filings for this 1,000 megawatt (MW)/US$1 billion project, named the Lake Erie Connector project, were made to regulators in both Canada and the United States in 2015 (Blackwell, 2015; see also National Energy Board, 2016a).[3] Other international projects are relatively small—the Soule River Hydroelectric Project (Alaska-British Columbia) is a case in point (CEA, 2016, p. 8).

In this chapter, I focus on three that occupy a middle ground between those done and those on the drawing board, namely, three projects in which proponents have plans and/or activities, opponents have concerns, regulators and others are reviewing, and the politics is most active.

Manitoba-Minnesota

A proposed electricity linkage between Manitoba and Minnesota consists of projects on both sides of the U.S.-Canadian border. North of the border, the so-called Manitoba-Minnesota Transmission Project would be 150 kilometers of a new 500 kV AC transmission line, running from the Dorsey Converter Station located near Rosser, northwest of Winnipeg, and running through southeastern Manitoba. The project would include upgrades to substations at Dorsey, Riel, and Glenboro. This project is being led by Manitoba Hydro. An environmental impact statement on this preferred route was completed and submitted to the provincial regulator in September 2015. Public hearings are scheduled to be part of the subsequent review process (Manitoba Clean Environment Commission, 2016). The in-service date for this C$350 million project is projected to be mid-2020. (For information about the project, see Manitoba Hydro, 2015; and Manitoba Wildlands, 2015. More general reflections on Manitoba's resources can be found in Molinski, Yebra, & Gole, 2012; and Turanli & Mazur, 2015.)

South of the border, the so-called Great Northern Transmission Line involves a 400 kilometer line, running from the Minnesota-Manitoba border to the Blackberry 500 kV substation near Grand Rapids, Minnesota; upgrades to the Blackberry substation would occur as well. The project is being led by Minnesota Power. The project was approved by the Minnesota Public Utilities Commission (MPUC) after a series of consultations. A presidential permit from the U.S. Department of Energy is also required for the international border crossing, and the decision was expected to be forthcoming in September 2016. (For information about the project, see Minnesota Power, 2016a; and Whieldon, 2015.)

The interconnection would be part of the MidWest Independent System Operator system and would help to stabilize the grid. It would also be the facilitator of a power purchase agreement that was reached between Manitoba Hydro and Minnesota Power in 2012. That agreement stipulated that Minnesota Power would purchase 250 MW of electricity from Manitoba Hydro for a period of 15 years beginning in 2020.

There are motivations for this project on both sides of the border. For Manitoba, it is an opportunity to exploit its hydropower resources for export, thus potentially keeping its provincial rates lower than would otherwise be the case, let alone generating greater returns for its shareholders through greater access to more export markets. For Minnesota Power, it is not only a firm supply of electricity in the face of expected rising demand, but it is also a decarbonizing strategy. Minnesota Power's fleet of power stations is dominated by thermal power (1,508 MW of 2,147 MW, or 70%), the vast majority of which is from coal (Minnesota Power, 2016b). The new supply not only reduces their average carbon intensity, but the agreement also allows for the potential to "store" wind during high production periods or low demand periods. Manitoba Hydro has agreed to take wind power and gear back its hydropower production during such times. And, more generally, increased diversification of supply can advance energy system reliability (see, for example, Marketwatch, 2015).

While Minnesota Power and Manitoba Hydro are in favor of the project, there is much opposition at both local and regional levels. Locally, on both sides of the border there are those who oppose particular routes being investigated. A group of residents of the Rural Municipality of Tache in Manitoba, for instance, say they were not "consulted properly about the route, which will cut through their properties . . . and they're concerned about the health effects, the impact in wildlife and their future property value" (Ladhani, 2014). Property owners on the U.S. side have also expressed concern (see Myers, 2014). Regionally, there are those who wonder whether a project of this scale is really needed. On the Manitoba side, some fear the "lock-in" that it will create—that is, that it will oblige the province to a large-scale, hydropower-intensive energy future, which will also drive, they argue, much of the province's economic strategy (see Pickford, 2014). And notwithstanding Manitoba's negotiations with, and involvement of, First Nations groups, not all such groups are engaged fully (Jossi, 2015). Among these kinds of protests south of the border, a citizen group entitled Residents and Ratepayers Against Not-so-Great Northern Transmission said the scope of the project "far exceeds local power needs, and could require more transmission line construction elsewhere to carry Canadian hydropower to Wisconsin or other states" (Shaffer, 2015).

Quebec-New York/Vermont

The second of the three projects I review is considered, by many, to be made up of two distinct entities. Because, however, these two projects are related by the fact that they share a common geographic core or spine, as well as a common proponent, I investigate them together.

The project's core or spine is a line that extends from the Canadian province of Quebec down to and across the length of Lake Champlain, which provides part of the border between the states of New York and Vermont. From there, the two projects split, with a southerly part (the Champlain Hudson Power Express [CHPE]) traveling down to New York City and an easterly part (the New England Clean Power Link [CPL]) making its way to a substation in Ludlow, Vermont, to deliver power to the New England grid.

The CHPE is a US$2.2 billion project that is expected to deliver 1,000 MW of power to the high-demand and supply-constrained New York City area. Its developer, Transmission Developers Inc. backed by the Blackstone Group, plans for the project to be in service by the fall of 2017. With approval from the U.S. Army Corps of Engineers received in early 2015, all necessary approvals were in place (see, generally, Transmission Developers Inc., 2016).

Proponents tout the project's many potential benefits. It would provide power to a congested area—one that has a heavy load and is located at the end of the grid—and bring with that power not only improved reliability (which has both social and economic benefits) but also financial advantages in terms of relieving some of the upward pressure on electricity prices in New York (London Economics International, 2012). Moreover, much of the route is being submerged underwater in Lake Champlain and the Hudson River and, elsewhere, buried underground, which addresses some of the visual aesthetic challenges that are often raised by local landowners and others in the case of transmission line siting. And it also has some local supporters who favor the displacement of fossil fuels within their communities or at least see this as a means to stop or to delay the construction of additional such facilities (e.g., Trapasso, 2014). New York State meets a significant share of its electricity needs with fossil fuel-powered generators, particularly during high demand periods. In 2015, across the state as a whole, 45% of the state's electricity generation came from gas, oil, gas and oil, or coal-powered facilities. Downstate the equivalent figure was 69% (NYISO, 2016, p. 24). Displacement of some of this could improve air quality on local, regional, and global scales. Finally, some believe that, in contrast with the approach of other developers, the proponent has generally had an open and engaged relationship with affected communities.

But there are critics. Initially, there were concerns that rate payers would be stuck with the cost of the project and would not necessarily benefit, which catalyzed the New York utility Con Edison to oppose the project during its early stages. While this has been mitigated to a significant extent, there are still those along the route who do not appreciate the fact that the transmission line is traveling through their communities but they are not able to access it for power (Harris, 2013). Among others, New York state–based power generators working together under the umbrella of the Independent Power Producers of New York are quick to highlight the fact that New York jobs may be sacrificed for the sake of foreign imports (Hirsch, 2014). Indeed, critics claim that there is already surplus generating capacity in upstate New York that will effectively be further shut out by the CHPE (Lungariello, 2014). In any case, some wonder whether the total cost will not actually surpass the present estimate, given previous experience with capital-intensive projects. If it does, they further wonder who will end up paying the bill. (For perspectives on the evolving Hydro Quebec position on the project, see, for instance, Hydro Quebec, 2016a; Waldman, 2015.)

There are other concerns, such as the potential for significant damage to ecological resources and social heritage. With respect to the former, if construction or operation of the new high-voltage transmission line interferes with the operation of the high-pressure gas lines already at the bottom of the Hudson River, environmental damage could result. And with respect to the latter, historical sites of importance in New York State could similarly be disrupted (Hirsch, 2014).

In addition to the CHPE, the New England CPL is also a 1,000 MW transmission line that runs 80 kilometers across the southern part of Vermont. It is a US$1.2 billion project, and it is also being developed by Transmission Developers Inc., and similar kinds of approval must be secured. The state-level public service board (in this case, the Vermont Public Service Board) and the U.S. Army Corps of Engineers have successfully completed a review and the decision regarding the presidential permit was expected in September 2016. Similar kinds of debates have also arisen, with supporters touting improved reliability through resource diversification, the cost savings for Vermont customers of these imports (Esperacion & Lustig, 2014), and the clean energy benefits (more than one-half of the electricity generation within New England in 2015 was fossil fuel-sourced [ISO New England, 2016]). Opponents, alternatively, have queried the cost savings and highlighted the relative dearth of local economic opportunities and the potential gravity of the environmental and social impacts. (See, for instance, Newsham, 2015. For more about the project, see TDI New England, 2016.)

Quebec-New Hampshire

The Northern Pass Transmission Project consists of a 300-kilometer transmission line that would travel from the Quebec-New Hampshire border to Deerfield, New Hampshire, connecting the New England electricity system (which is managed by the New England Independent System Operator) with the Quebec one (which is managed by Hydro Quebec). The line would have both a direct current (DC) component and an alternating current (AC) component and would have the capacity to carry 1,090 MW of electricity. As of August 2016, the U.S. regulatory approvals process had been characterized by a series of delays. The project had received approval from the New England Independent System Operator to connect to the regional grid, yet the U.S. Department of Energy had yet to finalize its environmental review. At that time, the proponent's representatives were hoping for an in-service date of 2019 for this US$1.4 billion project. (For more about the project, see Adams, Maheu, & McDougal, 2014; Northern Pass, 2016.)

Supporters point to a variety of benefits that would accrue from its construction and deployment. Economically, it would lessen New England's reliance upon natural gas for power generation; the price of natural gas can be quite volatile, for it is not only affected by developments in electricity markets, but given its important direct role in heating, cold spells can have a dramatic impact upon demand patterns and thus prices. Given that New England has some of the most expensive electricity rates in the 48 states of the continental United States (EIA, 2016a), anything that can potentially reduce the pressure upon prices can be viewed positively. This, in turn, can also stimulate other economic activity (Northern Pass, 2016). For Quebec, meanwhile, the prospects of even more export revenues in addition to, for instance, the CDN$1.6 billion generated in 2015 are appealing (Hydro Quebec, 2016b).

Environmentally, New England's power system makes extensive use of fossil fuels. In 2015, 49% of generation was from natural gas and 4% from coal (ISO New England, 2016). Thus, carbon dioxide emissions arose from one-half of the region's electricity generation. By accessing Quebec's relatively low-carbon hydropower resources, the Northern Pass transmission line has the potential to reduce net greenhouse gas emissions.

But opponents, especially those based in New Hampshire, have identified a number of problems with the proposed Northern Pass Transmission Project. Economically, it is argued that even if the modest economic benefits are forthcoming, many of them will accrue to the broader regional electricity market, particularly to those living and working in Massachusetts, rather than those in New Hampshire who, the argument continues, would bear the brunt of the costs. Moreover, the employment benefits touted by some proponents could well be minimal (Adams et al., 2014).

There are also many concerns about the route of the transmission line, particularly its impact through northern New Hampshire's White Mountain National Forest. A new plan has been researched, which would bury part of the line and re-route it slightly, but some concern still remains. Indeed, after the U.S. Department of Energy released a scoping report on the project, more than 7,500 comments were received in response. Concerns included: that alternatives had not been sufficiently examined (including the upgrading of existing interconnectors between New England and Canada), that economic impacts would not be positive (in addition to the points made here, there was broader concern about the impact on the tourism sector), and that there was no particular need for this project (as far as New Hampshire's energy needs were concerned) (USDoE, 2014). In a general sense, it was felt that New Hampshire's treasured rural way of life would be threatened. (For the range of such opposition perspectives, see Adams et al., 2014; Brooks, 2016; Sanders, 2015.)

MOVING FORWARD

This section sets out some suggestions for possible next steps. I propose four steps, and each subsequent step is to some extent dependent upon the successful completion of the previous one.

First, there should be better assessment of these kinds of international transmission projects. To date, most such projects have suffered from incomplete or inadequate assessment approaches. Specifically, the following three areas should be given greater attention:

a. A broad swath of factors should be taken into consideration; i.e., a variety of environmental and social impacts. Any immediate inability to monetize particular considerations should not dissuade analysts from investigating or including them in the analysis.
b. Multiple projects are being considered, but each is usually investigated in isolation. They should be examined collectively, so that more direct comparisons can be made and the ways in which each potentially affects the other can be revealed.
c. Attention to a number of major transmission projects should not divert attention from smaller projects that may achieve the same goal. Indeed, greater consideration of how local approaches (conservation, distributed generation, etc.) could make contributions must be made. Any decision should not necessarily require an either-or approach; i.e., a potentially important direction could be a plan that recognized how larger-scale grid developments could co-exist with distributed energy projects. Indeed, this would provide important learning and could potentially set precedents.

Second, after a rigorous and comprehensive assessment is completed and a particular project (or collection of projects, perhaps coupled with programs) is determined to be worthwhile, careful attention should be paid to the resulting distribution of related benefits and costs. A good assessment process would have considered this in any case, but I highlight it on its own because there is the opportunity to draw upon analogous multiactor issues in politics to learn lessons about ways in which strategies for distributive justice can be developed. Efforts to advance transborder projects to date have revealed that attention to the manner in which these same projects create winners and losers is critical to secure social acceptance.

Third, attention should be paid to the ways in which actors across scales can be involved in the projects. Studies into multilevel governance and collaborative governance could be used to make suggestions on how to create ways for meaningful participation. Sometimes individual jurisdictions (e.g., states and provinces) have their own procedures that may or may not approach accepted gold standards, but when there is a proliferation of actors across territories (i.e., multiple states and/or provinces) and across scales (i.e., municipal, state/provincial, regional, and national levels), new mechanisms may well be needed.

Finally, after these initial three steps have been completed, there should be reflection upon these same three steps and a thorough evaluation of their particular strengths and weaknesses to improve the processes and to transmit learnings to other projects. This class of opportunity is one that is widespread, worldwide.

These suggestions are not entirely new or original—Ek and Fergusson (2014), for example, note that many are calling for broader "master plans" of transmission, "on a wide geographic scope to facilitate renewable energy development and other purposes" (p. 53). Particular institutional fora, such as the New England Governors and Eastern Canadian Premiers Conference (Adams et al., 2014) and NERC (Ek & Fergusson, 2014), have also been identified as being appropriate to play a leadership role in advancing such ideas. Existing RTOs and ISOs already have some experience in this regard, and sets of recommendations from a variety of stakeholders continue to emerge (e.g., CEA, 2016). Additionally, these issues are all active and in play, with endogenous and exogenous developments having impact on project outcomes. For instance, the August 2015 U.S. decision on how to treat Canadian electricity under the terms of the Clean Power Plan, which recommended counting imports from nonemitting sources towards their targets if the sources were developed after 2012, will influence all of the case studies examined in this chapter (National Energy Board, 2016b; see also, Aarons & Vine, 2015). Thus, I do not mean necessarily to challenge any proposals already advanced nor to ignore broader developments; instead, I suggest that political scientists, policy analysts, and others can contribute to efforts by bringing their particular talents to bear. Contributing to policy debates in this way would enrich discussions and potentially lead to more sustainable outcomes that could be achieved more quickly.

CONCLUSION

The purpose of this chapter was to investigate the prospects for increased electricity transmission connections between Canada and the United States. After the general debate was reviewed, the focus turned to three projects in particular along the U.S.-Canadian border: connections between Manitoba and Minnesota, Quebec and NewYork/Vermont, and

Quebec and New Hampshire. For each, the factors encouraging and discouraging their respective development were highlighted. This was followed by suggestions on how to move the agenda forward, with a focus on a more rigorous and holistic assessment, a recognition of the need to involve and to treat justly many actors across multiple scales, and the value of self-reflection across the entire process. Such transborder projects show promise for advancing energy sustainability. Rigorous, transparent, participatory, and evidence-based investigation could help to reveal whether such promise can actually be realized.

ACKNOWLEDGMENTS

This chapter benefitted greatly from discussions the author had with Andrew Adams, Lyne Maheu, and Kieran McDougal as part of the 2013–2014 Centre for International Governance Innovation Junior Fellowship Programme. The author thanks them for their insights and ideas. An earlier version of this chapter was presented at the 24th World Congress of Political Science hosted by the International Political Science Association in Montreal, QC, on July 20, 2014, on a panel entitled, The Politics of Energy and Pollution on the Canada-U.S. Border. The author would like to thank the participants for their comments, particularly the discussant, Stephen Bird. The author would also like to thank Andrea Bale for research assistance. The author acknowledges, however, that he is solely responsible for the content of this chapter.

NOTES

1. For support, see, for instance, the world maps showing world energy trade in Grubler et al. (2012, pp. 128–129); oil dominates.
2. Intra-Canada exchanges of electricity are also getting attention (e.g., Nathwani, 2013; Pineau, 2012), at a smaller scale (e.g., Quebec-Ontario, see Pineau & Winfield, 2014), and at a larger scale (e.g., Canadian Academy of Engineering, 2009). This is within a broader political landscape that is considering a possible Canadian energy strategy, the likes of which have not been seen for at least three decades (Council of the Federation, 2015).
3. Another example is the proposed Atlantic Link—an underwater cable between New Brunswick and Boston (Alberstat, 2015).

REFERENCES

Aarons, K., & Vine, D. (2015). *Canadian hydropower and the Clean Power Plan*. Arlington, VA: Center for Climate and Energy Solutions.

Adams, A., Maheu, L., & McDougal, K. (2014). *A call for bilateral energy governance: Examining the Northern Pass project*. Waterloo, ON: The Centre for International Governance Innovation.

Alberstat, J. (2015, November 16). Emera plans 2nd subsea cable. *The Chronicle Herald (Halifax)*. Retrieved from http://thechronicleherald.ca/business/1322579-emera-plans-2nd-subsea-cable

Amor, M. B., Pineau, P.-O., Gaudreault, C., & Samson, R. (2011). Electricity trade and GHG emissions: Assessment of Quebec's hydropower in the Northeastern American market (2006–2008). *Energy Policy*, *39*, 1711–1721.

Antweiler, W. (2014, May 9). *Cross-border trade in electricity*. Vancouver, BC: Sauder School of Business, preliminary version.

Bahar, H., & Sauvage, J. (2013). *Cross-border trade in electricity and the development of renewables-based electric power: Lessons from Europe* (Trade and Environment Working Papers, no. 12). Paris, France: OECD.

Baker, B., Sklokin, I., Coad, L., & Crawford, T. (2011). *Canada's electricity infrastructure: Building a case for investment*. Ottawa, ON: The Conference Board of Canada.

Biette, D., & Finn, A. (2013). *Changing energy: Canada and the United States* [Policy brief]. Washington, DC: Wilson Center.

Blackwell, R. (2015, May 31). Lake Erie cross-border power-line project reaches milestone. *The Globe and Mail (Toronto)*. Retrieved from http://www.theglobeandmail.com/report-on-business/industry-news/energy-and-resources/lake-erie-connector-cross-border-power-line-project-reaches-milestone/article24715446/

Blanchard, J., & Jacobson, D. (2011–12). The future of the Canada-United States energy relationship. *Canada-United States Law Journal*, *36*, 235–242.

Brooks, D. (2016, January 8). What does the quick approval of a Vermont power line say about Northern Pass? *Concord Monitor*. Retrieved from http://www.concordmonitor.com/Archive/2016/01/vermont Electricity-cm-010816

Burn, P. (2014). It's time for a NAFTA deal on energy. *iPolitics*. Retrieved from http://www.ipolitics.ca/2014/02/07/its-time-for-a-nafta-deal-on-energy-2/

Canadian Academy of Engineering. (2009). *Report of the Canada power grid task force*. Ottawa, ON: Author.

Canadian Business. (2013, November 22). Former Energy Secretary calls for more Canada-U.S. co-operation on renewables. Retrieved from http://www.canadianbusiness.com/business-news/former-energy-secretary-calls-for-more-canada-u-s-co-operation-on-renewables/

Canadian Electricity Association. (2013). *The integrated electric grid: Maximizing benefits in an evolving energy landscape.* Ottawa, ON: Author.

Canadian Electricity Association. (2016). *The North American grid: Powering cooperation on clean energy & the environment.* Ottawa, ON: Author.

Council of the Federation. (2015). *Canadian Energy strategy.* Ottawa, ON: Council of the Federation Secretariat.

Demerse, C. (2016). *Backgrounder: Priorities for Canada-U.S. collaboration on clean energy.* Vancouver, BC: Clean Energy Canada. Retrieved from http://cleanenergycanada.org/wp-content/uploads/2016/03/US-CAN-Clean-Energy-Media-Backgrounder-09032016.pdf

Doucet, J., Kleit, A., & Firkirdanis, S. (2013). Valuing electricity transmission: The case of Alberta. *Energy Economics, 36,* 396–404.

Ek, C., & Fergusson, I. F. (2014). *Canada-U.S. relations.* Washington, DC: Congressional Research Service.

Energy Policy Institute of Canada. (2012). *A Canadian energy strategy framework.* Calgary, AB: Author. Retrieved from http://www.canadasenergy.ca/wp-content/uploads/2012/08/Final-Document-Aug-1.pdf

Esperacion, K., & Lustig, M. (2014, December 9). TDI files in Vermont for approval of New England Clean Power Link. *SNL Financial.* Retrieved from https://www.snl.com/InteractiveX/article.aspx?CDID=A-30118434-12343&KPLT=4/

Gattinger, M. (2012). Canada-United States energy relations: Making a MESS of energy policy. *American Review of Canadian Studies, 42,* 460–473.

Globerman, S. (2012). Strengthening innovation through closer bilateral integration. *American Review of Canadian Studies, 42,* 474–481.

Goodman, R. J. (2010). *Power connections: Canadian electricity trade and foreign policy* (Energy report no. 1). Ottawa, ON: Canadian International Council.

Government of Canada (2016). *Leaders' statement on a North American climate, clean energy, and environment partnership.* Ottawa, ON: Government of Canada. Retrieved from http://pm.gc.ca/eng/news/2016/06/29/leaders-statement-north-american-climate-clean-energy-and-environment-partnership

Grubler, A., Johansson, T. B., Mundaca, L., Nakicenovic, N., Pachauri, S., Riahi, K., Rogner, H.-H., & Strupeit, L. (2012). Energy primer. In *Global energy assessment—Toward a sustainable future* (pp. 99–150). New York, NY: Cambridge University Press.

Hale, G. (2012). *So near yet so far: The public and hidden worlds of Canada-US relations*. Vancouver, BC: UBC Press.

Harris, S. (2013, April 19). NYS board approves Quebec-NYC underground power line. *North Country Public Radio*. Retrieved from http://www.northcountrypublicradio.org/news/story/21824/nys-board-approves-quebec-nyc-underground-power-line

Hirsch, Z. (2014, November 17). Quebec-NYC underwater power line nearing construction phase. *North Country Public Radio*. Retrieved from http://www.northcountrypublicradio.org/news/story/26647/20141117/quebec-nyc-underwater-power-line-nearing-construction-phase

Hufbauer, G. C., & Schott, J. J. (2005). *NAFTA revisited: Achievements and challenges*. Washington, DC: Institute for International Economics.

Hughes L., & Lipscy, P. Y. (2013). The politics of energy. *Annual Review of Political Science*, *16*(1), 449–469.

Hydro Quebec. (2016a). Hertel-New York interconnection. Retrieved from http://www.hydroquebec.com/transmission-construction-projects/hertel-new-york-interconnection/

Hydro Quebec. (2016b). Québec-New Hampshire interconnection. Retrieved from http://www.hydroquebec.com/transmission-construction-projects/quebec-new-hampshire-interconnection/

International Energy Agency. (2015). *Key world energy statistics 2015*. Paris, France: Author.

ISO New England. (2016). Resource mix. Retrieved from http://www.iso-ne.com/about/key-stats/resource-mix

Jossi, F. (2015, May 15). Manitoba tribe lobbies against Minnesota hydro proposal. *Midwest Energy News*. Retrieved from http://www.midwestenergynews.com/2015/05/15/manitoba-tribe-lobbies-against-minnesota-hydro-proposal/

Ladhani, R. (2014, June 18). Residents angry over proposed power line route. Retrieved from http://winnipeg.ctvnews.ca/residents-angry-over-proposed-power-line-route-1.1875391

London Economics International. (2012). *Analysis of the macroeconomic impacts of the proposed Champlain Hudson Power Express Project in New York*. Boston, MA: LEI.

Lungariello, M. (2014, October 20). Canada-to-NYC power line draws scrutiny. *Westchester County Business Journal*. Retrieved from http://westfaironline.com/westchester-county-business-journal_1/

Manitoba Clean Environment Commission. (2016). Manitoba-Minnesota Transmission Project. Winnipeg, MB: Manitoba Clean Environment Commission. Retrieved from http://www.cecmanitoba.ca/hearings/index.cfm?hearingid=43#1

Manitoba Hydro. (2015). Manitoba-Minnesota transmission project. Retrieved from https://www.hydro.mb.ca/projects/mb_mn_transmission/index.shtml

Manitoba Wildlands. (2015). Manitoba Hydro projects: Manitoba Minnesota transmission project. Retrieved from http://manitobawildlands.org/develop_future_minnesota.htm

Marketwatch. (2015, May 15). Great Northern transmission line needed: MPUC [Press release]. Retrieved from http://www.marketwatch.com/story/great-northern-transmission-line-needed-mpuc-2015-05-15

McKinney, J. A. (2008). United States-Canada energy interdependencies. *Southern Journal of Canadian Studies*, 2, 2–10.

McLaughlin, D., & Page, B. (2010). The Canada-US trade and energy relationship. *Policy Options*. Retrieved from http://policyoptions.irpp.org/magazines/g8g20/the-canada-us-trade-and-energy-relationship/

Minnesota Power. (2016a). Delivering clean energy to Minnesota. Retrieved from http://www.greatnortherntransmissionline.com/

Minnesota Power. (2016b). Mix of fuels. Retrieved from http://www.mnpower.com/Company/Generation

Molinski, T., Yebra, T., & Gole, A. M. (2012). Using renewable energy sources in the Province of Manitoba. *International Conference on Renewable Energies and Power Quality*. Santiago de Compostela, Spain. Retrieved from http://www.icrepq.com/icrepq'12/803-yebra.pdf

Myers, J. (2014, April 17). New 220-mile Minnesota powerline would bring power from Manitoba. Retrieved from http://www.twincities.com/localnews/ci_25585045/new-220-mile-minnesota-powerline-would-bring-power

Nathwani, J. (2013). Beyond Keystone: Canada's clean electricity. *Policy Options*. Retrieved from http://policyoptions.irpp.org/magazines/nudge/nathwani/

National Energy Board. (2015a). Exports and imports of electricity. Calgary, AB: Author. Retrieved from https://apps.neb-one.gc.ca/CommodityStatistics/ViewReport.aspx

National Energy Board. (2015b). Export sales summary report. Calgary, AB: Author. Retrieved from https://apps.neb-one.gc.ca/CommodityStatistics/ViewReport.aspx

National Energy Board. (2015c). Import purchases summary report. Calgary, AB: Author. Retrieved from https://apps.neb-one.gc.ca/CommodityStatistics/ViewReport.aspx

National Energy Board. (2016a). ITC Lake Erie Connector LLC–Lake Erie Connector Project. Calgary, AB: Author. Retrieved from http://www.neb-one.gc.ca/pplctnflng/mjrpp/lkrcnnctr/index-eng.html#s2

National Energy Board. (2016b). Market snapshot: Electricity from Canadian non-emitting sources qualify under the U.S. EPA's final Clean Power Plan. Calgary, AB: Author. Retrieved from http://www.neb-one.gc.ca/nrg/ntgrtd/mrkt/snpsht/2015/08-02lctrct-eng.html?utm_source=All+Media&utm_campaign=05f48021ae-2016_06_28_3_Amigos_Reaction_CanCORE&utm_medium=email&utm_term=0_135bfb50a9-05f48021ae-347653925

Natural Resources Canada. (2015). *Energy fact book, 2015–2016*. Ottawa, ON: Author.

Newsham, J. (2015, June 4). Canadian power line project for New England advances. *Boston Globe*. Retrieved from https://www.bostonglobe.com/business/2015/06/04/canadian-power-line-project-advances/yh8YxapWGFoPByvEPJsDzO/story.html

Northern Pass. (2016). Project overview. Retrieved from http://www.northernpass.us/project-overview.htm

NYISO. (2016). *Power trends 2016: The changing energy landscape*. Rensselaer, NY: The New York Independent System Operator, Inc.

Pickford, A. (2014). *Pipe, dam and electricity dreams: Burdening Manitoba's next generation*. Winnipeg, MB: Frontier Centre for Public Policy.

Pineau, P.-O. (2012). Integrating electricity sectors in Canada: Good for the environment and for the economy. Montreal, QC: The Federal Idea. Retrieved from http://ideefederale.ca/documents/Electricity_ang.pdf

Pineau, P.-O., & Winfield, M. (2014, June 11). Ontario, Quebec, electricity and climate change: Time for a new relationship? Retrieved from http://marksw.blog.yorku.ca/2014/06/11/ontario-quebec-electricity-and-climate-change-time-for-a-new-relationship/

Sanders, B. (2015, February 20). Will N. H. really benefit from major energy projects? *New Hampshire Business Review*, *37*(4). Retrieved from http://www.nhbr.com/February-20-2015/Will-NH-really-benefit-from-major-energy-projects/

Shaffer, D. (2015, May 14). Regulators accept the need for big northern Minnesota transmission line. *Star Tribune (Minneapolis)*. Retrieved from http://www.startribune.com/regulators-accept-need-for-big-northern-minnesota-transmission-line/303817961/

Statistics Canada. (2015). Statistical tables. Retrieved from http://www.statcan.gc.ca/pub/57-003-x/2014002/tablesectlist-listetableauxsect-eng.htm

TDI New England. (2016). New England clean power link: Project development portal. Retrieved from http://www.necplink.com/index.php

Terry, A. (2012). Policy and practice in North American energy security. *International Affairs Review*, *20*(3), 52–70.

Transmission Developers Inc. (2016). Champlain Hudson Power Express Project: Project development portal. Retrieved from http://www.chpexpress.com

Trapasso, C. (2014, February 13). Plans to build $2 billion transmission line from Canada to Queens moving along. *New York Daily News*. Retrieved from http://www.nydailynews.com/new-york/queens/canadian-hydroelectric-power-astoria-article-1.1612074

Turanli, H., & Mazur, R. (2015). Manitoba Hydro's plans to meet provincial electricity demands and export opportunities. *IEEE Canadian Review*, *73*, 36–40.

UN Conference on Trade and Development. (2015). *Key statistics and trends in international trade 2015*. Geneva: Author.

U.S. Department of Energy. (2014, March 12). *The Northern Pass Transmission Line Project environmental impact statement (DOE/EIS-0463), scoping report*. Washington, DC: Author.

U.S. Energy Information Administration. (2016a). Electric power monthly. Washington, DC: Author. Retrieved from https://www.eia.gov/electricity/monthly/epm_table_grapher.cfm?t=epmt_5_6_a

U.S. Energy Information Administration. (2016b). Electricity: Data, summary. Washington, DC: Author. Retrieved from http://www.eia.gov/electricity/data.cfm

U.S. Energy Information Administration. (2016c). Electricity: Detailed state data. Washington, DC: Author. Retrieved from http://www.eia.gov/electricity/data/state/

U.S. Energy Information Administration. (2016d). Energy in brief: How much U.S. electricity is generated from renewable energy. Washington, DC: Energy Information Administration. Retrieved from http://www.eia.gov/energy_in_brief/article/renewable_electricity.cfm

Waldman, S. (2015, April 7). Hudson River power line project faces challenges. *Capital (New York)*. Retrieved from http://www.capitalnewyork.com/article/albany/2015/04/8565561/hudson-river-power-line-project-faces-challenges

Whieldon, E. (2015, May 19). Transmission line developer, DOE pilot more open siting strategy. *SNL Financial*. Retrieved from https://www.snl.com/InteractiveX/Article.aspx?cdid=A-32703704-12851

FIFTEEN

The Case for Continental

Examining the Potential for Climate Change Policy Integration in North America

MAT HUFF

INTRODUCTION

Climate change represents a unique and difficult challenge for policy makers. Forgoing the immediate benefits of further fossil fuel exploitation to avoid catastrophe at an indeterminate point in the future requires immense vision and leadership, virtues not always congruous with the political pressures of government. It evokes the ever-present fear of free-ridership, in which one country commits to and follows through with strong action to curb emissions, while other states renege on their commitments and still enjoy the benefits (i.e., lowered emissions and a reduced likelihood of runaway climate change). This "collective action" problem threatens to derail serious action to prevent climate disaster.

Globe-spanning treaties like the Kyoto Protocol are massive undertakings, and until recently, had failed to secure the buy-in of several key players, such as the United States and China. While the success of the Paris conference gives heart to onlookers by creating a new, inclusive, and globally binding regime, it is not expected to be in force until 2020, until which time the actual implementation of carbon-reduction policies is left up to the prerogative of signatory countries.

In North America, unilateral action on climate change has historically been slow, with strong opposition from certain domestic sectors that would be negatively affected by moves to strongly regulate emissions. Canada, Mexico, and the United States have highly integrated economies, and there is some measure of collaboration at the transnational level on climate change. But to suggest that an integrated climate change policy framework exists within North America would be an exaggeration, although recent developments suggest its potential in the future.

Some have dismissed the possibility of a highly coordinated and integrated climate change regime within North America as unlikely, given the highly decentralized and fluid nature of climate governance within the region and lack of demand for such a regime from influential economic actors within each respective country (Studer, 2013). However, there has been significant political movement to coordinate climate policy at the state and provincial level in Canada and the United States, and some measure of border cooperation between northern Mexican and southern U.S. states. Notably, there have been three regional cap-and-trade initiatives aimed at regulating and reducing emissions in certain sectors, including the Regional Greenhouse Gas Initiative (RGGI), the Western Climate Initiative (WCI), and the Midwestern Greenhouse Gas Reduction Accord (MGGRA). However, of these, only the RGGI is still functional in a meaningful way; the MGGRA has dissolved and the WCI is making slow progress after strong initial setbacks.

Fortunately, there recently has been increasing attention devoted to combating climate change and encouraging trilateral cooperation in mitigation and adaptation by the federal governments of the United States, Mexico, and, to a lesser extent, Canada, indicating that there might be potential for greater policy integration in North America. A cause for hope comes from the recently concluded "Three Amigos" summit, from which a trilateral agreement, the North American Climate, Clean Energy, and Environment Partnership, on methane emission reduction and clean energy production targets, among other goals, was announced (CBC, 2016).

This chapter will explore the case for North America as a political arena for combating climate change, outlining some advantages of this approach and noting certain obstacles to deeper integration. It begins with a discussion about the feasibility of a continental regime, and then moves on to examine the political economy of climate change policy at the federal level within the three NAFTA states. From there, it looks at the innovative subnational cap-and-trade systems that have been established in North America. The success of the RGGI where the others failed or struggled provides important insights into climate policy integration in North America. Next, the chapter examines existing trilateral institutions that deal with environmental issues and climate change, with particular focus on the Commission for Environmental Cooperation (CEC), and gauges their potential in facilitating a more integrated climate policy among the three countries. It ends with some thoughts on the future of continental climate change policy integration in North America.

There are significant benefits to trilateral cooperation relating to climate change in North America, including mitigating concerns regarding competitiveness of trade-exposed industries, lowered overall costs in Canada, access to best practices and carbon-accounting methodologies and funding for infrastructure through emissions trading and offset markets for Mexico, and greater energy security for the United States. There also exist significant, but not insurmountable, obstacles to a viable North American regime, including recalcitrant elements within the U.S. Congress, a change in the political direction of the U.S. executive branch on regulating emissions with the election of Donald Trump as president, reluctance on the part of North American states to create binding multilateral institutions, and economic actors that stand to lose money from, and thus lobby against, the regulation of emissions, as well as a lack of financial capacity from Mexico to achieve its otherwise ambitious targets without financial assistance from more developed nations.

IS A CONTINENTAL REGIME FEASIBLE?

Some scholars doubt the viability of an integrated regime to address climate change in North America. Isabel Studer's "supply-and-demand" analysis of the potential for climate change policy integration in North America notes several reasons why she is not optimistic for its prospects. Studer notes that opposition to strong climate action "arises chiefly as the result of the political and economic influences on the U.S. Congress, but also the disparate regional interests in Canada and constitutional constraints within the Mexican energy sector" (Studer, 2013, p. 35). Studer suggests this congressional opposition, coupled with the power asymmetry between the North American countries, where Canada and Mexico are "policy takers" requiring strong policy cues from the United States to act meaningfully on climate change, limits the potential for meaningful trilateral cooperation (Studer, 2013, p. 38). In addition, she notes that both Canada and Mexico lack the infrastructure and ability to diversify their energy exports, meaning that both countries rely on the United States as their primary customer.

Studer notes that North America, in terms of governance, is characterized by what she calls "soft regionalism," where interactions are informal and diplomatically led, rather than binding and institutionalized. She attributes this arrangement to a "strong U.S. preference for maintaining policy autonomy in both its foreign and domestic policies" and the preference of Canada and Mexico to avoid "the United States . . . encroaching on their national sovereignty through regional norms developed by supranational institutions dominated by the largest partner" (Studer, 2013, p. 36). Finally, she notes that in cases where cooperation and integration has occurred, such as with trade and investment through NAFTA, there tended to be strong demand internally from economic actors, which is generally not the case when discussing the integration of North American emissions policy. In fact, powerful fossil fuel lobbies in all three countries have historically opposed the implementation of strong climate change policy, for fear it might damage their profitability. With NAFTA, there was a "convergence of values and beliefs amongst political elites in the three countries regarding the overall social benefits to be accrued through freer trade and closer economic ties" (Studer, 2013, pp. 37–38). Studer claims this convergence of values has not yet happened at the federal level in relation to climate change policy.

While there are political roadblocks to creating a continental regime, largely in the U.S. and the Canadian legislative branches, there are also reasons to be optimistic. When Studer notes a lack of demand by internal constituencies for a continental climate change regime, she focuses mostly on economic actors. However, these actors are only one part of a broader political culture, and while influential, they are not the only relevant constituencies in relation to climate change policy. Increasingly, public opinion in the United States is in favor of action on climate change, with 83% of Americans surveyed by the Yale Project on Climate Change Communication stating that the United States should make "an effort to reduce global warming, even if it has economic costs" and that 56% of people surveyed said that "the U.S. should reduce its own greenhouse gas emissions, regardless of what other countries do" (Leiserowitz, Maibach, Roser-Renouf, Feinbein, & Rosenthal, 2015, p. 20). Additionally, there is significant demand from state and provincial governments in Canada and the United States for coordinated action on climate change. Twenty-three U.S. states and four Canadian provinces were once members of one or more regional cap-and-trade systems. In addition, eight other U.S. states, two Canadian provinces, six Mexican states, and the District of Columbia were formal observers (Rabe, 2013). An interesting fact regarding these subnational cap-and-trade regimes is that they anticipated federal preemption of their emissions trading programs into a national or international program, or explored convergence with the other regional programs. This shows significant demand for measures to combat climate change with a broad scope, from a wide range of important political actors. In addition, certain important economic actors are beginning to advocate for, or at least lessen their opposition to, emissions pricing. Recently, Steve Williams, the CEO of Suncor Energy Inc., one of Canada's largest energy firms, announced that Suncor would support the enactment of a carbon tax at the provincial level in Alberta, as long as it applies to both business and end users (Morgan, 2015).

Finally, elements within the United States, Canada, and Mexico that would lobby against a continental climate change regime also lobby against domestic initiatives to regulate emissions. Thus, Studer's argument does not highlight the unviability of a continental regime per se. Rather, it simply identifies the fact that industry will lobby against legislation that is perceived to harm their interests, which is a problem that policy makers would face regardless of whether action on climate change takes place at the subnational, state, or supranational levels.

In both Canada and the United States, opposition to national schemes to put a price on emissions often focuses on the potential for lost competitiveness when compared to other jurisdictions without similar regulation (Rivers & Jaccard, 2010, p. 411). There is significant concern that regulating emissions will cause leakage if emissions-intensive production is moved to jurisdictions with lax regulations. This fear is felt in a particularly acute fashion by highly trade-exposed and emissions-intensive industries that fear strong regulation on emissions will disadvantage them in a globalized market (Rivers, 2010, p. 1092). While this fear is likely overemphasized by industry lobbying to protect its interests, research suggests that leakage would occur should Canada impose a strong unilateral emissions policy. A report by the C. D. Howe Institute estimated that for every five tonnes reduced unilaterally by Canadian industry, one tonne would be leaked, primarily to the United States (Bataille, Dachis, & Rivers, 2009, p. 2). The severity of leakage naturally depends on the carbon pricing differential between countries, although Bataille, Dachis, and Rivers suggest that leakage to developing countries would be minimal.

By establishing a common regulatory area for carbon, Canada, the United States, and Mexico sidestep much of this concern. North America is already economically integrated through NAFTA. Canada, although recently having made efforts to diversify its trading partners, still overwhelmingly trades with the United States, and a significant portion of those exports are natural resources. For its part, Canada is still the top destination for U.S. exports, with Mexico running a close second. China has become an important trading partner to the United States, recently becoming its top source of imports; however, Canada and Mexico, combined, still constitute a greater source of total imports (International Trade Administration, 2016). Of particular note, the United States imported more crude from Canada than from anywhere else, and also imported a significant amount from Mexico (U.S. Energy Information Administration [USEIA], 2014a). The continental approach does not completely eliminate the potential for lost competitiveness, but it does lessen that potential significantly.

The North American Climate, Clean Energy, and Environment Partnership (NACCEEP), which was the result of the latest "Three Amigos" summit between Canada, the United States, and Mexico, represents a bold step in the right direction. It is an indicator that there is real and strong potential for meaningful cooperation on climate change within North America. Through it, the three partners pledge cooperation in many areas relating to climate change. These include achieving 50% of North America's power generation from clean sources, including nuclear, renewables, carbon capture and storage (CCS), as well as demand reduction from energy efficiency measures; reducing methane emissions from the oil and gas sectors by 40–45% by 2025 and to collaborate on monitoring, data-collecting, and reporting in regard to methane emissions; reducing methane from landfills and limiting food waste; reducing black carbon emissions in a number of key sectors; supporting infrastructure development for cross-border electricity transmission and cross-border energy integration; "greening" their respective governmental operations, including the purchase of more efficient products, cleaner power, and more fuel-efficient vehicles, as appropriate, with the United States and Canada pledging to purchase 100% of their electricity from clean sources by 2025; phasing out inefficient fossil fuel subsidies by 2025; aligning and improving energy efficiency standards in several sectors, both industrial and commercial, as well as encouraging energy efficiency through supply chains; supporting research, development, and collaboration regarding clean energy and CCS technology; reducing hydrofluorocarbons; reducing emissions from transportation through fuel-efficiency standards and promoting low-emissions vehicles, including development of zero-emissions vehicle infrastructure; reducing maritime and aviation emissions; committing to adopt the Paris agreement in 2016; and encouraging the G-20 countries towards greater climate action (Prime Minister of Canada, 2016).

This agreement is certainly extensive and ambitious. The regulation of key sectors under a firm cap (i.e., methane from the oil and gas industry) could constitute a precursor to regulation of other emissions-intensive sectors, and potentially a continental cap-and-trade system. However, it bears mentioning that this agreement is newly announced and the policies required to hit these targets have not been implemented. Time will tell as to the actual significance of this agreement.

THE POTENTIAL FOR CLIMATE POLICY INTEGRATION IN CANADA

Currently, the Canadian federal government is negotiating a sector-by-sector carbon intensity standard for heavy industry. An intensity standard differs from a traditional cap-and-trade system in that rather than imposing a cap on total emissions it sets a limit on how much CO_2 equivalent (CO2e) can be released per unit of production, and incrementally lowers that limit as time passes. However, the lack of a fixed cap allows for a potential overall increase in emissions. If production in emissions-intensive sectors expands significantly, it could wipe out any gains made in terms of per-unit energy efficiency (Rivers & Jaccard, 2010, p. 410). Given the recent emphasis shown at the federal level on developing Canada's unconventional oil reserves, with significant heavy oil and bitumen stores,[1] including generous subsidies and incentives, production in the oil and gas sector is likely to continue to expand. This is reflected in the recent Environment Canada report on national emissions trends, which notes that the oil sands in Alberta are projected to more than triple their output between 2005 and 2020, and that Alberta will steadily increase its emissions output during that same time period by an additional 55 megatonnes of carbon dioxide equivalent (CO2e) by 2020 (Environment and Climate Change Canada, 2016, pp. 18, 29). Industry greatly prefers intensity regimes, as they do not put a limit on expansion, and will not interfere with plans to ramp up production in the oil sands.

However, there has been some movement in Canadian federal politics towards a stronger and more comprehensive policy action for combating climate change. The federal election in 2008 saw an unprecedented move by the Liberal Party, under its leader Stephane Dion, to dedicate a significant portion of its electoral platform to combating climate change. Their "Green Shift" plan presented a series of policy measures, including a nationwide carbon tax. This wagered their electoral fortune on public concern over climate change. At the time, the wager did not seem to be unfounded. British Columbia, led by the center-right provincial Liberal Party, had just enacted its own province-wide carbon tax, with an initial price of C$10/tonne and with scheduled yearly increases of C$5 a tonne through 2012, where it reached C$30/tonne. Unfortunately for Dion's Liberals, the gamble did not pay off. Not only did they lose the election, but they also received the lowest share of the popular vote in the party's history and lost fully one-quarter of their seats in parliament (Harrison, 2012, p. 397). In both the federal and British Columbia cases, other parties opposed pricing carbon and lobbed vitriolic attacks, claiming that the tax disproportionately affected northern communities and let "big polluters off easy," as the provincial New Democratic Party claimed, or that it was a "tax on everything" and would "screw everybody across the country," as federal Conservatives alleged (Harrison, 2012, pp. 386, 391). Despite a recent groundswell of public concern regarding climate change, and the environment in general, the economy had reemerged as the primary concern among electors in 2008, with financial crises unfolding worldwide. Harrison (2012) notes a general preference for cap-and-trade systems over a carbon tax among the electorate, despite a widespread lack of understanding of how a cap-and-trade system actually works, beyond vague notions that it "makes big polluters pay" (pp. 403–404). Harrison further notes that "cap-and-trade again has significant political advantages, because the complexity of the system and the indirectness of costs to consumers render costs to individuals relatively invisible" (p. 387).

Finally, in 2016, the Government of Canada announced that it will require all provinces to have a price on carbon by 2018. It has set an initial "benchmark price" of C$10 per tonne of CO_2e in 2018, increasing in annual increments until it reaches C$50 tonne in 2022. Provinces have flexibility in how they meet this requirement, and can choose a carbon tax or a cap-and-trade system. Revenues from pricing carbon will be revenue-neutral and remain within the jurisdiction of origin (Government of Canada, 2016). In his first foreign visit as president, Barack Obama met with Stephen Harper to discuss a range of issues, including the environment and climate change. Out of these discussions came the announcement of the Clean Energy Dialogue in April 2009, which centered on the development and sharing of new green technology, with a particular focus on CCS (Childs, 2010, p. 427). Additionally, in that same year, Minister of Environment Jim Prentice stated that Canada would likely have to adjust its climate change policy to "align its reduction targets, reporting rules, enforcement mechanisms, and industry specific regulations with those of the United States" (Childs, 2010, p. 431). Indeed, both countries agreed in 2009 to the same reduction targets under the Copenhagen Accord, and Canada just recently announced new targets of a 30% reduction in emissions from 2005 levels by 2030 (McDiarmid, 2015). This again brings Canadian targets roughly in line with those of the United States, who pledged a reduction of 26–28% by 2025. Both of these targets were reaffirmed in the Paris Agreement, with the acknowledgement that they are not enough to stay below two degrees Celsius and that stronger targets will be needed in the future, with commitments on the part of signatories to review their progress towards staying below 1.5 degrees Celsius and to adjust their target accordingly. However, for policy integration that is more comprehensive than simply agreeing to similar targets, Canada would likely need to abandon intensity standards for something more easily harmonized, such as a traditional cap-and-trade.

It is too early to meaningfully make assertions on the impact of the defeat of Stephen Harpers' Conservatives by Justin Trudeau's Liberal Party in 2015. However, this new government seems more interested in averting serious climate change, as evidenced by signing the Paris Agreement, the NACCEEP at the recent "Three Amigos" summit, and the introduction of the Pan-Canadian Approach to Pricing Carbon Pollution. Further, the regime change in Alberta, where the right-wing Progressive-Conservatives were ousted by the center-left provincial New Democratic Party, is a significant event when it comes to climate change policy. Already, the Alberta government has moved from its previous intensity standard towards a provincial cap-and-trade system, including allowing the purchase of "made-in-Alberta" offsets as an alternative compliance mechanism. Further, it has implemented a broad carbon price, which will eventually cover 90% of the emissions generated by the economy by 2018, with revenues from that tax going towards mitigating any negative impact it might have on low- to medium-income households, as well as towards investing in further emissions reduction and training workers to transition their skills into low-carbon industries (Leach, Adams, Caims, Coady, & Lambert, 2015). As long as future provincial governments maintain these commitments, Alberta may no longer be an obstacle to tackling climate change on a broader scale.

However, some issues should be addressed to provide political space for Canada to enter into a continental climate regime. Canada's energy mix consists of much more hydroelectric power, and less overall reliance on coal and natural gas, than is the case in the United States (Studer, 2013, pp. 40–41). This means that the United States has greater opportunity to reduce its emissions at a lower cost through fuel switching. Additionally, most of Canada's power generation facilities in the energy sector are not due to be replaced until 2020–2025. This further increases mitigation costs for Canada relative to the United States (NRTEE, 2007).

The issue of higher abatement cost of Canada could be greatly mitigated by linking carbon markets between the two (or three) countries under a bilateral or continental cap-and-trade. In their analysis of the potential for a North American cap-and-trade system, Murray, Maniloff, and Monast (2013) note that, if Canada and the United States adhere to the Copenhagen target of a 17% reduction of 2005 levels, permit prices in the two countries would differ widely if each of them opted for strictly national systems. Permit prices in Canada would be an estimated US$60 per tonne, compared to an estimated US$30 per tonne in the United States. If the two countries linked their markets, the overall price of permits is estimated at US$31 per tonne, leading to substantial savings in Canada with only very minor price increases in the United States, due to Canadian industry getting access to the much larger U.S. permit market, which in turn has greater potential for cheaper emissions reductions (Murray et al., 2013, p. 253).

It is particularly important for Canada to coordinate climate change policies with the United States. By engaging in the formation of a continental regime, Canada can shape it to not harm Canadian interests. An example of this potential for U.S. climate legislation harming Canadian interests are provisions within the Waxman-Markey bill, the ill-fated comprehensive bill that dealt with climate change and which passed a vote by the U.S. House of Representatives but died in the Senate. These provisions were a cause for concern within Canada and Mexico, particularly those that granted "the President discretion to award special rebates to American industries when they are engaged in competition with foreign companies operating in jurisdictions with less-stringent emissions requirements" and required the executive branch "to impose fees on importers from countries with weaker climate change prevention regimes" (Childs, 2010, pp. 430–431). While this ostensibly prevents leakage, this provision could cause significant economic friction to industry in Canada and Mexico. Having a unified regime sidesteps these potential issues while reducing the potential for leakage.

THE POTENTIAL FOR CLIMATE POLICY INTEGRATION IN THE UNITED STATES

Integrating climate change policy with its closest trading partner makes as much sense for the United States as it does for Canada. Some regions of the United States face an immense challenge in transitioning away from coal, and are subsequently greatly concerned about the potential impacts of regulating emissions (Childs, 2010, p. 396). Overall, 33% of electricity generated in the United States is from coal and 67% from fossil fuel in general (coal, natural gas, and petroleum) (USEIA, 2016b). In addition, the United States produces and exports significant amounts of coal (USEIA, 2015b), and is predicted to become a net exporter of natural gas (USEIA, 2015a). In the case of a potential cap-and-trade system, energy producers in all three countries would gain access to a much larger pool of permit sellers, which would lower the cost of purchasing permits to cover excess emissions (Childs, 2010, p. 445).

An integrated North American climate change regime aligns well with U.S. foreign policy, as well as being good climate policy. The quest for "energy security" is a significant factor in recent U.S. foreign policy and an important element in the deepening relationship between the Canada and the United States. Energy security has become a priority for U.S. policy makers (Childs, 2010, p. 395) and Canada hopes to become an "energy superpower," primarily through shipping bitumen south from Alberta to be refined in the United States (Prime Minister's Office, 2006). Canada is a secure, politically stable source of oil in close proximity to the United States. It is also significant that Canada is a non-OPEC producer, with the third-largest proven reserves in the world, trailing Saudi Arabia and Venezuela (Natural Resources Canada, 2016). Potentially more significant, Canadian total reserves are estimated at 1.6 to 1.7 trillion barrels, greater than the rest of the world combined. While oil production from the oil sands region is more emissions-intensive than most other sources of oil, when one includes the increased carbon emissions in transporting oil from Saudi Arabia to the U.S. market, "the total life cycle of a barrel of oils sands' crude ultimately results in approximately a 9.7% greater carbon footprint than the average barrel of Saudi light crude shipped to the United States" (Childs, 2010, p. 409). So, while it is more emissions-intensive than other forms of domestic oil production, oil from the oil sands will likely play a continued role in the continental energy security without completely jeopardizing the climate. Fossil fuel production and distribution is already fairly integrated in North America, and integrating emissions policy helps prevent leakage, limits concerns regarding competitiveness, and could potentially increase public buy-in for continental energy projects.

As mentioned earlier, there has already been some movement towards an American national cap-and-trade program, through the proposed Waxman-Markey bill. Although that act died in the U.S. Senate, the Obama administration pushed forward with action on climate change by signing the Copenhagen Accord in 2009. Further, it began to regulate greenhouse gases through the Clean Air Act, via powers granted to the U.S. Environmental Protection Agency by the U.S. Supreme Court in the *Massachusetts v. EPA* case of 2007, which determined that the EPA had the authority, and the obligation, to regulate greenhouse gases, initially regulating fuel efficiency for passenger vehicles, and later for medium-to-heavy trucks (Cohen & Miller, 2012, p. 43). President Obama also announced regulations, again through the EPA, to regulate power plants, with the goal of reducing their emissions by 30% of 2005 levels, with the first compliance period beginning in 2020 (U.S. Environmental Protection Agency, 2015). These regulations essentially cap emissions from stationary power facilities. Once industry is regulated in this way, it might become more amenable to a continental cap-and-trade, or trilateral offset market, to lower their own compliance costs. Interestingly, the first U.S. cap-and-trade system, the highly successful sulphur dioxide regime, was introduced in 1995 via amendment to the Clean Air Act.[2]

However, the fossil fuel industry in the United States still has significant influence on the political process. During the Clinton administration, a "BTU" (British thermal unit) tax was proposed, which would have taxed all forms of energy based on BTU content. Viewed as a means to reduce pollution, among other goals, the tax was "savaged by industry groups including the oil companies, the U.S. Chamber of Commerce, and the National Association of Manufacturers," who defeated the bill in its original form (Cleetus, 2011, p. 26). Fossil fuel companies have a long history of paying to undermine climate science in the United States. Cohen and Miller (2012) note research that identifies "40 ExxonMobil-funded organizations that either sought to undermine the mainstream scientific findings on climate change or maintained affiliations with a small group of skeptic scientists" (p. 41). Additionally, the partisan gridlock in both houses of the U.S. legislature in the last few years has hamstrung progress on enacting new climate legislation, which was partially the reason the Obama administration opted to regulate greenhouse gases through the Clean Air Act, which bypassed Congress. Cohen and Miller note that many of the Republican presidential candidates in the 2012 election were climate change deniers, and the others were quick to disavow strong action to combat climate change, including moderate John Huntsman, who initially pushed for a cap-and-trade but withered under the backlash and withdrew his support (Cohen & Miller, 2012, p. 40). More recently, Kentucky Senator Mitch McConnell embarked on a campaign to push states to oppose the Obama administration's plan to regulate coal-fired power plants. This plan, which was heavily funded by the fossil fuel industry, saw the senator's office send every governor in the United States a detailed legal argument on why they ought to oppose President Obama's plan, claiming that it usurped state jurisdiction over energy policy and economically damaged areas that relied on coal extraction for jobs (Davenport, 2015).

Finally, it bears mentioning the uncertainty of climate change as a continued federal priority in light of the 2016 U.S. presidential election. Initially in support of measures to combat climate change, since accepting the Republican nomination, President Donald Trump has noted significant skepticism regarding climate change, referring to it interchangeably as a hoax, of minimal impact, and "just the weather" (Worland, 2016). Actions by the Trump administration since assuming office seem to confirm a hostile position towards regulating emissions. In the short period since assuming office, President Trump has signed executive orders rescinding Obama-era regulations on emissions, water, and air pollution; signaled the intent of the United States to leave the Paris Climate Accord and the United Nations more broadly; and appointed noted climate change skeptic Scott Pruitt to the head of the U.S. Environmental Protection Agency (EPA). Pruitt and the EPA have had an acrimonious history, with Pruitt having led multiple lawsuits on behalf of states' attempting to block the EPA's enforcement of emissions regulations (Meyer, 2017).

Further actions suggest the direction the Trump administration is heading regarding climate and energy policy. President Trump recently signed executive orders that cleared administrative barriers that had halted two major pipeline projects—the Keystone XL pipeline and the Dakota Access pipeline project—that were previously blocked by the Obama administration (Jones, Diamond, & Krieg, 2017). These projects have been lightning rods for debate surrounding the economic trade-offs of lowering emissions, and were halted by the Obama administration. By clearing the path towards their construction, the Trump administration seems to be signaling a significant shift in the White House policy towards a deregulated approach towards emissions.

President Trump's time in office has been tumultuous. Civil unrest and protests in relation to his actions relating to the environmental policy of this administration has occurred, and it is unclear what role the United States will play in combatting the rise of emissions globally in the near-term.

THE POTENTIAL FOR CLIMATE POLICY INTEGRATION IN MEXICO

Mexico has historically been a significant oil producer and exporter, with net exports peaking in 2003 at 1,792,017.2 barrels per day. However, since then, exports have declined significantly, hitting their lowest point since 1980 in 2011, at 847,433.5 barrels per day, before rebounding slightly. Total oil production is also down from a historical high of 3,847,993.2 barrels per day in 2004, to 2,624,700 barrels per day in 2015. Domestic consumption has leveled off and has begun to decline as well, down from the 2007 high of 2,172,789.6 barrels per day, to 2,007,000 barrels per day in 2014. Additionally, proven reserves are fast being depleted, falling from a historic high point of 56.99 billion barrels in 1982, to current 2015 proven reserves of 9.8 billion barrels (USEIA, 2016a). While still a significant oil producer, Mexico differs from both Canada and the United States in that production is on a steady decline. While this decline is likely to make Mexico more amenable to a North American climate change regime, the country still relies heavily on revenues from its state-owned oil company to shore up its public finances (Remirez, 2014, p. 148). However, the fossil fuel industry in Mexico is also significantly subsidized, to the tune of US$18.9 billion in 2014, which offsets the revenue value of industry somewhat (Ordonez, 2015). Some market liberalization in the energy sector has occurred in the last few years, as the government has allowed private companies to bid on projects, while still giving PEMEX, the state-owned oil company, the right of first refusal.

With that in mind, Mexico has made some progress towards combating climate change, likely due to the fact that many areas of Mexico are particularly susceptible to the impacts of climate change, including floods, droughts, and rising sea levels (Childs, 2010, pp. 446–447). In 2006, as greater understanding developed regarding the physical impacts of climate change, then-newly elected President Felipe Calderón committed to working multilaterally on progress in mitigating climate change. Although this enthusiasm was tempered somewhat by the financial crisis, Mexico continued to push for stronger measures on climate change (Remirez, 2014, p. 149). In 2008, Mexico announced emissions targets, stating that it would reduce CO_2 levels by 50 million tonnes of CO_2 from 2012 levels, without the use of international aid funds. In the same year, Mexico also proposed the creation of a global Green Fund, to help developing nations with investments in green infrastructure (Remirez, 2014, p. 152). Noting the gridlock at the United Nations Framework Convention on Climate Change Conference of Parties meeting in Copenhagen (COP15), Mexico embarked on a mission to "restore confidence in the multilateral system" by way of intensive diplomatic effort between Mexico and other countries, supervised directly by President Calderón, through the Foreign Ministry. In 2010, Mexico hosted COP16 in Cancun, and was praised for its enthusiasm and deft diplomatic skills in attempting to restore confidence in multilateral climate talks (Remirez, 2014, pp. 154–155).

Mexico has lobbied internationally to ensure transfers of wealth to developing countries for the purposes of low-carbon, sustainable development, and also embraced market means to emissions reductions, endeavoring to become an attractive site for the Kyoto Protocol Clean Development Mechanism (CDM) investment (Remirez, 2014, p. 154). While Mexico is the only developing country to have taken on binding commitments, it is also important to realize that these plans are unlikely to come to fruition without significant external funding. Involving Mexico in a continental regime benefits all participants, particularly in the case of a cap-and-trade or trilateral offset pool. A wider pool of permits would lead to decreased cost, increased efficiency, and a reduction in potential leakage.

Interestingly, PEMEX has been a vocal advocate for action on climate change, becoming "the first and only developing country oil company to have developed a company-wide carbon emission reduction target" and "piloted an internal corporate emissions trading system, which was implemented between 1999 and 2002" (Studer, 2013, p. 55). Studer notes significant potential for GHG reduction across PEMEX facilities through cogeneration, which is beginning to materialize; PEMEX recently created an internal business division to develop its cogeneration potential (Iliff, 2015). Many of these projects were originally put forth as CDM candidates, and could feasibly find funding through a North American offset pool, or cap-and-trade system.

Mexico is limited in its potential to reduce its own emissions unilaterally, due to its limited resources. This is why it embarked on a sustained campaign to garner multilateral buy-in for action on climate change. It stands to benefit significantly from further integration, whether that is sharing information and technical knowledge or deeper integration, such as an emissions-trading regime, green development fund, or continental offset pool.

SUBNATIONAL CLIMATE CHANGE COOPERATION IN NORTH AMERICA

North American climate change governance has been described as "a set of mechanisms that are profoundly multi-level, highly diverse in the range of actors and institutions involved, as well as the objects and means of cooperation, and also dynamic in the sense that governance arrangements change in response to shifts in political and economic conditions" (Craik & VanNijnatten, 2013, p. 6). This dynamic system has fostered significant policy experimentation, with North America being home to trailblazing sub-national governments. Of particular note are the three sub-regional cap-and-trade programs: The Regional Greenhouse Gas Initiative (RGGI)[3] in the U.S. Northeast, the Western Climate Initiative (WCI),[4] and the Midwestern Greenhouse Gas Reduction Accord (MGGRA).[5] As mentioned earlier, only the RGGI, and to a lesser extent, the WCI, still function in a meaningful way. Examining these sub-national cap-and-trade systems provides important lessons about the potential viability of a continental system.

Barry Rabe notes several reasons why the RGGI outperformed the other regional cap-and-trade programs. These include experience in common policy development, a high degree of trust and familiarity, and a scope that was limited but more manageable, focusing solely on regulating greenhouse gases emitted by the power generation sector (Rabe, 2013, p. 72). Not only has the RGGI been successful at maintaining its cohesion where other regional agreements have stalled or failed, but it also has succeeded in auctioning permits to raise capital for projects related to climate change mitigation and adaptation—a first globally.[6] It also has managed to successfully renegotiate its cap in light of reduced emissions due to the recession of 2007–2010 (Rabe, 2013, pp. 82, 104). Of additional interest, the RGGI created a nonprofit organization to manage the day-to-day implementation of the program, RGGI Inc., which in turn is monitored by an executive board consisting of two representatives from each member state (Rabe, 2013, p. 82). This reduced the administrative burden on individual states, ensured greater institutional memory and policy continuity in the face of changing state officials, and added greater transparency and impartiality to the system.

By contrast, the WCI attempted to bring together a more diverse group of states and provinces under the auspices of a more ambitious program. The scope of the WCI included not only power generation, as the RGGI did, but encompassed "a wide-range of manufacturing and related entities" (Rabe, 2013, p. 90). Additionally, the members of the WCI had little in common and little experience in common policy development at the state/provincial level. Unfortunately, the WCI lost significant momentum when members were unexpectedly slow in passing implementation legislation. This lethargic process was further confounded by gubernatorial changes in several states, in some cases bringing governors who were not enthusiastic about the concept of cap-and-trade into power. This is evidenced by the withdrawal of Arizona from the cap-and-trade provision of WCI membership. Governor Jan Brewer noted in the executive order initiating the withdrawal that "imposing costs on Arizona's economy associated with a GHG cap-and-trade system that are not borne by national and international rivals would cost investment and jobs in Arizona and put Arizona at a competitive disadvantage without effectively addressing what is a national and global issue" (Rabe, 2013, pp. 93–94). After Arizona's withdrawal, one by one the other states dropped out of the WCI or signaled their unwillingness to participate in its cap-and-trade program, leaving only California and four Canadian provinces as members. Efforts towards establishing actual emissions trading seem to have stalled for the time being, with only Quebec and California passing authorizing legislation. California and Quebec concluded another joint permit auction in August 2016.

However, newly elected Ontario premier Kathleen Wynne announced that Ontario would adopt the WCI cap-and-trade legislation (Rand, 2015).

The Government of Ontario tabled Bill 172, which would enact the Climate Change and Low-Carbon Economy Act 2016 to establish, among other things, the foundation for Ontario's cap-and-trade program. Alongside this bill, Ontario released the Draft Cap and Trade Regulation, and a discussion paper on cap-and-trade program design options, which outlined the program in greater detail. Ontario's first emissions allowance auction is set to occur in March 2017. This auction will only be open to firms in Ontario. Once the program is implemented satisfactorily with Ontario, auctions will be held quarterly with Quebec and California (Coop, King, Sadikman, Fairfax, & Hall-McGuire, 2016).

The MGGRA was essentially dead on arrival, having been launched in 2007 and then abandoned in 2011 before entering its first compliance period. It modeled itself after the RGGI, basing its targets on reductions from 2005 levels and proposing a nonprofit entity similar to RGGI Inc. to administer the program. Commitment from legislators in participating states quickly waned, and significant blows to the regime were dealt by gubernatorial changes in the 2010 midterm elections, where almost all of the governors who initially supported the initiative were replaced. Additionally, several members were in fiscal crisis, and finding funds, staff, and political will to enact the cap-and-trade system proved an insurmountable challenge (Rabe, 2013, p. 100).

Subnational governments can act as policy laboratories, experimenting and innovating with a speed and agility that larger governments have trouble replicating. If we analyze these three regional cap-and-trade regimes, we learn valuable insights relating to the potential viability of a North American regime. The RGGI succeeded (or at least endured) where the WCI and MGGRA lagged or failed partially due to the fact that RGGI states had a significant degree of familiarity with each other and experience in shared policy design together. This is also true of the relationship between the three North American countries, which have significant shared policy design experience, particularly in the area of trade and investment, air pollution, and national security. However, these issues are geographically bound to North America, while climate change is global (Craik & VanNijnatten, 2013, p. 5). This might present a challenge to operating at a continental level, but no more so than it would for subregional or national programs, and the increased geographical scope of the program might serve to quell objections to regulation like those expressed by Governor Brewer. If serious progress is to be made on climate change, harmonizing and integrating policies and scaling up what has been shown to work at the subregional level is an integral step.

CROSS-BORDER INSTITUTIONS AND THEIR ROLE IN CLIMATE POLICY COOPERATION

RGGI Inc. was a highly successful policy innovation, providing monitoring and technical support that enabled the smooth running of the RGGI. North America has an existing institution that could play a key role in harmonizing climate change policy and promoting further integration, the Commission for Environmental Cooperation (CEC). The CEC was created by the North American Agreement on Environmental Cooperation (NAAEC), itself created as a "side agreement" to NAFTA, designed to allay fears of an environmental "race-to-the-bottom" due to trade and investment liberalization.

While the CEC does not function as a regulator, it nonetheless influences policy outcomes in its role as a producer and conveyor of credible and actionable knowledge (Craik, 2013). The CEC has experience in facilitating cross-border environmental cooperation, particularly in the development of common biodiversity mapping tools, work that crosses the borders of all three states and has "resulted in the development of specific North American-scale conservation strategies" (Craik, 2013, p. 221). In addition, the CEC has been effective in compiling and making comparable national inventory data on the "release and transfer of toxic substances from the three national tracking programs" and compiling "the data in comparable form, allowing for laggard jurisdictions and facilities to be more easily identified. This, in turn, created pressure for standards harmonization at higher levels" (Craik, 2013, p. 222). While other initiatives did not focus on climate change, the CEC's expertise as a creator and clearinghouse of credible information could prove valuable in harmonizing standards and disseminating best practices in relation to climate change mitigation.

The CEC has begun to make climate change a greater priority in its work. This began in 2009 at the North American Leaders Summit, where the heads of NAFTA signatories "refocused their attention on the importance of climate change issues and instructed officials to develop a trilateral working plan for consideration at their next summit," and at the CEC ministerial meeting in April 2010, where "North American Environment Ministers also committed to improving the comparability of data gathering and inventories for mitigation and adaptation projects" (Fickling & Schott, 2010, p. 10). This strategy builds on past CEC success in harmonizing and disseminating information in a format that is usable by policy makers. Currently, the CEC is focused on initiatives such as modeling and assessing carbon stocks and sinks in North American forests and oceans, the reducing emissions from maritime transport, and building systems for identifying extreme heat events and helping communities adapt to these conditions (CEC, 2016).

However, some obstacles prevent the NAAEC and CEC from reaching their full potential in facilitating climate policy integration. Arguably, the strongest and most entrenched area of trilateral governance in North America is the trade and investment regime exemplified by NAFTA. The CEC has limited ability to influence NAFTA's Free Trade Commission (FTC), which in turn is not obligated to work with the CEC. Therefore, trade and investment issues are often handled separately from environmental issues (Carpentier, 2006). Further, large-scale resource extraction is excluded from the mandate of the NAAEC, limiting its usefulness in enforcing environmental standards in sectors of the economy that have a large-scale negative impact on the environment (Phillips, 2015). Moreover, while the NAAEC is authorized to establish a tribunal to deliberate on potential environments violations and deliver binding decisions, this dispute mechanism has never been invoked and is subject to NAAEC Council interference, which can halt the panel process during the research phase (López-Vallejo, 2014).

Much of the CEC's past effectiveness stems from its carefully cultivated reputation for providing information that is salient, credible, and legitimate. This reputation was developed over time with a generally narrow range of actors who were involved with niche issue areas such as transborder biodiversity mapping or creating regional transport plans relating to cross-border movement of toxic chemicals. Climate change, however, has captured the attention of a much broader range of actors, with whom the CEC must now establish a similar reputation (Craik, 2013, pp. 221–222). In addition, climate change as an issue area is much more contentious than any other on which the CEC has acted, with strong vested interests opposing action to curb emissions. The CEC will have to expend significant effort to establish itself as a credible and unbiased source of information if it is to have a greater impact on climate change policy in North America.

Other promising, if halting, trilateral institution building related to climate has occurred. The North American Energy Working Group (NAEWG), which later was superseded by the broader Security and Prosperity Partnership (SPP), is working towards cooperative development of tidal and biofuel energy. Even more directly related to climate change, the three North American countries have developed a common CCS map with "a common methodology and the goal of sharing and comparing data" (López-Vallejo, 2014, p. 78). In addition, the NAEWG has facilitated standards harmonization in various consumer sectors. Further, in addition to the CEC, the NAAEC created the Border Environment Cooperation

Commission (BECC), which facilitates border cooperation in environmental areas, including the management of methane and its conversion into biogas and helping local governments to develop climate action plans. This second activity with local governments is particularly important, as through the BECC northern Mexican states have access to EPA methodologies for drafting their own emissions standards, which in turn harmonizes them methodologically with those of Canada and the United States (López-Vallejo, 2014, p. 77).

In its current form, the CEC is relegated to a largely passive role, providing information and hoping that, if the information is useful enough, the NAFTA countries will act upon it. There is value in its work, in that comparable information about GHG levels, policies, and initiatives allows for more informed policy making and builds trust between the three partners in this area. It will be interesting to see if it plays a greater role in regulating North American climate change policy integration. The NAC-CEEP gave the CEC a role in creating a North American black carbon registry. But outside of its current monitoring function, it cannot take a more active role without NAFTA partners granting it greater regulatory authority. However, if that were to occur, the CEC's capacities and location in continental policy making could give it a key role in facilitating and managing more comprehensive and deeper integration, such as a continental cap-and-trade.

CONCLUSION

The recent IPCC report, released in November 2014, again reaffirms the need to bring North America, and indeed the world, into the battle against climate change. North America is a critical region in this fight: The United States and Canada have the highest per capita emissions in world, and it was only recently that China surpassed the United States as the top gross emitter.

Also, until very recently, both countries have been obstinate in global climate talks, preferring bilateral discussions and nonbinding agreements. Although the signing of the Paris Climate Agreement is a step in the right direction, there is some significant uncertainty regarding the U.S. government's ongoing position regarding climate change since the 2016 presidential election.

Concerns surrounding competitiveness and leakage have dogged the discussion on pricing emissions. Both the United States and Canada have significant internal constituencies that are resistant to regulating emissions for economic reasons. Raising revenue through carbon pricing, either auctioned permits in a cap-and-trade or through a tax, and redistributing them to fossil fuel dependent states and provinces would help mitigate some of the disproportionately negative economic impacts on these regions. Mexico, for its part, has been an effective and steadfast proponent of climate multilateralism, due to both its diminishing oil supply, vulnerability to climate change impacts, and inability to successfully transition away from fossil fuels without significant external funding.

This chapter set out to describe the potential for climate change policy integration in North America. There are significant benefits to a trilateral regime, including greatly reduced mitigation costs for Canada under cap-and-trade, access to mitigation and adaptation funding through offsets or emissions trading in the case of Mexico, and assurance for the United States that its primary trading partners will be included. Further, a regime at the national or supranational level can enforce regulation on laggard jurisdictions, something that more voluntary regional systems cannot do. Crafting such a system to regulate a limited range of significant sectors, as accomplished by the RGGI, would likely increase its political viability. The "Three Amigos" deal gives hope that such a system might be possible.

A continental climate change strategy would not preclude other initiatives to limit emissions on a broader scale, as North American efforts can later be integrated with global regimes. In fact, showing that North America is serious about curbing emissions might bolster global talks. As the clock ticks, supporters of decisive action to avert climate disaster can only hope that will be the case.

NOTES

1. Bitumen is a heavy viscous form of oil, often mixed with sand or clay. It is energy- and cost-intensive to refine compared to conventional oil stocks.
2. There are, however, key differences between the SO_2 regime and any potential CO_2 cap-and-trade system. SO_2 emissions were largely produced by a small number of electrical utilities, which made them easier to regulate. CO_2 emissions are generated by a much more diverse and widespread set of actors. Further, SO_2 abatement was largely based on the implementation of already existing and proven technology, such as scrubbers. No analogous technology has been proven on a widespread commercial basis for CO_2. While carbon capture and storage technology is promising, it is currently very costly to retrofit old plants with it (Hanemann, 2010, p. 237). Thus, compared to the

sulphur dioxide regime, GHG emissions require a more active regulatory approach.

3. The RGGI began in 2005 with seven initial members (Connecticut, Delaware, Maine, New Hampshire, New Jersey, New York, and Vermont), and later expanded in 2007 to include Massachusetts and Rhode Island as members. New Jersey has since left, and Maryland has joined.
4. At its peak in 2010, the WCI had eleven members, including the states of Arizona, California, Montana, New Mexico, Ontario, Oregon, Utah, and Washington, and Canadian provinces Quebec, Manitoba, and British Columbia, as well as 15 formal observers, including Alaska, Colorado, Idaho, Kansas, New York, and Wyoming; Nova Scotia and Saskatchewan in Canada; and Baja California, Chihuahua, Coahuila, Nuevo Leon, Sonora, and Tamaulipas in Mexico. Currently, its membership has diminished to one U.S. state, California, and four Canadian provinces, British Columbia, Manitoba, Quebec, and Ontario (Rabe, 2013, p. 91). Only Quebec and California are currently trading permits.
5. The MGGRA was formed in 2007 and initially consisted of Illinois, Iowa, Kansas, Michigan, Minnesota, Wisconsin, and Manitoba. Indiana, Ohio, and South Dakota become observer states. In 2010, Ontario became an observer province (Rabe, 2013, p. 99).
6. Although New York and New Jersey ended up using most of the funds to shore up deficit, which led to some controversy (Rabe, 2013). New Jersey has since left.

REFERENCES

Bataille, C., Dachis, B., & Rivers, N. (2009). *Pricing greenhouse gas emissions: The impact on Canada's competitiveness.* Toronto, ON: C. D. Howe Institute.

Canadian Broadcasting Corporation. (2016, July 27). U.S., Mexico to source 50% of electricity from clean energy by 2025. Retrieved from http://www.cbc.ca/news/politics/three-amigos-summit-climate-policies-1.3654166

Carpentier, C. L. (2006). NAFTA and its environmental side agreement: Trade and foreign investment in the Americas—The impact on indigenous people and the environment. *Michigan State Journal of International Law*, 199–223.

Childs, J. (2010). Continental cap-and-trade: Canada, the United States, and climate change partnership in North America. *Houston Journal of International Law*, *32*(2), 393–457.

Cleetus, R. (2011). Finding common ground in the debate between the carbon tax and cap-and-trade policies. *Bulletin of the Atomic Scientists*, *67*(1), 19–27.

Cohen, S., & Miller, A. (2012). Climate change 2011: A status report on US policy. *Bulletin of Atomic Scientists*, *68*(1), 39–49.

Commission for Environmental Cooperation. (2016). Climate Change. Retrieved from http://www.cec.org/our-work/climate-change

Coop, J., King, R., Sadikman, J., Fairfax, J., & Hall-McGuire, R. (2016, March 3). Ontario reveals proposed legislation and regulations for its cap and trade regime. *Osler*. Retrieved from https://www.osler.com/en/resources/regulations/2016/ontario-reveals-proposed-legislation-and-regulatio

Craik, N. (2013). Climate policy facilitation: The role of the North American Commission on Environmental Cooperation. In N. Craik, I. Studer, & D. VanNijnatten (Eds.), *Climate change policy in North America: Designing integration in a regional system* (pp. 213–246). Toronto, ON: University of Toronto Press.

Craik, N., & VanNijnatten, D. (2013). Designing integration: The system of climate change governance in North America. In N. Craik, I. Studer, & D. VanNijnatten (Eds.), *Climate change policy in North America: Designing integration in a regional system* (pp. 5–34). Toronto, ON: University of Toronto Press.

Davenport, C. (2015, March 19). McConnell urges states to help thwart Obama's "war on coal." *New York Times*. Retrieved from http://www.nytimes.com/2015/03/20/us/politics/mitch-mcconnell-urges-states-to-help-thwart-obamas-war-on-coal.html?_r=0

Environment and Climate Change Canada. (2016). *Canada's emissions trends 2014*. Retrieved from https://ec.gc.ca/ges-ghg/E0533893-A985-4640-B3A2-008D8083D17D/ETR_E%202014.pdf

Fickling, M., & Schott, J. J. (2010). *NAFTA and climate change*. Washington, DC: Peterson Institute of International Economics.

Government of Canada. (2016). Pan-Canadian approach to pricing carbon pollution. Retrieved from http://news.gc.ca/web/article-en.do?nid=1132169

Hanemann, M. (2010). Cap-and-trade: A sufficient or necessary condition for emission reduction? *Oxford Review of Policy Research*, *26*(2), 225–252.

Harrison, K. (2012). A tale of two taxes: The fate of environmental tax reform in Canada. *Review of Policy Research*, 29(3), 383–407.

Iliff, L. (2015, May 15). Mexico oil firm Pemex creates cogeneration unit, shuffles executives. *Wall Street Journal*. Retrieved from http://www

.wsj.com/articles/mexico-oil-firm-pemex-creates-cogeneration-unit-shuffles-executives-1432332696

International Trade Administration. (2016). Top US trade partners. Retrieved from http://www.trade.gov/mas/ian/build/groups/public/@tg_ian/documents/webcontent/tg_ian_003364.pdf

Jones, A., Diamond, J., & Krieg, G. (2017, January 24). Trump advances controversial oil pipelines. *CNN.com*. Retrieved from http://www.cnn.com/2017/01/24/politics/trump-keystone-xl-dakota-access-pipelines-executive-actions/

Leach, A., Adams, A., Caims, S., Coady, L., & Lambert, G. (2015). Government of Alberta. Retrieved from http://www.alberta.ca/documents/climate/climate-leadership-report-to-minister-executive-summary.pdf

Leiserowitz, A., Maibach, E., Roser-Renouf, C., Feinbein, G., & Rosenthal, S. (2015). *Climate change in the American mind*. New Haven, CT: Yale University and George Mason University.

López-Vallejo, M. (2014). *Reconfiguring global climate governance in North America*. Surrey, UK: Ashgate.

McDiarmid, M. (2015, May 15). Canada sets carbon emissions reduction target of 30% by 2030. *CBC*. Retrieved from http://www.cbc.ca/news/politics/canada-sets-carbon-emissions-reduction-target-of-30-by-2030-1.3075759

Meyer, R. (2017). As the planet warms, Trump's EPA pick hedges. *The Atlantic*. Retrieved from https://www.theatlantic.com/science/archive/2017/01/as-the-planet-warms-senators-shrug/513746/

Morgan, G. (2015, May 22). Carbon tax should apply to companies and consumers, says Suncor Energy Inc's CEO. *Financial Post*. Retrieved from http://business.financialpost.com/news/energy/carbon-tax-should-apply-to-companies-and-consumers-says-suncor-energy-incs-ceo?__lsa=6583-6623

Murray, B. C., Maniloff, P. T., & Monast, J. (2013). Design issues for linking carbon markets. In N. Craik, I. Studer, & D. VanNijnatten (Eds.), *Climate change policy in North America: Designing integration in a regional system* (pp. 246–273). Toronto, ON: University of Toronto Press.

National Roundtable on the Environment and the Economy. (2007). *Getting to 2050: Canada's transition to a low-emissions future*. Retrieved from http://nrt-trn.ca/wp-content/uploads/2011/08/Getting-to-2050-low-res.pdf

Natural Resources Canada. (2016, August 7). *Oil resources*. Retrieved from http://www.nrcan.gc.ca/energy/oil-sands/18085

Ordonez, C. D. (2015). *G20 subsidies to oil, gas and coal production*. Retrieved from https://www.odi.org/sites/odi.org.uk/files/odi-assets/publications-opinion-files/9967.pdf

Phillips, F.-K. (2015). Climate change, sustainable development, and NAFTA: Regional Policy harmonization as a basis for sustainable development. In H. L. Kong & L. K. Wroth (Eds.), *NAFTA and sustainable development: History, experience, and prospects for reform* (pp. 244–266). New York, NY: Cambridge University Press.

Prime Minister of Canada. (2016). Leaders' statement on a North American climate, clean energy, and environment partnership. Retrieved from http://pm.gc.ca/eng/news/2016/06/29/leaders-statement-north-american-climate-clean-energy-and-environment-partnership

Prime Minister's Office. (2006, July 14). Address by the Prime Minister at the Canada-UK Chamber of Commerce. Retrieved from http://pm.gc.ca/eng/news/2006/07/14/address-prime-minister-canada-uk-chamber-commerce

Rabe, B. (2013). Building on sub-federal climate strategies: The challenges of regionalism. In N. Craik, I. Studer, & D. VanNijnatten (Eds.), *Climate change policy in North America: Designing integration in a regional system* (pp. 71–107). Toronto, ON: University of Toronto Press.

Rand, T. (2015, April 14). *The provinces get it: Carbon pricing can be simple and efficient. The Globe and Mail.* Retrieved from http://www.theglobeandmail.com/globe-debate/the-provinces-get-it-carbon-pricing-can-be-simple-and-efficient/article23956553/

Remirez, B. T. (2014). Mexico and climate change: Was the country a multilateral leader? *Global Governance*, *20*, 147–162.

Rivers, N. (2010). Impacts of climate policy on the competitiveness of Canadian industry: How big and how to mitigate? *Energy Economics*, *32*(5), 1092–1104.

Rivers, N., & Jaccard, M. (2010). Intensity-based climate change policies in Canada. *Canadian Public Policy*, *7*, 409–428.

Studer, I. (2013). Supply and demand for a North American climate change regime. In N. Craik, I. Studer, & D. VanNijnatten (Eds.), *Climate change policy in North America: Designing integration in a regional system* (pp. 35–67). Toronto, ON: University of Toronto Press.

Tobin, P. (2015). The politics of climate change: Can a deal be done? *Political Insights*, *6*(1), 32–35.

U.S. Energy Information Administration. (2014a). *Mexico*. Retrieved from http://www.eia.gov/countries/country-data.cfm?fips=mx#pet

U.S. Energy Information Administration. (2014b). Petroleum and other liquids. Retrieved from http://www.eia.gov/dnav/pet/pet_move_impcus_a2_nus_ep00_im0_mbbl_m.htm

U.S. Energy Information Administration. (2015a). Projections show U.S. becoming a net exporter of natural gas. Retrieved fromhttp://www.eia.gov/todayinenergy/detail.cfm?id=20992

U.S. Energy Information Administration. (2015b). *Quarterly coal report*. Retrieved from http://www.eia.gov/coal/production/quarterly/

U.S. Energy Information Administration. (2016a). International energy statistics. Retrieved from http://www.eia.gov/cfapps/ipdbproject/iedindex3.cfm?tid=5&pid=57&aid=6

U.S. Energy Information Administration. (2016b). What is U.S. electricity generation by energy source? Retrieved from http://www.eia.gov/tools/faqs/faq.cfm?id=427&t=3

U.S. Environmental Protection Agency. (2015). Fact sheet: Clean power plan & carbon pollution standards key dates. Retrieved from http://www2.epa.gov/carbon-pollution-standards/fact-sheet-clean-power-plan-carbon-pollution-standards-key-dates

Worland, J. (2016, June 9). Donald Trump supported addressing climate change before calling it a "hoax." *Time Magazine*. Retrieved from http://time.com/4362393/donald-trump-supported-addressing-climate-change-before-calling-it-a-hoax/

SIXTEEN

Reflections and Projections on North American Environmental Governance Research

PETER STOETT AND OWEN TEMBY

The title of this book, *Towards Continental Environmental Policy? North American Transnational Networks and Governance*, encapsulates the two broad dimensions motivating the investigations it gathers; namely, the scalar expansion of environmental governance across the U.S.-Canadian and U.S.-Mexican borders, and the relevance of transnational networks of actors (including bi- and trinational institutions) to this process.[1] The chapters of this book seek to provide answers to the following questions, identified in Chapter 1:

- What transnational networks and international organizations are significant in the governance of transboundary environmental issues in North America?
- Has the proliferation of these networks and intergovernmental organizations facilitated a transition of North American environmental governance towards integrated continental environmental policy? And,

  - To the extent this has happened, what is its scope in terms of stakeholder inclusion, organizational and network activities and functions, and issue comprehensiveness?
  - To the extent this has *not* happened, what alternatives have proliferated, and which policy directions can take us closer to realizing coherent, sustainable arrangements?

In this chapter we assess some of the conclusions reached and lessons learned. We begin with the first two questions, on the transnational networks and organizations found significant by the volume's contributors, and whether this constitutes a transition towards continental environmental policy. Following this, we group the final two questions together and discuss the scope and stakeholder inclusion of these networks and organizations, and existing alternatives to these institutions. We conclude by briefly looking forward, laying out a partial roadmap for future research on North American environmental governance.

INTEGRATED NORTH AMERICAN ENVIRONMENTAL POLICY?

This volume's contributors identify several binational and trinational organizations and transnational networks active in North American environmental governance. In the recent *Review of Policy Research* special issue on natural resource and biodiversity conservation in North America, we summarized the findings about several organizations in a table assessing their function and behavior on two institutional traits (Stoett & Temby, 2015). Here we include a revised version of this table, adapted to account for the findings and featuring most of the binational and trinational organizations discussed in the present volume (Table 16.1).[2]

Clearly the existing organizations are mostly for water and wildlife, some with formal regulatory authority and some without. Their substantive focus reflects in no small part the political salience of boundary waters and the economic value of binational fisheries, and very likely other features of these issues that render them more manageable in a bilateral or multilateral context than other environmental challenges. Noticeably absent are organizations for managing energy development, climate change mitigation, and agriculture—in particular, genetically modified organisms. International institutions at this scale for addressing these issues are clearly underdeveloped.[3] For instance, although Lopez-Vallejo notes the U.S.-Mexican Bilateral Framework on Clean Energy and Climate Change has served as the basis for bilateral task forces, it lacks a secretariat and other defining features of international organizations (see Lopez-Vallejo, Chapter 12). Healey, VanNijnatten, and Lopez-Vallejo (2014) observe that in the climate change policy area, "the transboundary framework is ad hoc, informal, and piecemeal" (p. 145). In their review of several policy areas in North America, the reasons Healey et al. give for the variation in institutional development is the relative experience the

Table 16.1
Bilateral and Trilateral Environmental Organizations in North America

Organization	Parties	Environmental Issues	Geographic Scope	Tasks	Dominant Function		"Interactive"?
					Capacity Building	Regulation	
Commission on Environmental Cooperation	Canada, Mexico, United States	Wide range, including ecosystem conservation, marine biodiversity, pollution measurement, and environmental hazards	Ecosystems of all three member states	Facilitating the generation and sharing of technical knowledge, developing uniform standards, educating vulnerable populations	Yes	No	Yes, but with limitations for citizen engagement
Trilateral Committee for Wildlife and Ecosystem Conservation and Management	Canada, Mexico, United States	Wildlife and habitat conservation, including migratory birds, endangered species, and wetland conservation	Ecosystems of all three member states	Facilitating the exchange of scientific and other technical information and facilitating inter-agency coordination	Yes	No	Yes
Border Environment and Cooperation Commission and the North American Development Bank	Mexico, United States	Water quality and waste processing	U.S.-Mexican border region	Funding environmental infrastructure development projects	Yes	No	No
International Boundary and Water Commission	Mexico, United States	Water supply, use, and quality; Flood prevention; Border integrity	Colorado River, Tijuana River, Rio Grande	Measuring water flow and reservoir storage, dam and water treatment plant operation and maintenance, and water quality monitoring	No	Yes	Increasingly, although it is unclear whether this will continue

(*continued*)

Table 16.1 (*continued*)

					Dominant Function		
Organization	**Parties**	**Environmental Issues**	**Geographic Scope**	**Tasks**	**Capacity Building**	**Regulation**	**"Interactive"?**
International Joint Commission	Canada, United States	Water supply, use, and quality	U.S.-Canadian shared waters, including Great Lakes	Developing policy recommendations addressing shared water issues and directing their implementation	Yes	Yes	Yes
Great Lakes Fishery Commission	Canada, United States	Ecosystem health, invasive species	Great Lakes	Facilitating the generation and sharing of technical knowledge, developing policy recommendations	Yes	No	Yes
Pacific Salmon Commission	Canada, United States	Ecosystem health, salmon fisheries harvesting	U.S.-Canadian shared waters in the Pacific Northwest	Setting fishing quotas and monitoring fishery health	No	Yes	Yes

Source: Adapted from Stoett and Temby (2015).

three countries already have in addressing these issues and cooperating in transboundary governance arrangements over them (e.g., biodiversity and wildlife conservation are old issues; GMO governance and climate change mitigation are relatively new). The contributors to this volume suggest a different explanation.

Although these organizations are created through international treaties or executive agreements (and thus have a degree of permanence), the same is not true of networks. The latter are a persistent feature of North American environmental governance, yet are individually ephemeral to varying degrees. They are under constant construction, and communication patterns shift within them as issues evolve, science advances, technology changes, and extra-continental factors emerge. As such their existence and distribution is more difficult to verify. Nevertheless, a few generalizations can be made. First, they tend to be issue-specific and regional—and nearly always binational, not trinational. This is observable in the multi-stakeholder and interagency networks managing U.S.-Canadian binational fisheries and working to prevent the introduction of invasive species (Song et al., Chapter 7; VanNijnatten & Stoett, Chapter 8), seeking solutions to the problem of water flow in rivers shared by Mexico and the United States (Gerlak, Chapter 9), the grassroots efforts to deal with a host of environmental problems affecting economically disadvantaged populations on the U.S.-Mexican border, and numerous regional multi-stakeholder watershed councils on the U.S.-Canadian border (Brown, 2015). Second, they are substantially informal, with fluid membership prioritizing participants with resources suited for the task of addressing the environmental challenge. This informality and fluidity has considerable (and paradoxical) implications for stakeholder representation and inclusion within these governing arrangements, a point to which we return later.

If there was evidence of substantial coordination among the binational and trinational institutions discussed in this book, it might seem feasible to talk about integrated North American water, wildlife, and biodiversity policy. Yet while we list many of these organizations as "interactive" with relevant networks, we must qualify this with an often-overlooked fact: they rarely communicate with one another and do not formally coordinate programs. This is especially striking when considering that several of them work in ostensibly overlapping policy domains. The Commission for Environmental Cooperation (CEC) does not noticeably communicate with the Trilateral Committee for Wildlife and Ecosystem Conservation and Management or the Pacific Salmon Commission over wildlife issues; it does not communicate with the Canada-United States Air Quality Committee over its air pollution programs;

and the International Boundary and Water Commission (IBWC) is similarly closed off. Thus, if these organizations are interacting within the same networks, they are degrees apart. The only obvious exception, the unavoidably close relationship between the International Joint Commission (IJC) and the Great Lakes Fishery Commission (GLFC), is the exception that proves the rule. While the two organizations both have mandates for the management of Great Lakes water quality, habitat availability, ecosystem integrity, and other pressing concerns, their diverging purposes suggest different indicators of these values. The IJC measures aspects of fisheries under the Great Lakes Water Quality Agreement; the GLFC is concerned with stocking for recreational withdrawal and commercial harvesting—two very different functions with different measures.[4] The entrepreneurship so pervasive in international organization secretariats and other network participants has not been sufficient to overcome whatever potential institutional factors, such as conflicting mandates, institutional myopia, and stultifying underfunding, prevent integrative policy making across binational and trinational environmental organizations. As long as this is true, North American environmental policy will remain radically fragmented, despite occasional network overlaps and collaboration.

SCOPE, INCLUSION, AND ALTERNATIVES

Among the water and wildlife issues, binational and trinational organizations and other transboundary network members are demonstrably active players. As several chapters show, they disseminate information, develop policy, and work with other actors to implement scientifically informed measures addressing environmental challenges (Jinnah & Lindsay, Chapter 2; Mumme, Chapter 5; Olive, Chapter 6). As Gerlak informs us, even the famously insular IBWC has integrated more public participation in recent years. However, inclusion in the activities of these networks and organizations are, for the most part, limited to technical experts, government agencies, and powerful stakeholders. Lacking rigid rules of participation, networks operate in a realm less constrained by bureaucratic standards. They facilitate interactions among network members but potentially cut out stakeholders whose participation is ostensibly unnecessary for decision making. Furthermore, attempts to introduce citizen participation through organizational features have been met with limited success. As Chapter 3 demonstrates, the CEC and Border Environmental Cooperation Commission/North American Development Bank (BECC/NADB) mechanisms for inclusion have been at times stymied by their inaccessibility to the very people they were ostensibly designed to engage.

This points to an uncomfortable feature of trilateral environmental governance: It often occurs either through selective networks and institutions, or without them, through means that are arguably less democratic than we might consider ideal. The inclusion of stakeholders is limited to those the networks engage or allow, or those able to utilize the citizens' mechanisms in the CEC, BECC/NADB, IJC, IBWC, and other organizations.[5] This is a tall order given the lack of clarity about what these organizations accomplish in the first place (hence, the need for scholarship on the topic). Sure enough, among the most important members of these collaborative networks are public agencies of democratic governments, but the environmental issues addressed in a transboundary context tend to be the "below the radar" elements of environmental governance that give preference to those with specialized knowledge or substantial resources, lending some credence to the assertion that we are still in a technocratic, much more than a democratic, policy milieu.

Beyond water and wildlife issues, for (sustainable) energy, climate change mitigation, and genetically modified organisms (GMOs), the prospects for continentally integrated public policy are less immediately promising. The same can be said about the utility of scholarly attempts to examine these areas through the lens of collaborative public management networks. Water and wildlife are tangible commons that cut across national boundaries and must be managed if they are going to continue to serve society's needs and provide ecosystem services and values. It is less clear that this is the case with the environmental issues that are not well represented in the continent's bilateral and trilateral policy infrastructure. Contemporarily, air pollution in Canada and the United States is an increasingly invisible troublemaker—more like a toxic chemical than the smoke that blackened city skylines before the 1970s. Corporations and trade associations can take care of GMO and energy governance themselves (see Gonzalez, Chapter 11), with little obvious downside. And while there is presently a move in the United States to mitigate greenhouse gases nationally, it is not clear that North America is a sensible scale for collaboration (notwithstanding Huff's Chapter 15). Not coincidentally, there is no binational or continental environmental assessment treaty, as we are reminded by Collins and Kennedy in Chapter 4. Implementing one would potentially expand the scope of North American environmental policy beyond water and wildlife areas to those related to the production and trade of commodities, for which there is little political incentive (see Studer, 2013); the creation of the CEC was supposed to assuage concerns that increased trade would have a deleterious effect on ecology, and the International Organization for Standardization (ISO) gives corporations a ready-made blueprint for self-evaluation.

Thus in contrast to Healey et al.'s (2014) argument that the reason for the lack of policy infrastructure in these neglected areas is their relative newness, an alternative explanation emerges: They are inherently different policy problems that tend to be governed by different types of actors. This was visible in this volume's contributions on energy (notably, Gonzalez [Chapter 11], Lopez-Vallejo [Chapter 12], Macfarlane [Chapter 13], and Rowlands [Chapter 14]). Consistent with Gonzalez's examination of "policy planning networks" of economic elites, scholarly inquiry into how this policy domain operates on the continental scale needs to locate who makes policy and the lines and spokes through which related political power is circulated, and to develop the appropriate tools for making sense of these processes.

WHAT'S NEXT? AVENUES FOR FUTURE RESEARCH

This volume suggests that a robust agenda for future research on North American environmental governance is emerging. While the individual styles and aspirations of researchers retain their prominence, it is possible to suggest that a community of scholars, often integrated with practitioners, is making headway into the overarching task of better understanding the utility, efficacy, and sustainability of the hundreds, if not thousands, of transnational interlinked networks that count natural resource and ecological management as their primary concern.

However, even the numerical imprecision of the previous sentence reflects the need for more empirical work in this area. Put bluntly, no one really knows the full extent of the operative and formative networks that have sprouted between the two borders in recent decades. A mapping exercise, built on painstaking data collection, would help us get a more accurate, panoramic, view of the extent of activities.[6] This could result in the formation of an authoritative database that can be modified over time. Quantifying governance itself, of course, is not as simple. But we should at least have a more inclusive vision of the overall picture, even if the links between different networks and nodes are not as easy to identify. Again, a panoramic mapping exercise would help researchers make better-informed decisions about where, exactly, they should engage the complex formal and informal systems in place in order to pursue work grouped by various identifiers, such as issue area, support base, political orientation, and others.

In general, future research will be accompanied by the onset of big data in environmental governance studies. With the advent of widespread drone technology, vastly increased data computation abilities, and improvements in every aspect of scientific research, we will know more about North America's ecosystems and the interconnections between them than ever before, a point strongly stressed in the UNEP Global Environmental Outlook 6 Regional Assessment for North America released in 2016. Indeed North America is clearly a leader in global terms. The interesting question for many of us is whether there will be a substantial lag between leaps in knowledge and data collection (and, one presumes, dissemination) in the natural sciences and in the social sciences, in particular the study of governance. This would not be unusual; at the same time, however, there is greater focus on the role and potential transformations of the science-policy interface than ever before, and, returning to the big-picture frame once again, it is certainly incumbent on researchers to study how they can best contribute to this aspect of sustainable development.

Most future work will not, however, be so broad-based in aspiration, but will continue the case study approach pioneered so well by Don Munton (see 2007) and others in the 1980s. Here, several new developments are worth mentioning. First, the sheer scope of case study material continues to expand. Climate change adaptation has pushed myriad issues to the fore, in particular water management (including extensive droughts and sudden floods, sea rise, and eutrophication), forestry (related to invasive species and forest fire prevention), and disaster relief (especially in hurricane-prone coastal regions). We still lack any solid form of trilateral dialogue on these issues, which is every bit as shortsighted as it sounds. But responses to these and other problems associated with global warming will no doubt give researchers ample material for case studies. Beyond this, there will be new issues associated with increased population pressures in some areas, Arctic natural resource exploitation, North America's role in global efforts, responses to technological change such as synthetic biology, and many other relatively "new" issue areas ripe for case study treatment. Meanwhile older topics such as shared water resources, cross-border migratory species, and energy production will continue to drive scholarship and policy development. Of special interest will be how these more familiar themes and networks interact with the emerging ones: hybrid networks may be formed, jostling for policy capture and public attention may ensue, and solidarities might be forged or tested.

Second, the bulk of work in the preceding decades has focused on the relationship between Canada and the United States; this is hardly surprising, as there is a long pedigree of scholarly work in this area, and most of the academics engaged in the topic were typically located in one or the other country. This is changing. The constant tensions over the U.S.-Mexican border, cognizance of shared problems, and the rise of a new generation of energetic Mexican scholars is bringing Mexico into the picture with more clarity than ever before. Part of this is no doubt a reflection of the consistent efforts of the Mexican government to publicize its biodiversity conservation programs, and its superb representation in this field in international venues. Part of it might also be that, put next to an oscillating United States and a seriously regressive Canada, Mexico (despite its immense internal political problems) looks better by the decade. But the simple fact remains that, for most people engaged in the study of North American environmental governance, Mexico—which, as we indicated in our introduction, is not even considered part of North America according to the formal United Nations' categorization—is the great unknown. This is slowly changing and we can expect the dialogue to assume a more pan-continental dimension in the future (and to involve the Caribbean states in more depth as well). This is a very welcome development indeed.

In general, there is much room for more detail and depth in case studies of trilateral and bilateral governance networks in North America. Scholars have only begun to scratch the surface at this stage, and we need to encourage case studies in all the issue areas covered in this and other books and journals. Another mapping exercise would involve increasing our understanding of evolving ideational traits of networks, such as formality or informality and trust, and their effects on mutual learning and adjustment to changing policy and fiscal landscapes. But we need nuanced, deep case studies of the actors and nodes in these networks to get near the point at which we can draw reliable maps of their combined traits. For the most part, we still lack authoritative accounts of the major secretariats discussed in this volume, let alone the many other networks with substate origins and orientations. Can a new generation of scholars be enticed to conduct this demanding work, perhaps through time-consuming observer-participant research at the agencies and organizations, governmental and nongovernmental, involved? Perhaps the continued rise of the study of the science-policy interface mentioned earlier can help push them in this direction.

North America's place in the broader context of global environmental politics is another area in which network analysis can play a key role. While we are more aware of the interlinkages between the actors across a variety of issue areas and fields, their connections to international organizations and less formal networks are often undervalued or hidden from plain sight. These links can serve to reinforce and even construct organizational culture as well as agendas. For example, there are few governmental agencies or environmental non-governmental organizations that did not follow the convoluted but high-profile process of determining the post-2015 United Nations Sustainable Development Goals (SDGs; see Fox & Stoett, 2016).

The resulting formulation of the SDGs will have a concrete impact as governments seeks to pursue policy goals that help meet at least some of the many indicators accepted by the UN General Assembly and, by extension, each and every UN agency. There are hundreds of other, less visible, examples. During the Harper Government years, Canada's rather extreme position on UN matters, such as withdrawing from the Kyoto Protocol, or pulling out of the Convention to Combat Desertification and even the World Tourist Organization, is interesting in this regard: These actions from Ottawa limit the impact of many actors within Canada, yet they also prompt renewed criticism of the government and may even force nongovernmental groups to seek stronger transnational networks (see Stoett & Kersten, 2014). The 2015 change in federal government is a promising development for Canadian engagement abroad; yet the election of Donald J. Trump in November 2016 strongly suggests it is the United States that will take a decidedly non-multilateralist turn in the near future.

Finally, as always in studies of governance, questions swirl around the concept of legitimacy. Surely we need more on this, as we improve information gathering and communication skills across the continent, yet often see both promising and problematic programs implemented without adequate public consultation. The explosion in fracking sites is but one example of how natural resource use has come to permeate entire landscapes with limited explicit public dialogue. Throughout this text, the contributors have emphasized the role that professional bureaucrats play in the development of policy, often in a semitechnocratic manner (semi, because they are still subject to politicization), within and across borders, in environmental governance. What does this imply for democracy, including environmental, ecological, climate, and social justice? Is a technocratic approach even possible in countries where government corruption is as deeply embedded as notions of civic duty? Can inclusive, yet technocratic, expert networks that transcend borders escape the charges of elitism and social engineering that have been thrown at similar processes in other areas, such as finance and development? Are there innovative ways to get more citizen science content in program implementation, scaling up their scope and increasing their legitimacy at the same time?

It is clear, then, that there is ample room for the fresh, advanced analysis of North American environmental governance, whether or not it is leading to continental policy convergence and transborder networks whose authority challenges that of each individual nation-state. It is our hope that this volume has inspired this future research agenda, and we look forward to seeing its fruition reflect the collective challenges faced by the citizens of North America.

NOTES

1. Notably, Emma S. Norman, Alice Cohen, and Karen Bakker have asked similar questions about U.S.-Canadian water governance. In their edited volume on the topic, they observe a simultaneous "scaling out" towards more inclusive processes (similar to our observations about networks) and a "scaling down" to lower levels of government (reflected in our contributors' observations about interagency participation in these networks; Norman, Cohen, & Bakker, 2013, p. 11). As noted in Chapter 1 of this volume, several studies of environmental policy in other transnational contexts have also observed similar trends in natural resource governance.
2. We exclude from this table subnational-transnational arrangements and binational/trinational agreements lacking secretariats. We also exclude the U.S.-Canadian Air Quality Committee (AQC) because it was not discussed by any of the authors in this volume. As Munton (2007) and Temby, Munton, and Weibust (2016) have explained elsewhere, the AQC has minimal participation in the clean air policy process and no detectable influence.
3. This is consistent with Bow and Anderson's (2015) observation about the failure of North American economic integration, post-NAFTA, to yield additional formal binational and trinational institutions.
4. We acknowledge and thank Gail Krantzberg for pointing this out and clarifying the relationship between the two organizations.
5. Recent research by Emma S. Norman (2015) has examined the extent to which one of the IJC's recent initiatives, its International Watershed Boards, which rescales water governance to subnational levels, enhances the potential for greater inclusion in decision-making processes. However, she leaves the question mostly open, instead spelling out ways in which indigenous communities across the U.S.-Canadian border are improving their capacity for self-governance.
6. For recent attempts to quantitatively map binational fishery networks, see Temby, Rastogi, Sandall, Cooksey, and Hickey (2015) and Mulvaney, Lee, Höök, and Prokopy (2015).

REFERENCES

Bow, B., & Anderson, G. (2015). Building without architecture: Regional governance in post-NAFTA North America. In B. Bow & G. Anderson (Eds.), *Regional governance in post-NAFTA North*

America: Building without architecture (pp. 1–30). New York, NY: Routledge.

Brown, C. (2015). Scale and subnational resource management: Transnational initiatives in the Salish Sea Region. *Review of Policy Research*, *32*(1), 60–78.

Fox, O., & Stoett, P. (2016). Citizen participation in the UN SDG process: Toward global democratic governance? *Global Governance*, *22*(4), 555–574.

Healy, R. G., VanNijnatten, D. L., & Lopez-Vallejo, M. (2014). *Environmental policy in North America: Approaches, capacity, and the management of transboundary issues*. Toronto, ON: University of Toronto Press.

Mulvaney, K. K., Lee, S., Höök, T. O., & Prokopy, L. S. (2015). Casting a net to better understand fisheries management: An affiliation network analysis of the Great Lakes Fishery Commission. *Marine Policy*, *57*, 120–131.

Munton, D. (2007). Acid rain politics in North America: Conflict to cooperation to collusion. In G. R. Visgilio & D. M. Whitelaw (Eds.), *Acid in the environment: Lessons learned and future prospects* (pp. 175–201). New York, NY: Springer.

Norman, E. S. (2015). *Governing transboundary waters: Canada, the United States, and indigenous communities*. New York, NY: Routledge.

Norman, E. S., Cohen, A., & Bakker, K. (2013). Introduction. In E. S. Norman, A. Cohen, & K. Bakker (Eds.), *Water without borders? Canada, the United States, and shared waters* (pp. 3–24). Toronto, ON: University of Toronto Press.

Stoett, P., & Kersten, M. (2014). Surviving ideological fixation: Ecology, justice, and Canadian foreign policy under Harper. *Canadian Foreign Policy Journal*, *20*(2), 229–232.

Stoett, P., & Temby, O. (2015). Bilateral and trilateral natural resource and biodiversity governance in North America: Organizations, networks, and inclusion. *Review of Policy Research*, *32*(1), 1–18.

Studer, I. (2013). Supply and demand for a North American climate change regime. In N. Craik, I. Studer, & D. VanNijnatten (Eds.), *Climate change policy in North America: Designing integration in a regional system* (pp. 35–67). Toronto, ON: University of Toronto Press.

Temby, O., Rastogi, A., Sandall, J., Cooksey, R., & Hickey, G. M. (2015). Interagency trust and communication in the transboundary governance of Pacific salmon fisheries. *Review of Policy Research*, *32*(1), 79–99.

Temby, O., Munton, D., & Weibust, I. (2016). Air pollution policy in Canada: Government leadership or smoke and mirrors? In D. VanNijnatten (Ed.), *Canadian environmental policy and politics: The challenges of austerity and ambivalence* (pp. 329–346). Don Mills, ON: Oxford University Press.

Contributors

CHRISTOPHER BROWN is an associate professor and academic department head of the Department of Geography, New Mexico State University. Brown began researching environmental and water resource issues on the U.S.-Mexican border while working on his dissertation in the joint PhD program offered by the University of California, Santa Barbara, and San Diego State University. He has published extensively in this area, including articles in the *Natural Resources Journal*, *Environment*, *Social Science Journal*, *Review of Policy Research*, and *International Review of Comparative Public Policy*.

OLIVIA COLLINS has a master's degree in environmental impact assessment from Concordia University, Montreal. She has worked in the San Francisco area on food security projects, natural building, and climate change issues.

IRASEMA CORONADO is a professor in the Department of Political Science at The University of Texas at El Paso. From 2012 to 2016 she served as executive director of the North American Commission for Environmental Cooperation. She is co-author of the book *Fronteras No Mas: Toward Social Justice at the U.S.-Mexico Border* (2002) and numerous academic articles.

ANDREA K. GERLAK is an associate professor in the School of Geography and Development and associate research professor with the Udall Center for Studies in Public Policy at the University of Arizona. Her research agenda examines the causes of—and innovative solutions to—some of our world's most pressing water problems. Her work has appeared in journals such as *American Review of Public Administration*, *Ambio*, *Third World Quarterly*, *International Environmental Agreements*, and *Environmental Management*.

GEORGE A. GONZALEZ is associate professor of political science at the University of Miami. Dr. Gonzalez's area of research specialization is U.S. environmental politics and policy (e.g., energy, pollution, global warming). He is the author of numerous books including *Urban Sprawl, Global Warming, and the Empire of Capital* (2009), *Energy and Empire: The Politics of Nuclear and Solar Power in the United States* (2012), *Energy and the Politics of the North Atlantic* (2013), and *The Politics of Star Trek: Justice, War, and the Future* (2015).

GORDON M. HICKEY is an associate professor and William Dawson Scholar in the Department of Natural Resource Sciences at McGill University, Canada. His international research applies mixed-method techniques to explore the institutional processes affecting sustainable natural resource–related policy making and implementation, with a particular focus on integrating scientific knowledge for innovation. His work has appeared in journals such as *Social Studies of Science*, *Science and Public Policy*, *Ecological Economics*, *Regional Environmental Change*, *Land Use Policy*, and *World Development*.

MAT HUFF holds a bachelor of arts from Simon Fraser University and a master of arts from the University of Victoria. He has held a number of research positions, including work on carbon offsetting, transnational commodity chains, and international investment arbitration. He currently works in the area of First Nations health, supporting governance and systems transformation in British Columbia.

SIKINA JINNAH is an associate professor of politics at the University of California at Santa Cruz. Her first book, *Post-treaty Politics: Secretariat Influence in Global Environmental Governance* (2014), received the 2016 Harold and Margaret Sprout Award for best book in international environmental affairs from the International Studies Association. She also co-edited (with Simon Nicholson) *New Earth Politics: Essays from the Anthropocene* (2016).

WILLIAM V. KENNEDY currently serves as the director of the Office of Accountability at the U.S. Overseas Private Investment Corporation and is a former executive director of the North American Commission for Environmental Cooperation. He also served as head of the Environmental Policy and Strategy Unit of the European Bank for Reconstruction and Development in London and has held senior posts with the Dutch ministries of Environment and Foreign Affairs, the Organization for Economic Cooperation and Development, and the United Nations Environment Program.

GAIL KRANTZBERG is a professor at McMaster University, where she leads the Engineering and Public Policy master's program. She has worked for the Ontario Ministry of Environment as a Great Lakes scientist and senior policy analyst and served four years as director of the Great Lakes Regional Office of the International Joint Commission. Her recently published journal articles have appeared in *International Journal of Water Governance*, *Journal of Great Lakes Research*, and *Sustainability*.

ABBY LINDSAY is a PhD candidate at the School of International Service, American University, where she specializes in global environmental politics, water governance, and trade and environment. Previously she worked at the U.S. Department of State on trade-related environmental cooperation. Her current research focuses on urban water governance in Peru.

MARCELA LÓPEZ-VALLEJO is an associate professor of the Division of International Studies at Centro de Investigación y Docencia Económicas in Mexico. She belongs to the Mexican National Research System and is associate editor of *Latin American Policy*. She has been visiting fellow at the Oxford Institute for Energy Studies, at Wilfrid Laurier University, and at Université de Montréal. Her two latest books explore climate and energy policy, carbon transregional markets, and environmental policy in North America.

DANIEL MACFARLANE is an assistant professor in the Institute of the Environment and Sustainability at Western Michigan University. He is the author of *Negotiating a River: Canada, US, and the Creation of the St. Lawrence Seaway* (2014) and co-editor of *Border Flows: A Century of the Canadian-American Water Relationship* (2016).

STEPHEN P. MUMME is professor of political science at Colorado State University where he conducts research on U.S.-Mexican cooperation on environment and natural resources management. His most recent articles appear in *Global Society*, *Water*, *Globalizations*, and the *Journal of Water Law*.

ANDREA OLIVE is an assistant professor of political science and geography at the University of Toronto. Her main areas of interest are conservation policy, private property rights, and natural resource policy. She is the author of two books, *Land, Stewardship, and Legitimacy* (2014) and *The Canadian Environment in Political Context* (2015), and has recently published manuscripts in *Ecology and Society*, *The Canadian Geographer*, and *Review of Policy Research*.

IAN H. ROWLANDS is a professor in the Faculty of Environment at the University of Waterloo (Canada). With interests in energy policy and management, corporate sustainability and international environmental relations, Rowlands has had his recent work published in *Applied Energy*, *Energy and Buildings*, and *Renewable Energy*.

SUZANNE SIMON is an associate professor of cultural anthropology at the University of North Florida in Jacksonville. She is the author of *Sustaining the Borderlands in the Age of NAFTA* (2014) and various articles examining sustainable development challenges and opportunities in Mexico.

ANDREW M. SONG is a research fellow at the Australian Research Council Centre of Excellence for Coral Reef Studies, James Cook University, Australia, who is working on the issue of fisheries governance in the Asia-Pacific region. Previously he was a postdoctoral fellow at McGill University. Also affiliated with WorldFish, his work has appeared in *Marine Policy*, *Political Geography*, and *Journal of Great Lakes Research*.

PETER STOETT is Dean of Social Science and Humanities at the University of Ontario Institute of Technology in Oshawa. In 2012 he was Fulbright Chair in Canadian-American relations at the Woodrow Wilson International Center for Scholars in Washington, DC, and from 2013–2017 he was the founding director of the Loyola Sustainability Research Centre at Concordia University in Montreal. He co-edited (with Philippe Le Prestre) *Bilateral Ecopolitics: Continuity and Change in Canadian-American Relations* (2006).

OWEN TEMBY is an assistant professor in the Department of Political Science at The University of Texas Rio Grande Valley. His current research focuses on air pollution politics and transboundary ecosystem governance. His co-authored (with Ryan O'Connor) *Journal of Policy History* article, "Property, Technology, and Environmental Policy," won the Ontario Historical Society's Riddell Award for the best article of the year. Other recent articles have appeared in *Review of Policy Research*, *Environment*, *Urban History Review*, *Organization & Environment*, *Cambridge Review of International Affairs*, and *Journal of Great Lakes Research*.

DEBORA VANNIJNATTEN is an associate professor at Wilfrid Laurier University and chair of the Department of Political Science. Her research and publications have focused on transboundary environmental governance in North America, at the cross-border regional, bilateral (U.S.-Canadian and U.S.-Mexican) and continental levels. Her recent books include the edited collection *Canadian Environmental Politics and Policy* (4th edition, 2016), the co-authored (with Robert Healey and Marcela López-Vallejo) *Environmental Policy in North America* (2014), and the co-edited collection (with Neil Craik and Isabel Studer) *Climate Change Policy in North America* (2013).

Index

www.ingramcontent.com/pod-product-compliance
Lightning Source LLC
Chambersburg PA
CBHW030856270326
41929CB00008B/438